When the War Was Over

When the War Was Over

Women, War and Peace in Europe, 1940–1956

Edited by
CLAIRE DUCHEN
and IRENE BANDHAUER-SCHÖFFMANN

Leicester University Press
London and New York

Leicester University Press
A Continuum imprint
Wellington House, 125 Strand, London, WC2R 0BB
370 Lexington Avenue, New York, NY 10017-6503

First published 2000
© Claire Duchen, Irene Bandhauer-Schöffmann and the contributors 2000

British Library Cataloguing-in-Publication Data
A catalogue record for this book is available from the British Library.

ISBN 0-7185-0179-9 (hardback)
    0-7185-0180-2 (paperback)

Library of Congress Cataloging-in-Publication Data
When the war was over : women, war and peace in Europe, 1940–1956 / edited by Claire Duchen and Irene Bandhauer-Schöffmann.
    p. cm.
    Includes bibliographical references and index.
    ISBN 0-7185-0179-9 – ISBN 0-7185-0180-2 (pbk.)
    1. Women–Europe. 2. Reconstruction (1939–1951) I. Duchen, Claire.
    II. Bandhauer-Schöffmann, Irene, 1958–

HQ1587.W53 2000
305.4'094–dc21   00-021836

Typeset by BookEns Ltd, Royston, Herts.
Printed and bound in Great Britain by TJ International Ltd, Padstow, Cornwall

Contents

Plates

1. One of the first pictures of the capture of Chartres (23 August 1944). Two women collaborators

2. One of the first pictures of the capture of Chartres (23 August 1944). Two women collaborators

3. Axis collaborationists denounced in Cherbourg

4. 'Normandy haircut' for anti-French women

5. Collaborationist in Paris

6. Montereau

Contributors

Irene Bandhauer-Schöffmann lectures in history at the Department of Social and Economic History, Johannes Kepler University, Linz, Austria, and is currently working as researcher and project leader for the Historical Commission of the Austrian Federal Government. She has published widely on women in Austria during the immediate post-war period. Her most recent edited volumes are *Auf dem Weg zur Beletage: Frauen in der Wirtschaft* (Vienna, Sonderzahl Verlag, 1997) and, with Regine Bendl, *Unternehmerinnen: Geschichte und Gegenwart selbständiger Erwerbsarbeit von Frauen* (Vienna, Peter Lang Verlag, 2000). She is currently preparing a book on Austrian businesswomen in the nineteenth and twentieth centuries.

Ingrid Bauer is Director of the Boltzmann-Institut Salzburg, Research Centre for Social History and Cultural Studies, and Assistant Professor in the History Department, University of Salzburg, Austria. Her publications include several on the phenomenon of the 'GI bride'. Her current research concentrates on gender constructions and arrangements in post-war societies, ethnological and intercultural aspects of Occupation periods and post-1945 gender history. Her most recent book, *Welcome Ami Go Home: Die amerikanische Besatzung in Salzburg* (Salzburg, Pustet, 1998) is based on oral history interviews.

Sylvie Chaperon teaches history at the University of Toulouse, France. She is a historian specializing in the French women's movement from 1945 to 1970, on which she wrote her PhD at the European University Institute in Florence. Her book *Les Années Beauvoir* will be published by Fayard in 2000. She has published widely on feminism and other subjects and was the co-organizer of the colloquium on the fiftieth anniversary of *The Second Sex*, held at the Sorbonne in Paris in January 1999. With Christine Delphy she is co-editor of *Cinquantenaire du Deuxième Sexe* (Paris, 2000).

Claire Duchen, who died in March 2000, was Honorary Senior Research Fellow in French Studies at the University of Sussex. After working on contemporary feminism in France for many years (see her *Feminism in France from May '68 to Mitterrand*, London, Routledge, 1986), she became more interested in the immediate post-war years and published articles and chapters on this period, as well as her book *Women's Rights and Women's Lives in France 1944–1968* (London, Routledge, 1994).

Barbara Einhorn is Director of the Research Centre in Women's Studies at the University of Sussex and Associate Editor of the *European Journal of Women's*

Studies. She specializes in gender and citizenship, and also gender, nation and identity in narratives of exile and return. She has acted as a consultant on gender to the United Nations women's programme, the International Labour Organisation and the World Bank. She is the author of *Cinderella Goes to Market: Citizenship, Gender and Women's Movements in East Central Europe* (Verso, 1993) and is currently writing a book entitled *Gender, Power and Democracy in Europe* (Sage, 2001).

Helga Embacher is Assistant Professor in the Department of History, University of Salzburg. She is particularly interested in Austrian studies, gender studies, Jewish studies, National Socialism, and migration and emigration. Her books include *Neubeginn ohne Illusionen: Juden in Österreich nach 1945* (Vienna, 1995); with Margit Reiter, *Gratwanderungen: Die Beziehungen zwischen Österreich und Israel im Schatten der NS-Vergangenheit* (Vienna, 1998).

Ute Gerhard is Professor of Sociology and Director of the Centre for Women's Studies, University of Frankfurt/Main. She has written extensively on women's rights, the history of women and social policy, and the history of feminism in Germany. Among her books are *Unerhört: Die Geschichte der deutschen Frauenbewegung* (Reinbek, Rowolt, 1990) and *Frauen in der Geschichte des Rechts: Von der Frühen Neuzeit bis zur Gegenwart* (Munich, 1997).

Ela Hornung is historian for research on the consequences of wars at the Ludwig Boltzmann-Institut für Kriegsfolgen-Forschung in Vienna. She has published widely on women in post-World War Two Austria. Her particular research interests are in oral history methodology, prisoners of war, wartime influences on the construction of male and female biographies and the politics of daily life in post-war Austria. Her book *Penelope und Odysseus: Erzählungen über Warten und Heimkehren aus dem Zweiten Weltkrieg* will be published in 2000.

Elina Katainen is currently teaching at the University of Helsinki and has long been involved in gender and labour history in Finland. She is the author of a history of the Finnish Women's Democratic League (*Akkain aherrusta aatteen hyväksi: Suomen Naisten Demokraatinen Liitto 1944–1990*, Helsinki, KSL, 1994) and of several articles on the first women members of the Finnish Parliament. She is now completing her PhD on the gender discourse of the Finnish Communist movement in the 1920s.

Ronit Lentin is an Israeli-Jewish writer and sociologist living in Ireland. She is course co-ordinator of the MPhil in Ethnic and Racial Studies, Trinity College Dublin, and has published widely on women and the Shoah, gender and racism, and feminist research methodologies. She is Europe and Middle East Editor of *Women's Studies International Forum*. She has most recently edited *Gender and Catastrophe* (London, Zed Press, 1997); her latest novel is *Songs on the Death of Children* (Dublin, Poolberg, 1996). Her next book is titled *Israel and the Daughters of the Shoah: Re-occupying the Territories of Silence* (Oxford, Berghahn Books, 2000).

Andrea Petõ is Assistant Professor and teaches both history and gender studies at the Central European University, Budapest. She has published extensively on post-World War Two women's history, the history of Communism and the theoretical problems of gender relations. Her first monograph *Nõhistóriák: A politizáló magyar nõk története (1945–1951)* (Women's Stories from the History of Hungarian Women in Politics) was published in 1998. She is currently serving as president of the Feminist Section of the Hungarian Sociological Association.

Anna Rossi-Doria is Professor of Women's History, the University of Bologna. Her research focuses primarily on Italian political history of the nineteenth and twentieth centuries and on women's history. Her books include *La libertà delle donne: voci della tradizione politica suffragista* (Torino, Rosenberg e Sellier, 1990) and *Diventare cittadine: il voto alle donne in Italia* (Firenze, Giunti, 1996).

Penny Summerfield is Professor of Modern History, Manchester University. She has published extensively on British women and World War Two. Her latest book is *Reconstructing Women's Wartime Lives: Discourse and Subjectivity in Oral Histories of the Second World War* (Manchester, Manchester University Press, 1998). Her current research includes a major project on the gendering of home defence in Britain in the Second World War and another on the culture of conscientious objection in Britain, 1939–45.

Penny Tinkler lectures in the Department of Sociology, University of Manchester. She has written extensively on aspects of twentieth-century girlhood, including girls' popular literature, leisure, citizenship, and consumerism. She is the author of *Constructing Girlhood: Popular Magazines for Girls Growing up in England 1920–1950* (London, Taylor and Francis, 1995). She is currently researching the feminization of smoking in Britain, 1900 to 1970.

Tasoula Vervenioti is a historian and educational advisor in Athens. She has also held the post of Visiting Research Fellow at Princeton University. Her research on the history of Greek women and politics has been published as *I Gynaika tis Antistasis: I Eisodos ton Gynaikon stin Politiki* (Athens, Odysseas, 1994). Her current research focuses on women and children during the Greek Civil War (1946–49).

Jolande Withuis is a historian, based in Amsterdam, specializing in gender and World War Two and its aftermath. She is currently working as a researcher at the National Institute of War Documentation. She is the author of *De jurk van de kosmonaute: Over politiek, cultuur en psyche* (Amsterdam, Boom, 1995) and of many publications on the war and post-war years. Her main fields of interest are women's history, Communism and psychiatry. In her work, she combines historical, sociological and psychodynamic perspectives. Her current research is on the post-war organizations of concentration camp survivors.

Acknowledgements

This book has been a long time coming. The two editors met at the First European Feminist Research Conference at Aalborg, Denmark, in August 1991, where we found that our research interests coincided in several ways. We said, 'Let's write a book together.' Four years later, Claire went to Vienna and with Irene began to commission chapters. We would like to thank the many people who helped us locate the scholars who figure in the book. Working in difficult conditions, it has taken a further four years to complete the writing and editing of this volume.

For help in preparing the English-language edition of the book, Claire would particularly like to thank Siân Reynolds, who took on some editing when Claire was not well enough to work; as well as Siân, Barbara Einhorn has been a tremendous source of support. Both gave helpful, critical comments on the Introduction, as did Judith Miller. Mark Mazower helped both locate Tasoula Vervenioti and provide extra information about Greece; Perry Willson did the same for Italy.

Finally, we would most of all like to thank the contributors, who have not only provided the scholarship so evident in the book, but answered endless queries patiently and with good humour, and waited for what must seem like a terribly long time to see their work in print. Many thanks to them all.

The editors and publisher would like to thank:

Yale University Press for permission to include extracts from Charlotte Delbo, *Auschwitz and After* (1995), on pages 179, 187 and 190.

The Imperial War Museum, London, for permission to reproduce the photographs on pages 238, 239, 242, 243, 244 and 245.

Magnum Photos for permission to reproduce the two photographs by Robert Capa, on pages 238 and 239.

London, November 1999

Claire Duchen died on 15 March 2000 just as this book reached proof stage. Claire fought cancer and the clock to complete the editorial work, continuing to the very end and inspiring everyone who worked with her.

Thoughtful as ever, she had arranged for Siân Reynolds to take over the final proofreading when she became too ill to continue.

I will always remember the meetings we had – in London, in Vienna and in the Tyrolean Alps.

When the War Was Over and its German edition (*Nach dem Krieg: Frauenleben und Geschlechterkonstruktionen in Europa nach dem Zweiten Weltkrieg.* Herboltzheim: Centaurus Verlag, 2000) are dedicated to Claire's memory.

Irene Bandhauer-Schöffmann

1 Introduction

Claire Duchen and Irene Bandhauer-Schöffmann

The end of World War Two was celebrated in Europe on 8 May 1945. On newsreels and in reminiscences we can see and hear those moments: the euphoria tempered with sadness; reunions that were joyful, those that were not and those that never took place; scenes of pleasure contrasting with scenes of devastation and horror.

The chronology of the end of the war is untidy: we cannot say that it 'ended' on a particular date, nor that peace meant the same thing for the populations of different countries. Liberation, for some, meant welcoming Allied soldiers while for others the Nazi Occupation was replaced by occupation by the Soviets. In Greece, one war was followed by another. There were winners and losers, national borders shifted, allegiances reshaped on personal and political levels.

Simone de Beauvoir has called the war 'an unburied corpse' (1963, p. 49), lingering on and seeping into the post-war present, contaminating possible arrangements for the as-yet-unknown future. The lines between war and peace, then, were blurred and the disruptions of war persisted long after peace treaties had been signed. Wartime conditions still largely obtained throughout Europe, vast numbers were uprooted from their homes and on the move – going to or fleeing from their homes – and personal relationships were altered by war, sometimes irrevocably. Changes wrought by war in status, in household groupings, in occupation, all had to be reconsidered once the war was officially over.

While the post-war transformation of nations – the planning of new democracies, the work of reconstruction, the settling of Europe into two mutually hostile political camps, the battles of the decolonizing decades – is well documented (see General Bibliography), questions remain to be asked about transformation on more local and personal levels. In *When the War Was Over*, we are interested in the awkward space between war and peace. The war may have been over, but, we ask, 'What happened next?' These transitional years – loosely covering the 1940s, including the Communist takeover in Hungary and continuing up to the granting of women's suffrage in Greece in 1956 – are too often considered as an afterthought in work on World War Two or as a prelude in work on the post-war period. They have rarely been considered in their own right. The gendered dimension of experience during these years is even more absent. During the war years, women had been active in armed conflict, supporting the troops in the field, participating in Resistance movements. They had been victims of political oppression and violence, of bombs and of sexual aggression and abuse. They had supported fascism or communism or liberal democracy or had been apolitical. They had looked after families, shouldered unpredictable responsibilities, endured harsh living conditions, and sustained personal loss.

And then it was over. The ways in which women came to terms with these upheavals – how they survived, how they accounted for and spoke of their wartime behaviour and actions and how their wartime experiences affected their post-war lives – are among the many threads followed in the book. The contributors explore some of these gender issues, arising out of ongoing research undertaken in different European countries. In many cases, archives are only just opening up, releasing previously untapped sources of information. In others, it is now becoming possible to investigate issues which have long been taboo, shrouded in silence.

The archaeology of the immediate post-war years demands work of different kinds: discovering the unknown, uncovering the hidden, listening to the witnesses, telling and decoding the stories, analysing the evidence. Elements of each of these aspects of the historian's work are present throughout the chapters in this book. We approached historians who are currently involved in research on women in the post-war years and asked them to write a chapter of their own choosing. We wanted this volume to represent the cutting edge of ongoing research, and to raise the issues and identify the areas of inquiry that are currently preoccupying researchers. Three key areas of inquiry emerged and run through the book: the question of the varied discourses of war and gender (by which we mean ways of narrating war and post-war experiences which support women's view of their own history, or a nation's view of appropriate roles for women); the altered relationship of the 'women, politics, feminism' triad, which figures importantly in the book; and how communities are reconstructed, both literally and symbolically.

Discourses of war and gender

The language of war and gender is a key feature of many chapters, whether as focus or context. Gender is a peculiarly plastic concept, and can be shaped, reshaped, analysed and understood in contradictory ways. The gender assumptions that underpinned attitudes towards women and their wartime activities persisted in the ways in which the post-war world assessed gender roles both in the home and in public. Assumptions about masculinity and femininity affect in a number of ways both individual memories of the war and post-war years, and the analysis later historians bring to them. During the war, or Occupation, there were women in every country who were stoical, heroic, helping others to hide or escape, working or waiting; and there were also women who took part in acts of betrayal, discrimination or violence against others. Women could be as heroic or as culpable as men, as varied in their political and personal actions and responses as men.

In the gendered discourse of the post-war world, however, a number of symbolic stereotypes about women in wartime surface: female figures are taken to represent suffering, endurance and selflessness, or conversely, guilt, betrayal and helplessness. The female figure is further invoked as representing the future, in particular in women's role as mother, creating and nurturing the new world. In all these manifestations, the feminine becomes invested with a significance that occasionally passes unnoticed or unspoken.

World War Two undoubtedly meant the disruption of traditional gender roles (Higonnet *et al.*, 1987). But how was that disruption reflected in the discourses of the post-war world? On the one hand, wartime experiences might lead to a rhetoric of 'returning to normal', implying pre-war domestic arrangements, while on the other there was clearly a strong desire to build new societies based on greater equality and justice. Even notions such as 'normal' were fraught with difficulty and had to be questioned, while visions of a new, more equal and just society were rarely consensual. Personal testimonies, whether at the time or elicited later on, might not sit easily with national or 'official' discourses about the proper relations between the sexes. Diverse mythologies were created for a number of post-war purposes and gender lent itself to such mythologizing. In a war which, to a greater extent than any previous one, involved civilians and therefore women, the generally assumed polarities of public and private, political and personal, masculine and feminine, combatant and non-combatant, war and peace had been comprehensively confused. The years that immediately followed the war saw complex negotiations on a personal and national level as individuals and communities attempted to settle into new or reasserted patterns. In the same way, the hierarchy of identity markers that make up the individual – gender, nationality, politics, class, among others – had to be reconfigured after the war.

The first five chapters deal most specifically with these discourses of war and gender, each in a different way. Penny Summerfield re-examines the question of the impact of the war on women's lives in Britain. This topic has often been addressed in British women's history for the past fifteen years or so, leading to three dominant theses in the historiography of the period: the transformation thesis (war changed women's lives); the continuity thesis (after 1945, life reverted to the status quo ante); and the polarization thesis (war accentuated gender differences rather than minimizing them). In her analysis of women's narratives, elicited via oral testimony in the 1990s, Summerfield suggests that testimonies can be used to support any of the three interpretations.

Jolande Withuis, by contrast, looks at an external discourse about women, which has been used, she suggests, to incorporate women's wartime work as a seamless extension of a natural caring nature and role (which Withuis calls 'symbolic motherhood'), rather than as either anomalous or emancipatory. A return to conservatism in the 1950s could therefore seem simply to follow on, and not to appear as a setback to women's freedoms and opportunities. She offers an analysis which explains this shift as due to the way in which women's considerable activity in the Dutch Resistance was interpreted: it was always embedded in traditional ideas of gendered behaviour and nature.

Ela Hornung's chapter approaches the question of perceptions of gender roles from yet another perspective. She focuses on couples and how women and men recollect and narrate their experiences of Nazism, war and the post-war period. Using the prototype of Ulysses and Penelope – the homecoming man and the waiting woman – she asks questions not only about how each partner remembers and relates his/her own particular set of experiences, but about how each narrative strategy sustains and confirms the other. This mutual support, she suggests, was an integral part of the reconstruction of Austrian identity after the catastrophe of the war. Her chapter concentrates on the narratives of one married couple as a case study of how discourse analysis can contribute to our understanding of how individuals come to terms with the experience of war, separation and the guilt of association (if not always collaboration) with the Nazis.

Penny Tinkler looks, rather, to discourses about the future and to the prescriptions offered by those in charge of girls' formal and informal education. Adolescence, the time young people moved, in the main, from full-time education to work, was considered by educationalists to be a period of instability, a view which encouraged the raising of the school-leaving age and the provision of continuing part-time education and organized leisure. The visions of womanhood proposed for British girls approaching adulthood in the late 1940s contained some ambivalence about their role as paid workers, pitting the needs of home and family against the needs of an expanding economy, and, once again, the attention paid to the feminine reveals the anxieties and hopes for society in a reconstructed Britain.

Irene Bandhauer-Schöffmann's chapter looks at the relationship between two kinds of discourse on food and hunger in post-war Austria. On the one hand, while investigating the apparently ungendered question of the food supply, she found it to be deeply gendered; on the other, in her interviews with women about food shortages, she found that the 'heroic stories of survival labour' that women related drew attention away from the 'real victims of the Nazi regime'. Furthermore, women's victimization stories – hunger, living in bombed cities, rape by Russian soldiers – cast them as victims themselves and, by the same token, as not guilty of collusion and collaboration. In this way, Bandhauer-Schöffmann argues, the politics of everyday life in Austria during World War Two were underplayed, and submerged under layers of stories of individual suffering.

Women, politics, feminism

When surveying the political landscape of post-war Europe, a number of themes highlight the complexities of the relationship between women, politics and feminism. Among them are suffrage and women's entry into national political institutions, the significance of Communism after the war and feminisms, both old and new.

Suffrage

The formal political arena was clearly a crucial area for potential change for women throughout Europe. Despite the continent's political and economic diversity and each nation's specific history, certain features are common to many European countries and recur in the texts in this book in varying ways. Women's suffrage, for instance, was a hot topic in the immediate post-war years in the countries which had not yet granted citizenship rights to women.

Finland had been the first European country to accord women the vote (1906), followed by other Scandinavian countries (Norway in 1913, Denmark in 1915), the Soviet Union (1917), Austria, Poland and Ireland (1918), Germany, the Netherlands and Luxembourg (1919), Czechoslovakia (1920), Sweden (1921) and the United Kingdom (1928). A second wave of enfranchisement followed World War Two: France and Bulgaria in 1944, Italy and Hungary in 1945, Romania in 1946, Belgium in 1948 and Greece, after much confusion, in 1956. By the end of the 1940s, the majority of European countries therefore claimed to have achieved equal political rights between the sexes, though in fact none had equality in practice.

Women were not really welcomed to the political world as equal partners with men; in Western Europe, politics remained overwhelmingly masculine, judging by the number of women elected to office. In spite of brief applause for women's wartime work and Resistance activities, prejudices and gender-bound assumptions were evident throughout Western Europe and were reflected in the very low numbers of women in parliaments and governments once elections had been properly re-established.

These questions are explored through the cases of Italy and Greece. Anna Rossi-Doria's chapter considers the way in which Italian women entered politics, a process similar in many respects to the experience of women in France. Enfranchised in 1945, women turned out to vote in 1946 in similar numbers to men, but the early enthusiasm for politics dwindled over the next few years, at least partly due to the difficulties experienced by women in office. As in France, the numbers present on the political stage declined steadily over the next two decades, demonstrating a clear disaffection from the political process. While the late 1940s and the 1950s represented a time of lost opportunities and disappointments for women, Rossi-Doria argues that in the short period between the end of the war and the beginning of the Republic, women in politics laid the groundwork for much of the legislation concerning women that followed. Their achievements must not be forgotten.

Greece offers a singular experience among European nations, in that World War Two was followed immediately by civil war between Communists and Republicans. The very bloody and bitter conflict concluded with the victory of the Republicans in 1949. Tasoula Vervenioti's chapter traces the complicated trajectory of the suffrage question in Greece, from the demands made by women's groups in the 1920s through to the final inclusion of women's political rights in the Constitution and the first trip to the ballot box on the same terms as men in 1956, a trajectory made all the more uncertain by the succession of conflicts. She reminds us that while Greek women never appeared to be overly interested in politics or concerned by the issue of suffrage, yet when they perceived that their own interests were at stake, they could be as forceful, determined and involved as men.

Communism, feminism and gender

In much of Western Europe, Communism had a strong presence in Resistance to the Nazis and provided a focus for the hopes expressed by many after the war for the creation of a new, more equal and just society. After the war, the various Communist Parties sought to consolidate their wartime influence in peacetime politics, with some initial success which, on the whole, did not last. In Finland, however, and in East Central Europe, Communism had a completely different history and completely different resonances.

Communism in Finland, in the context of its peculiar relationship to the Soviet Union, is explored in Elina Katainen's chapter. Through the life of Olga Virtanen, Katainen reflects on the particularities of women cadres' life and work inside the Party. Her life story mirrors experiences throughout Europe as Communist Parties sought to gain broad-based support of the 'masses' and sent women activists out to 'work among women'. Many Communist women activists had previously led lives somewhat distinct from other 'ordinary' women and had been conscious of their difference. Katainen suggests that when they were made to work among ordinary women and lead ordinary lives themselves, many women (Olga among them) were brought into conflict with the Party. The conflict illustrates a little discussed disillusionment experienced by women activists in relation to the Party hierarchy.

Communism features again in Andrea Petö's chapter on Hungarian women's associations. The mechanisms by which the Communist Party took control of women's groups throughout East Central Europe are dissected, moment by moment, through the example of Hungary. As the Communist Party began to dominate national politics, so it gradually demobilized the independent women's associations, seizing their usually meagre assets, banning them in turn and then replacing them with the new (Communist) Democratic Association of Hungarian Women (MDNZ), whose role was to mobilize women for Communist electoral purposes. Throughout East Central Europe, variations of this process could be observed.

Feminisms old and new

Feminism in East Central Europe was noticeable either by its absence or by its incompatibility with the new circumstances of the post-war era. In Western Europe and the USA, feminism is said to have been 'in the doldrums' (Rupp and Taylor, 1990) between World War Two and the late 1960s. The dominant image of women associated with the 1950s is that of the homemaker – women retreating to the private sphere, raising their 'baby boom' children and polishing their new domestic appliances.

The apparent quiescence of feminism is examined and questioned by Sylvie Chaperon in her chapter on France and by Ute Gerhard for Germany. Chaperon analyses the French women's groups active at the Liberation, characterizing them as both fragmented among themselves and polarized between the twin influences of Communism and Catholicism. Caught up in the broader post-war political divisions, self-defined feminists – belonging to centrist Republican groups from the pre-war period – were little heard and little heeded in the clamour for attention from the heavy hitters. The disaffection from political life noted by Rossi-Doria in Italy was repeated in France; many women activists who might have pursued battles for women's rights in the political arena chose instead to operate outside it. Chaperon's chapter reminds us not to overlook the accomplishments of women in and out of the formal political arena, on behalf of all women in this period of perceived inactivity.

Ute Gerhard's opening question concerns the 'waves' of feminism and whether the legacy of earlier feminists could be seen in the second wave of the late 1960s and 1970s. Gerhard argues that while certain of the forms of activism and styles of argument belonging to the immediate post-war generation of feminists were rejected by women of the so-called second wave, other aspects of the work accomplished by the post-war generation remained crucial for those who came later, whether they recognized it at the time or not. Daughters inevitably reject their mothers. Feminist 'daughters' were no exception.

Reconstructing communities: exile and return, belonging and betrayal

Five chapters take up the theme of community, exile and exclusion, and the strategies deployed so that the symbolic reconstruction of national identity could take place. The 'before and after' caesura caused by the war was very clear for some, less obvious for others. Survivors of concentration camps and prisoner of war camps lived with failure, death and bereavement, with survivors' guilt, with the horror of what they had lived through, a horror they were frequently unable to express. This was compounded by a sense of betrayal, a suspicion of those around them, and an inability to adapt to 'normal' life after the trauma of the camps. For Jewish survivors – their families destroyed, their homes occupied (or 'Aryanized'), their possessions stolen, their jobs vanished – the extent of their dispossession is still unfolding, more than fifty years later. Survival itself had been the goal during the war; after the war they had to learn not merely to survive but to live again.

Ronit Lentin's chapter speaks of the re-silencing of concentration camp survivors: caught between the imperative of telling and the impossibility of telling, silence prevailed. Furthermore, 'the things they have to tell are the things we don't want to hear', so that even when survivors have felt able to externalize the horror, nobody has been prepared to listen. This sobering essay contributes to the relatively new scholarship on the gendered nature of the Shoah experience, pointing out how women were targeted as mothers and as sexual objects, how they were robbed of their femininity and were sexually vulnerable. Lentin argues that while suffering was terrible for both sexes, those sufferings were not identical for men and women.

Helga Embacher deals specifically with Jewish women who returned to Vienna after years of exile. Jews were resented because anti-Semitism remained rife and because their presence made non-Jews feel guilty; those Jews who had fled or emigrated before the 1938 Anschluss and then returned in 1945 received little sympathy for their years in exile, imagined as full of comfort and safety, unlike the lives of those Viennese who had remained in Vienna and experienced the full impact of the war. Embacher, like Lentin, tells of women whose camps stories weren't believed; of the suspicion and disgust which greeted those women whose survival was due to their work as prostitutes; and of the prevailing sense that those who had been deported must have 'done something' or they wouldn't have been deported in the first place.

Barbara Einhorn's interviewees did not return in the same way. Exiled from Hitler's Germany, they chose to return to post-war Germany in order to build socialism in the East. Blending theory with personal testimony, Einhorn's essay seeks to elucidate the relationship between three key identity markers discussed by her interviewees – Communist, Jew and woman. Foregrounding their political self, their Judaism emerged only as they experienced continuing anti-Semitism, while the gendered dimension of their new lives went largely unremarked by the women themselves. That dimension is, nonetheless, clear in their narratives of life in post-war East Germany.

Claire Duchen and Ingrid Bauer's chapters look at the ways in which French and Austrian society tried to come to terms with Occupation, guilt and collaboration; both picked on young women seen to have transgressed, usually sexually, with the enemy. These two chapters echo each other even as the detail differs. The overarching conclusion is that women's sexuality provided a necessary scapegoat, allowing society to transfer guilt and blame from the collective to the designated outsiders and thus exonerate itself. Ingrid Bauer's chapter focuses on the female form as a 'surface projection' of Austrian fears and hatreds at the end of the war, looking specifically at the figure of the GI bride. In the American sector of occupied Austria, GIs were considered by the population not as liberators but as new occupiers. The GI bride was therefore the antithesis of the faithful wife of the returning soldier: she was, rather, the disreputable girlfriend of the Occupation soldier, the 'whore who sold herself for a piece of chocolate'. Recipient of the same loathing and resentment as the French *femme tondue*, or woman with a shaved head, the GI bride destroyed the Austrian male's last position of power – his hereditary right to possess 'his' women. Bauer suggests that the hatred of the GI bride allowed Austrians to project their 'abyss' outwards and thereby avoid confronting their own inner conflicts over their wartime behaviour.

Duchen's chapter examines one form that retribution took in the war's closing months: the headshaving of French women for alleged collaborationist activities, usually assumed to involve sexual relationships with the German occupiers. Their punishment symbolically allowed the reconstruction of the community and the re-establishment of gendered as well as political order. She suggests that in this attack on women considered to be both politically and sexually deviant, the latent association of the sexual and the political, the personal and the political, has rarely been more overt. Duchen's chapter also takes on the question of the visual nature of these punishments, by consideration of contemporary photographs.

The ways in which women have attempted to make sense retrospectively of their experiences of the war and post-war years, how they speak of those years and construct an acceptable self in their narratives, are issues present throughout the book. Many authors have used oral testimony as their primary source, sometimes revealing glaring discrepancies between individual memory and 'official' discourses. Women's memories are foregrounded and placed in the political as well as the social history of the period. Memory itself is problematized and its complex nature recognized.

Several of the contributors bring the forgotten or the repressed back to history by lifting the veil on hitherto taboo subjects. Chapters deal with the literal work of survival and with the symbolic dimension of reconstruction. Using a wide variety of theoretical approaches and source material, the range of issues raised by this book indicates the breadth and depth of current research on this rich and exciting period in European women's history.

References

de Beauvoir, S. (1963) *La Force des choses*, vol. 1. Paris: Gallimard.

Higonnet, M. and Higonnet, P. (1987) 'The double helix'. In M. Higonnet *et al.* (eds), *Behind the Lines: Gender and the Two World Wars*. New Haven: Yale University Press, pp. 35-51.

DISCOURSES OF WAR AND GENDER

2   'It did me good in lots of ways': British Women in Transition from War to Peace[1]

Penny Summerfield

Controversy surrounds the issue of the impact of World War Two on British women. Historians have advanced at least three different interpretations. The most optimistic is that the war had a transformative effect. According to this thesis, British women's participation in unprecedented numbers in paid employment officially designated 'essential work', their involvement in national defence as members both of military auxiliaries and, more generally, of the Home Front, and the extension of state policies to support women and children (such as separation allowances and nurseries), profoundly altered women's social status (Titmuss, 1958: 84; Myrdal and Klein, 1968: 52–4; Marwick, 1968: 291–4). Opponents of this view advanced the continuity thesis. According to this interpretation, the paid employment offered to women during the war was, in the main, an expansion of the relatively unskilled, repetitive industrial and clerical work which had absorbed increasing numbers of women in the interwar years. Those women who obtained access to work normally done by men, in industry or in the military, were not normally trained for the full range of skills required of men in such work, rarely received equal pay and were allowed to do the work on only a strictly temporary basis. In the area of social policy, allowances for the wives of servicemen may have been a welcome source of regular income but they did not keep the women dependent upon them out of debt (Madge, 1943: 17, 39), and wartime nursery places, which were provided for only about a quarter of the children under five of women war workers, were phased out after 1945 (Summerfield, 1989: 67-98; Riley, 1983: 109–49). Some historians have taken this critical approach to the transformation thesis even further. According to them, not only did the war contribute nothing to greater equality between the sexes, it actually deepened inequality. The logic of the expansion of a military role for men in wartime, argued J. B. Elshtain, is that war polarizes rather than equalizes gender identities and relations (Elshtain, 1987). Harold Smith's interpretation of the specific case of Britain in the period 1939 to 1945 accorded with this polarization thesis: 'The war's most important legacy for women was a strengthening of traditional sex roles rather than the emergence of new roles' (Smith, 1986: 225).

A statistical summary indicates the wartime expansion in the numbers of British women in paid work, and its fate afterwards. The size of the female workforce increased from approximately 6.25 to 7.75 million between 1939 and 1943, and then shrank to approximately 6 million by 1947. The shrinkage was partly due to the smaller size of the younger age groups in the population and possibly also to undercounting, as many women left insured wartime employment to find casual, unregulated post-war jobs, but there was considerable job loss for women at the end of the war. Within the overall picture of post-war decline, however, there were some important and lasting changes. Only 16 per cent of working women were married in 1931. During the war, the proportion of wives in the female workforce rose to 43 per cent in 1943, and although it dipped to 40 per cent in 1947, it returned to 43 per cent in 1951, rose to 48 per cent in 1955 and continued to rise thereafter. Part-time work, introduced with official encouragement during the war, absorbed increasing proportions of all adult women: 5 per cent in 1951, 9 per cent in 1961. Accompanying this trend, the age profile of women workers altered. Whereas before the war 41 per cent of women workers were under 25, by 1943 only 27 per cent were in this age group and by 1947 only 24 per cent. The war permanently enhanced the participation of older married women in the workforce. The war also hastened long-term decline in industries such as textiles and domestic service, which had traditionally employed more women than men. But wartime increases in the numbers and proportions of women in other industries, such as engineering, transport, and local and national government, were not completely reversed. The sections of these industries which employed women (at lower rates of pay than men) contracted slightly after the war, but remained larger than they had been in pre-war Britain (Summerfield, 1988: 97–102; 1993a: 66–70; 1994: 62–3).

Such a statistical snapshot cannot settle the debate about the effects of the war on gender relations. Indeed interpretations of it have been hotly disputed (Smith, 1986; Summerfield, 1988). Personal testimony has featured as strongly as quantitative evidence, if not more so, in the claims made for the three rival interpretations discussed above. Women's memories of the changes (or lack of them) brought by the war, and of what those changes meant to them, were obviously germane to the debate. But each thesis depended upon a selective reading of the wartime surveys, diaries, memoirs and oral histories from which conclusions about the effects of the war on individual lives were drawn. There is no consensus to be found within personal testimony on this subject: it is possible to produce evidence to support all three conflicting interpretations from the forty-two oral histories which will be discussed here. Rather than seeking to settle the debate once and for all, this chapter will approach the relationship of such personal testimony to historical interpretation by means of a methodological and theoretical path which will help us to understand the different interpretations, rather than accord precedence to any one of them.

Recent work on oral history encourages us to regard it not as unmediated testimony which can reveal the truth about the past in any simplistic sense, but as the product of a series of cultural interactions (Passerini, 1992; Portelli, 1981; Sangster, 1994). Experience cannot be communicated or understood without language, and the meanings central to language are formed within culture. The cultural sociologist Bronwyn Davies (1992: 54) has written, 'When I talk about the experience of being "a woman", I refer to the experience of being assigned to the category female, of being discursively, interactively and structurally positioned as such, and of taking up as one's own those discourses through which one is constituted as female'. Furthermore, audience is important. Narrators produce stories about their pasts with which they can live 'in relative psychic comfort' (Dawson, 1994: 22–3) and which 'they perceive to be of interest to their audience'

(Coleman, 1991: 121). The extent to which audience and narrator hold cultural values in common, and, feminist oral historians would add, can share and exchange meanings intersubjectively (Minister, 1991: 36; Chanfrault-Duchet, 1991: 78), are crucial to the ways in which life experiences can be told.

Using this theoretical framework, we can analyse the impact of discursive constructions of the relationship between women and wartime change upon women's understandings and explanations of what happened to them in the transition from war to peace in Britain in the 1940s. We can also investigate the contribution of the interaction between interviewee and interviewer to the account offered. In short, we can explore the interplay of culture with memory in British women's reconstructions of their personal histories of the war and its aftermath.

The oral history interviews used here were conducted in the early 1990s as part of a project funded by the Economic and Social Research Council on women's wartime training and work.[2] The forty-two interviewees were mostly drawn from over 300 responses to a short piece in a women's magazine popular with women over 60, *Woman's Weekly*, asking women with memories of doing any sort of work, manual or non-manual, military or civilian, to contact the research team (of three). We interviewed equal numbers in each of these occupational categories, drawn from all over Britain, and in addition two women who had come from the Caribbean to work in the Women's Auxiliaries to the Armed Forces. The purpose of the project was to examine the effects of wartime training and work on women's longer term work histories. The results supported the continuity rather than the transformation thesis (Summerfield, 1993b). However, the women spoke about much more than wartime work and training because of the approach to interviewing which we adopted. The interviews were not based on a structured questionnaire, but used a series of prompts concerning pre-war, wartime and post-war life, punctuated by some direct questions. One of these questions concerned whether the women felt that the war had changed them. The answers illuminate women's uses of the popularly available stories about the effects of the war on women to compose their personal accounts.

Modernizing and traditional discourses

Two versions of the effects of the war on women were current in the 1940s and have been popular ever since. In one, the war hastened women towards modernity; in the other, it stimulated a return to traditional feminine life styles. The transformation thesis summarized on p. 13 can be seen as part of the modernizing discourse, while both the continuity and the polarization theses are more closely linked to the traditionalist version.

Contemporary accounts of the modernizing trends hastened by the war emphasized the desirability of women's emergence from domestic seclusion into public life. A recurrent motif in these accounts was of women enclosed within the home and literally liberated by war; common metaphors were of the war lifting a curtain or opening a door. For example, writing in 1942, the Labour MP Edith Summerskill presented a brief history of women in the twentieth century, the theme of which was the vital role of both world wars in women's release from domestic bondage into citizenship. Both wars, especially the second with its opportunities for military service, had produced a 'new woman' who had 'a mind of her own' which led her to desire participation in reconstruction and the promotion of peace, and therefore to want a voice in politics and the professions. Summerskill sketched a future in which, while women would not have lost the urge to be feminine (meaning to dress nicely, to marry and to have children), they would demand egalitarian marriages. The traditional position of the housewife would 'not satisfy the post-war housewife who has tasted the joys of economic independence in the factories and the services' (Summerskill, 1942: 213). Summerskill contributed, with no reservations, an image of the modern woman freed by the war to discover her own value and her importance as a citizen. Others, such as the journalists and popular writers J. B. Priestley and Peggy Scott, followed her lead, although, as we shall see, not without some qualms.

However, a quite different version of war and social change was available, one in which the war figured as a period not of freedom, but of constraint and instability; its end signalled a welcome return to secure domesticity. For example, in 1945 Dorothy Paterson, founder of the Council of Seven Beliefs for the Guardianship of Family Life, published a book called *The Family Woman and the Feminist: A Challenge*, in which she explicitly rejected the construction of the home as a cage: 'Our friends the Feminists appear to think that the average home is built without doors or windows and that a woman in a home sits alone all day in a perpetual mental and social blackout!' (Paterson, 1945: 13). Paterson argued that the domestic sphere was a 'natural outlet' for women, and the most important task in a woman's life was to build a home into 'a landmark of security' for herself and her husband and within it fulfil her destiny by creating a family (Paterson, 1945: 33, 35). The war, with its loss of life adding to the long-term decline in the birthrate, gave special urgency to women's home-making and reproductive mission. Wartime developments, which replaced the family with communal facilities such as hostels, restaurants and nurseries, undermined women's position and must be swept away. For Paterson the matrimonial and maternal role, rather than economic or political participation, qualified women for citizenship and was central to post-war reconstruction.

Paterson's text was embedded in a context in which ideas of the re-establishment of family life after the stress and worry of wartime were presented as deeply comforting. The rebuilding of homes, physically and emotionally, and the birth of children within the security of the familiar gender order, were essential to post-war reconstruction. The reassurance derived from such a view was in large part directed at male members of the armed forces. It was for their wives and sweethearts, their children and their homes, that men were allegedly fighting. As Gledhill and Swanson (1984: 57) have argued, the hearth, and the gendered social structure for which it was a metaphor, was at the centre of national identity.

The idea that women were waiting anxiously for men to return home was an unquestioned piece of commonsense. It pervaded accounts of the effects of the war on women, not only those like Paterson's, but also those like Scott's and Priestley's which suggested that the war had caused great changes. As well as applauding new opportunities for women arising from the war, both these authors expressed the view that women's response to peace would be an overwhelming desire to 'go home'. They differentiated their views of 'women', however, by age, although they did not agree on the effects on the various groupings proposed. Priestley thought that older women would return permanently to their pre-war life styles whereas younger women would soon discover that they wanted more than home life (Priestley, 1943: 54). Scott thought that older women who had experienced the isolation of home life before the war would be readier to welcome change (1944: 7–8, 147).

The public opinion research organization Mass-Observation, founded in 1937, also took a keen interest in the effects of war on women. In *The Journey Home* published in 1944, Mass-Observation asserted that most women wanted to return home, but made yet more subtle distinctions according to age and occupation than Scott and Priestley. Women under 25, especially servicewomen, were unsettled. We shall return to them shortly. Mass-Observation contrasted their worries and fantasies with the 'calm and "sensible"' attitude of those over 25 who wanted to 'settle down', that is, to exchange paid work for the occupation of homemaker. Women in their forties and fifties were different again. As in Scott's version, so in that of Mass-Observation: these older women valued the wartime release from seclusion and confinement in the home (Mass-Observation, 1944: 55).

The women in whom these observers of social life variously believed they perceived signs of change, included, of course, the wives to whom many servicemen would be returning. Traditionalists invested these women with a natural store of comfort, reassurance and stability which they believed vital to post-war life. But it was possible that the flow of this essential goodness had been jeopardized by the consequences of war, as proposed by the modernists. Writers like the 'medical psychologist', Kenneth Howard, who published *Sex Problems of the Returning Soldier* in 1945, advised the serviceman about how 'to resume his rightful place as the breadwinner of the household', countering his wife's resentment of 'her loss of her newly-found prestige and power' in such a way as to re-establish a happy and lasting marriage (Howard, 1945: 63).

It is striking that nowhere in his book did Howard conceptualize the 'returning soldier' as a woman, in spite of the 450,000 women serving in the Auxiliary Forces in 1945 (Central Statistical Office, 1995: Table 3.4). Any problems of readjustment that servicewomen might have had were rendered invisible in accounts like Paterson's or Howard's and were marginalized in the Parliamentary discussions of demobilization in November 1944. In this debate, the message concerning servicewomen was consistent with the return to gender norms expected of all women. It was encapsulated in an announcement by John Profumo, Secretary of State for War, of a government proposal to give servicewomen a cash award for clothing rather than a 'demob suit' of the sort that would be issued to men when they relinquished their military uniforms. He stressed the importance of assisting women to become 'once again individually, adequately and gracefully dressed' (Hansard, 1944: col. 1988; see also Swindells, 1995).

It was to servicewomen, however, that Mass-Observation attributed particular restlessness. 'Service women are, on the whole, much more interested in the future than their counterparts in factory and war-job' (1944: 117). Servicewomen had rejected the idea of settling down, they had a 'longing for adventure' and a desire for change. In the Mass-Observation account, it was within this group that the new feminine sense of citizenship was growing. 'These women have been taken from their homes, often for the first time in their lives, and for the first time are being forced to think for themselves instead of falling back on some opinion taken ready made from husband or father' (61). This had led to political awareness, and, in Mass-Observation's view, to aspirations for 'equal competition between the sexes' (64).

The idea that the war had produced a modern woman (the transformation thesis) was restated academically and popularized in the 1950s and 1960s, for example by the sociologists Myrdal and Klein (1968), in a continuing dialogue with traditionalist views. The 1970s feminist rethink of women's history, however, interacted in an interesting way with these strands within the discourse of women, war and social change. The feminist critique of the advocacy of women's dual role, and reinterpretation of it as a double burden which underpinned women's subordination, had the effect of obliterating the difference between the modernist and traditionalist accounts, and of treating them as a monolithic discourse supporting women's marginalization and oppression. What is more, although World War Two assumed a place of importance within feminist discussion, by the 1980s the dominant feminist interpretation was the continuity thesis (Lewis, 1984; Mitchell, 1975; Riley, 1983; Summerfield, 1989). In spite of an appearance of wartime change due to labour shortages and state policies directed to the relief of domestic tasks, it seemed that there was little long-term change in the identification of women with domesticity and in women's subordinate position within paid work.

Such a construction left little space for the idea of personal change for women occurring as a result of the war. The suspicions voiced by feminists of the 1970s and 1980s of claims that women had been emancipated by the war suggested that any individual who believed this was true for her was likely to be deluded. There was, as a result, an uncomfortable gap between the generalized feminist account of little or no change, and individual accounts of the war as a special experience in women's lives, necessarily drawn from other sources. The narratives of modernization and traditionalism reviewed here were possibilities. Of special interest in the modernizing one was the position of servicewomen.

Personal oral histories: servicewomen [3]

Twenty-two of the forty-two women interviewed had served in the Women's Auxiliaries to the Armed Forces during World War Two. In view of the attention given to servicewomen in accounts of the modernizing effects of the war, I shall begin my analysis of the relationship of personal accounts to discursive constructions with them.

All but two of the ex-servicewomen interviewed took up enthusiastically the idea that their wartime experiences had changed them. One of the changes was the idea of the emergence of women from seclusion in the home, release from the controls normally imposed on women by parents and husbands. One of the ways such an experience was portrayed was through telling a story of development from a shy and inarticulate personality to an outgoing one as a result of experiences of meeting people within the Services. Such accounts came from across the social spectrum. They were sometimes further embellished by stories of not only rising to the challenge of self-expression and conviviality, but of freeing the body itself from the confines of modesty and prudishness in the public world of the Forces.

Ivy Jones, daughter of working-class parents in Cardiff conjured up the sheltered, limited world which she left behind on entering the Women's Auxiliary Air Force (WAAF) as a meteorologist. By the end of the war, she said, 'I suppose I must have had more confidence, I'd mixed more, I'd got used to dealing with men, because you see at home I had three sisters and I went to an all girls' school and in those days you weren't encouraged to mix ... yes, it brought me out, I was a different person at the end, and I felt differently ... I'm sure it did me a lot of good' (Jones, 362, 364).[4]

In accounts like Ivy's, there was a strong view that experience in the Services had had a corrective effect on what were perceived (with hindsight) as deficiencies in a woman's character caused by the sheltered lives imposed on them by their parents and schooling. It was summed up in the phrase used by Ivy and several others: 'It did me a lot of good'.

Marion Paul was one of several women who commented on the enforced adjustment to exposing one's body to the public gaze in the Services. She vividly reconstructed her feelings when, on first joining the Auxiliary Territorial Service (ATS, the women's branch of the British Army) from a clerical job in a mines office, she was told to change into her new uniform in a room full of other women: 'This was very embarrassing, because I'd never changed, I'd never taken my clothes off in front of other people. And most of the others were the same, they – they were all very embarrassed, and we all sort of got against walls and in corners, and turned our backs to the middle of the room and sort of gingerly took everything off and put all these other ones on' (Paul, 179).

Usually such reflections related to accepting the personal and communal exposure of one's body in the company of other women. But the process of shedding inhibition and arriving at improved understanding of self and society could also relate to women's growing knowledge of men's bodies and of sexual behaviours. Ivy Jones referred specifically in this context to the benefits of an enlarged understanding of embodied masculinity. Between flights, Royal Air Force (RAF) pilots slept on the airfield in the flying control building where Ivy worked as a 'Met girl' or meteorologist: 'They had these little cots and things and they relied on us to get them up in the morning at 6 o'clock, you see the Met girl was the one who was awake. Because there was this room just full of – really smelly because everybody went to sleep in their clothes, you know. And you sort of got used to this sort of thing that you'd never been used to, and you'd sort of get on with men as people, yes it was a good thing. Didn't have any brothers! I think we learned a lot' (Jones, 364). Kate Lomax, a photographer in the WAAF, implied that the specific awareness she gained was less of different types of body than of different types of sexual behaviour: 'I thought I knew – I went into the Service say 21, and I thought I knew it all, and I learnt more about people and their way of life than I ever would have done in a private life. And there's all sorts – I met lesbians, and things like that. I met married women, married men ...' (Lomax, 788).

Modernists believed that a consequence of wartime release from the domestic cage was that women were becoming less bounded by their own individual concerns and more socially responsible. In these constructions the content of the new citizenship in servicewomen fostered by the war was vague. At its most precise it did not go beyond a sketchily defined concern with social justice and equality (Calder, 1971; Smith, 1975; Summerfield, 1981).

The ex-servicewomen interviewed spoke in similarly general terms about the effects of their service on their social consciousness. They drew on the idea of the enlargement of social awareness to express how they felt the Services had changed them. A prevalent theme was the idea of growth in their capacity to feel a sense of commonality with other people. This could involve levelling up or levelling down. For example Katharine Hughes, from a working-class background, said of the Women's Royal Naval Service (WRNS), 'I think it made me more confident myself, and I don't consider anyone better than I am. They might have a bit more money than I have but they're no better than me, because I've proved to myself that I can do these things and I can hold my own with people' (Hughes, 354). Estelle Armitage on the other hand, described an experience of 'levelling down'. The major change for her resulting from joining the ATS in Jamaica and coming to Britain, was her re-evaluation of her relationship as a coloured woman (as she described herself) to the white people who, as a middle-class Jamaican, she regarded as her social inferiors. Speaking of her upbringing in Jamaica, Estelle said 'some white people, I wouldn't associate with some of them. I thought I was a better class than them' (Armitage, 66). Estelle explained that the ATS made a great difference to this: 'I ... learned to respect people that I thought were below me. Nobody is below you, people are what they are, and you accept them at face value' (Armitage, 312). Estelle was sure that this change in herself was beneficial: 'It made me a better person' (Armitage, 330).

The theme of growing up was strong in the servicewomen's accounts. Descriptions of the development of new understandings of common humanity and the dawning of political awareness were often accompanied by the comment 'I grew up'. So too were descriptions of leaving a former state of greater dependency and uncertainty about personal competence. The changes accompanying wartime service were cast in terms of maturation, implying self improvement and manifest in feelings of greater confidence and self-sufficiency. Competence, confidence and independence were central to the theories of maturity normally applied to boys and men (Dyhouse, 1981: 122).

The currency of the idea that war service gave women a sense of equality with men is indicated by negative testimony about change. Amy O'Connor responded to the question 'Did war service change the way you thought about yourself' with an emphatic 'No'. She went on to refer without prompting to a pre-existing sense of the injustice of the idea that women were the inferior sex. 'Just felt the same. I've always felt like that. Always thought women were more important than men' (O'Connor, 813).

Personal oral histories: civilian war workers

So far we have explored the accounts of personal change of women in the Services. The other women interviewed had been civilian workers of various types. In some of the public accounts of women and wartime change (such as those of Summerskill and Scott) no distinction was drawn between military and civilian women. It was suggested that all women who did war work would emerge from the war as new feminine citizens. Among the interviewees who had done civilian war work, a small group expressed themselves in similar terms to the ex-servicewomen. They spoke of gaining a deeper knowledge of humanity as a result of their war work, of developing new competences, of release from restricted homes and of a sense of growing up. Marianne Lloyd, clerical worker turned engineering draughtswoman, summed up their responses in her statement: 'It took me out into the world which I wouldn't have been out in before' (Lloyd, 391). This small group had in common the determination to contribute to the war effort in ways which were relatively unusual for women (engineering draughtswoman, member of the Aeronautical Inspection Directorate, storekeeper in a Royal Ordnance Factory, Postal Censor). Even though they did not go into quasi-military roles, they, like most of the servicewomen, gave relatively 'heroic' accounts of their war service. Like the servicewomen, they subscribed, to a high degree, to the ideas about change ensconced in the public account of war and modernity. They became better and more complete people, losing the inhibitions of a secluded existence, understanding their common social and physical, spiritual and corporeal humanity with others, gaining a sense of national identity and acquiring a new gender identity. The presentation of 'heroic' wartime lives involved the construction of stories of personal purification which were also stories of modernization. The hero sought a high standard of performance in pursuit of the honourable goal of war service; the dross of personal imperfections must be left behind. The discourse of expanded horizons leading to improved social consciousness, to a new sense of feminine citizenship, provided a framework within which to cast the account. If wartime experiences produced none of these changes in individual women, it was not because they did not occur, but because these women already possessed these attributes.

A great deal more doubt about whether the war had changed their lives in positive ways characterized the accounts of the other women who had done civilian work in wartime, as well as two of the ex-servicewomen. In contrast to the small group of civilian women discussed above, the majority told stories of stoically putting up with war work rather than entering it with patriotic enthusiasm. Scepticism about the idea that war service might have had a transformative effect was as pervasive among these women as the confidence of the 'heroes' in the profoundly positive personal effects of war service, military or civilian. The short, terse comments of the 'stoics' on the matter are striking.

For example, Evelyn Mills, pre-war clerk and wartime duplicator operator at the Admiralty, said in response to the question 'Did the war change you?', 'I don't think so, no' (Mills, 297). Dorothy Rose, clerical worker in the Ministry of Food, said it was 'hard to say' (Rose, 679). Hester Hamilton, who reluctantly left university to become a 'progress chaser' with the job of monitoring the pace of production in an aircraft factory, said, 'not at all, I don't think so' (Hamilton, 257). Helena Balfour, pre-war domestic servant and wartime aircraft assembler, was also doubtful about whether the war had changed her: 'I don't think so, I don't think so really' (Balfour, 655). Similarly Wilma Harrison, who moved from upholstery to engineering, said 'I don't know, I can't think, just part of your life, isn't it?' (Harrison, 497). Elizabeth Little, who was sent from a grocer's shop to an engineering factory, said, 'I don't know that it changed me' (Little, 843), and Ethel Singleton, who also left shopwork, in her case for welding in an engineering works, said emphatically, 'No it didn't change me at all' (Singleton, 353). Fiona Thomas, who moved from shopwork to an aircraft factory and eventually became a wartime bus conductress, was equally negative about the idea that wartime experiences changed her: 'No, not really, no I don't think so' (Thomas, 443).

Just two members of this group readily assented to the idea of personal change. However the changes they described were not positively transformative ones. One of them was Sadie Bartlett, a working-class woman who moved during the war from hairdressing into the Timber Corps of the Women's Land Army (a non-military organization which sent women to do agricultural labour on farms). Sadie's account appeared to be informed by feminist understandings of sexual politics in the 1970s and 1980s. Sadie's response to the question about change was 'I think I grew up a lot, because after having been in a village, I think I was quite innocent when I went out into the world' (Bartlett, 270). She went on to explain that her wartime experiences replaced innocence about the nature of relations between the sexes with an understanding that they were prejudicial to women. Men had control at work, and used this to their own advantage; men also had sexual power over women. Sadie spoke of learning about sexual harassment in a number of contexts – at work in the woods, in her billet and while hitch-hiking. Learning the ways of the world, for Sadie, involved developing a particular kind of gender awareness. The war made no difference to the gender hierarchy, which remained based on men's sexual, economic and political power, linked to their greater strength. War work revealed to Sadie the implications of that hierarchy for her as a woman. When asked if war service changed her in any other ways she said 'No, I don't think so, really' (Bartlett, 275).

How do we understand the remarkably consistent negative replies of these civilian women? None of them had chosen war work, but were sent into it by the state under regulations introduced in 1941. From April 1941 all women aged 18 to 45 were required to register at an Employment Exchange, where those who did not have children under 14 were interviewed. Unless they could convince the interviewer that they had compelling household responsibilities, they were 'directed' into 'essential' work. In December 1941, this state compulsion was tightened with the introduction of the National Service (Number 2) Act, under which single women aged 19 to 30 were conscripted for war work in the women's auxiliaries to the Armed Forces, in the munitions industries or in civil defence (Summerfield, 1989: 29–37). The women interviewed who were recruited to war work in this way, rather than by volunteering, perhaps not surprisingly gave 'stoic' accounts of their experiences. War service was an unfortunate necessity. They did not want or expect it to have a transformative effect. The story of the modernizing effects of the war on women was not useful to them as a language and set of concepts in which to frame their experiences. They expected to maintain their existing sense of identity, which most of them constructed as conventionally feminine. The war left intact their pre-war sense of themselves as women. Only in Sadie's account, informed by the concepts of 1970s feminism, did the war have an 'educational' effect, but the lesson it taught her was a negative one, about the 'real world' of unequal power relations between the sexes.

Part of the maintenance of identity involved retaining a sense of social (as well as gender) position. Barbara Wilson was one of the two servicewomen in the sample to give a 'stoic' account. Her story started from the reluctance with which she left her studies as an architecture student to join the WRNS and culminated in the relief with which she resumed her studies at the end of the war. She spoke, like some 'heroes', of receiving an 'education' in social differences as a servicewoman, but indicated that her own superior social position was confirmed rather than 'levelled'. Barbara was middle-class, but such a view could be taken by working-class women too. Helena Balfour referred even more explicitly to the way in which her wartime education in social difference confirmed her own position. If she had not been sent by the state, 'No way would I have gone into factory work. Well when I saw some of the young people, and as I say there was nothing wrong with their character or anything, they were just a wee bit rough and ready in their speech, but I wouldn't have been happy mixing with them all the time on a conveyor belt or something like that' (Balfour, 655).

Another characteristic of the 'stoic' accounts was reference to the menace of war: to death and fear, to loss and grief. Yvette Baynes was the other 'stoic' who, like Sadie Bartlett, did not emphatically deny change, but her account differed from Sadie's as well as from the positive accounts of the 'heroes'. Her answer to the question about whether the war changed her was, 'Oh I'm sure yes. They were very very happy days, apart from the fact that you had a lot of friends killed, and you never knew when you were going to be killed, and you never knew when you were going to wake up and find that your best friend had gone, as I did one day. You know, I think it changed everyone' (Baynes, 700). Recall of such experiences of shared suffering in the context of 'personal change' gave a different meaning to the process of maturation from that attributed to it by the 'heroes'. Peggy Peters, secretary at a naval base, said that the proximity to death made you 'more grown up': ' The boy I was engaged to was killed … I think it makes you older really before your time' (Peters, 227, 230).

It was not the case that those who told 'heroic' stories of their wartime work did *not* experience anxiety and loss, or felt that they had no effect on them. For example, Joyce Greaves, one of the servicewomen who said war service had helped her to put issues in political perspective, suffered a personal tragedy. She related this to personal change and the war: 'Oh it changed you, definitely. It must have done. You can't have all those experiences and particularly getting married and being widowed by the time you're 21 – it all has an effect on you. It's bound to do isn't it. It either makes or mars you I think. I think I got quite a lot out of it really' (Greaves, 348). It is perhaps characteristic of a 'heroic' narrative to present setbacks and problems as trials which temper and refine the character, as Joyce did. Her construction 'It either makes or mars you … I think I got quite a lot out of it' is quite different in its robustness from Peggy Peters' view of wartime tragedy making you 'grow up before your time', or Yvette Baynes' lament for the almost unbearable loss of friends during the war.

Marriage, as we have seen, was regarded as a vital, almost inevitable, part of a woman's life in both the modernizing and the traditional strands of the discourse of the effects of war. The orientation to marriage within each was, however, quite distinct. The modernizing story gave it a less dominant position than the traditional account: marriage and motherhood could be combined with outside activities; modern marriages were to be relatively equal and companionate. The traditional account rejected such a prospect. Marriage and motherhood represented fulfilment for women; a gendered hierarchy and a division of labour within marriage embodied happiness for men and women, and stability for society.

The differentiator between the two groups in terms of the ways they reconstructed the effects of the war upon them and their expectations of life after the war, was not in itself the factor of marriage, or even the combination of marriage with paid work. All but four of the forty-two women married and all but two of those who married combined paid work (either part-time or full-time) with marriage at some point after the war. The small sample thus conformed to post-war social trends, in which, as we have seen, the proportion of women in the total workforce, the proportion of married women, and the proportion of women working part-time all increased. The differences between the 'heroes' and the 'stoics' were in the ways they spoke of marriage – who they married, how they felt about marriage, motherhood and home life.

Several women who gave 'heroic' accounts referred to making very different marriages from those which had been expected of them. For example Katharine Hughes got married in 1943: 'I mean I was engaged to someone else when I was called up. I never married him. I married someone else. We met and married within about six weeks' (Hughes, 356). She described a truly whirlwind romance. A similar sense of the fun of Forces courtships came through other accounts. The excitement was enhanced by the need to break disciplinary rules in order to pursue the romance, which was special in part because it was an independent liaison with someone from outside the family circle. In the case of Mary Mackenzie, one of those who met and married her husband while she was in the Forces, the man himself was part of the effect she felt that her war work had on her: 'It gave me more confidence in myself, plus the husband that I've got, he has given me an awful lot of confidence' (Mackenzie, 213).

Another characteristic of the accounts of marriage and motherhood by several 'heroes' was ambivalence and restlessness. For example Heather McLaren said that, on leaving the WAAF, she 'was quite excited about getting home to be with my husband and expecting my baby, that sort of helped a lot from leaving my job. But I'll say this much, when I came home I found it very difficult to settle. I felt I always had to be on the go. I missed all the company … civilian life seemed very humdrum after what we had had. And yet I mean I was happy, I was happily married. It was very difficult trying to settle' (McLaren, 682). This restlessness was exactly what the account of the modernizing effects of war on women predicted: it would lead, according to this story, to huge changes in feminine identities, in which marriage and motherhood no longer dominated women's lives.

The recollections of courtship and marriage offered by those who gave 'stoic' accounts of their wartime experiences were more sedate. They spoke of relationships with men they had known for many years, who were already part of their home lives. Edith Dixon is a case in point. She volunteered enthusiastically for war work in the WRNS, and sounded at the beginning of the interview as though she was going to construct a 'heroic' story. But as she described enduring what she felt to be an unimportant job in terrible conditions, her account became decidedly 'stoic'. She spoke of her relief in obtaining her discharge to marry 'a Church of Scotland Minister who had been our Minister in the Church at Prestwick where I taught in the Sunday School and sang in the choir and my father was the treasurer' (Dixon, 19). In the war, this man became an army chaplain but was disabled out of military service in 1943, at which point the couple married and, over the next thirteen years, had five children. Edith (like many of the heroes, as we have seen) said that her experience of war work 'did me a lot of good'. But the 'good' it did her was not to do with it taking her 'out into the world'. On the contrary, the negative features of war work 'made me very very much more appreciative of my home afterwards' (Dixon, 440). Those who, like

Edith, told 'stoic' stories did on the whole experience the war as 'long and weary years of separation' as the traditionalists put it, and they did welcome the restoration of home and family at its end. 'It was such a feeling of relief when the war was over' said Yvette Baynes (717).

The references the 'stoics' made to their marriages suggested that, even if there was a sense of inevitability about getting married, that was what they wanted at the time, and whatever happened to the marriage later had not altered this view. An interesting exception, however, was the case of Caroline Woodward. After a reluctant start in war work, she eventually became enthusiastic about her wartime job as a welder and regretted having to leave it at the end of the war. Reflecting on the subject of whether war work changed her, she said: 'Aye I wished it had ... Maybe I could have stood up for myself a wee bit better. But no, I just got married you see and that was that' (Woodward, 510). Caroline Woodward constructed herself as an unconfident person after the war as before it, in her marriage as in her single life. Her account contrasts both with the 'heroic' stories of personal development prompted by the war and with the 'stoic' accounts of contented acceptance of a return to a traditional feminine role. Caroline's comment placed her between the two narratives of war and social change. While acknowledging the personal change that might have happened as a result of war work, she communicated the idea that marriage as an end in itself was what she had expected and even wanted at the time. It was as if the interview caused her to review the life she understood within a traditionalist framework from the vantage point of the modernizing narrative, and to regret retrospectively the opportunities she felt she had denied herself in the past.

In conclusion, there was a distinct polarization in the responses of the women who offered us their oral histories to the question 'Did the war change you?' Those who were required by the state to join the war effort, and who saw it as something to be endured until the welcome release of demobilization, did not construct the war as having changed them. If it taught them anything new, the lessons were negative. They were about coping individually and collectively with adversity, with tragedy and with fear, whether produced by military aggression, by perilous war work, or by the iniquities of men. For these women, personal change of the sort posed by the discourse of modernity was not on the agenda. They did not expect the war to lift a curtain or open a door. For the most part they framed their wartime stories in terms of continuity with what women had always been: low paid workers for whom the satisfactions of marriage, children, home-making and family life were sufficient. On the other hand, women who welcomed the war effort, who strove to participate as close to the front line as a woman could get, whether in military or civilian work, presented narratives structured by the concept of change. The process of transformation began with the welcome upheaval of leaving one life for another, and continued with the story of learning and applying new skills, of mixing with unfamiliar social groups, and of discovering a new humanity and a new self.

The story a woman told depended not on simple determinants like social class, age or education. It was a consequence of how she took up as her own the models of womanhood available to her during and after the war. It depended on the 'modes of female identification' which she adopted, that is 'the different ways in which women confront the institutions that reproduce and dictate social models of and for women' (Chanfrault-Duchet, 1991: 90). Since the models available to explain the effects of the war on British women contradict each other, it is perhaps not surprising that women mainly followed one or other of these discursive formulations. Nevertheless, as we have seen, some women's narratives shifted from one account to the other, as if they were searching for an alternative story to the dominant versions, for other ways of accounting for their personal transition from war to peace.

Notes

1. This chapter is closely related to Chapter 7 of my book *Reconstructing Women's Wartime Lives: Discourse and Subjectivity in Oral Histories of the 1940s* (Manchester: Manchester University Press, 1998). The book as a whole discusses the relationship of women's subjective accounts of their wartime lives, given in oral history interviews, to discursive constructions of British women and the war produced at the time and since. I should like to thank members of the Cardiff University History Department Seminar held in February 1997 for their stimulating discussion of an early draft of material relating specifically to this chapter. I should also like to thank Hilary Arksey and Nicole Crockett for their part in the interviewing project and, above all, the forty-two women who agreed to be interviewed.

2. Economic and Social Research Council grant number R000 23 2048, 1990–1992, project title 'Gender, Training and Employment 1939–1950: An Historical Analysis'.

3. All the women interviewed have been given pseudonyms. For biographical details of each woman quoted, see my *Reconstructing Women's Wartime Lives: Discourse and Subjectivity in Oral Histories of the Second World War*, Appendix 2, pp. 300–12.

4. The numbers following the name refer to the text unit numbers assigned to the interview transcripts by the qualitative data analysis package NUDIST.

References

Calder, A. (1971) *The People's War: Britain 1939–1945.* London: Panther.

Central Statistical Office (1995) *Fighting with Figures: A Statistical Digest of the War.* London: HMSO.

Chanfrault-Duchet, M.-F. (1991) 'Narrative structures, social models, and symbolic representation in the life story'. In S. B. Gluck and D. Patai, *Women's Words: The Feminist Practice of Oral History.* London: Routledge, pp. 77–92.

Coleman, P. (1991) 'Ageing and life history: the meaning of reminiscence in late life'. In S. Dex (ed.), *Life and Work History Analyses: Qualitative and Quantitative Developments.* London: Routledge, pp. 120–43.

Davies, B. (1992) 'Women's subjectivity and feminist stories'. In C. Ellis and M. G. Flaherty (eds), *Investigating Subjectivity: Research on Lived Experience.* London: Sage, pp. 53–76.

Dawson, G. (1994) *Soldier Heroes: British Adventure, Empire and the Imagining of Masculinities.* London: Routledge.

Dyhouse, C. (1981) *Girls Growing up in Late Victorian and Edwardian England.* London: Routledge and Kegan Paul.

Elshtain, J. B. (1987) *Women and War*. Brighton: Harvester Wheatsheaf.

Gledhill, C. and Swanson, G. (1984) 'Gender and sexuality in Second World War films: a feminist approach'. In G. Hurd (ed.), *National Fictions*. London: BFI, pp. 56–62.

Hansard (1944) vol. 404, House of Commons Debates, 5s, 15 November 1944, Manpower (Release from Forces).

Howard, K. (1945) *Sex Problems of the Returning Soldier*. Manchester: Sydney Pemberton.

Lewis, J. (1984) *Women in England 1870–1950: Sexual Divisions and Social Change*. Brighton: Harvester Wheatsheaf.

Madge, C. (1943) *Wartime Patterns of Saving and Spending*. Cambridge: Cambridge University Press.

Marwick, A. (1968) *Britain in the Century of Total War: War, Peace and Social Change 1900–1967*. London: Bodley Head.

Mass-Observation (1944) *The Journey Home: A Mass-Observation Report on the Problems of Demobilisation*. London: John Murray.

Minister, K. (1991) 'A feminist frame for the oral history interview'. In S. B. Gluck and D. Patai (eds), *Women's Words: The Feminist Practice of Oral History*. London: Routledge, pp. 27–41.

Mitchell, J. (1975) *Psychoanalysis and Feminism*. Harmondsworth: Penguin.

Myrdal, A. and Klein, V. (1968) *Women's Two Roles: Home and Work*. London: Routledge and Kegan Paul (first published 1956).

Noakes, L. (1996) Gender and British national identity in wartime: a study of the links between gender and national identity in Britain in World War Two, the Falklands War, and the Gulf War. Unpublished DPhil thesis, University of Sussex.

Pargeter, E. (1942) *She Goes to War*. London: Heinemann (reprinted London: Headline Books, 1989).

Passerini, L. (ed.) (1992) *Memory and Totalitarianism*. Oxford: Oxford University Press.

Paterson, D. (1945) *The Family Woman and the Feminist: A Challenge*. London: Heinemann.

Portelli, A. (1981) 'The peculiarities of oral history'. *History Workshop*, 12, 96–107.

Priestley, J. B. (1943) *British Women Go To War*. London: Collins.

Riley, D. (1983) *War in the Nursery: Theories of the Child and Mother*. London: Virago.

Sangster, J. (1994) 'Telling our stories: feminist debates and the use of oral history'. *Women's History Review*, 3(1), 5–28.

Scott, P. (1944) *They Made Invasion Possible*. London: Hutchinson.

Smith, A. C. H. (1975) *Paper Voices: The Popular Press and Social Change 1935–1965*. London: Chatto and Windus.

Smith, H. (1986) 'The effect of the war on the status of women'. In H. L. Smith (ed.), *War and Social Change: British Society in World War Two*. Manchester: Manchester University Press, pp. 208–29.

Summerfield, P. (1981) 'Education and politics in the British Armed Forces in World War Two'. *International Review of Social History*, 26, Pt. 2, 133–58.

Summerfield, P. (1988) 'Women, war and social change: women in Britain in World War Two'. In A. Marwick (ed.), *Total War and Social Change*. London: Macmillan, pp. 95–118.

Summerfield, P. (1989) *Women Workers in the Second World War: Production and Patriarchy in Conflict.* London: Routledge (first published 1984).

Summerfield, P. (1993a) 'Approaches to women and social change in World War Two'. In B. Brivati and H. Jones (eds), *What Difference Did the War Make?* Leicester: Leicester University Press, pp. 63–79.

Summerfield, P. (1993b) 'The patriarchal discourse of human capital: women's work and training in World War Two'. *Journal of Gender Studies* 2(2), 189–205.

Summerfield, P. (1994) 'Women in Britain since 1945: companionate marriage and the double burden'. In J. Obelkevich and P. Catterall (eds), *Understanding Post-war British Society.* London: Routledge, pp. 58–72.

Summerfield, P. (1998) *Reconstructing Women's Wartime Lives: Discourse and Subjectivity in Oral Histories of the Second World War.* Manchester: Manchester University Press.

Summerskill, E. (1942) 'Conscription and women'. *The Fortnightly*, vol. 151, March, 209–14.

Swindells, J. (1995) 'Coming home to heaven: manpower and myth in 1944 Britain'. *Women's History Review*, 4(2), 223–34.

Titmuss, R. (1958) *Essays on 'The Welfare State'.* London: Unwin.

3   Mothers of the Nation: Post-war Gendered Interpretations of the Experiences of Dutch Resistance Women

Jolande Withuis

When Queen Wilhelmina returned to the newly liberated Netherlands in the spring of 1945 after five years of exile in London, she was generally named *Mother of the Resistance*. Sometimes she was even called *Mother of the Fatherland*, a respectful reference to the honorary title 'Father of the Fatherland' of Willem van Oranje, the founding father of Dutch national independence in the sixteenth century 'Eighty Years' War' against Catholic Spain. However, the Queen was by no means a *motherly* woman. On the contrary, Churchill is said to have called her 'the only man' in the Dutch wartime government in London. In her own eyes she was primarily a soldier. Before the war others had found her authoritarian and very stand-offish, a 'Royal Highness', living at quite a distance from her 'subjects'. But Wilhelmina's role during the war had changed her image, as the war had changed the lives of many Dutch women.

In this chapter, I want to show that a form of *symbolic motherhood* played a major part in the interpretation of these changes.[1] After a short sketch of pre-war Dutch society, the chapter goes on to describe the part that Dutch women played in the Resistance against German oppression and the circumstances in which non-Jewish women lived during the years of Occupation.[2] Subsequently, I will show how the changes the war brought about in many lives were interpreted in terms of *gender*. All this throws new light on a paradox also encountered in other Western Allied countries: from 1940 to 1945, female participation in public life increased, while the decades between 1950 and the so-called second feminist wave were mainly characterized by conservative opinions and practices when it came to gender and the relations between the sexes.

Pre-war society

Before the war, Dutch society was characterized by a strong degree of *pillarization* (*verzuiling*). People mainly lived within what historians and social scientists have called their 'pillar'. There were four such pillars: Roman Catholics, Protestants, Socialists and Liberals. Family and friends usually shared the same religion or world view, and Dutch culture, education, political life, mass media and even sports were organized along these ideological dividing lines. These were strict divisions: Socialist parents would never send their children to Catholic or Protestant schools, nor were churchgoers supposed to send their offspring to a 'public' (e.g. neutral, or non-pillarbound) school.[3]

Society was segmented and also hierarchical: the majority of the population was non-political, law-abiding and deeply shocked by the sudden confrontation with war, a threat that had long been denied by government authorities. The Netherlands had stayed out of World War One and had formally followed a policy of neutrality in the 1920s and 1930s.

Women's and men's worlds in the 1930s were still strongly divided according to the principles of the traditional separate spheres. Participation in the labour market and in politics by women, especially married women, was extremely low; only 2 per cent of all married women engaged in paid employment. Both Catholic and Protestant women almost never held paid jobs outside the home, though they did work in small family businesses like shops and farms (Posthumus, 1977: 391). Dutch women, unlike women in France and Belgium, had had the vote since 1919 but this had not put many women in parliament (only four out of the hundred seats in 1940), nor were women usually members of political parties (Posthumus, 1977: 270). They were largely confined to their family and neighbourhood.

However, this restricted circle was slightly enlarged by contacts within the pillar-bound women's organizations that (rivalling the suffrage movement) were founded between about 1910 and 1930. Especially for Calvinist (*Gereformeerde*) women, these outside contacts played an important role in their later Resistance activities. It was the Chairwoman of the Gereformeerde Women's Organisation, Mrs H. Th. Kuipers-Rietberg, who initiated the largest national underground organization to hide people from the Germans. (She herself died, Christmas 1944, in the infamous Ravensbrück concentration camp.[4])

Feminism in Holland, as elsewhere, had practically died after about 1920. There had been a revival, however, which is relevant to the role of women during the war. In reaction to government proposals during the Depression to forbid all paid labour for married women, a broad-based committee was set up in 1935, uniting old and new feminists from different social and political backgrounds. Some of these contacts resulted in important initiatives before and during the German Occupation to save Dutch and refugee Jewish children. Interesting from a sociological viewpoint is the fact that, for this category of women, the unity created through gender partly cut through the strong social divisions of pillarization. Women of different cultural and religious backgrounds joined forces in all kinds of Resistance activities, having previously met each other *as women* in different kinds of women's activities. Nevertheless, we can conclude that the German Occupation of the Netherlands in May 1940 befell a society in which women in general were still strongly bound to family and pillar.

The Occupation

From May 1940 onwards, the Netherlands was completely occupied. That is, there was no division between a home front and a battle front, as in Great Britain and the United States. The nation was not fighting. Only a few days after the German invasion on 10 May 1940 and the bombing of the city of Rotterdam, the Dutch army capitulated. Civil servants in the main continued working, but the Queen and her government fled to London to become a government-in-exile.

The Netherlands did not have a 'Rosie the Riveter' phenomenon: no husbands, sons and fiancés had gone away to war and no war industry had to be kept going. By and large, the Dutch economy came to work for the Germans; there were no jobs to be taken for patriotic reasons. On the contrary, the Germans tried to force Dutch men to work in Germany by way of the *Arbeitseinsatz* (forced labour) and then tried to make Dutch girls and women take the men's jobs at home or go to Germany as well. These measures met with no success with women: taking over a man's job was considered to be collaborating with the occupying power. A pamphlet, probably written by a prominent feminist member of the Resistance movement, urged girls to refuse men's work and if necessary go into hiding.[5] Though more research is certainly required, we can safely assume that the war did not cause a shift in female labour force participation.

From a comparative perspective, this lack of female war labour is an interesting fact, for the post-war period exhibited certain striking similarities throughout Western Europe and the United States: full-time mothers, male breadwinners, baby boom and restrictive stereotypes with regard to femininity. Does this mean that it made no difference that women had held jobs during the war as they did in Great Britain and the United States? I will return to this question later.

Women's part in the Dutch Resistance can best be analysed in relation to military and political developments because the Resistance developed largely in reaction to changes in Nazi-German policy (Blom, 1977; Hirschfeld, 1988). During the *first* period of the Occupation, up to about February 1941, the Nazi Occupation forces had exhibited a certain restraint. The preparation for the persecution of the Jewish population was not yet very visible and the population as a whole was left in relative peace. World-wide, Germany was militarily successful and the expectation of long-lasting German domination led the majority of the Dutch population to seek ways to adjust to the situation. (Or worse: in the first two years of the Occupation, the Dutch National Socialist Women's Organisation grew from 1500 to 20,000 members, about whom we know as yet regrettably little (Marrenga, 1988).) In this period there was hardly any organized Resistance.

In the *second* period, when Nazi policy hardened and anti-Jewish measures were introduced, the Resistance began to grow. In this expanding Resistance movement, women mainly played roles in line with traditional gender expectations. These expectations were often cunningly exploited for quite opposite purposes. There are numerous anecdotes (now funny) about German officers kindly helping women they thought pregnant, who in fact had filled their corsets with guns or illegal papers and documents, or cuddling attractive blond babies lying on mattresses covering illegal papers. There are also stories about Germans charmed by that shy girl on the train who, when her luggage was examined, would rather not have men's eyes on that one tiny packet apparently containing sanitary towels, but in reality containing Resistance papers.

One of the most important life-saving activities mainly dependent on women (initiated by the chairwoman of the Christian Organization of Academic Women, Gesina van der Molen) was the smuggling of Jewish infants and toddlers out of the deportation centre in Amsterdam. Under the nose of their persecutors, these children were taken away from their parents and delivered to addresses all over the country, mainly by female students who did not look suspicious when walking down the street holding a baby.[6]

The same holds true for another particularly female Resistance activity: taking children (infants and older children) and adults into hiding in their homes. It has been estimated that during the Occupation around 25,000 Jewish and about 350,000 non-Jewish Dutch people were in hiding from persecution and forced labour in Germany, the latter mostly men (Blom, 1977: 498, 506). What does this mean? We can only guess at how many people were involved in helping them; figures showing the exact number of people involved in underground activities are, of course, not available. People who sought shelter usually moved from address to address, and some families had more than one person in hiding. But for the sake of argument let us say that about 100,000 Dutch families sheltered at least one person. That implies that 100,000 women, most of whom had never been involved in politics before and had always lived protected law-abiding lives, were suddenly active accomplices in illegal activities, which on discovery could bring death or imprisonment to themselves or their loved ones. One could say that by 'just' doing their daily housework, be it under difficult circumstances and sometimes for quite 'extended' families, they became involved in international politics. We can also assume – the more so in light of the fact that most of the time it was the *wife* who decided whether her family took someone in hiding – that this affected marital relations.

A lot of support was necessary for people to go into hiding. It took great effort to find trustworthy addresses, and for every single address a complete network of assistance was needed to provide transport, food, false identity cards, ration cards and sometimes also medical care or money for the wives and children left behind by those who were hidden. A lot of women were involved in these activities, such as the illegal industry set up to provide false identity cards. They all lived in constant fear of betrayal, of neighbours hearing an unusual sound, of people seeing a strange movement behind the curtains, of visitors remarking on creaking in the attic. They lived in constant fear of arrest or of comrades being arrested, tortured and naming names.

As Nazi rule and oppression intensified, the significance of women in the organized Resistance increased. Before 1943, women had not been very welcome. They had remained mainly background helpers or hosts of illegal meetings, offering refuge, emotional support and food to commandos in a country where food became more and more scarce. However, the more difficult it became for adult men to move about and travel freely, which happened after 1943 when Germans stepped up their terrorist tactics against non-Jewish Dutch society, the more indispensable women became to underground work. Hundreds of women couriers biked through the country, often on wheels without tyres, with guns, information, messages, warnings, lead for printing and copy for illegal periodicals. In the last period of the war, underground organizations, for instance the underground Communist Party and the Protestant-Christian Resistance paper *Trouw* (*Faithful*), depended almost completely on the courier activities of women. Another task carried out by women, often pretending to be girlfriends, was to accompany English and American pilots, whose planes had been shot down, out of the country. When detected, this 'helping the enemy' (in war language) meant the death penalty. Unlike their male comrades, women seldom became full-time members of the Resistance. The number of women actually participating in the *armed* Resistance remained small throughout the war. At least six young Dutch women were shot, most because of their involvement in the killing of Dutch Nazis or in sabotage (Withuis, 1995: 170).

During the final year of the Occupation, before the liberation in May 1945, Dutch society was disrupted; chaos, scarcity and hunger were rampant in the western provinces of the country. More than 20,000 people died during the 'hunger winter' of 1944–45 (De Jong, 1969–1988, Vol. 10b: 209). Keeping your family healthy, warm, fed and clean was the main task of women and that task became more and more difficult to fulfil. Since virtually all basic supplies were lacking, housekeeping required great creativity. Women turned tulip bulbs into biscuits, chopped down trees for firewood, made new clothes from old ones. They had no nappies, no soap, no food, no fuel, no medical care. And what is more, no husbands. Many women had to keep their families alive while the men were away in Germany or in hiding, and even when the husband was at home, he could no longer leave the house without running the risk of being arrested and sent to Germany. Women and children often had to walk for days from the western cities to the countryside in the east to beg the farmers for food or exchange linen, gold or jewellery for a bit of bread and butter.

All this meant that even the lives of non-Jewish women who did not participate in anti-Nazi activities were deeply influenced by this phase of total war. Women had to manage by themselves, while in pre-war Holland men had usually done most of the business outside the home. They had to become autonomous, sometimes finding themselves unintentionally the sole person available to take care of their families. Moreover, they were sometimes unsure about the fate of their husbands.

This description is based on the little information about Dutch women in the years between 1940 and 1945 that is currently available. For a long time, historical research into the Second World War paid little attention to women. Even simply trying to find details about individual women – Who did what? What were the backgrounds of women Resistance fighters? – is frustrated by a lack of specific factual material. In the official multi-volume Dutch national war history (De Jong, 1969-1988), women are mostly referred to anonymously. They are presented as the friends, fiancés or wives of individual men (who are certainly mentioned by name). Furthermore, historians usually define 'Resistance' in such terms as to exclude the activities of many women.[7] Sheltering people and other homely forms of anti-German behaviour are usually not included and a distinction is often made between 'organized' and 'individual' Resistance, the former being looked upon as 'the real thing'. Many exploits executed by women are not included in the category 'Resistance' as, often acting alone or with a few trusted friends, they aimed at saving *people* rather than liberating the nation.

'Reconstruction feminism'

How was the post-war social and political position of women affected by their wartime experiences? It has often been observed that despite women's active role in the Resistance in countries like Holland and France, and even despite their large-scale participation in the war industry in the United Kingdom and the United States, World War Two did not basically change the position of women.

According to Françoise Thébaud in her comparative overview in Volume 5 (*Towards a Cultural Identity in the Twentieth Century*) of *A History of Women in the West*:

> The end of a world war signalled a return of women to the private sphere. Since the children of the next generation were declared to be the key to national reconstruction, women were told that it was their civic duty to return home, just as it had been their duty a few years earlier to join the workforce. (Thébaud, 1993: 8)

This was certainly true for the Netherlands as is borne out by the hard facts of the limited female participation in paid labour and politics. Women's participation in these sectors only began to grow around 1980, after a decade of modern feminism. But reality is considerably more complex, if we take into account the new gender consciousness of 1945 that I observed in my research into some women's organizations founded during or immediately after the war (Withuis, 1994, 1995).

This new gender consciousness can be seen in the feelings of responsibility and self-confidence former Resistance women expressed at the time. Some of these women, having survived concentration camp hardships, were in very poor health. Nonetheless, the refrain of the *Women's Hymn*, the song of the Nederlandse Vrouwenbeweging (NVB, Dutch Women's Movement, an organization founded in 1946 mainly by survivors of Ravensbrück concentration camp), was: '*No longer weak women but a new and proud sex*'. Like women in other post-war circles, the NVB founders, among whom were some important Communist Resistance fighters, believed that their gender was deeply transformed.[8] Furthermore, women expected to get 'paid' for their wartime efforts. They felt their equality had been proven: 'We'd rather have rights than memorial statues', was their bitter observation when around 1950 they realized how much men had re-established their former positions (Posthumus, 1977: 350).

The NVB was founded after the war, but already during the Occupation other prominent Resistance women of various cultural and religious backgrounds had organized illegal meetings in order to discuss the position of women after liberation. In 1944, for example, the Nederlands Vrouwencomité (NVC, Dutch Women's Committee) was founded at the home of feminist Marie Anne Tellegen. This committee was to bring together women from all pillars and from all walks of life in order to fight for equal economic and legal rights for women in post-war Holland. Until the 1970s, when modern feminism replaced it, the NVC spoke to the government on behalf of women. Tellegen, who had been the leader of the pre-war committee in defence of women's labour, was a very important figure in the national Resistance movement. The fact that in 1946 Queen Wilhelmina appointed Tellegen Director of the Queen's Cabinet, a high position of trust, while Tellegen at the same time remained chairwoman of the NVC, illustrates the significance of women's participation in the Resistance movement. Tellegen was the first woman to hold this politically delicate position between Queen and Prime Minister, and was the first Director who did not belong to the nobility.

Also in 1944, some members of the same group of Resistance women formed the Unie van Vrouwelijke Vrijwilligers (UVV, Union of Women Volunteers). Whereas the NVC was primarily politically oriented, the UVV was to focus on post-war social reconstruction. Like the predominantly working-class NVB, the upper-class chairwoman of the UVV declared that women had been profoundly changed by their wartime responsibilities; she also optimistically assumed that pre-war prejudice about 'the weaker vessel' had by now disappeared (de Iongh, 1948: 272).

The NVC and UVV were female variations of a broader movement focusing on the renewal of Dutch society after liberation. This 'breakthrough' movement aimed at breaking through the restrictive pre-war divisions of strict hierarchy and pillarization. In the Resistance, people had associated with men and women of other denominations often for the first time – the poor with the rich, Protestants with Catholics or Communists – and for a short while many fostered this ideal of social 'renewal' and political and cultural 'depillarization'. However, this 'breakthrough' failed and very soon the old political parties and institutions came to retake their former positions (Blom and Ten Have, 1990).

Interestingly, women kept these 'breakthrough' ideals longer than the general organizations. They also brought them more often into practice. In my view this is because they consciously considered *gender* to be their unifying basis. For that reason, depillarization was a matter of principle to the NVC as well as the UVV.[9] Their views on women's situation in the post-war Netherlands were two-sided: they wanted to improve the position of women and they wished to draw women's attention to their duties and responsibilities in society, their duties *outside* their homes. The same holds true for the original NVB, but the NVB post-war gender goals dwindled when during the Cold War escalation the NVB turned into a Communist suborganization (Withuis, 1990; 1994: 308-9).

The war-inspired gender consciousness that I observed is not only seen in these three new organizations (NVC, UVV, NVB). Between 1945 and 1947 a striking number of political activities targeted women or were initiated by them. The future of Dutch women formed one of the issues that Queen Wilhelmina, after her return to her liberated country, discussed with prominent women members of Dutch society. Questions such as 'How should women vote?' that seemed to appear in the 1970s after more than half a century of feminist silence, surprisingly turn out to have been raised in the late 1940s too. There were election meetings for women and pamphlets on the theme 'What Do Women Want?' There was even a women's political party, Practical Politics (Withuis, 1990: 50-6). It was established in Amsterdam in the summer of 1946 by the famous Ravensbrück survivor Mrs Mies Boissevain-van Lennep. Though it never won a seat in parliament (just as the feminist parties founded after 1919 failed to do), the party, whose propaganda first of all referred to women's Resistance role, raised considerable interest and debate.

In more conservative confessional circles, a new female political awareness dawned as well. As the representative member of the Dutch Calvinist so-called Anti-Revolutionary Party, Mrs Diemer-Lindeboom, a former Resistance fighter herself, put it:

> Women silently took up their places within the Resistance movement beside the men and no one would have thought of refusing this help because it was offered by women. And for women it went without saying that after the war they would carry on with this work … but then they soon bumped their heads. (cited in Schwegman, 1980: 88)

The new collective gender consciousness was also manifest during the exhibition 'De Nederlandse Vrouw (Dutch Woman), 1898-1948'. This exhibition was held in honour of the Queen's Golden Jubilee and also commemorated the great feminist exhibition of 1898 when Wilhelmina, only eighteen years old, succeeded to the throne. The commemorative book *Vrouwen van Nederland 1898–1948* (*Women of the Netherlands*) (Schenk, 1948) was dedicated to Wilhelmina with the significant words: 'To Queen Wilhelmina, Mother of the Fatherland, the Women of the Netherlands dedicate their work for the people and humanity.' Instead of belonging only to a family and a pillar Dutch women now had a bond with the *nation*, and so with each other. Despite political and religious dividing lines they had come to know and appreciate each other as Dutch *citizens*. 'Women, help your land with head, heart and hand', summoned a post-war poster of the emphatically 'general' (as opposed to 'pillar-bound') Union of Women Volunteers.

So at the end of the war and during the first years of the rebuilding of the nation, gender was a category for political identification. Women felt that gender had been a basis for subordination and exclusion and therefore considered it as a basis for collective organization. I have defined this consciousness and its manifestations as *reconstruction feminism*. But by 1950 this short upsurge of feminism between the two well-known feminist waves, at least in its public manifestation, was over, as was the general move towards equality. Although immediately after the war, more jobs in the civil service were opened to unmarried women, it wasn't until 1956 that the NVC demand to grant women complete civil rights received a new impetus. It took a new feminist wave to complete the NVC equal rights programme. The Cold War was certainly one of the causes for the collapse of this small upsurge of feminism, as during that period, women's rights came to be associated with the 'unfeminine' Soviet form of emancipation.[10] A further reason for the collapse must be sought in the way women themselves perceived the place of their gender in society.

Symbolic motherhood

In order to explore the paradox that during and after the war quite a lot and at the same time very little changed for women, we must look into the various meanings of *gender* rather than try to establish the influence of 'the war'. Viewing gender as a fundamental category of historical analysis, as Joan Scott (1986, 1987) has put it, and as a prestige structure, as Michelle Rosaldo (1980) and Nathalie Davis (1976) have suggested, can make clear why the new female autonomy and even armed female heroism did not automatically entail a breach in tradition.

Analysis of the autobiographical and biographical literature, for instance, as well as the national history written directly after the liberation of Holland, shows that women's activities in the Resistance were framed in terms of traditional gender stereotypes. In the light of the silence between 1950 and 1975, it is remarkable that in the earliest post-war years, the part women played in Dutch Resistance was acknowledged; most of the important commemorative books of those years devoted a chapter to women in the Resistance. But it is just as remarkable that the descriptions of what these women did, and why, were embedded in traditional ideas about the nature of women. Women in the Resistance were described (not only by men) as emotional, irrational and reckless, and therefore only useful under male leadership. Women were courageous, certainly, but their courage had to be kept in check by the sensible and calm decisions of men. At the same time women were praised for their stamina, their solicitousness and their readiness to comfort their comrades and offer them *ersatz* coffee, even when the women themselves were the ones returning from a dangerous mission.

We find this description in the chapter 'Women and girls in the Resistance' in *Onderdrukking en verzet (Repression and Resistance)*. This widely-read standard work was written just after the war by a diverse group of authors. The chapter on women was written by a member of the Resistance herself, Mrs A. M. J. Ten Holt-Taselaar. Explaining why a separate chapter was devoted to this subject, Ten Holt noted:

> From the very beginning, by virtue of their nature, women's reactions to the German Occupation differed from men's. Their anger was more violent and deeper, and their strong emotions initially tempted them to reckless and dangerous demonstrations. They did not set targets, they did not reason. They did not ask themselves whether their attitude brought harm to the enemy. They reacted emotionally and primitively, but because of that their reaction was often more direct than the more rational male reaction. (Ten Holt-Taselaar, no date: 818)

In fact, Ten Holt illustrated her point with an example of very courageous women's behaviour in a situation where men acted in a cowardly and selfish way, but she only admits this hesitantly. Subsequently, the author contrasts 'young' with 'adult' Resistance women. Although young and unmarried women proved themselves particularly suited and willing to take on dangerous and important courier services, Ten Holt's appreciation is half-hearted. 'Many girls involved in this work were young and attracted by the heroism of it.' And by the heroic males, she later suggests. Older women, on the other hand, were 'a haven where the men could be attended to; due to the fact that they combined courage, enthusiasm and warm motherliness, they were a stimulating impulse and a source of encouragement to men at hard times when they felt downcast' (824-6).

This positive emphasis on 'warm motherliness', in which Ten Holt was by no means unique, explains, I think, to a large degree, the relatively minor impact of the years 1940 to 1945 on the post-war years. *Onderdrukking en verzet* shows us how women's new roles during wartime came, in the reconstruction era, to be ideologically fitted into old stereotypes. Women accomplished a great deal during the Occupation years but what they did could nearly always be interpreted as an extension of what they had previously done in the pre-war tradition of separate spheres. Even their crossing of pre-war gender boundaries could be interpreted as extending the essence of traditional womanhood. Motherhood in particular seemed a fitting frame, as Resistance names amply illustrate: the mother of the commando group, Sister Mammy, Mother of the Resistance.

Hence in the Dutch edition of *Storia delle donne* (1993), Marjan Schwegman and I concluded that, at the end of the war, some variant of the first-wave feminist ideal of *symbolic and social motherhood* had unintentionally been realized on quite a large scale. This concept of motherhood, sometimes also referred to as *spiritual* motherhood, was based on the idea that all women, regardless of whether or not they had children, did possess a kind of intuitive motherliness, an urge to protect the weak and those in need of help. Moreover, this ideal sought recognition for the social importance of motherhood and wanted society to acknowledge how essential this undervalued women's work was for the functioning of the public sphere.

The difference between being a housewife before and during the war was that household tasks and taking care of people, especially at the end of the Occupation period, were looked upon as publicly or nationally charged. The public–private distinction faded as war invaded even households where no one took part in illegal activities, where no one had disappeared, or where no one was persecuted or killed. The increased burden of household tasks (sometimes for families enlarged with refugees) was no longer endured as the isolated toiling of individual women but as a collective female effort to maintain the fatherland until it was liberated. During the war, Queen Wilhelmina, speaking to her occupied homeland on Radio London, sometimes directly addressed housewives to encourage them and to underline the importance of their tasks. She even called them 'sisters-comrades-in-arms' (Posthumus, 1977: 311–12).

The notion of a symbolic motherhood (unconsciously fostered) is tellingly illustrated in the autobiographical novel *Partisanen-Vrouwen* (*Partisan Women*), published shortly after the war. In this book the pious Protestant Jacqueline Kuyck described her Resistance activities. Apart from having a house full of Jewish children in hiding from their German persecutors, the two ex-nurses 'Aunt Jacq' and 'Aunt Nettie' also hid a group of commandos in the woods of the Veluwe, a rural area in central Holland. In order to save the children 'Aunt Jacq' had herself arrested. Looking back on those experiences and the time she spent in prison, Kuyck writes:

> The fatherland was in danger and a long, long line of simple women, unknown to anyone, honoured by no one, silently formed a bond and offered unbreakable Resistance to the enemy ... They fought unflinchingly because all of them, regardless of whether they had children, were mothers. (Kuyck, *c.* 1945: Foreword).

Her formula echoes the classic Dutch feminist tradition of seeing all women as 'spiritual mothers', yet Kuyck had no relationship with feminism.

The more explicit feminist varieties of the 1945 gender consciousness, the activities I have labelled *reconstruction feminism*, also show a feminism of *difference*. The welfare work of the UVV for instance intended to bring 'the feminine' into the nation, and to exert female care outside the family circle and pillar. The women's party, Practical Politics, aimed at 'diminishing the short-comings of the party system with its male origins, by making women's practical intelligence exert influence on all parties' (Withuis, 1990: 52). Party leader Mrs Mies Boissevain, a well-known feminist before the war, was one of Holland's most notable Resistance fighters. Boissevain, beloved among her fellow prisoners because of her strong and supportive personality, was generally called Mammy Boissevain; prisoners even called her 'Sister Mammy' because of her work at the hospital in the Dutch concentration camp at Vught. 'We take it that men and women are completely different', Boissevain wrote in a left-wing periodical, introducing her plans for the Party (Boissevan-vain Lennep, 1946: 550). At a meeting in the city concert hall in July 1946 'Mammy' unfolded her view that women's 'self-confidence' and 'public responsibility' had increased so much by their difficult experiences, that they could stop trying to be like men. Boissevain presented her post-war feminism as a modern feminism. The desire for equality (in the sense of 'sameness') was over now, she explained to her audience. In this new phase of human development, the feminine element should balance the masculine. Boissevain's women's party would stand above the party system and would contain no 'intellectual masculinized women', no women 'assimilated into the masculine way of life'. Women also would stand above traditional social distinctions; femininity meant harmony. If 'consciously womanly women' were given the positions they were entitled to, the world would be a better place.[11]

Boissevain herself certainly was a mother – two of her sons were shot by the Germans because of their part in the armed Resistance – but even her motherhood was perceived as highly symbolic. As her pre- and post-war feminist companion Mrs W. Posthumus-van der Goot wrote on the occasion of her death:

> From her immense trial [besides her own imprisonment and the death of two sons, she also lost her husband in a German concentration camp, JW] she gained insights which she subsequently tried to share. Her experience was that our feminine diversity is based on unity . . ., women can, because of their motherly feelings, give strength and warmth in every situation to everybody who needs it.[12]

However, this feminist emphasis on the difference between men and women was not the whole story – women wanted equality as well. In their view, difference was strictly linked to equal rights. Because of their qualities, women should be more equal, more important. As they saw it, the fact that femininity had had so little influence over politics and society had meant disaster.[13] As *mothers* in politics, as *mothers* of the nation, the 'Women of the Netherlands' would prevent new wars and unhappiness. They also wanted work. The title of an article in an emancipatory women's journal written on the occasion of Queen Wilhemina's Jubilee in 1948, 'Our Queen, mother and working woman' can be read as a programme of what these women envisaged: to be mothers, to be working women, and to have political influence (Withuis, 1994, 1995; Schwegman and Withuis, 1993).

Regrettably the equality part of their programme was not fulfilled. Difference in a restrictive sense prevailed in the reconstruction era. It certainly prevailed during the Cold War years and came to a peak during the 1950s. This holds true for all Western countries. Until about 1970, equal rights disappeared almost completely from the public stage, regardless of women's wartime role. In all Western countries, the 1950s was the decade in which the so-called 'feminine mystique', the myth of 'femininity', reached an unprecedented high.

Gender

In this chapter, I have attempted to explain that the post-war developments which so heavily emphasized the role of housewife and mother were a consequence of the specific way in which Dutch women during the war had committed themselves to the nation. This 'nationalization' of Dutch women (the term 'nationalization' is used by Thébaud (1993) in *Storia delle donne*) was a two-sided process. On the one hand, women's Resistance activities were undervalued and reduced to a form of extended motherhood (and then forgotten), while at the same time people realized the extent to which women's household activities had formerly been undervalued (Withuis, 1995).

In viewing gender as a grid for interpretation and as a prestige structure – in other words, by not looking at isolated activities but by analysing the meanings attached to these activities – I think we can also explain the similarities among various Western countries.

Penny Summerfield, for instance, has shown that the massive participation of women in industries to which they had formerly had no access had no lasting influence on post-war family policy and pro-natalism. Summerfield too ascribes this to the fact that the work these women did continued to be interpreted along traditional gender lines: work was defined as temporary, the nurseries were never meant to replace the mother but were services on behalf of the child, and part-time work came in vogue because no matter how much work women did, their role in the home was never questioned.

By means of her oral history project and through her analysis of large-scale interview material gathered during the war, Summerfield has been able to trace women's subjective response to the war years: 'Women's own testimony speaks volumes about the emotional and psychological changes they experienced.' Summerfield chose *Out of the Cage* as her title because 'wartime experiences ... felt like being let out of the cage for many women even though ... all the objective data indicated strong continuity in the subordination of women at work and at home ...' (Summerfield, 1993; Braybon and Summerfield, 1987).

Research on the French and Italian Resistance shows that just as in Holland, the Resistance activities of female partisans tended to be labelled as 'motherly care'. Jenson (1987: 279) writes:

> While the Resistance may have allowed women to show themselves as capable as men in wartime, reference to their activities also contained notions of specificity. The heroic exploits recited were often actions of women in support of their male *compagnes* [*sic*] or against the occupier who had diverted to his own use bread that was rightfully due to French children.

Or, as Paula Schwartz has noted, 'Partisan fighters in the bush, most of whom were men, required an immense support apparatus. The survival of maquis groups in the country-side depended on support of the surrounding population ... some maquis groups had "godmothers" or "guardian angels"' (Schwartz, 1987: 146). One woman was nicknamed 'Mother of the Maquis', another 'Mother of the Patriots'.

Marjan Schwegman and I (1993) have analysed Dutch post-war 'social motherhood' as the last flourishing of the old feminist ideal of symbolic motherhood. With our analysis, we modify the notion that women were 'sent back to the kitchen'. The 'feminine mystique' of the 1950s and 1960s was no male conspiracy but the unhappy result of a variety of historical factors, not the least of them that women themselves also interpreted their role in terms of motherhood and femininity. In the shattered world of 1945, the fear and insecurity caused by infringements of gender divisions – so fundamental to ourselves and our world view – were mitigated by a familiar interpretation scheme: gender worked as a grid which could select, interpret and evaluate activities. These interpretations channelled real transformations in gender into the safe mainstream of continuity. Our soldier queen Wilhelmina was changed back into a 'mother'.

Notes

1. This argument was first advanced in M. Schwegman and J. Withuis 'Moederschap van springplank tot obstakel: Vrouwen, natie en burgerschap in twintigste-eeuws Nederland', in G. Duby and M. Perrot (eds) (1993), *Geschiedenis van de vrouw, Dl. V: De twintigste eeuw* (Amsterdam: Agon), pp. 557–83. (Dutch translation of Volume 5 of *Storia delle donne in occidente*, Rome: Laterza, 1992.) See also Withuis, 1995.

2. This chapter, analysing the meaning of women's experiences in the Dutch underground, does not include the largely unwritten war history of Dutch Jewish women. A larger percentage of the Jewish population was deported from the Netherlands than from any other country in Western Europe. Of the 160,000 people classified as Jews, 140,000 had four Jewish grandparents and were thus in Nazi terminology referred to as *Volljuden* (full-blooded Jews). A total of 102,000 were murdered in Nazi concentration camps. On the genocide of Dutch Jewry, see Presser, 1965.

3. For an analysis of Dutch 'pillarization', see Lijphart, 1968.

4. Data on the social and political history of Dutch women and Dutch feminism comes mostly from Posthumus-van der Goot, 1977. On Mrs Kuipers-Rietberg (her Resistance name was 'Aunt Riek'), see *Het grote gebod*, 1989.

5. Posthumus, 1977: 338.

6. Van Ommeren and Scherphuis (1986). It is estimated that between 600 and 1000 children were saved in this way. See Verhey, 1991: 223.

7. In her study of the French Resistance, Paula Schwartz (1987) has made the same point.

8. On the NVB, see Withuis, 1990.

9. This fact has been neglected in Dutch historiography. Obsessed as they were with questions concerning the political dichotomy of 'left' and 'right' and the 'Breakthrough', historians and social scientists failed to see the different attitudes women held towards pillars and politics, and the fact that for them, another social distinction (gender) was crucially important. See Withuis, 1994.

10. For a similar argument, see Wilson, 1980.

11. Mrs Boissevain's handwritten notes on her speech, IIAV Amsterdam; the meeting was of Praktisch Beleid at the Concertgebouw, Amsterdam, 11 July 1946.

12. Posthumus wrote this in the Dutch newspaper *Algemeen Handelsblad*, in February 1965. On Mies Boissevain's feminism, see Withuis, 1990: 50–6; 1994; 1995: 72–7.

13. We might, I think, compare their philosophy to that of the 'women reformers' described by Wendy Sarvasy, who 'wanted social reform *and* equality' and so, in Sarvasy's view, show a possible synthesis in the equality–difference dilemma. See Sarvasy, 1992: 331.

References

Blom, J. C. H. (1977) 'The Second World War and Dutch society: continuity and change'. In *Britain and the Netherlands VI*. Den Haag, pp. 228–48.

Blom, J. C. H. and Ten Have, W. (1990) 'Making the new Netherlands: ideas about renewal in Dutch politics and society during the Second World War'. In M. L.

Smith and P. M. R. Stirk (eds), *Making the New Europe: European Unity and the Second World War*. London: Pinter, pp. 98–111.

Boissevain-van Lennep, A. M. (1946) 'Meer vrouwen in de Gemeenteraden'. *De Vrije Katheder*, 5, 22 February.

Braybon, G. and Summerfield, P. (1987) *Out of the Cage: Women's Experiences in Two World Wars*. London: Pandora.

Davis, N. Z. (1976) ' "Women's history" in transition: the European case' *Feminist Studies*, 3 (3/4), 83–103.

de Iongh, J. (1948) 'De maatschappelijke positie der vrouw'. *Vijftig jaren* Amsterdam: Scheltens & Giltay, pp. 265–74.

De Jong, L. (1969-1988) *Het Koninkrijk der Nederlanden in de Tweede Wereldoorlog 1939–1945*, 13 vols. 's-Gravenhage: Staatsuitgeverij.

Het grote gebod: Gedenkboek van het verzet in LO en LKP (1989) Kampen: Kok (reprint of 1951 edn).

Hirschfeld, G. (1988) *Nazi Rule and Dutch Collaboration: The Netherlands under German Occupation, 1940–1945*. Oxford: Berg.

Jenson, J. (1987) 'The Liberation and new rights for French women'. In M. R. Higonnet *et al.* (eds), *Behind the Lines: Gender and the Two World Wars*. New Haven: Yale University Press, pp. 272–84.

Kuyck, J. Th. [probably 1945] *Partisanen-Vrouwen*. Den Haag: M. Z. de Pagter.

Lijphart, A. (1968) *The Politics of Accommodation: Pluralism and Democracy in the Netherlands*. Berkeley: University of California Press.

Marrenga, E. (1988) 'De Nationaal-Socialistische Vrouwenorganisatie'. In M. Grever and C. Wijers (eds), *Vrouwen in de twintigste eeuw. De positie van de vrouw in Nederland en de Verenigd Staten van Amerika, 1929–1969*. Ijsselstein: VGN, pp. 37–42.

Posthumus-van der Goot, W. H. (ed.) (1977) *Van moeder op dochter: De maatschappelijke positie van de vrouw in Nederland vanaf de Franse tijd*. Nijmegen: SUN (reprint of 3rd edn, 1968; 1st edn, 1948).

Presser, J. (1965) *Ondergang: De vervolging en verdelging van het Nederlandse jodendom 1940–1945*. 2 vols, 's-Gravenhage: Staatsuitgeverij.

Rosaldo, M. Z. (1980) 'The use and abuse of anthropology: reflections on feminism and cross-cultural understanding'. *Signs* 5(3), 389–417.

Sarvasy, W. (1992) 'Beyond the difference versus equality policy debate: postsuffrage feminism, citizenship and the quest for a feminist welfare state'. *Signs* 17(2), 329–62.

Schenk, M. G. (ed.) (1948) *Vrouwen van Nederland 1898–1948: De vrouw ijdens de regering van Koningin Wilhelmina*. Amsterdam: Scheltens & Giltay.

Schwartz, P. (1987) 'Redefining resistance: women's activism in wartime France'. In M. R. Higonnet *et al.* (eds), *Behind the Lines: Gender and the Two World Wars*. New Haven: Yale University Press, pp. 141–53.

Schwegman, M. (1980) *Het stille verzet: Vrouwen in illegale organisaties Nederland 1940–1945*. Amsterdam: SUA.

Schwegman, M. and Withuis, J. (1993) 'Moederschap: van springplank tot obstakel. Vrouwen, natie en burgerschap in twintigste-eeuws Nederland'. In G. Duby and M. Perrot (eds.), *Geschiedenis van de vrouw. Dl. 5: De twintigste eeuw*, Amsterdam: Agon, pp. 557–83.

Scott, J. W. (1986) 'Gender: a useful category of historical analysis'. *American Historical Review*, 91(5), 1053-75.

Scott, J. W. (1987) 'Rewriting history'. In M. R. Higonnet *et al.* (eds), *Behind the Lines: Gender and the Two World Wars*. New Haven: Yale University Press, pp. 19-30.

Summerfield, P. (1993) 'Research on women in Britain in the Second World War'. Lecture, Stuttgart.

Ten Holt-Taselaar, A. M. J. (no date) 'Vrouwen en meisjes in het verzet'. In J. J. van Bolhuis *et al.* (eds), *Onderdrukking en verzet: Nederland in oorlogstijd III*. Arnhem: Van Loghum Slaterus/Meulenhoff, pp. 818-27.

Thébaud, F. (1993) 'Inleiding'. In G. Duby and M. Perrot (eds), *Geschiedenis van de vrouw, Dl. 5: De twintigste eeuw*. Amsterdam: Agon, pp. 1-13.

Van Ommeren, A. and Scherphuis, A. (1986) 'De creche 1942-1943'. *Vrij Nederland*, 18 January.

Verhey, E. (1991) *Om het joodse kind*. Amsterdam: Nijgh & Van Ditmar.

Wilson, E. (1980) *Only Halfway to Paradise: Women in Post-war Britain, 1945-1968*. London: Tavistock.

Withuis, J. (1990) *Opoffering en heroïek: De mentale wereld van een communistische vrouwenorganisatie in naoorlogs Nederland, 1946-1976 (Sacrifice and Heroism: The Mental World of a Communist Women's Organization in the Post-War Netherlands, 1946-1976)*. Amsterdam: Boom.

Withuis, J. (1994) 'Patchwork politics in the Netherlands, 1946-1950: women, gender and the World War II trauma'. *Women's History Review*, 3(3), 293-313.

Withuis, J. (1995) *De jurk van de kosmonaute: Over politiek, cultuur en psyche (The Cosmonaut's Dress: On the Psychology of Politics and Culture)*. Amsterdam: Boom.

4 The Myth of Penelope and Odysseus: An Austrian Married Couple Narrate Their Wartime and Post-war Experiences

Ela Hornung

The staging of a pair relationship in post-war Austria

The mythic figures of 'the homecoming man and the waiting woman' form a particular heterosexual pair relationship which marked Austrian discourse in the immediate post-war years. Homecoming assumes departure, and thus movement, separation, foreign lands and homeland. The meaning of the word 'homecoming' today has taken on pathetic, heroic and manly connotations. In contrast, the 'other', the 'waiting', indicate woman's continuity, unmoving faithfulness, and sexual passivity. The latency of this bi-polar pair construct is driven by sexual uncertainty and competition (Bauer, 1996). It is the old fairy tale of male polygamy and female virtue, the representation of the collective male desire for a 'Penelopisation' (Schaetzing, 1957) of women. What traces have these dialogues left in pair relationships? How were they promoted by the couples themselves? The Austrian state aided the construction of this imaginary couple based on the widely staged, (de)politicized bringing-home-to-Austria of the soldier fathers and sons who, as prisoners of war,[1] came to be officially incorporated as war victims in the construction of the Austrian victim mythology. The iconography of this antithetical couple is not just that of the 'healing nurse'/'sick man' – necessary and functional in the immediate post-war period – but a 'central element in the Austrian concept of economic, social and psychological reconstruction' (Bauer, 1996). The 'Family Austria' (Kos, 1994) first needed to reconstruct its national entity. Not included, quasi-extraterritorialized, were those not thought of as 'homecomers' since they had never been thought of as 'natives' – the Jews and other victims of Nazism, whose life stories vehemently repudiate the lies of Austria as victim (Embacher, 1995).

Interviewing couples

My interest in the analysis of interviews with married couples is primarily based on the overlapping and mutual inter-relations of men's and women's biographies in this period. How and to what extent did men and women reciprocally construct their biographies? Oral history is increasingly adopting the methods of sociological biographical research and concentrating on the recording of life stories with the aid of narrative interviews and their interpretation through textual analysis. This lends itself particularly well to the investigation of 'sychronisation stabilisation processes' (Dausien, 1996) in the interrelationship of men's and women's biographies.[2]

Under Nazism and during the war and the post-war period, the usual separation of female and male spheres was intensified by geographical separation: with men in the army and in POW camps, and women in the 'hinterland'.[3] Men's and women's recollections differ. I wanted to compare oral autobiographies of married women and men[4] to discover how their narrative strategies differ. After carrying out extensive case studies on women's recollections,[5] I examined the differences between female and male accounts about Nazism, the war and the post-war period. How do women today relate their experiences under Nazism? Did they talk to their husbands about this period of their lives and if so, in what terms? What did women know about men's experiences and thoughts during the war and in the POW camps in the Soviet Union? What stories do men tell? What possibilities for decision or action did women and men have in the mesh of the 'hierarchical relationship' of marriage in this particular period? What did the end of the war mean to women and men? Are the silences 'gendered'?

With the aid of one specific case study, the differences in the life story accounts of a Viennese couple on the war and post-war period and their relationship patterns are followed. How did the physical separation of 'battle front and home front' affect the narrated life stories of Gertrud and Otto Tischer? Were there any ascertainable effects on their life together in the period after 1945? Can old mythological tales of pair relationships in wartime (like that of Odysseus and Penelope) which dehistoricize the different forms of behaviour of the sexes, serve as narrative foils and construction aids for the married couple's treatment of their separation in World War Two?

In feminist discussions on gender history in wartime, the binary gender concepts of 'battle front – home front', 'peace-loving woman – warlike man', etc., have been investigated in their multiple connections and points of contact, and criticized as cultural codings which help form and maintain gender-specific dialogue (Cooke and Woollacott, 1993). Joan Scott has encouraged reflection on the way experiences are constructed in different discourses, and thus have always had to be regarded as historical, never as unchangeable, essentialized, fundamental categories (Scott, 1992). The couple separated by 'battle front and home front' behaved in a gender-specific way in terms of division of labour, but not independently of each other (Zipfel, 1995).

What do the women's struggles to secure the survival of their families in the war and the post-war period mean in comparison to the everyday life of the male soldier, and what influence do these experiences have on their accounts? True, the women interviewed talked about their everyday experiences under Nazism and during the war, but they preferred to describe situations experienced in the immediate post-war period in much greater detail, seeing them as atypical for women and thus as particularly unusual. The reticence of men of this generation in talking of certain wartime experiences stands in sharp contrast to the often traumatic experiences of Wehrmacht soldiers.[6] The majority of former Wehrmacht soldiers use a narrative form in which one's own person, one's own culpable actions and the terrible side of the war do not become a subject of discussion (Schröder, 1991, 1992; Rosenthal, 1995b; Hornung, 1996a, b). In the field of the collective memory of the war generation, the blackout still needs to be lifted.

As interviewees, I chose couples who had mostly married at the beginning of or during World War Two. There is barely any theoretical discussion or literature on methodological questions involved in interviewing couples.[7] It is neither a 'one-to-one' interview nor a 'group' interview; it is something 'in between'. It means interfering with a stable communication dynamic and dealing with the competition that often arises between the two interview partners. I opted, finally, for interviewing each person separately and giving them as much time as possible (at least two meetings each).

At the beginning, I was interested in the question of whether there had been any communication at all between the married couple about their experiences during the periods of separation. How far did women psychologically support their men, and thus psychologically reproduce the 'warriors', and afterwards support their exoneration strategies? I started, in fact, from the expectation that couples would have attempted to come to an understanding of each other's differing experiences in order to rebuild a common basis of trust and understanding. I had imagined that two people who felt close to each other would exchange ideas and build their relationship in this way. If they lived at particular times inside different milieux – as was the case for many men and women during the war – 'they would need to identify with one another – whether through letters, descriptions, through their accounts on seeing each other again, to be able to let each other know every detail of the circumstances in which they found themselves when they were no longer in contact with each other – in order to allow everything in their experiences that was alien to the one or the other to be absorbed into their common thinking' (Halbwachs, 1995: 25). I had, in fact, imagined the communication of these alien experiences and areas to be the foundation of a functioning relationship.

Gertrud and Otto Tischer: a biographical approach

The qualitative approach – characterized by openness – means neither quantification nor representativity. It offers the opportunity to carry out nuanced research on male and female biographies. The narrated story of one's life is always a selective presentation of biography in a specific context as seen by the narrator in the present perspective.

I always use the interviewees' total biographies for interpretation. In open biographical interviews, the women and men interviewed structured their life story narratives without intervention on the part of the interviewer. This was then supplemented by a series of topic-centred follow-up questions concerning the Nazi, war and post-war periods. The 'remembered' and 'narrated' (Rosenthal, 1995a) is not merely recalling an event, it implies a meaningful structure in terms of situation and articulation, which is subject to constant change.

For this chapter, I have chosen interviews with one married couple who had a similar political and ideological background. In 1938, Gertrud Tischer's father became a member of the NSDAP (National Socialist German Workers' Party) and she lived in a so-called 'Aryanised'[8] apartment, which had previously belonged to a Jewish family. Otto Tischer's family, who belonged to the German minority, came from Bohemia. They were so-called Sudeten Germans, most of whom welcomed the annexation by Hitler's Germany.

I carried out several biographical narrative interviews with each of them in separate meetings, each lasting a number of hours. Certainly by their marriages in 1941, common as well as separately experienced histories and stories turn up in matching accounts (e.g. 'family legends' or anecdotes).

Otto Tischer was born in 1913, in a Sudeten German family. His parents immigrated from Bohemia to Vienna before World War One. Being an only child and a son, he was given the chance to study to become a surveyor, although his family was poor. Because of the shortage of jobs in this profession, he interrupted his studies in 1934. He then enrolled in the military academy and began a military career. In 1938 he welcomed the annexation of the Sudetenland and the take-over of the old-fashioned Austrian army by the modern German Wehrmacht – the latter he compared to Austria's good fortune in entering the European Union. [The interview was held in 1993 when discussions had begun on Austria joining the EU.] In 1945, he was held prisoner in a British POW camp near Denmark. He was released in May 1946 and returned to Vienna. As Austria had no armed forces until 1955, he had to look for another job and so he tried to finish his studies in surveying at the Technical University. Having been a staff officer in the German Wehrmacht, he had difficulty enrolling because of denazification measures (Stiefel, 1981).[9] Finally, he got the permission needed and quickly graduated. After 1946, he worked as a civil servant and became head of the Department of Topography in the Government Office of Standards and Surveying.

In the main part of his biographical narrative, he presented his life as a success story – an 'apolitical soldier and a successful civil servant'. In the sequence about his time in the German Wehrmacht – one of the longest parts of the whole interview – he sought to emphasize that he had always been a responsible officer. He chose 'the bird's-eye view' as the perspective for his descriptive account of the war, typical perhaps of officers having and representing a strategic view, and typical also of his profession as a surveyor. He told no stories about his daily war life, with injured men, blood and the dead. He explained that the soldiers at the front had no information about the criminal acts that were being committed and, even though he had been an officer, he did not consider himself a decision-maker. Like many Wehrmacht soldiers I interviewed, after 1945 Otto Tischer never spoke about his negative war experiences to his wife or his children.

Otto Tischer narrated hardly anything about his private life during the entire set of interviews. He concentrated on the description of his military career and his later working life as a civil servant, which fitted his biographical presentation. He only mentioned his wife, marriage and difficulties with his children shortly before the end of our talks, and then only because of a question I had asked: 'Yes, I married in 1941 in Vienna. This was when it became critical.' Otto Tischer married in 1941, at about the same time as he was sent to the Soviet front. This sentence also reflects interesting links and delicate relationships between the 'private life of soldiers' and the 'official course of the war'.

As he had been an officer in the Wehrmacht, he and his wife received no additional ration cards when the war ended. He was dependent on his wife's survival labour in the immediate post-war period, as he started to study very soon after his return. Otto Tischer did not talk about her or her work. I got the impression that he found it difficult to admit to himself that he was the weaker of the two during this period, which was contrary to his image of a man – being strong and the bread-winner.

Gertrud Tischer was born in 1919. Her father was director of a technical college, her mother was a housewife. In 1938 her father (formerly a Social Democrat) became a member of the NSDAP. After school, under the Nazi regime, she trained as a physical education teacher and met Otto Tischer. He prevented her from studying medicine. Then she taught in a technical college and tried to finish her studies as a teacher at night school. In 1941 she married Otto. Their son was born in 1942, their daughter in 1944. Gertrud told me how difficult her life became when her son was born. At that time she was still giving lessons at a commercial college. Fearing the growing intensity of the air raids and not wanting to be separated from her child, she then gave up her job. In May 1944 her daughter was born. She recalled: 'There were heavy air raids on Vienna, and we had to run to the air raid shelters. When I came home from the hospital I had to breastfeed and change the baby in the shelter. Her eyes started to water because it was much too cold there for such a small baby – it was terrible; and so I decided I wouldn't stay in Vienna.' As the air raids on Vienna became heavier, she moved to her grandparents' house in the countryside. Later she was joined by her sister and her parents, and they stayed until the end of the war.

She told some stories about how the whole family cooperated in order to survive and how she managed to get enough food for her family. In 1954 she began teaching again because her son was ill and needed to go to a special school. She left her job in 1960.

Gertrud Tischer opens her biographical narrative with the story of her father, who returned as a disabled soldier from World War One and married a young woman, her mother, in order to have someone to look after him. Why does she open her narrative with this 'mother-nurse figure' and how can this be interpreted? One interpretation could be that she characterized herself as a nurse figure, unconsciously comparing herself to her mother, although Otto Tischer was not a physical invalid when he returned from war.

A little later in the interview, she touched upon how she had met her future husband at a dance in 1941. This part is within the narrative context of her university medical studies, which she had liked but had willingly given up because her husband was adamantly opposed to her continuing.

Although she had been a strong and independent woman during the war and the immediate post-war period, she always made her husband the centre of her narrated life story, even if he had been absent for years. He was always, in her mind and imagination, the centre of her life, although not in the 'lived' reality. This indicates the discrepancy between the 'lived' and the 'narrated life story'.[10] Only in rare moments, identifying herself with a 'strong mother figure', was she able to talk about her own strength and authority.

Gertrud and Otto Tischer both narrated one major story which seems to be an important 'family legend', the story of Gertrud's adventurous escape with her two little children from the 'Russians' at the end of the war. This narrative figure, the 'strong mother', shows their ideological tie and their acceptance of this type of female strength. This 'family legend' also perhaps helped them to handle their situation as a couple in the post-war years. Their narratives are able to visualize – in the frame of this milieu – typical constructions of female and male biographies and the gendered reactions to historical proceedings.

Narratives about National Socialism

Needless to say, the confrontation with Nazism also follows gender-dependent lines: for women, it was easier to withdraw from responsibility, because their collaboration on the Nazi home front seemed largely apolitical. Yet, are the narratives of men and women concerning the Nazi period really different? If so, what are the differences?

Even today most women are not aware of how household duties were functionalized and militarized by Nazi girls' and women's organizations. Women's services in the 'hinterland' – in fact as important for the war as those of men at the front – did not seem to call for collective self-analysis after the war (Bandhauer-Schöffmann and Hornung, 1994). Gertrud and Otto Tischer each told me during chats over coffee, in response to a question of mine, that they had never been 'Nazis', meaning never being members of the NSDAP, and both used the 'see no evil, hear no evil, speak no evil' collective narrative figure that is typical of Austrians who were neither opponents of nor persecuted by the Nazi regime. Both told stories which revealed their knowledge of the discrimination and persecution of the Jews. I was told by Otto Tischer in another sequence:

> I do not know, we were told that they [the Jews] were transferred from Döbling to the second district, because that was where most of the Jews had lived since coming to Vienna. So that was what they told us, giving vague explanations. The exact version of what had happened was given to us after the war.

In this passage, Otto Tischer uses only the passive form, in order to distance himself from any responsibility. It is interesting to note that Otto begins his narrative using a present verbal tense, 'I do not know', which could be interpreted as his still not accepting the historical facts about the persecution of the Jews in Austria. During the interview, Otto often referred to this theme without being asked. He always tried to differentiate between the 'political' Nazi organizations, such as the NSDAP and the SS, and the 'clean' Wehrmacht.[11] He said: 'I have NEVER been a member of a political party, I have always been a soldier.' Otto Tischer constructed his exculpation with the often-used figure of 'the myth of the clean German Wehrmacht', in contrast to the 'dirty, political' Nazi organizations, like the SS. He told me that he was particularly struck by the fact that in American films the soldiers of the German Wehrmacht were characterized as 'horrible enemies'. This did not correspond to his recollections or to his values.

Women who were not persecuted by the Nazis and/or who were not opposed to them, often make comments to the effect that in 1938 they knew nothing of the persecution of the Jews, or that 'the Jews simply disappeared'. Thus, Gertrud Tischer recollects, 'I only knew about those – that much I did know, from school – well, we had Jewish girls in class, in school. But listen. That was interesting, and there were suddenly three of them who were gone. We never learned where [they went to].'

Gertrud Tischer avoided speaking about National Socialism and did not mention the fact that she had lived in an Aryanized flat. But Otto Tischer did tell me the story about her flat.

In 1945, the war was lost and most of the soldiers felt like losers. They had to admit, 'We lost the war'. Women said more often, 'The war has been lost', thus expressing emotional distance, and apparent detachment. Even today, veterans' associations (the so-called *Kameradschaftsbünde*) and public bars provide the settings where men can experience socially accepted collective reminiscences, where they can shape their wartime memories into heroic male myths, completely ignoring their acts and their fears. Since post-Fascist society – unlike Nazism – ignored women's support of the war, women have, on the one hand, had no opportunity for self-glorification, but, on the other, they have also been allowed to ignore their share of responsibility (Bandhauer-Schöffmann and Hornung, 1994).

While the end of the war meant an interruption in the lives of most men who had served in the German Wehrmacht (Rosenthal, 1987), women had no such collective experience (Bandhauer-Schöffmann and Hornung, 1992). For men, the outward event of the defeat of the German troops brought about the loss of military structures and the collapse of their soldierly life. As with any break in a life story, this one also offered a chance for reorientation. After the defeat of the Wehrmacht, Otto Tischer had to reorientate his life, but this does not mean that he also reorientated his world-view. Since Austria had no army until 1955, he could not continue his military career. This did not mean that he changed his ideological and political views as well. Many sequences of his interviews indicate that he only formally accepted 'the right of the victor'. He would often say, 'Winners are always right, and losers are always wrong', but even today he still cannot admit that he had been wrong.

Is there any gender difference in their narratives about the Nazi period? Otto spoke extensively about his military career without speaking about his personal war experiences. 'Silence' or 'not telling' means that most soldiers tried to find a form of narrative which avoided personal memories and their direct involvement as actors in the war.

Like many of the women I interviewed, Gertrud Tischer talked mostly about her tough struggle for survival and her daily life at the end of the war, its immediate aftermath in particular. Many women narrate 'adventure stories' (Bandhauer-Schöffmann and Hornung, 1991, 1992) about this period when life was extremely hard. In general, daily life as a routine is difficult to relate. Changes, crises, extraordinary events are easier to remember (Rosenthal, 1995a; Knoch, 1988). But both Otto and Gertrud epitomized the collective figure of having 'seen nothing' of the persecution of the Jews, and presented themselves as innocent.

The first reunion after the war

From the moment men were drafted, women had to learn to provide for and make decisions for themselves and their families. It seemed for a brief period as if the traditional relations of the sexes had become cloudy. In 1945, the distribution of power and authority within the family had unmistakably altered. Most of the women interviewed, however, interpreted this change for greater independence as one of sheer necessity.

Being separated from one's spouse, often for years, naturally caused feelings of alienation, deepened by different intervening experiences. After a number of years, the couple was reunited: men hoped for safety, a homely atmosphere, and an unchanged, pretty, young, loving wife to coddle them after all the physical and mental strains at the front and in POW camps (Bandhauer-Schöffmann and Hornung, 1996).[12]

Narratives about the reunion differ greatly between women and men. In most cases, men have a very exact picture of this event, recalling the precise time and place. It is important to them, so they narrate elaborate stories about it. Otto Tischer remembered his arrival in a very detailed way: the date, that he was wearing a leather air force coat, the names of the streets he took on his way home. He told me:

> On 8 May 1946, I arrived at Westbahnhof, in a cattle truck … I still had that leather air force coat and I was glad to have it, because you could wrap it around you. And in Hütteldorf they deloused us when we arrived. Well, and then I came here, she lived there in Peter-Jordan-Street with her in-laws … And I walked up there, you have to take that small path up there, it still exists. Although there are buildings there now – there's a rented villa, it once belonged to her grandparents. And I entered, I don't recall that precise moment. But they were at home. She was there, but I don't remember about the children, they were in the garden – the house had a garden. Well, yes, of course the reunion was incredible. You can understand that, at that moment one fell into an abyss and had to start all over again. I was lucky, though, that I had interrupted my university studies, so for me the first thing was to try and continue my studies.

Otto begins his homecoming story with the date of his return: the anniversary of the liberation by the Allied troops. He contrasts the negative experience of his arrival in a cattle truck to the positive connotation of his leather air force coat, which could symbolize his former idealized position as an officer in the German Wehrmacht and could express a symbolic protective function against the uncertain future. In the next sequence, he describes in detail his walk home and his story reaches a climax of emotions as he enters his home. He says: 'She was there'. He does not remember the children, or where they were at his arrival. His 'emotional armour' as a soldier at this moment seems to break down. He expresses his inability to find the right words by choosing the impersonal 'one' to get more distance. He summarizes this emotional experience as 'one fell into an abyss'. This last sentence could express his break from a soldier identity to the unknown future as a civilian, the very point where he had to start again. This could also indicate a 'status passage' (Sieder, 1994) from an officer to a 'loser of war', from a soldier to civilian status. This metaphor of an 'abyss' indicates his lack of words, expresses his helplessness. In general it seems difficult for men to find representation forms for biographical changes which involve strong, deep emotions. This is even more so for men coming home from war or POW camps.

For many former soldiers, the return is a determining life experience (Rosenthal, 1987); they feel a rupture and/or crisis to a much greater extent than women (Bandhauer-Schöffmann and Hornung, 1992). The Wehrmacht soldiers had lost the war. They had been forced to forfeit the military as a prop to their virility. They lost their affiliation to the men's collective of the Wehrmacht and POW camp. Most women, who were neither Nazi victims nor Nazi activists, had, in contrast, more continuity in their social environment. The experience of military discipline, of oppression and violence in the Wehrmacht often found its sequel on the family stage (Hornung, 1995). The instructional 'ideals' of the Wehrmacht 'men's house'[13] (Weber, 1976) found easy access to the private house of the family and lent themselves particularly to the raising of sons. The military, warlike ideal of manliness was personality-forming for Otto Tischer. Brought up in World War One, marked by the conflicts in the First Republic, professional soldier under Austro-Fascism, taken over into the German Wehrmacht, his whole life was geared to a military career. For Otto Tischer, this military career plan ended abruptly with the end of the war. In a certain sense he never 'came home'; his real 'home' was actually the military 'men's house', which was now closed to him.

Over the years, what was expected from women had risen beyond measure. Correspondingly, women's expectations were by no means any less great: strained by their hard life to the point of breakdown, they hoped for relief when their husbands returned from captivity. For them, it was not such a caesura in their exhausting struggle for survival. Symptomatic of this is that Gertrud Tischer has even forgotten the year of her husband's return. She told me that he came back in 1948, which was wrong. The first fact she remembered in the context of their first meeting were the conflicts between her husband and daughter. She told me:

> The funny thing was, my daughter was still so little, and she always said, she could hardly speak then, 'Go away, stranger'. She always pushed him away. She always came to me, I had to take her in my arms. 'Go away, stranger'. Then she would say, 'What do we need that man for? We have Mummy, we don't need a man.' She always wanted him to go away, she did not like him. In the beginning it was terrible. And today (laughs) they are so close – but she did not want him. His presence disturbed her, she wasn't used to that situation, no. She was not used to that.

In describing her daughter's reactions she perhaps expresses her own feelings of distance. She seems to emphasize the importance of her position in the family as the person of reference. Perhaps this situation entailed more strain for her because she had to harmonize the relationship between the two.

Many war returnees had problems with their children. In many cases, the unknown fathers were at first experienced as 'strangers', as 'intruders' (Fishman, 1991; Preuss-Lausitz *et al.*, 1983), as the 'others', often characterized by an estranged appearance or a behaviour that could not be placed in the normal scheme of things. In a certain way, many returnees fitted the stigmatized individual investigated by Erving Goffman, who 'defines himself as nothing more than any other human being, whereas he is defined at the same time by himself and by people in his surroundings as someone apart' (Goffman, 1994).

In Gertrud's biographical narrative, the homecoming of her husband does not seem to be an important 'biographical point of interpretation' (Sieder, 1994). Her daily life went on as before.

'The starting point of a couple is the transformation of the other into a holy object' (Kaufmann, 1994)

Like most couples during the war, Gertrud and Otto Tischer had some information about each other, through letters and from men on leave. That does not mean that they really had any knowledge of their different experiences, as both women and men tried to make leave periods a time only for pleasure and tried not to talk too much about their sorrows and fears. The long separation and communication gap created an open field for gendered idealizing fantasies and projections of each other. The collapse of the postal system at the end of the war interrupted the flow of communication and this inevitably heightened fears concerning the fate of the other. In addition, Gertrud and Otto Tischer were terrified of the approaching Soviet troops. This was a typical reaction for many Austrians. Racist Nazi propaganda filled men and women with ideological images about the 'Russian subhumans' and advised all women to leave Vienna. Men were personally afraid of being captured in the Soviet Union and were obsessed by acts of retaliation at home, above all of rape. Women were afraid of the 'Russian rapist and plunderer' (Bandhauer -Schöffmann and Hornung, 1995). In reality, Gertrud Tischer managed to save her family and never had any terrifying experiences with Soviet soldiers.

After the end of the war, Gertrud Tischer had no news of her husband. She told me, 'I did not receive any letters any more. I only knew where he was when the war came to an end. He had told me before that he would not leave me alone, and so I had always waited for him to come and fetch me. But that was not possible. He did not come … He was in Germany, somewhere – still on duty at that time. And so I thought, maybe he'll come by plane one day and fetch me. Since he was a high-ranking officer then, that was how I imagined it. He had said he wouldn't leave me by myself, especially in the Russian Zone. But he never came, nothing, it was all in vain. In spite of everything, I had to stay in the Russian Zone.'

Gertrud Tischer described her husband using the fantastic figure of 'the rescuer', of 'the prince charming', who would come by plane and save her (using the figure of the waiting princess or Penelope) from the 'Russians', which reveals her gender constructions and their ideological background.

Otto Tischer also styled himself as a 'brave soldier fighting for the fatherland and the family', who had to protect his wife against the 'Russians'. But he had problems in admitting that he could not do anything for his family. He told me, 'But then, in the end the situation was such that, well yes, for God's sake, it concerned your own family back home as well! To surrender at this moment concerned not only myself, but also my family – the Russians had a bad reputation: they had *also* been attacked. We didn't know this at the time, we learned only later, that WE had raided them.' In this sequence, he expresses his own fears over whether to surrender or not and his ideological background of fighting against the 'red menace'. Using the word 'also' in this context could mean that after the war he had to accept that the German Wehrmacht had attacked the Soviet Union, but that even today he is not fully sure about the correct version of the facts.

Conclusion

With these exaggerated, unrealistic expectations, disappointment was a foregone conclusion. Instead of the hoped-for help, the men coming home from war often turned out to be an additional burden. Many couples did not manage to get along and divorced.[14] Marriages broke down either because partners had become estranged during the long separation, or because they could not come to an agreement on the distribution of power within the family. Moreover, men coming home from the war had difficulties with their mother-fixated children, as we saw with Otto Tischer.

Gertrud and Otto Tischer's marriage continued. To my question as to whether their marriage had suffered from any difficulties immediately after her husband's return, Gertrud answered that it had been easy for her because her husband was away a lot because of his job after the end of the war. She explained: 'I was alone quite a lot. Because then, as a surveying engineer, his job took him out of Vienna for six months, and I could not join him, I had to stay home. Well, that was my fate. And so I said to him, now you are retired, now the best time has come for me. Because now we can be together.' Gertrud and Otto Tischer's married life survived perhaps because of his frequent absences, which possibly helped them to avoid conflicts. Only now during retirement have they really started to live an everyday kind of marriage.

This couple's silences and stereotyped forms of communication when talking about the period of separation, where their experiences did not fit their own gender images and roles, are a necessary structural element of their relationship. Silences in this type of context are often, more than words, the basis of the relationship. Both had difficulties accepting experiences incompatible with their role: Gertrud could only speak about her competence and power at that time using the 'strong mother figure'. Otto could not even speak about his weak position in the immediate post-war period, and simply avoided it. In their use of gendered fantasies, Otto and Gertrud Tischer each reflect the image of the other. Both adopted these gendered narratives, developed and used during their Nazi and wartime experiences. Their relationship survived despite silences, perhaps because of the silences.

Paradoxically in general the poor economic situation, through the housing shortage and mobility in the post-war years, favoured new, differentiated forms of relationship and cohabitation, and thus first made the discrepancies and contradictions with the social norms and role demands on men and women visible. The (re)formation of heterosexual pair relationships and the realization of the nuclear family idyll of the late 1950s was only slowly put in train through the complex negotiation processes of the distribution of power between men and women in the post-war period.

Notes

1. Thus, for example, the minutes of the Ministry for Home Affairs on the meeting of the Prisoners of War Commission repeatedly state the common aim of disregarding all party political interests, as well as questions of judgement of war crimes where the return of POWs was concerned. Cf. the minutes of the first meeting of the Commission for Prisoner of War Matters at the Ministry for Home Affairs, on 5 July 1947, No 188, 386 – 12/K/47.

2. By this I do not want to suggest, however, that questions of gender may not also be investigated in interviews exclusively with women or men.

3. This chapter is based on my dissertation 'Penelope and Odysseus, Waiting and Returning: Influences of WWII on Biographies of Women and Men' and on the research projects 'The Situation of the Wives of the Austrian POWs in the USSR' and 'Austrian Prisoners of War in the USSR: Problems of Reintegration'. The projects were financed by the Austrian Ministry of Science and by Fonds zur Förderung der wissenschaftlichen Forschung, and conducted under the super-

vision of Stefan Karner, Institut für Wirtschafts- und Sozialgeschichte, University of Graz and Ludwig-Boltzmann Institut für Kriegsfolgen-Forschung, Graz-Wien.

4. I refer to a corpus of thirty recollective interviews with both men and women. The sample includes interviewees from different social classes and different age groups, most of them from Vienna.

5. For the research project 'Women in post-war Vienna' and its follow-up 'The fight for food: governmental nutrition policies and individual strategies for survival', Irene Bandhauer-Schöffmann and I used a corpus of sixty recollective interviews with women and men.

6. The research concerning men carried out by Gabriele Rosenthal and Hans Schröder confirms that men hardly ever spoke about negative war experiences with friends or relatives.

7. Cf. B. Dausien (1996) *Biographie und Geschlecht. Zur biographischen Konstruktion sozialer Wirklichkeit in Frauenlebensgeschichten*, Bremen: Donat; J. C. Kaufmann (1994) *Schmutzige Wäsche. Zur ehelichen Konstruktion von Alltag*, Konstanz: UVK; Günter Burkart (1995) Biographische 'Übergänge und rationale Entscheidungen' *BIOS* 1, 59–88; M. Bock (1987) *Macht in der Ehe*, Gießen: Focus.

8. In Vienna alone 70,000 apartments were 'Aryanized'. These were flats that had belonged to Jewish families before 1938, which they had been forced to abandon by non-Jewish Austrians. Cf. G. Botz (1978) *Wien vom „Anschluß" zum Krieg. Nationalsozialistische Machtübernahme am Beispiel der Stadt Wien 1938/ 39*, Wien: Jugend & Volk, pp. 453ff.

9. These denazification measures affected university lecturers as well as students. For the teaching staff, the general conditions for government service applied. After the first denazification at the Vienna Technical University, thrity-one of the fifty-six lecturers were dismissed. In February 1946 a commission, consisting of the Rector and one student representative from each of the three political parties, was established to check on student admissions. Cf. D. Stiefel (1981) *Entnazifizierung in Österreich*, Wien: Europa, pp. 171ff.

10. For a more exact differentiation between the 'lived' and the 'narrated' life story, cf. G. Rosenthal (1995) *Erlebte und erzählte Lebensgeschichte. Gestalt und Struktur biographischer Selbstbeschreibung*, Frankfurt: Campus.

11. In Austrian research, the difference between the 'clean Wehrmacht who conducted the regular war' and the 'dirty troops of ideology, the SS, etc., who conducted the ideologically motivated Genocide', has only recently been criticized. Cf. H. Safrian (1988*) Österreicher in der Wehrmacht*, in Wolfgang Neugebauer (ed.), *Österreicher und der Zweite Weltkrieg*, Wien: ÖBV; W. Manoschek (1993) '*Serbien ist judenfrei'. Militärische Besatzungspolitik und Judenvernichtung in Serbien 1941/42*, München: Oldenbourg; W. Manoschek (ed.) (1996) *Die Wehrmacht im Rassenkrieg*, Wien: Picus; W. Manoschek (1995) "Gehst mit Juden erschießen?" Die Vernichtung der Juden in Serbien', in H. Heer and K. Naumann (eds), *Vernichtungskrieg. Verbrechen der Wehrmacht 1941 bis 1944*, Hamburg: Hamburger Edition, pp. 39–56; W. Manoschek and H. Safrian (1995) '717./117. ID. Eine Infanteriedivision auf dem Balkan', in H. Heer and K. Naumann (eds), *Vernichtungskrieg. Verbrechen der Wehrmacht 1941 bis 1944*, Hamburg: Hamburger Edition, pp. 359–73; B. Boll and H. Safrian (1995) 'Auf dem Weg nach Stalingrad. Die 6. Armee 1941/42', in H. Heer and K. Naumann (eds), *Vernichtungskrieg. Verbrechen der Wehrmacht 1941 bis 1944*, Hamburg: Hamburger Edition, pp. 260–96.

56   *Ela Hornung*

12. Austrian war prisoners were in general released earlier than Germans. By 1948 all Austrians from American, British and French POW camps were released; most of the 335,270 war prisoners returned in 1945 and 1946. By 1949, the Soviets had released 136,270 prisoners of war; the remaining were released little by little until 1956. Cf. K. Böhme 'Die deutschen Kriegsgefangenen in sowjetischer Hand: Eine Bilanz', in E. Maschke (1966), *Zur Geschichte der deutschen Kriegsgefangenen des Zweiten Weltkriegs*, München: Verlag Ernst und Werner Gieseking, pp. 127ff. S. Karner (1995) *Im Archipel GUPVI: Kriegsgefangenschaft und Internierung in der Sowjetunion 1941–1956*, Frankfurt, München: Oldenbourg, p. 201; *Bundesministerium für Inneres (ed.) (1949) Das Buch des österreichischen Heimkehrers* Wien, p. 61.

13. Meaning the whole world of the military, where everything is done by men.

14. The divorce rate in Austria increased reaching a high point of 14,162 divorces in 1948. This was a 72 per cent increase by comparison with the 8226 divorces in 1939. In Vienna in 1946, 6357 marriages, and in 1950, 5014 marriages ended in divorce. Cf. *Statistisches Jahrbuch der Stadt Wien* (1950), p. 42.

References and further reading

Bandhauer-Schöffmann, I. and Hornung, E. (1991) '"Von der Trümmerfrau auf der Erbse": Ernährungssicherung und Überlebensarbeit in der unmittelbaren Nachkriegszeit in Wien'. *L'Homme: Zeitschrift für feministische Geschichtswissenschaft*, 2(1), 77–105.

Bandhauer-Schöffmann, I. and Hornung, E. (1992) 'Von Mythen und Trümmern. Oral History Interviews zum Alltag im Nachkriegs-Wien'. In I. Bandhauer-Schöffmann and E. Hornung (eds), *Wiederaufbau Weiblich*. Dokumentation der Tagung 'Frauen in der österreichischen und deutschen Nachkriegszeit' (Veröffentlichungen des Ludwig Boltzmann Institutes für Geschichte der Gesellschaftswissenschaften, Erika Weinzierl (ed.), vol. 22). Wien: Geyer-Edition, pp. 24–54.

Bandhauer-Schöffmann, I. and Hornung, E. (1994) 'Women of the ruins: daily life of Viennese women after World War Two'. *Women's Studies International Forum*. Special Issue 17(2/3), 204–15.

Bandhauer-Schöffmann, I. and Hornung, E. (1995) 'Der Topos des sowjetischen Soldaten in lebensgeschichtlichen: Interviews mit Frauen'. In *Jahrbuch 1995*. Wien: DÖW, pp. 28–44.

Bandhauer-Schöffmann, I. and Hornung, E. (1996) 'War and gender identity: the experience of Austrian women, 1945–1950'. In D. F. Good, M. Grandner and M. J. Maynes (eds), *Austrian Women in the Nineteenth and Twentieth Centuries*. Oxford: Berghahn Books, pp. 213–33.

Bauer, I. (1996) 'Die "Ami-Braut": Platzhalterin für das Abgespaltene?' *L'Homme: Zeitschrift für feministische Geschichtswissenschaft*, 7(1), 107–21.

Bock, M. (1987) *Macht in der Ehe*. Gießen: Focus.

Böhme, K. (1966) 'Die deutschen Kriegsgefangenen in sowjetischer Hand: Eine Bilanz'. In E. Maschke (ed.), *Zur Geschichte der deutschen Kriegsgefangenen des Zweiten Weltkriegs*. München: Verlag Ernst und Werner Gieseking, pp. 127ff.

Boll, B. and Safrian, H. (1995) 'Auf dem Weg nach Stalingrad: Die 6. Armee 1941/
   42'. In H. Heer and K. Naumann (eds), *Vernichtungskrieg. Verbrechen der
   Wehrmacht 1941 bis 1944*. Hamburg: Hamburger Edition, pp. 260-96.

Botz, G. (1978) *Wien vom Anschluß zum Krieg: Nationalsozialistische Machtübernahme am Beispiel der Stadt Wien 1938/39*. Wien: Jugend & Volk.

Bundesministerium für Inneres (ed.) (1949) *Das Buch des österreichischen
   Heimkehrers*. Wien: Jugend & Volk.

Burkart, G. (1995) 'Biographische Übergänge und rationale Entscheidungen'.
   BIOS, 1, 59-88.

Cooke, M. and Woollacott, A. (eds) (1993) *Gendering War Talk*. Princeton:
   Princeton University Press.

Dausien, B. (1996) *Biographie und Geschlecht: Zur biographischen Konstruktion
   sozialer Wirklichkeit in Frauenlebensgeschichten*. Bremen: Donat.

Embacher, H. (1995) 'Unwillkommen. Zur Rückkehr von Emigrantinnen und
   Überlebenden aus den Konzentrations- und Vernichtungslagern'. In Histor-
   isches Museum der Stadt Wien (ed.), *Frauenleben 1945: Kriegsende in Wien*.
   Katalog zur 205. Sonderausstellung des Historischen Museums der Stadt Wien.
   Wien: Eigenverlag, pp. 133-49.

Fishman, S. (1991) *We Will Wait: Wives of French Prisoners of War, 1940-1945*.
   New Haven: Yale University Press.

Goffman, E. (1994) *Stigma: Über Techniken der Bewältigung beschädigter
   Identität*. Frankfurt am Main: Suhrkamp.

Halbwachs, M. (1995) *Das kollektive Gedächtnis*. Frankfurt am Main: Fischer (first
   published Stuttgart 1967).

Hornung, E. (1995) 'Trennung, Heimkehr und danach: Karls und Melittas
   Erzählungen zur Kriegs- und Nachkriegszeit'. In Historisches Museum der
   Stadt Wien (ed.). *Frauenleben 1945: Kriegsende in Wien*. Katalog zur 205.
   Sonderausstellung des Historischen Museums der Stadt Wien. Wien: Eigen-
   verlag, pp. 133-49.

Hornung, E. and Kerschbaumer, G. (1995) '"Ich bin erst zu Haus, wenn ich
   über'm Semmering bin!" Stationen des Heimkehrens in die "britische"
   Steiermark'. In S. Beer (ed.), *Die 'britische' Steiermark 1945-1955*. Graz:
   Selbstverlag der Historischen Landeskommission für Steiermark, pp. 261-75.

Hornung, E. (1996a) 'Trümmermänner: Zum Schweigen österreichischer Soldaten
   der Deutschen Wehrmacht'. In W. Kos and G. Rigele (eds), *Inventur 45/55*.
   Wien: Sonderzahl, pp. 233-50.

Hornung, E. (1996b) 'Das Schweigen zum Sprechen bringen: Erzählformen
   österreichischer Soldaten in der Deutschen Wehrmacht'. In W. Manoschek
   (ed.), *Die Wehrmacht im Rassenkrieg*. Wien: Picus, pp. 182-205.

Karner, S. (1995) *Im Archipel GUPVI: Kriegsgefangenschaft und Internierung in
   der Sowjetunion 1941-1956*. Frankfurt: Oldenbourg.

Kaufmann, J. C. (1994) *Schmutzige Wäsche: Zur ehelichen Konstruktion von
   Alltag*. Konstanz: UVK.

Knoch, P. (1988) 'Kriegserlebnis als biografische Krise'. In A. Gestrich (ed.),
   Biographie – sozialgeschichtlich. Göttingen: Vandenruprecht, pp. 86-108.

Kos, W. (1994) *Eigenheim Österreich: Zu Politik, Kultur und Alltag nach 1945*.
   Wien: Sonderzahl.

Manoschek, W. (1993) *'Serbien ist judenfrei': Militärische Besatzungspolitik und
   Judenvernichtung in Serbien 1941/42*. München: Oldenbourg.

Manoschek, W. (1995) ‘"Gehst mit Juden erschießen?"': Die Vernichtung der Juden in Serbien'. In H. Heer and K. Naumann (eds), *Vernichtungskrieg: Verbrechen der Wehrmacht 1941 bis 1944*. Hamburg: Hamburger Edition, pp. 39–56.

Manoschek, W. and Safrian, H. (1995) '717./117. ID: Eine Infanteriedivision auf dem Balkan'. In H. Heer and K. Naumann (eds), *Vernichtungskrieg: Verbrechen der Wehrmacht 1941 bis 1944*. Hamburg: Hamburger Edition, pp. 359–73.

Manoschek, W. (ed.) (1996) *Die Wehrmacht im Rassenkrieg*. Wien: Picus.

Preuss-Lausitz, U. *et al.* (eds) (1983) *Kriegskinder, Konsumkinder*. Weinheim, Basel: Beltz.

Rosenthal, G. (1987) ‘"... Wenn alles in Scherben fällt ..." Von Leben und Sinnwelt der Kriegsgeneration. Typen biographischer Wandlungen'. In *Biographie und Gesellschaft*, 6. Opladen: Leske und Budrich.

Rosenthal, G. (1995a) *Erlebte und erzählte Lebensgeschichte: Gestalt und Struktur biographischer Selbstbeschreibungen*. Frankfurt am Main: Campus.

Rosenthal, G. (1995b) ‘Vom Krieg erzählen, von den Verbrechen schweigen'. In H. Heer and K. Naumann (eds), *Vernichtungskrieg. Verbrechen der Wehrmacht 1941–1944*. Hamburg: Hamburger Editon, pp. 651–63.

Safrian, H. (1988) ‘Österreicher in der Wehrmacht'. In W. Neugebauer (ed.), *Österreicher und der Zweite Weltkrieg*. Wien: ÖBV.

Safrian, H. (1993) *Die Eichmann-Männer*. Wien: Fischer.

Schaetzing, Eberhard (1957) ‘Die Frau des Heimkehrers, Die Sexualität des Heimkehrers'. In H. Prinz and H. Giese (eds), *Beiträge zur Sexualforschung*. Stuttgart: Ferdinand Enke Verlag, pp. 42–50.

Schütze, F. (1976) ‘Zur Hervorlockung und Analyse relevanter Geschichten im Rahmen soziologisch relevanter Lebensweltforschung'. In Arbeitsgruppe Bielefelder Soziologen (ed.), *Kommunikative Sozialforschung*. München: Fink Verlag, pp. 159–260.

Schütze, F. (1983) ‘Biographieforschung und narratives Interview'. *Neue Praxis*, 3, 286.

Schröder, H. J. (1992) *Die gestohlenen Jahre: Erzählgeschichten und Geschichtserzählungen im Interview: Der Zweite Weltkrieg aus der Sicht ehemaliger Mannschaftssoldaten*. Tübingen: Niemayer Verlag.

Schröder, H. J. (1991) ‘Die Vergegenwärtigung des Zweiten Weltkrieges in biographischen Interviewerzählungen'. *Militärgeschichtliche Mitteilungen*, 1(25), 9–37.

Scott, Joan W. (1992) ‘Experience'. In J. Butler and J. W. Scott (eds), *Feminists Theorize the Political*. New York: Routledge, pp. 22–40.

Sieder, R. (1994) ‘Anmerkungen zur sozialwissenschaftlichen "Feldforschung"'. In A. Linhart, E. Pilz and R. Sieder (eds), *Sozialwissenschaftliche Methoden in der Ostasienforschung: Beiträge zur Japanologie*, vol. 32, 165–80.

Stiefel, D. (1981) *Entnazifizierung in Österreich*. Wien: Europa.

Weber, M. (1976) ‘Wirtschaft und Gesellschaft: Grundriß der verstehenden Soziologie'. Tübingen, p. 684. Quoted in K. Köstlin (1989) ‘Erzählen vom Krieg - Krieg als Reise II'. *BIOS*, 2, 173–82.

Zipfel, G. (1995) ‘Wie führen Frauen Krieg?' In H. Heer and K. Naumann (eds), *Vernichtungskrieg: Verbrechen der Wehrmacht 1941–1944*. Hamburg: Hamburger Edition, pp. 460–74.

5   Girlhood in Transition? Preparing English Girls for Adulthood in a Reconstructed Britain

Penny Tinkler

'Girls'[1] aged between 14 and 20 years of age were constructed in the 1940s as key to the successful transition of Britain from war to peace. As such, they embodied anxieties and also aspirations concerning the future of Britain. The standing of Britain as an internationally competitive industrial nation was of particular import, but so too were the stability of family and gender relations, and the preservation of democracy, national integrity, security and peace. Adolescent girls stood at this juncture because, as was also true of their male peers, their teenage years were endowed with a special social significance.[2] Adolescence was widely perceived as a crucial phase of female development characterized by a number of transitions which occurred for most girls in their mid- to late teens. The most important of these were the transition from full-time schooling to full-time paid or unpaid work and initiation into heterosexual relationships as a prelude to marriage, mother-hood and domesticity. Since adolescence was perceived as crucial to the shaping of future adults, adolescents were central to plans for the reconstruction of Britain. The importance placed on individuals aged 14 to 20 years was heightened by concerns that they were particularly vulnerable because most were removed from the relative security of full-time schooling and cast out into the unsupervised world of paid work, with the attendant accessibility of what were regarded by many middle-class commentators as commercialized, sexualized and potentially corrupting leisure pursuits (see note 8). In 1951 only 19 per cent of 16-year-old girls were in full-time education, less than 10 per cent of 17-year-olds and 6 per cent of 18-year-olds (Census, 1951, Table 53); roughly three-quarters of all girls aged 15 to 19 were in full-time employment (Tinkler, 1995: 27). The intersection of concerns about the transitions facing both adolescents and British society significantly shaped approaches to girls growing up in the period between 1940 and 1950.

This chapter examines how preoccupations with the transitions of female adolescence, in the context of concerns and hopes of reconstruction in the late war and immediate post-war period, were manifest in three 'education initiatives' which targeted girls aged between 14 and 20 years. Firstly, it looks at informal education provided by the few commercial magazines that catered specifically for *girls* during the 1940s:[3] the *Girl's Own Paper* (henceforth, *GOP*) which targeted mainly middle-class schoolgirls and young workers throughout the war and in the period up to December 1947; its successor, *The Heiress,* which addressed upper-working-class and middle-class teenaged workers from January 1948 until 1956;

and the 'Teen Page' which featured in the widely read upper-working-class and middle-class magazine *Woman* in 1949 and 1950.[4] The second education initiative to be addressed is the government plan, set out in the Education Act of 1944 and elaborated in *Youth's Opportunity* (1946), for the introduction of a nation-wide system of part-time continuation education in county colleges catering for 15- to 18-year-olds removed from full-time education.[5] Leisure organizations which catered for girls are the third education initiative to be considered. Before the war, girls' leisure provision had largely been the province of voluntary organizations such as the Girl Guides and Girls' Church Brigade; many of them had religious associations. At the outset of hostilities the Board of Education (Ministry of Education after 1945), the government department responsible for the design and implementation of education policy in England and Wales, established an umbrella scheme, the Service of Youth, to protect the welfare and extend the education of young people removed from full-time education (14 to 20, then in 1947 after the raising of the school leaving age, 15 to 20). This scheme, which was administered by the National Youth Committee (Youth Advisory Committee after 1943), aimed to encourage and extend the work of voluntary agencies and supplement it with local authority youth clubs and pre-Service organizations which prepared young people for work in the wartime Services (women's services included the Auxiliary Territorial Service, Women's Auxiliary Air Force, Women's Royal Navy Service). By 1944 this scheme had dramatically increased the membership of youth leisure organizations. In Nottinghamshire, for example, less than 15 per cent of boys and girls were members of youth clubs in 1939 compared to 52 per cent and 46 per cent in 1944 (Tinkler, 1994: 397).

Although part-time continuation education plans, youth leisure initiatives and commercial publishing differed in many ways, these three 'education projects' shared a concern to manage or supervise the transitions associated with female adolescence. This chapter is organized around the two key transitions – school to paid work and preparation for marriage, motherhood and domesticity – and the ways in which the education initiatives conceptualized and aimed to manage them in the context of reconstruction.

School to paid work

Transition from full-time schooling to full-time paid employment was a feature of adolescence for the majority of girls throughout the 1940s, a pattern established in the interwar period. In 1931, 75 per cent of 15- to 20-year-old girls were recorded as in full-time employment; in 1951, after the raising of the school leaving age to 15 in 1947, 78.7 per cent of 15- to 19-year-olds (Tinkler, 1995: 27–8). For most girls in the 1940s this meant employment in industry, especially the clothing industry (20 per cent) or, increasingly, office (25 per cent) or retail work (14 per cent). Jobs in these sectors had been staples of girls' work prior to the war (24 per cent, 12 per cent and 10 per cent respectively in 1931) although the 1940s were significant for accelerating the expansion of service sector, and especially clerical, opportunities (Tinkler, 1995: 28–9).[6] Although middle-class girls often had better prospects than their working-class peers, those who left school at 16 or 17 usually entered office work following in the footsteps of their pre-war counterparts (Pratt, 1934: 28–9; Ministry of Education, 1954: 53).

The early transition from school to paid work, which occurred for most working-class and middle-class girls by their seventeenth birthday,[7] was perceived throughout the 1930s and 1940s to exacerbate the trauma and vulnerability commonly associated with adolescence. Conditions of employment, particularly in the unskilled and semi-skilled work for which most working-class girls were destined, were blamed for encouraging physical and mental stultification during this key period of development. Entrance into full-time paid work was also perceived to jeopardize the moral development of young people who, it was feared, were exposed to unwholesome influences in the workplace and, once they started earning, to unhealthy influences in their leisure.[8] Such concerns were not new. However, the war acted as a catalyst to change in that it heightened concerns about the preservation of social stability, moral standards and economic efficiency, which in turn increased fears about the consequences of ignoring the deleterious effects of paid employment on the malleable adolescent. Echoing pre-war concerns and demands for change, post-war commentators insisted on the raising of the school-leaving age and the introduction of measures to ease this transition in ways which allowed the further and full development of youth and protection of young people from undesirable influences. It was in the context of these concerns that the introduction of a nation-wide system of part-time continuation education and youth leisure provision were widely promoted for young people (e.g. Morgan, 1943; Jephcott, 1942, 1948; Ministry of Education, 1946, 1947).

Proposals for part-time continuation education, set out in *Youth's Opportunity*, clearly indicate that most working-class girls were assumed to be temporary paid workers, a view which was consistent with pre-war approaches: 'average' girls, the pamphlet explained, regarded their employment in unskilled and semi-skilled work as short term and therefore they did not need or want vocational training (Ministry of Education, 1946: 43). As Miss Hammond, HMI school inspector and member of the committee set up to research continuation education, explained to the Youth Advisory Council in 1943,

> Far more girls were engaged on repetitive work which irked them less because usually a girl regarded this work as temporary and looked forward to marriage and a home. Her mind was on the future and on her prospects as an individual. This made it easier for her to be content with monotonous and uninteresting work. (PRO ED 136/ 344 YAC II Minutes 2/43: 4)

This perspective, which was rearticulated in *Youth's Opportunity*, rather conveniently shifted attention from the conditions of girls' work, which Miss Hammond and her colleagues acknowledged were not exciting, to the girls themselves who, trapped in boring jobs, hankered after marriage. John Newsom, County Education Officer for Hertfordshire, reiterated these sentiments in his book *The Education of Girls* (1948). Although sometimes tongue-in-cheek, as implied by R. A. Butler (architect of the 1944 Education Act) in his preface to this book, Newsom clearly subscribed to the view that most girls were destined for temporary semi-skilled or unskilled work. An average girl, he maintained, therefore required continuation education which would enable her 'to endure the frustrations of her "temporary work" while preparing her for her main job of marriage' (p. 120). Endurance was not the primary concern of *Youth's Opportunity*; it stressed that average girls required education which would compensate them for their premature expulsion from full-time schooling[9] as well as instruction in subjects suited to older girls, for example parenthood and citizenship.

Newsom's dismissal of girls' prospects as paid workers was shortsighted. In the late 1940s it became increasingly clear that girls in semi-skilled and unskilled work were not necessarily 'temporary' workers. Labour shortages, arising in particular from the post-war export drive and the establishment of the welfare system, led to married women and even mothers being called back into the labour market as part-time unskilled and semi-skilled workers in the textile industry, and in institutional cleaning and clerical posts. Indeed, in the post-war period and in marked contrast to the interwar years, married women part-time workers were established as a permanent and significant feature of the female workforce. In 1951, 43 per cent of the female workforce were married compared to 16 per cent in 1931 (Summerfield, 1984: 188).

The work prospects of girls in skilled employment, probably upper-working-class and lower-middle-class girls, were, however, taken more seriously by *Youth's Opportunity*. Unlike their semi-skilled and unskilled counterparts, these girls were seen to need vocational instruction alongside a general education within county colleges. Attention to skilled workers was consistent with approaches to more 'able' schoolgirls. Amidst widespread concerns in the late 1940s about Britain's ability to maintain its position as a leading industrial nation and demands, created by the setting up of the welfare state, for women to enter skilled and professional work as nurses and teachers, the Ministry of Education pondered ways in which to develop human resources. In this context, official reports considered means of encouraging able schoolgirls, particularly grammar-school girls, to pursue advanced studies and, where appropriate, to continue in maths and science education and into science-related careers (e.g. Ministry of Education, 1954: v). Hence Butler, in his preface to Newsom's book, attempted to counter the domestic excesses of Newsom's message: 'Even though our girls may be taught to be good cooks and mothers, we cannot with our present limited man-power resources risk leaving undeveloped the mind of any girl who can serve her homeland as well as Mr. Newsom would wish her to serve her home' (Newsom, 1948: 10).

Youth organizations varied in their approaches to young women's prospects in the labour market, although the ambivalence noted in official education policy was also apparent in leisure policy. In *Looking to the Future* (1944), the National Association of Girls' Training Corps offered a positive work identity for its mainly working-class and lower-middle-class members whilst encouraging girls to take domestic and familial responsibilities seriously. In its reconstruction training programme it suggested the provision of specialized vocational or cultural training: instruction in child care, home nursing and technical work (geared towards fitting girls for opportunities in light engineering) were advocated alongside training in housecraft, the arts and foreign languages (PRO ED 124/90).

Consistent with the aim of formal education to promote the careers of 'able' girls in the post-war years, the *GOP* was vocal on the subjects of training and employment. Throughout the 1940s, as it had in the 1930s, it articulated a clear and positive vision of middle-class girls as adult workers and enthusiastically encouraged readers to pursue professional careers.[10] It was this commitment that underpinned the introduction of a regular careers page advising readers about prospects in a host of areas including teaching, horticulture and medicine. In an editorial entitled 'What Next?', the editor described the new opportunities awaiting girls on leaving school and contrasted these with the options available forty years previously:

> By the nineteen-twenties girls were being given more opportunities, but even then there were many difficulties confronting those who chose work off the well-beaten track of home, office and school. Remembering how hard I had to plead to take the kind of job that was then regarded as 'not quite suitable for a girl', I know how very fortunate you are to be starting out at a time when almost every profession and trade is open to you, and when there are so many training schemes to fit you for useful responsible work. (July 1944: 5)

In some respects the *GOP* was right. More women were employed in the male-dominated professions: at the end of the war there were 7198 women doctors and 549 women dentists, compared with 2580 and 82 in 1928; the number of women solicitors and architects increased significantly (Braybon and Summerfield, 1987: 261). Nevertheless, women professionals remained a minority and the only professions readily accessible to (mainly middle-class) girls in the 1940s, as in the interwar years, were teaching and nursing. Even service women equipped with new technical skills were not expected to transfer these into civilian jobs; instead they were encouraged to retrain for, or return to, the feminized spheres of nursing, teaching and clerical work which underwent dramatic expansion towards the end of the war owing to the rising birthrate and the reform of the health and education services (Braybon and Summerfield, 1987: 266).

'Teen Page', which targeted upper-working-class and lower-middle-class readers, was also positive about young women's work but, in contrast to the *GOP*, it principally advocated careers in the expanding feminized sectors of retail and clerical work. Ambitious girls of 15 and 16 were addressed in 'Your Success is in Your Hands' and advised on ways to ensure promotion: 'One day *you'll* be the one who dictates the letters; *you'll* be the one who designs the goods which now cause you so much anguished pencil-sucking before you hand them over the counter' (*Woman*, 'Teen Page', 7 January 1950). Similarly in 'Can I Help You Madam?' the author wrote that an enthusiastic and conscientious school leaver could make 'the job of selling into a fascinating career': this 'job can be a career … Most of the big stores have a carefully organized system whereby a girl with ability can, through the years, make her way right up to the top of the tree' (*Woman*, 'Teen Page', 4 February 1950). Elsewhere in its pages, however, *Woman* revealed that most of its readers were expected to marry and leave the labour market to have children, although it did acknowledge the possibility of returning to employment later in life. The mixed messages conveyed in the pages of *Woman* contrasted sharply with the *GOP*s wholehearted endorsement of life-long careers for middle-class women. Undaunted by evidence of obstacles which women encountered in employment, the editor and contributors of the *GOP* even insisted that readers should attempt to combine a career with marriage (November 1945: 6-7). *Woman*, however, more accurately reflects the wider ambivalence about women's adult role as paid worker which was evident in education policy and in government plans for the 'welfare state'. (Lewis (1992: 21) and Wilson (1980: 19) describe how the graduate wife seemed more of an embarrassment than a welcome addition to post-war British society.)

Preparing for marriage, motherhood and domesticity

Consistent with earlier approaches to social reconstruction and engineering (e.g. Lewis, 1986), the family was identified by wartime social reformers as key to the preservation of British life in the post-war period: 'for only on the foundation of good homes can a sound nation be built' (PRO ED 136/345, YAC Paper 13, n.d. 1943[?]). However, it was widely feared that the family had become fragmented and destabilized during the war from the effects of bombing, the evacuation of children, the mobilization of men and women into war work and, more specifically, the temporary replacement of traditional family services by state nurseries, work canteens and restaurants (Summerfield, 1984). Fears about the declining birthrate in the early years of the war contributed a further dimension to concerns about the family and provided the rationale for the setting up of the Royal Commission on the Population in 1945; however, by the time this committee reported in 1949, the birthrate had dramatically recovered.[11] Perennial concerns about juvenile delinquency and, in the case of girls, sex-related delinquency, heightened the significance attributed to the family. As the Board of Education explained in 1943, 'the root causes of children's misbehaviour are to be found in the broken home, the unhappy home and the home where, for one reason or another, they [youth] are deprived of affection and wise guidance' (p. 96). The equation of family and delinquency, and the preoccupation with 'decent homes' and 'family life', were echoed in other quarters in the post-war years (Ministry of Education, 1949: 4–5; Jephcott, 1948). Restoring the family was seen then, in different ways, as key to reconstruction and the restitution of social stability. Consistent with the prevailing sexual division of labour, education reforms and youth leisure initiatives identified women and girls as central to the healthy functioning of the family.

Promotion of the family was high on the Ministry of Education's agenda for the education of young workers. The aims and objectives of education in county colleges outlined in *Youth's Opportunity* stressed the importance of strengthening home life and parental responsibility: young people should, by the age of 18, have 'acquired an appreciation of the place and responsibilities of the family in a healthy community' (Ministry of Education, 1946: 31). Not surprisingly, girls were the focus of discussions about family life and youth's transition towards the responsibilities of parenthood. *Youth's Opportunity* was explicit that home and family were chiefly a female domain. In an appendix on 'the special needs of girls', the authors stressed that an important gender difference which had to be borne in mind in planning female education was 'women's unique function in the home', presumably domestic and caring work in the service of husband and children. The message conveyed was that post-war continuation education was not aimed at challenging the sexual division of labour in the home. For the most part, the appendix confined itself to discussing 'average girls', that is the 'unintellectual type of girl' who left school at 15 and became a wage earner in repetitive and monotonous work: 'Such girls form the majority of 15-year-old school-leavers, and all of them are future homemakers. Their own happiness, as well as the good of the community, requires that they should be much better equipped for this particular career than many who undertake it at the present time' (p. 43). Education for these girls, especially as they grew older, was to have a practical bearing on life; domestic studies and home-making were highly recommended. Even the 'more mentally alert type of girl' was perceived to need domestic instruction: 'Home-making for her is just as important as it is for everyone else. She will enjoy it as much as her slower companion, but she will be ready sooner for more advanced work' (p. 45). The familial note also emerged in guidelines as to the presentation of lessons. Girls, the reader was assured, required an approach to education which was linked to their interest in their appearance, boys, family life and home. Newsom rearticulated these views in *The Education of Girls* (1948). Continuation education, he claimed, should be organized around a 'centre of interest' which, for most girls, was the home:

> Women possess certain particular needs based on their particular psychology, physiology and their social and economic position. These will not be the same for all girls, but there is probably a sub-stratum of common experience which cannot be ignored. The fundamental common experience is the fact that the vast majority of them will become the makers of homes. (p. 110)

As this suggests, even grammar-school girls required instruction in domestic arts and, Newsom insisted, a social bias to their school and university studies.

Post-war plans for youth organizations set out in the Youth Advisory Committee review of the Service of Youth (PRO ED 136/345, YAC Paper 13) and by specific girls' leisure organizations (voluntary groups as well as local authority youth clubs and pre-Service organizations), also reveal a strong concern for strengthening home life, interpreted as preparing girls to more ably assume domestic and maternal responsibilities. This represented a significant departure from wartime policy which had aimed to encourage girls to contribute to the war effort and/or equipped them with skills which would fit them for adult war work in the women's Services. Although such work and training often had a domestic aspect, there was no explicit emphasis placed on preparing girls for marriage and motherhood. Reflecting on the post-war prospects of the Girls' Training Corps, the Youth Advisory Council advised that its training programme be converted to include a domestic policy to recognize the girl 'as a potential wife and mother' (PRO ED 136/345, YAC Paper 9, 1942); this was subsequently implemented.[12] In a similar vein, the National Association of Girls' Clubs commented that the 'girls' special province of domestic work would need to be explored' in the post-war world (PRO ED 124/70, *NAGC Annual Report* 1941–2: 9), while the National Association of Girls' Training Corps envisaged, and later introduced, a reconstruction programme for girls which included training in housecraft: 'To a woman her home is often her vocation, as well as a means of expressing her personality' (PRO ED 124/90, *Looking to the Future*, 1944: 3).

Boys were not totally excluded from discussion of the home. An inquiry into the education of the young worker conducted by the Central Advisory Council for Education (England) in 1948 rather predictably noted that girls should be prepared for marriage and instructed in the care of children, but proceeded to call for an inquiry to consider whether boys required such instruction (PRO ED 136/738, CACE Third Inquiry: Education of the Young Worker, letter 21 October

1948). This echoed the tone of *Youth's Opportunity* which admitted that in the past there had probably been too much emphasis in school education on domesticity for girls, and not enough for boys (Ministry of Education, 1946: 43). In his assessment of leisure provision in Birmingham, Reed (1950: 179) similarly stressed that boys needed to learn more about parenthood and housekeeping.

Although these sources do not explicitly discuss marriage, their reference to parenting and a domestic education for boys seems to draw upon models of companionate marriage which had gained ground in the 1930s, displacing more traditional notions of marriage characterized by a strict division of labour and a rigid hierarchy with the husband at its pinnacle. However, given the lack of detail, it is not possible to identify which variety of companionate marriage was being referred to as there were a number of models in circulation ranging 'from the notion that there should be greater companionship between partners whose roles were essentially different, through the idea of marriage as "teamwork", to the concept of marriage as based on "sharing" implying the breakdown of clearly demarcated roles' (Finch and Summerfield, 1991: 7). A companionate model of marriage also seems to have been favoured by the middle-class *GOP*. This was conveyed in the way that 'Youth Forum', a fictional discussion group, brought young women and men together as equals to debate topical issues; it is also suggested by a comment in a feature on married women and careers, that men should contribute to the care of a home (*GOP*, January 1946: 40–1). Informal and formal proposals for broadening the male role in family and home do not, however, indicate that the traditional sexual divisions of labour and responsibility were being radically challenged and they certainly tell us nothing about lived relations between the sexes. Braybon and Summerfield (1987: 272) argue that, although the basic structure of marriage did not change and that in many occupational groupings marriage remained as segregated as ever in the post-war years, the war did hasten the trend towards companionable marriage.

Marriage formed the bedrock and backbone of the nuclear family and gender relations. Rising divorce rates throughout the 1940s (1.5 per 10,000 of the British population in 1938, 3.6 in 1945 and 13.6 in 1947; Summerfield, 1995: 314) and an increased rate of illegitimacy (4.4 per cent of all live births in 1939, 9.1 per cent in 1945; Braybon and Summerfield, 1987: 215)[13] fuelled anxieties about the preservation of marriage and family life (Summerfield, 1987, ch. 12). Character-istic of the sexual double standard, it was female sexuality that was pinpointed for attention. Although before the war adolescent girls were perceived as sexually at risk arising from the destabilization popularly associated with adolescence, the war years were characterized by panics about an increase in premarital sexual activity among girls and worries about the incidence of sexually-transmitted diseases. Instilling the significance of marriage and regulating premarital sexual relations was, in this context, very much to the fore in initiatives to guide girls through the transitions of adolescence.

One response to the perceived problem of girls' sexuality which received widespread support from educationalists and youth workers was the provision of mixed-sex youth clubs. During the 1940s there was a dramatic expansion in mixed-sex provision (although most youth clubs retained some single-sex provision); in 1944 the National Association of Girls' Clubs (NAGC) became the 'NAGC and Mixed Clubs' and by 1950 it had twice as many mixed as girls' clubs (Reed, 1950: 153). Those who worked with girls rather than boys were the most avid supporters of mixed-sex provision. This was on the grounds that girls matured earlier than boys and were therefore in need of more guidance and that working-class girls, who were perceived as most at risk of sexual delinquency, were hostile towards single-sex clubs. Countering opposition to mixed-sex clubs, youth worker Josephine Brew (1943: 58–9) explained how ' "incidents" are far less likely to occur in a well-lit club than in shop doorways and back alleys'. This view was reiterated by the Ministry of Education (1947) and youth workers in the post-war years (Jephcott, 1948; Reed, 1950).

A further response to concerns about girls' sexuality was the provision of instruction about sexual matters. In 1943 the Board of Education published a pamphlet which encouraged schools and youth organizations to provide sex education: 'The stress of war and the social dislocation arising from it have given a new importance to the question of sex education'. Sex education, the Board insisted, was a means of protecting and guiding young people during their transition to adult sexual relations enjoyed within marriage; sex education was necessary to safeguard current and also future generations. *Youth's Opportunity*, published in 1946, specifically pinpointed young women aged between 15 and 18 years as sexually at risk; these girls, the report stressed, were often 'anxious and half-informed about sex, about their relations with boys and the vaguely understood connection between "having a good time" and the menace of disease' (Ministry of Education, 1946: 44). Significantly, this report contained no specific reference to the sex education of boys.

Grooming girls for heterosexual relations as a prelude to marriage was also a particularly strong theme in the case for mixed-sex leisure provision. Experience of the opposite sex was presented as an essential preparation for chosing a marriage partner and sustaining a marriage in the longer term. Mixed-sex clubs, it was claimed, would prepare girls to live with the opposite sex in platonic rather than romantic relations; they would also help to promote marriage and dissuade young people from undesirable sexual unions. As Morgan (who served as head of the Ministry of Information in the Northern Region during the war) had explained in his 1943 study precipitated by concerns about the wastage of youth, the acquisition of qualities 'basic to mating' was an important part of training for adult life; 'natural instinct', he insisted, could not be relied upon to safeguard the structure of marriage in a civilised community (p. 139). Pearl Jephcott (1948: 93), girls' club worker and author of two studies of girls, reiterated these sentiments and argued that clubs had a role to play in providing girls with standards: 'what so many need is an ideal of love and of marriage that is fiery and exalting', one that was distinct from 'crooner-style romance'. Such inspiration, Jephcott implied, was necessary to dissuade girls from premarital sexual activity.

The *GOP* and its successor, *The Heiress*, reiterated these themes in a few articles which were clearly influenced by wartime and post-war concerns about the sexuality of adolescent girls.[14] The *GOP*, for example, featured an article on boyfriends written by the youth worker, Josephine Brew, which articulated the need for girls to learn how to develop friendships with boys: 'If you have become interested in boys – and it is right and proper that you should (most girls want to marry and have a home of their own some day) – try to think of them as human beings with whom you *do* things, not curious creatures whom you show off with and show off to!' (*GOP*, July 1946: 12–13). It went without saying that girls did not '*do*' sex. Characteristic of youth workers, Brew suggested to the readers of the

GOP that girls and boys do things together such as join an evening class, a dramatic society or discussion group: 'It is the experience of friendship with boys which helps one to judge and decide carefully before taking the solemn step of marriage' (*GOP*, July 1946: 46). In a more explicit article on teenage petting in *The Heiress*, girls' sexuality was acknowledged but at the same time contained: 'There's not the slightest harm in an occasional kiss or some hand-holding or hugging. But it should be a climax to an evening – not the aim and occupation of the evening' (*The Heiress*, July 1948: 56). In a less intimate manner, 'Teen Page' also offered guidance on boyfriends and 'dates'.

Conclusion

Concerns about the transitions facing female adolescents were not specific to the late war or post-war years. Nevertheless, the war heightened their significance – the successful transition of girls into womanhood was crucial to the shaping of future citizens and a reconstructed Britain. Reflections on the effects of war and hopes about the future of Britain, in combination with the importance attached to adolescence, acted as the catalyst for change – the extension of youth leisure provision which laid the foundations of the modern youth service, the raising of the school-leaving age, renewed efforts to introduce part-time continuation education and official encouragement to schools and youth organizations to provide sex education. Although there was a consensus about the key transitions facing adolescence, the 'education initiatives' examined in this chapter reveal certain tensions about what womanhood entailed and how girls should be prepared for adulthood. This tension stemmed, in part, from the different ways in which women were expected to contribute to society amidst the pressing demands for both the reconstruction of the family and the expansion of the economy. It also arose from the ways in which social class cut across the transitions of adolescence and post-war expectations of girls as adults-in-the-making. Social class differentiation was apparent in magazines and also in formal education policy which distinguished between 'average' and 'more able' girls, a distinction which was a thinly-veiled differentiation by social class. The transitions associated with the teenage years were constructed as aspects of a shift from one state of being to another (although it might not be experienced as such). However, the transitions of Britain from the conditions of war to peace did not herald a radical departure from pre-war approaches to the shaping of women.

Notes

1. The term 'girls' is used here to denote adolescents. This is partly for convenience and also because adolescents were described as 'girls' in popular and official discourses of the 1940s.

2. The term 'teenager', used mainly to refer to the adolescent worker, appeared in the late 1940s and was popular by the 1950s.

3. Girls' magazines flourished before the war but most had folded by 1940. The resulting paucity of magazines continued until the late 1950s when new types of schoolgirl and teenage-workers' magazines emerged. Until the late 1950s most

magazines for 14- to 20-year-old girls were aimed at upper-working-class and middle-class readers. Working-class readers were catered for in romance magazines which targeted a broader female audience (see Tinkler, 1995).

4. In 1939 sales of *Woman* reached 750,000 (White, 1970: 97); by 1951 this had risen to 2,150,000 (Winship, 1987: 166). Fenwick (1953: 30) showed that roughly 50 per cent of 14- to 16-year-olds read *Woman*.

5. Due to financial constraints, universal part-time continuation was never introduced. Interest in part-time continuation education predated the war although proposals set out in the Fisher Education Act (1918) were similarly abandoned.

6. Wartime regulations and controls and the development of the welfare state led to a dramatic increase in the number of women clerks and typists in local and national government.

7. Ministry of Education (1954: 5) statistics indicate that the percentage of grammar school intake that left school at 16, 17 and 18 years for 1947 was 21 per cent, 64 per cent and 82 per cent respectively compared to 35 per cent, 74 per cent and 90 per cent in 1930. Although the percentage that stayed on at school increased between 1930–47, it nevertheless remained low.

8. There was particular concern from 1930 to 1950 about the staples of working-class girls' leisure activities – films, romantic magazines and dance halls – which were seen to encourage materialism and an unhealthy and romantic preoccupation with boys. See, for example Jephcott, 1942, 1948; Brew, 1943; Ministry of Education, 1946.

9. Education to enable them to concentrate on a piece of work and carry it through responsibly; to stimulate their imagination; and to improve their knowledge and use of the English language.

10. It is not possible to compare the *GOP* with other magazines as no comparable papers survived the war. The few remaining schoolgirl papers targeted principally at a working-class readership of girls aged 10 to 14 were dominated by fiction.

11. In 1941 the birthrate (including illegitimate births) reached an all-time low of 14.4 per 1000. By 1942, however, the decline ceased and the birthrate started to rise, reaching 15.9 per 1000 (highest point since 1931) and 17.9 per 1000 in 1944 (Braybon and Summerfield, 1987: 215).

12. During the war its training included general and physical movement and preparation for the women's Services – mechanical subjects, typing, cooking, book-keeping, elementary maths, physics, first aid, Morse code and wireless (PRO ED 136/322 Formation of the GTC).

13. Braybon and Summerfield (1987: 215) suggest that this should not be seen as a shift in morals as it was seen by many contemporaries. Pre-war, 30 per cent of mothers conceived out of wedlock but 70 per cent subsequently married. During the war there were merely fewer marriages before the birth (37 per cent).

14. Whereas pre-war the *GOP* had presented girls as too young to bother with boys (contrasting sharply with pre-war papers for working-class girls which were dominated by heterosexual romance), during the 1940s it acknowledged that many of its intended middle-class readers would be courting.

References

Board of Education (1943) *The Youth Service after the War*. London: HMSO.

Board of Education (1943) *Sex Education in Schools and Youth Organisations*. Educational Pamphlet No. 19. London: HMSO.

Braybon, Gail and Summerfield, Penny (1987) *Out of the Cage: Women's Experiences in the Two World Wars*. London: Pandora.

Brew, J. Macalister (1943) *In the Service of Youth: A Practical Manual of Work Among Adolescents*. London: Faber and Faber.

Census of England and Wales (1951) *General Report*. London: HMSO.

Fenwick, L. (1953) 'Periodicals and adolescent girls.' *Studies In Education*, (University College Hull), 2(1), 27–45.

Finch, Janet and Summerfield, Penny (1991) 'Social reconstruction and the emergence of companionate marriage, 1945-1959'. In D. Clark (ed.), *Marriage, Domestic Life and Social Change: Writings for Jacqueline Burgoyne*. London: Routledge, pp. 7–32.

Jephcott, Pearl (1942) *Girls Growing Up*. London: Faber and Faber.

Jephcott, Pearl (1948) *Rising Twenty*. London: Faber and Faber.

Lewis, Jane (1986) 'The working-class wife and mother and state intervention, 1870-1918'. In J. Lewis (ed.), *Labour and Love: Women's Experiences of Home and Family 1850–1940*. Oxford: Blackwell, pp. 99–120.

Lewis, Jane (1992) *Women in Britain since 1945*. Oxford: Blackwell.

Ministry of Education (1946) *Youth's Opportunity: Further Education in County Colleges*. Pamphlet No. 3. London: HMSO.

Ministry of Education, CACE (1947) *School and Life: A First Enquiry into the Transition from School to Independent Life*. London: HMSO.

Ministry of Education (1949) *Juvenile Delinquency*. London: HMSO.

Ministry of Education (1954) *Early Leaving: A Report of the Central Advisory Council for Education (England)*. London: HMSO.

Morgan, A. E. (1943) *Young Citizen*. Harmondsworth: Penguin.

Newson, John (1948) *The Education of Girls*. London: Faber and Faber.

Pratt, M. (1934) 'Reflections of a Headmistress on vocational guidance'. *Journal of Occupational Psychology*, 13(4), 285–94.

Reed, B. (1950) *Eighty Thousand Adolescents: A Study of Young People in the City of Birmingham by the Staff and Students of Westhill Training College for the Edward Cadbury Charitable Trust*. London: George Allen & Unwin.

Summerfield, Penny (1984) *Women Workers in the Second World War: Production and Patriarchy in Conflict*. London: Croom Helm.

Summerfield, Penny (1995) 'Women and war in the twentieth century'. In J. Purvis (ed.), *Women's History: Britain, 1850–1945: An Introduction*. London: UCL Press, pp. 307–32.

Tinkler, Penny (1994) 'An all-round education: the Board of Education's policy for the leisure-time training of girls, 1939-1950'. *History of Education*, 23(4), 385–403.

Tinkler, Penny (1995) *Constructing Girlhood: Popular Magazines for Girls Growing Up in England, 1920–1950*. London: Taylor & Francis.

White, Cynthia (1970) *Women's Magazines*. London: Michael Joseph.

Winship, Janice (1987) *Inside Women's Magazines*. London: Pandora.

Wilson, Elizabeth (1980) *Only Halfway to Paradise: Women in Post-war Britain 1945–1968*. London: Tavistock.

6 Women's Fight for Food: A Gendered View of Hunger, Hoarding and Black Marketeering in Vienna after World War Two

Irene Bandhauer-Schöffmann

This chapter will examine discrimination against women in a society of post-war shortages by analysing the distribution of food rations and supplementary food ration cards. That the ever-present hunger in post-war Vienna affected men and women differently can be observed not only in relation to hunger – that is, that women, as those responsible for reproduction, as mothers and housewives, had to respond to the shortage situation quite differently from men – but also in relation to gender-specific differences, even before the shortages, in state distribution of the meagre provisions among the population. Finally, I examine the survival strategies of the population and ask how hunger is remembered and which anecdotal themes concerning these times of hunger recur in the Viennese collective memory. My study is based on the archive material of the provincial food office of Vienna, and on the oral testimony of both women and men who spent the war and post-war period in Vienna.

From the reorganization of the provision system in post-war Vienna to the abolition of ration cards

The battle for Vienna, which had lasted nine days, ended on 13 April 1945 (Rauchensteiner, 1995a). The population spent these last days of the Third Reich in cellars and provided for itself from hoarded food stocks and from the slaughter of army horses. After the end of the regional battle, the Soviet military commanders' offices were established, and as soon as possible transferred administrative activity to the district mayors whom they had installed.[1] These mayors immediately arranged for requisitioning of such food stocks as there were, put out a call to the population to hand in looted food (with little success), and on the basis of the Nazi ration cards distributed what food was still available. The rations handed out differed widely from district to district as they were essentially dependent upon whether the district mayors possessed the organizational talent and the transport to get food into the city from the surrounding agricultural areas (Bandhauer-Schöffmann and Hornung, 1991).

In the second half of April, the bakeries and bakers in Vienna started up limited production again, in so far as they still possessed supplies (the Viennese people had looted more than two million kilos of flour from the stocks of the biggest bakery alone). But the weekly bread ration, which was organized at district level, amounted to only 500 grams per person at the beginning of May, raised to one kilogram in the second half of May. The first centrally organized distribution for the whole city was the Red Army's so-called 'May donation', comprising 200g beans, 200g peas, 50g cooking oil, 150g meat and 125g sugar per head, also handed out on the basis of the Nazi ration cards (Bandhauer-Schöffmann and Hornung, 1995a). Including this May donation the average daily ration in Vienna in May amounted only to 350 calories per person.[2] Diaries from this period, which record this donation with painstaking exactitude, show the significance of this hand-out from the Red Army.[3]

Subsequently, new ration cards were issued but the ration card system was only properly re-established in June 1945. From July, they were also differentiated according to consumer group.[4] Until 21 July 1946, each of the four Vienna Occupation zones had its own ration cards, which could only be used in the appropriate zone, an additional bureaucratic burden for people whose homes and workplaces were in different districts.[5]

The people of Vienna could not have survived without the assistance of the Allies, as Austrian agriculture was not in a position to feed the population for years after the end of the war. Until the end of August 1945, Vienna was provided with emergency rations by the Red Army. Until the end of June 1946, provision was taken over by all four Allies; then the United Nations assumed responsibility. Before the aid of the United Nations Relief and Rehabilitation Administration (UNRRA) was fully operational in June 1946, there was a serious supply crisis, the so-called '1946 May crisis', which meant that the normal consumer ration, already amounting to only 1500 calories at the beginning of 1946, had to be massively reduced and could not be raised to the earlier level until November.[6] From 1948, the ration book economy was gradually dismantled, and in December 1949 the Ministry of Food was dissolved. The period 1950 to 1951 was the first time there was something approaching free consumer choice, and from 1 July 1953 there were no more ration cards (Frenzel, 1947; Sandgruber, 1985b; Bandhauer-Schöffmann and Hornung, 1995b).

However, living conditions for wide sections of the population remained mean and frugal, and the statistics contradict images of an economic miracle and feeding frenzy: of the coveted foods such as meat, fat, sugar and fresh vegetables, only fresh vegetables had reached pre-war levels by the end of the 1940s, thanks to the initiative of the Viennese people who had laid out some 50,000 vegetable plots. Meat consumption only reached the pre-war average in 1956/57.[7]

Classification of the population into consumer categories

The ration card system was based on the consideration that people involved in heavy physical labour had a higher calorie consumption than others and should thus receive more calories on their ration cards. One section of the working population received so-called supplementary cards in addition to the cards given out to everyone, there being different classification methods in different Austrian provinces until May 1946. In Vienna, the highest calorific values were provided to 'heaviest labourers'; followed by the categories 'heavy labourer', 'labourer' and 'clerical worker'. The first list drawn up on 20 September 1945 by the Allied provisions committee included 28 occupations in the highest category, for example asphalter, boiler cleaner, wood-cutter, blacksmith and civil engineer. The list also included categories affecting women, namely pregnant women and breast-feeding mothers (who at the time did not receive their own 'mother's card'). Tuberculosis nursing was the only job in this category also carried out by women.

Such classification lists were drawn up by the Allies for the Austrian administration, which had to proceed in accordance with them. As self-evidently not all professions could appear on the list, the classifiers acquired great importance as they decided whether particular employees received a supplementary card, and, if so, which one. In Vienna, these committees were dominated by the trade unions until the end of 1947, after which an employers' representative was also included (Bandhauer-Schöffmann, 1995). All committees were made up exclusively of men as, in the slowly normalizing food administration, women had again lost the positions they had occupied during the period of upheaval between the end of Nazism and the establishment of Allied control. Discrimination against women in the distribution of ration cards for food and tobacco was *firstly* a direct result of gender-specific division of labour, and *secondly* a result of political decisions directed against women which were clearly illegal in that they contradicted the principle of equality.

It can be assumed from this that discrimination against women in the ration card system, which was a result of the structure of the labour market, was further exacerbated by the anti-woman position of the trade union officials who largely determined the distribution of supplementary ration cards in Vienna. Representation of women in higher trade union functions, as in all administrative systems directly based on the structure of the labour market, was noticeable by its absence.

Ration cards and the gender-segregated labour market

As a logical consequence of the gender-specific division of labour, 'men only' occupations received the highest food allocations; 'women only' occupations were in the lowest category. The 'heaviest labourer' category was occupied almost exclusively by men. But the second highest category, 'heavy labourer', was also understood by the responsible authorities as the prerogative of men. This is illustrated not only by the classification of occupations, but also in the reasoning for the ban on employing women in the building trades. Although women wanted to work in the auxiliary building trades, and although there was a shortage of labour in this area, the central trades inspectorate believed that women were in principle not in a position to earn the heavy labourer ration cards. 'Employment of women would result in an increase in food bonuses for heavy labourers, which would not be justified by the results of their labour' says the statement.[8]

The fact that housewives and maids received no supplement cards was in no way justified by the work that women actually did (which had extended enormously) but was a result of the socially inferior status accorded to women's work. Whereas maids did not receive a supplement card, teaching staff, who were well organized in a union, received a worker's supplement card in the summer holidays as well. Housewives and maids only received a supplement card from the end of May 1948 until it was discontinued in September 1948 because food conditions in general had improved.[9]

As the number of calories people were entitled to buy was established on the concept of typical wage–labour relations, those working in the non-social-insurance-paying jobs represented a problem group for the food administration. The people in these un- or little protected labour relationships were, above all, women: they worked, for example, as domestic servants or laundresses in varying households. With constantly changing employers, proof of full employment was hard to provide, but supplementary ration cards were not distributed without this proof.[10] Family workers too, again mostly women, failed to correspond to the 'norm'. Whereas in 1945 the wives who ran a trade or farm in the absence of their husbands had no problem being classified by the food administration as employed and receiving the appropriate supplementary ration cards, the attitude of the provincial food administration changed at the beginning of 1946. Although many men were still prisoners of war, a job description such as 'owner's wife' now no longer represented entitlement to a supplement card.[11]

Violation of the principle of equality in distribution of food and tobacco ration cards

Alongside discrimination against women in the gender-specific division of labour, clear legal infringements which put an added burden on women can also be ascertained. Male police officers on office duty received higher supplement cards than their female colleagues carrying out the same duties. When the provincial food office wanted to correct this clear bending of the law in favour of male office workers (in 1948 when the supply situation had in any case improved) and when the police union called for male and female employees to be classified in accordance with the law 'regardless of sex', the Viennese police refused for months to carry out this law.[12]

A similar case of law-bending was the fact that women received a smaller allocation of cigarettes, which not only discriminated against them as smokers but, in a period of 'cigarette currency', also put them at a disadvantage in the barter trade. Women received their own women's smoker card on which fewer cigarettes were allocated than on men's cards. In addition, different age limits applied. Men received smoker cards from the age of 17 until the end of their lives; women only from the age of 24 to 55. This not only took over the Nazi gender-specific discrimination against women but extended it, since from March 1942 women over 55 had received smoker cards if they could prove that they were smokers or if they had a husband or unmarried son serving in the Wehrmacht.[13]

In 1947, the Constitutional Court rejected a complaint of infringement of the right of equality before the law on the following argument: as we know from experience that women on average smoke less than men it is not a case of 'the granting of a prerogative to the male sex'.[14] The argument of the Constitutional Court, that the actual consumption behaviour was taken into account, can be considered specious. It could be added ironically that although women in general ate more confectionery than men, they did not receive a higher sugar allocation.

The politics of female abnegation

In trying to establish the reasons for this discrimination against women where distribution of ration cards was concerned, we first have to look at the level of women's political understanding and to recognize that women were excluded from all relevant political and administrative committees. The fact that exclusively male bodies in the Ministry of Food took all the decisions on the composition of the foodstuffs that could be received on the ration cards led to some grotesque allocations. Small babies, for example, received a sauerkraut allocation.

Women who had helped to ensure an improvised distribution of food during the last days of the war and in its immediate aftermath no longer carried out these functions in the 'normalized' food administration. As they understood their work in the district and provincial food office as a continuation of their unpaid 'natural' housework, they surrendered the chance of achieving influence and paid work in a male-dominated organization structure.

It has long been recognized that the women politicians of the two major parties adhered to a right-wing tradition and to the gender politics of the conservative and moderate women's movement, which emphasized 'female nature' and the difference between the sexes (Hauch, 1995; Bauer, 1995b; Thurner, 1995). The image of women in the post-war period was characterized by the assumption of a special feminine aptitude for gentleness and motherliness. But it was not only in the assignation of roles, but in association with political power that post-war political women adhered to the traditions of the bourgeois women's movement, which set up the motherly task of world salvation in compensation for the exclusion from concrete politics and influence. Women fulfilled a 'cultural mission', while politics remained 'men's business'. Whereas all women's organizations, regardless of political orientation, protested over discrimination against housewives, other injustices against women did not come into political discussion at all. Discrimination against housewives (less so than that against maids) united left and conservative women's organizations as a political fact and took up considerable space in the mainstream press, not just in women's magazines. The demands for increased food rations for housewives were not for the most part supported by arguments about equality, but were part and parcel of a discourse about mothering, population policy and patriotism.[15]

Self-help strategies

Nobody could survive on the food received via ration cards. In addition, individual self-help by means of hoarding, barter and the black market was unavoidable. Estimates from the Institute for Economic Research on the basis of surveys carried out by the Vienna Chamber of Workers assume that less than a third of the food consumed in 1945-46 was obtained through official ration cards.[16] Two-thirds must have been organized by the population itself, falling within the kind of self-help allowed and promoted by the authorities (as, for example, the planting of vegetable plots on unused land and in parks), but the greater part of self-organization was illegal and liable to prosecution.

The grey area between recorded cultivation and the actual harvest represented an additional source for the city population, which could be exploited through the black market or natural barter. Food also reached Austria from abroad, for example by smuggling over the Burgenland border (Sandgruber, 1985a) and by barter with Occupation troops around the camps for Displaced Persons. The clichés of 'well-provided-for foreigners' which were common in the western provinces (Reiter, 1995; Knight, 1988), played no part in the memories of the Viennese men and women interviewed.[17]

Black market prices varied from province to province and reflected the differing food-stocks situation. In Vienna they were almost always the highest. In August 1945 food prices on the black market were 264 times the official price; in April 1946 they were still 168 times higher than the official price.[18] At the end of 1946, there was a reduction in the exorbitant black market prices, which cannot exclusively be explained by improvement in the food supply, but rather resulted from a fall in demand because people's involuntary savings, accumulated during the war because of the shortage of buying opportunities, had been exhausted.[19] Soon the family jewellery, clothing, bed-linen and even the simplest kitchen appliances had been bartered for food.

Those who didn't want to starve was thrown back on their own resources as never before and had to attempt at least in part to make up the food deficit through their own efforts. People were differentiated by their ability to offer remaining objects of value or possible services in exchange for food. In the provisions crisis, aptly described as the 'provisions class society', traditional strata and class lines shifted – social position was determined in the short term according to access to food and consumer goods.

In a reconstruction of the collective survival strategies outside of state control, the question should obviously also be asked as to how this unregulated 'supply work', carried out partly on the borders of legality and partly clearly illegally, was divided between the sexes. With the exception of feminist work on the hunger crisis after 1945, the gender aspect has hardly been considered. In feminist research, by comparison, women's contribution to survival forms the core of a 'Trümmerfrauen legend' of the brave heroines of the reconstruction period (Bandhauer-Schöffmann, 1996).

Survival work – women's work

'Survival work' as an extension of housework was women's business, on the one hand owing to the gender-specific division of labour, in which looking after the household and caring for the family fell to women, on the other, simply through the demographic fact of the female majority in the population. In 1945, there were 1562 women for every 1000 men; in 1947, after the return of the majority of the prisoners of war, the number still was as high as 1333. The debates in Vienna City Council show not only a verbal recognition of housewives' achievements, but also display a defamation of the same women. The women were praised as responsible mothers and at the same time pilloried as illicit traders. The so-called 'rucksack trade' primarily carried out by hoarding women equipped with rucksacks gathering food in the surrounding areas of Vienna, was used in political discussion as a synonym for black marketeering and illicit trading.

Even worse slanders were directed against women who used their contacts with Occupation troops to improve their supply situation. Contact could be established in the Ressel Park, the biggest black market in the centre of Vienna, in the appropriate coffee houses and in the Allied soldiers' clubs, to which Austrian men were not admitted. These women broke out of the prescribed gender arrangements of the post-war period: they were not prepared to wait patiently like Penelope for the returning soldier, nor to accept the fate of the single women who numbered among the 'surplus female population' (Bauer, 1995a and 1996). These 'Chocolate Girls' are remembered in a negative light even today and women are seldom prepared to talk about such contacts.

The fact that securing food and housework became publicly discussed problems in the post-war period, and that housework was in the public eye to a much greater extent than before, did not lead to any fundamental critique of the accepted understanding of labour that implied only waged labour. The extension of reproductive labour in the immediate post-war period into many areas of activity which demanded enormous efforts and imagination, and which was a precondition for the reproduction and efficiency of the labour force, received no adequate social recognition. The official reconstruction legend referred exclusively to the 'heroic' male labourers, who were embodied in exemplary fashion in Austria by the workers on the great construction site of the Kaprun power station in the Alps. Against this, however, are the familiar anecdotal stories of strong women who carried their families through the times of hardship.

The hungry years in the collective memory of Viennese women

Whereas memories of food and taste experiences lodge themselves in our memories in a special way and relating these stories mainly elaborates the ideal world of childhood and a lost idyll (Hartmann, 1994), experiences of hunger, as unpleasant bodily feelings, are more difficult to relate (Rosenthal, 1995: 178). Anyone who goes hungry cannot look after themselves, and this situation of helplessness is socially stigmatized even today. For women, speaking of their experiences of hunger also means making their failure as a woman the topic of discussion, because the female gender role is that of the provider whose motherly sacrifice is to look after the physical well-being of the family.

In the life story interviews with women who spent the war and post-war period in Vienna, explicit hunger stories hardly appear; the women shy away from actualizing the role conflict between the providing woman and the actual possibilities available to women in the hunger crisis. If hunger is referred to directly, then it is the hunger that those of the older age group in the interview sample experienced during and immediately after World War One. In these accounts, the role conflict in the claim to be a caring and providing wife and mother does not arise, because the interviewees are talking of themselves as children who were not responsible for looking after themselves. (Similar account structures can also be found among men, who talk in detail about hunger in the prisoner of war camps.)

Hunger after World War Two was a discussion topic only indirectly in the life story interviews with women; the effect of hunger on the altered social relationship was the most frequent starting-point for such a story. The infringement of norms committed by women in the black market or by looting, or the conflicts in the family over sharing out the food, were the story-generating factors in all interviews. In these accounts, women also made their changed roles and increased authority the topic of discussion.

The following section discusses the question of how the hunger period is found in the collective memory of the Viennese population, and sets out some of the typical subjects of the narratives.

Narratives about the breakdown of supplies

For Nazi fellow-travellers, the breakdown of supplies represented the most significant memory of the end of the war; women who were opponents or victims of Nazism, on the other hand, described the liberation not the collapse of the food stamp system.

One motif in the discussion of hunger was the ideologically loaded comparison of the provisions situation under Nazism and in the post-war period. In contrast with the total breakdown of supplies at the end of the war and in the immediate post-war period, women who were not opponents or victims of Nazism talked about the comparatively good supply situation during the war and said that the Nazi state provided well for its citizens. These women, whose recollections do not include the non-Aryan population and who gloss over the supply situation in the last years of the war, formulated sentences such as: 'In the war nobody went hungry' or 'We had food right up until the end'.

Naturally, the supply situation for the fellow-travellers was better before the breakdown of the Nazi administration. However, it was by no means as good as women describe in interviews today. The recurrent comparison of being provided for in the Nazi state primarily expresses the worry of the story-teller who fears being held responsible as a Nazi and fellow-traveller. In this, feeling politically secure and well provided for go together.

A comparison with diary entries, in which the experience of hunger before the end of the war is reported without inhibitions,[20] and with official statistics too, clearly shows that the breakdown in the supply situation was much less drastic than the interviewees suggested.[21]

Remembering moral conflicts within the families

Quite often hunger became an issue in interviews in so far as it raised the question of moral conflict. On the one hand, there are activities that were actually infringements of the law (for example, looting); on the other hand, there were memories about internal family conflicts that the interviewee even today recalls as being morally wrong.

Moral conflicts that arose within the family also generate stories, because the sharing out of too little food was so difficult – there was unfairness in the portions allocated, or individual family members took food that didn't belong to them. In one family, the daughter reported that food was even weighed on scales to ensure fair shares. People who were young at the time have no problem recalling today how they took more from the food rations than belonged to them. Helga Eder, then an 18-year-old student, remembered how during the 1946 hunger crisis, her father crept secretly into the kitchen at night and ate up the week's supply of dripping. Such stories about stealing from other family members are only related in the interviews with young women or young men who were not responsible for sharing out the food. Adult women and mothers who were in charge of sharing out the short supplies either didn't do such things or do not speak of them. Nor are such family stories to be heard from men who were adult at the time, as they construct a healthy family picture where everyone looked after one another.

In analysing stories of how food was shared out in the family, age was the most important differentiating factor: those who were children or young people delegated the supply problem to the adults and still talk today from the standpoint of children. This is remarkable in as far as children in the immediate post-war period had to contribute much more to the survival of the family than they do in normal times.

Memories of looting

Given the fact that memories are always constructed in terms of the present, it is not surprising that the tension and discrepancy between today's moral values and remembered behaviour gave rise to numerous stories.

Looting from food warehouses and shops was illegal, but in the days in and around the battle for Vienna it was general practice. The official reports of the supply situation in Vienna differentiated precisely as to whether opportunities for looting existed in particular districts. On 25 May 1945 the market office reported, 'Especially in those areas where no possibilities for looting existed, people complained bitterly about the poor supply situation.'[22] In areas where people had no opportunity to participate in the looting of stores, warehouses and goods on railway stations, they were clearly worse off as far as their supplies were concerned. Women who took part in the looting of stores and private homes could thus ensure their supplies, at least in the short term, in periods when there were no more official food rations on the stamp system.

'Oral memory' confirms the importance of illegal provisions: looting is talked about in all the interviews. In using the example of looting, the women interviewed also referred to the conflict between the legal norms valid then and now. In the last weeks of the war, bending the rules was generally tolerated in everyday life.

In the immediate post-war period looting was considered normal behaviour. Women's personal narratives showed that it is difficult to justify this short-lived negation of legal norms today. All the women talked about looting and, typically, they tried to make it look as if they themselves had not participated.

The narrative figure of the
'raping and plundering Russian soldier'

The women interviewees displayed no inhibitions in speaking of the Russian soldiers as plunderers. This hierarchy of culprits is embedded in the hierarchy of collective negative images that the Vienna population had of 'the Russians' and of the farmers supposedly growing rich at the expense of the 'poor' city-dwellers. With the exception of women from left-wing circles, the interviewees often shifted responsibility for robberies and looting carried out in the immediate post-war period by the Vienna populace onto members of the Soviet Army, something that was already normal practice in the post-war period. Actual attacks by Soviet soldiers and the justified fear of rape (Baumgartner, 1995) mingled with the motif of the plundering, raping Russian.

That it was Austrians and not Soviets who robbed you and stole from you ran counter to the general attitudes and expectations people had of the 'plundering Soviets', and that conflict between ideological image and experience produced detailed stories. The fact that Soviets were made scapegoats for property offences committed, for example, by neighbours, produced many more stories in the interviews than looting and thefts by Soviets, which were seen as an experience in accordance with expectations.

The Austrian State Treaty of 1955 obliged Austria to maintain a monument (put up in August 1945) on the Vienna Schwarzenbergplatz in remembrance of the liberation of Vienna by the Soviet army and in honour of the soldiers who had died fighting for it. This liberation monument, with a base 20 metres high and a 12-metre-high statue of an unknown Soviet soldier, had always been nicknamed somewhat contemptuously 'the Russian monument' depicting the 'unknown plunderer'.

The symbol of the hunger crisis

In eastern Austria, memories of the hunger crisis, for women above all, are inextricably connected with dried peas; in contrast, there is a wide range of foods that, for the interviewees, symbolized an improvement of the food situation. The conquest of hunger also meant that individual choice could open up again.

'Oh my beloved Austria, land of yellow and green peas!' runs a poetic line in the Socialist women's magazine *Die Frau* in December 1945. A competition was held in 1946 to find a new national anthem and people sent in poems about peas (Steinbauer, 1997). Indeed, no other food stuff is a better symbol of the famine of 1945/46 in eastern Austria than those dried, worm-eaten peas. In the period immediately after the war, the inhabitants of Vienna fed themselves mostly on bread and peas which, following an order of the market office, were also turned into processed peas, pea flour and pea sausage.

A comparison of the consumption of main foodstuffs between 1937 and 1946, taking the official rations in Vienna, shows that the people had only 16.4 per cent of the sugar consumption of 1937, only 22.8 per cent of the fat consumed in 1937, only 25.4 per cent of the meat consumption and only 72.6 per cent of the bread consumption at their disposal. Instead, consumers received by way of official rationing almost three times the amount (263.8 per cent) of peas, compared to the average consumer of 1937. The reason for the composition of food rations was the understandable intention to import as many calories as possible with the funds provided by UNRRA. Immediately after the end of the war, when the Soviets had ensured that the Viennese population survived on their 'donation of peas', hardly any other foodstuffs apart from dried peas were available.

The importance of these food rations in ensuring survival is reflected in the diary of Mrs K., who meticulously listed the food rations received. On 22 April 1945, she wrote, 'Now I have received the May donation for the two of us: 40 dkg beans, 40 dkgs peas, a quarter kg sugar, 10 dkg oil. Apart from that, since the beginning of April we have only had one small ration of peas, pasta, salt, soda and dehydrated soup, and half a kilo of bread per person per week.' On 11 August 1945, she points out, 'We eat peas almost every day. We do not get anything else but peas and bread, and even of the latter we should only be eating 11 dkg a day.' She also refers a couple of times to the enormous amount of work which preparing the peas meant for a housewife. For example on 29 September 1945, we read, 'Today I spent three hours in the morning pulling worms out of almost every single pea. ... And still the peas do not taste nice, they can't be cleaned completely. In public canteens, even inns, the worms stay in, and gather at the bottom of the plate.'

The pea rations deeply engraved themselves into 'oral memory': times of hunger mean times of peas. Typical stories about hunger in the post-war period are centred around the disgust about the worms, the tedious job of removing them and the monotony of the pea meals in general. Renate Svanda remembered her way of preparing them: 'The famous and notorious worm-eaten peas; you put them into water overnight, and that drove them out, and the rest you picked by hand, just like Cinderella, and then you formed burgers of peas or – well, till today I just can't have any dried peas, I am traumatised ... Well, this is what we lived on, as long as the Russians were here.'

All the women interviewed talked about the 'worm-eaten peas of the Russians', although it was not only the Soviets who provided the peas – they were shipped to Austria in much larger quantities by UNRRA. The element of the 'wormy peas' is woven into a narrative context of general fears of 'the Russian'. In women's narratives the anti-Communist atmosphere of the post-war period, real experiences like plundering and rape by Soviet soldiers are mingled with the negative, racist images as propagated by the Nazis. The pea stories are specifically women's recollections, since some of the men were still prisoners of war during the hungry years and the men who were already back home did not have to bother themselves with arduous food preparation such as de-worming peas.

Narratives about hoarding and the female reconstruction mythology

Hoarding expeditions to the farmers, to barter for food or to beg, were widely used by the city population for improving their official rations. For oral historians, these elaborate accounts of hoarding expeditions represent a rewarding field of analysis of the relationship between producers and consumers, which is particularly rich in conflict during wartime, and for the analysis of the self-presentation of the 'rubble-women' generation. The many negative accounts of grasping, greedy farmers enriching themselves at the expense of the poor city women, do not correspond to real experience, but also incorporate unbelievable slanders against the farmers, who were said, for instance, to have pianos and Persian carpets in their cow-sheds.

The general recognition that the exceptional is more easily related than the everyday also holds true for recollections of bartering or black-market trade. Anyone who was given a particularly rough time and received candle wax instead of fat for their pearls, still tells the story today in all its details. The exchange rates for the exorbitantly expensive goods on the black market remain as clear in the memory today as the dangers the women had to go through during hoarding expeditions lasting one or more days.

Reconstruction mythology has a specifically female configuration in the way that housework became survival work in the immediate post-war period. Female self-presentation in the field of housework and caring for the family is more easily reconcilable with the traditional image of female identity. Hoarding, in particular, displays the characteristic that makes good material for female self-presentation: hoarding was extremely time and labour intensive, adventurous and the subject of public discussion. This enforced mobility, through the freedom of action in the household and family, was made a discussion topic by the women in their 'adventure stories', by which they prove how clever and hard-working they were. Mostly, these stories begin with the classic introduction, 'Once ...'. They mostly emphasize the negative circumstances attendant on the enterprise (such as travelling on the roof of a truck, the greedy farmers, the fear of check-points, etc.), and in general follow the story-line corresponding to the myth of the self-made man or woman (Samuel and Thompson, 1990; Bandhauer-Schöffmann, 1993).

Concluding remarks

Finally, I would like to put my analysis of Austria in a wider context. The fact that women's relation to factors of food sharing and caring for food and the impact of these duties on their self-perception is different from men's, turns out to be even more important for the crisis years when women's private problems gained a new dimension in the public domain. Furthermore, the discursive connection of being a victim and of being hungry gives women's memories a key role in the reformation of Austrian national identity.

The fact that, for women, food and the securing of food takes on special significance is underscored by feminist researchers. Women's feelings of self-worth are much more connected with providing food for the family than men's. During the immediate post-war period, this task of providing for others, defined as part of the female role, meant a major challenge for women. The labour-intensive performance in providing food was particularly important in the time span between the end of war up to the currency reform in 1948. In Austria (exactly the same as in Germany) *Trümmerfrauen* (rubble women) were praised for their efforts, but their work was not formally recognized, and was seen as a simple outcome of female nature. The ignorance about women's work can be seen not only in that housewives and house maids, who were directly and daily connected with the lack of everything, got the lowest food rations, but also in the classification of the female workforce. Women were disadvantaged, because they had to worry more about food supply due to their gender role obligations, and they were discriminated against, because they got fewer calorie rations from governmental provisions.

The criterion for rationing the food stamps, namely that those who did heavy labour should receive more rations, was not at all objective, but merely reproduced the gendered labour market. With regard to definition of the segregation of labour, woman's work could not be included in the 'best' category of ration cards.

Partly due to the worse supply situation in the defeated countries – and Austria was from time to time still more badly supplied than Germany – the value placed on the supply crisis in public discussion and political discourse was higher than in the winner states. Whereas de Gaulle, who made only one speech in which he addressed the supply problems in France, said that he had not returned to France in order to distribute macaroni rations (Duchen, 1994: 18), Austrian and German politicians dedicated many of their public speeches to the hunger crisis. Everybody in Austria remembers the famous radio address by Chancellor Leopold Figl in 1945, in which he enumerated all the things that the Austrian government could not give to the population due to the supply crisis.

In order to explain the importance of the hunger crisis in public discourse in post-war Austria, this discourse about suffering should be connected to the fact that the Nazi regime had had tremendous support from the Austrian people. The public discourse about suffering from lack of food and from all other post-war shortages and the personal narratives of women interviewed today about their heroic survival labour drew attention away from the real victims of the Nazi regime (Heineman, 1996). Because people wanted to repress memories of guilt, they exaggerated the stereotypically female experiences of victimization after the war (i.e. hunger, living in bombed cities, rapes by Soviet soldiers, etc.). Public discourse and personal narratives about the poor supply situation at the end of World War Two and the myths about Austria's victimization and the denial of any responsibility for the Nazi past influenced and reinforced each other.

Notes

1. For the Occupation period in Austria, cf. M. Rauchensteiner (1995b) *Der Sonderfall: Die Besatzungszeit in Österreich 1945 bis 1955,* Graz: Styria Verlag, first printed 1979; A. Pelinka and R. Steiniger (eds) (1986) *Österreich und die Sieger,* Wien: Braumüller Verlag; G. Bischof and J. Leidenfrost (eds) (1988) *Die bevormundete Nation: Österreich und die Alliierten,* Innsbruck: Haymon Verlag. On the post-war period in Austria, cf. W. Kos and G. Rigele (eds) (1996) *Inventur 45/55. Österreich im ersten Jahrzehnt der Zweiten Republik*, Wien: Sonderzahl Verlag. On the effects of the war and the end of the war on Austria in general, cf. M. Moll (1997) 'Sozialgeschichtliche Folgen des Kriegsendes in Österreich', in F. Petrick (ed.) *Kapitulation und Befreiung: Das Ende des Zweiten Weltkriegs in Europa,* Münster: Verlag Westfälisches Dampfboot, pp. 77–97.

2. *Monatsberichte* (Monthly reports of the Institute for Economic Research) 1/ 2 (1945), pp. 18ff; *Die Verwaltung der Bundeshauptstadt Wien vom 1. April 1945 bis 31. Dezember 1947. Verwaltungsbericht,* Wien 1949, p. 389.

3. The Vienna City and Provincial Archive (WrStLA) collected diaries and personal accounts of the year 1945.

4. Letter from the Food Office of Vienna to Vice-Chancellor Adolf Schärf, 15.1.1948, Landesernährungsamt (LEA; food office of Vienna), A 5, File 18. Schärf had asked for a report on the supply situation in April 1945.

5. Two laws in May 1946 decreed the standardization of distribution of rations and food cards throughout Austria, cf. BGB. 139/1946 and 138/1946.

6. *Monatsberichte* 1/6 (1946), pp. 49, 60. On the changeover from UNRRA aid to the Marshall Plan, cf. W. Wilfried Mähr (1989) *Der Marshallplan in Österreich,* Wien: Styria.

7. *Economic and Social Statistics Handbook 1945–1969,* pub. Chamber of Workers and Employees for Vienna, Vienna 1970, pp. 448ff.

8. Statement of the Central Trades Inspectorate, 23.12.1946, Archive of the Republic, BMfsV, Sozialpolitik, SA 11/1947. The Nazi regulation limiting changes of workplace remained in force until June 1947. Employees could only be taken on with the agreement of the Employment Office.

9. Ministry of Food to the Food Office of Vienna, 4.9.1948, line 42.714-3/48, LEA Vienna, A5, File 53.

10. For this see the difficulties of the committee in dealing with the application for supplementary ration cards in the classification of domestic servant Anna Mahn from Vienna XVIII, who worked a 50-hour week in five different workplaces. Record notes in File 5, LEA Vienna.

11. Instruction No. 11, 7.2.1946, LEA Vienna, File 5.

12. Letter from Chief Councillor Werner, leader of the Vienna LEA, to City Councillor Jonas, 25.6.1948; and letter of an anonymous member of the Vienna police force to the Minister for Food, 31.1.1948, LEA Vienna, A5, File 5.

13. Administration of the capital, Vienna 1 April 1945–31 December 1947. Administration report, Vienna 1949, p. 363; The Municipal Administration of the Vienna Reichs District from 1 April 1940 to 31 March 1945. Typewritten administrative report, p. 393. WrSt LA.

14. Finding No. 1526 of 11 February 1947, e.g. 12/46, in: Collection of findings and most important decisions of the Constitutional Court, Book 12, years 1946 and 1947, Vienna 1948, pp. 21 ff.

15. Cf. the speeches of women members of the Vienna Municipal Council, stenographic reports of the public sittings of the Vienna Municipal Council, sitting of 15.6.1946, p. 1211, 17.12.1946, pp. 2063ff, 22.10.1946, pp. 1581ff. WrStLA.

16. *Monatsberichte* 1/3 (1947), p. 16.

17. The food allocations for people who came out of the concentration camps had to be higher than the rations given to the Austrian populace; but this was not at the expense of the Austrians as the camps were under the supervision of UNRRA or the Allied armies, and were provided for by them. In Ischl in Upper Austria there were demonstrations against Displaced Persons because they received more milk than the locals.

18. *Monatsberichte* 5 (1947), p. 79.

19. *Monatsberichte* 1/3 (1947), p. 12.

20. Cf. the diaries collected by the Vienna City Archive, WrStLA, small holdings, reports of private individuals on the years 1945–1955.

21. *Monatsberichte* 1/2 (1945), p. 18.

22. Situation report on the food supply in Vienna on 25.5.1945, based on the daily report of the market office department. WrStLA, Körner estate, file 26.4.

References

Bandhauer-Schöffmann, I. (1993) 'Gedächtnis – Geschichten – Geschlecht. Erzählmuster und Selbststilisierungen von Frauen in lebensgeschichtlichen Interviews'. In G. Hauch (ed.), *Geschlecht – Klasse – Ethnizität* (Internationale Tagung der Historikerinnen und Historiker der Arbeiter- und Arbeiterinnenbewegung 28). Wien: Europaverlag, pp. 115–28.
Bandhauer-Schöffmann, I. (1995) 'Schlechte Karten für Frauen. Die Frauendiskriminierung im Lebensmittelkartensystem im Nachkriegs-Wien'. In Historisches

Museum der Stadt Wien (ed.), *Frauenleben 1945. Kriegsende in Wien.* Katalog zur 205. Sonderausstellung des Historischen Museums der Stadt Wien. Wien: Eigenverlag, pp. 41-57.

Bandhauer-Schöffmann, I. (1996) 'Weibliche Wiederaufbauszenarien'. In W. Kos and G. Rigele (eds), *Inventur 45/55. Österreich im ersten Jahrzehnt der Zweiten Republik.* Wien: Sonderzahl Verlag, pp. 201-31.

Bandhauer-Schöffmann, I. and Hornung, E. (1991) ' "Von der Trümmerfrau auf der Erbse". Ernährungssicherung und Überlebensarbeit in der unmittelbaren Nachkriegszeit in Wien'. *L'Homme: Zeitschrift für feministische Geschichtswissenschaft,* 2(1), 77-105.

Bandhauer-Schöffmann, I. and Hornung, E. (1995a) 'Der Topos des sowjetischen Soldaten in lebensgeschichtlichen Interviews mit Frauen'. In *Jahrbuch 1995,* Wien: DÖW, pp. 28-44.

Bandhauer-Schöffmann, I. and Hornung, E. (1995b) 'Von Erbswurst zum Hawaiischnitzel: Geschlechtsspezifische Auswirkungen von Hungerkrise und "Freßwelle" '. In T. Albrich *et al.* (eds), *Österreich in den Fünfzigern* (Innsbrucker Forschungen zur Zeitgeschichte, vol. 11). Innsbruck: Studienverlag, pp. 11-34.

Bauer, I. (1995a) ' "Ami-Bräute" und die österreichische Nachkriegsseele'. In Historisches Museum der Stadt Wien (ed.), *Frauenleben 1945. Kriegsende in Wien.* Katalog zur 205. Sonderausstellung des Historischen Museums der Stadt Wien. Wien: Eigenverlag, pp. 73-83.

Bauer, I. (1995b) 'Von den Tugenden der Weiblichkeit. Zur geschlechtsspezifischen Arbeitsteilung in der politischen Kultur'. In T. Albrich *et al.* (eds), *Österreich in den Fünfzigern* (Innsbrucker Forschungen zur Zeitgeschichte, vol. 11). Innsbruck: Studienverlag, pp. 35-52.

Bauer, I. (1996) 'Die "Ami-Braut": Platzhalterin für das Abgespaltene?' In Zur (De-) Konstruktion eines Stereotypes der österreichischen Nachkriegsgeschichte 1945-1955. *L'Homme: Zeitschrift für feministische Geschichtswissenschaft.* 7(1), 107-21.

Baumgartner, M. (1995) 'Vergewaltigung zwischen Mythos und Realität. Wien und Niederösterreich im Jahre 1945'. In Historiches Museum der Stadt Wien (ed.), *Frauenleben 1945. Kriegsende in Wien.* Katalog zur 205. Sonderausstellung des Historischen Museums der Stadt Wien. Wien: Eigenverlag, pp. 59-71.

Bischof, G. and Leidenfrost, J. (eds) (1988) *Die bevormundete Nation: Österreich und die Alliierten 1945-1949.* Innsbruck: Haymon Verlag.

Charles, N. and Kerr, M. (1988) *Women, Food and Families.* Manchester: Manchester University Press.

Duchen, C. (1994) *Women's Rights and Women's Lives in France 1944-1968.* London: Routledge.

Frenzel, H. (1947), *Das tägliche Brot: Gesetze und Verordnungen für die österreichische Ernährungswirtschaft.* Wien: Österreichische Staatsdruckerei.

Hartmann, A. (ed.) (1994) *Zungenglück und Gaumenqualen: Geschmackserinnerungen.* München: Beck Verlag.

Hauch, G. (1995) 'Frauenbewegungen: Frauen in der Politik'. In E. Talos (ed.), *Handbuch des Politischen Systems Österreichs. Erste Republik 1918-1933.* Wien: Manz Verlag, pp. 277-91.

Heineman, E. (1996) 'The Hour of Woman: Memories of Germany's "Crisis Years" and West German National Identity'. *American Historical Review*, 101(2), April, 354–95.

Knight, R. (1988) ' *"Ich bin dafür, die Sache in die Länge zu ziehen": Wortprotokolle der österreichischen Bundesregierung von 1945-52 über die Entschädigung der Juden.* Frankfurt am Main: Athenäum Verlag.

Kos, W. and Rigele, G. (eds) (1996) *Inventur 45/55: Österreich im ersten Jahrzehnt der Zweiten Republik.* Wien: Sonderzahl.

Lufton, D. (1996) *Food, the Body and the Self.* London: Sage.

Mähr, W. (1989) *Der Marshallplan in Österreich.* Graz: Styria Verlag.

Moll, M. (1997) 'Sozialgeschichtliche Folgen des Kriegsendes in Österreich'. In F. Petrick (ed.), *Kapitulation und Befreiung: Das Ende des Zweiten Weltkriegs in Europa.* Münster: Verlag Westfälisches Dampfboot, pp. 77–97.

Pelinka, A. and Steiniger, R. (eds) (1986) *Österreich und die Sieger.* Wien: Braumüller Verlag.

Rauchensteiner, M. (1995a) *Der Krieg in Österreich '45.* (3rd edn, first pub. 1970) Wien: Verlag Der Graph.

Rauchensteiner, M. (1995b) *Der Sonderfall: Die Besatzungszeit in Österreich 1945 bis 1955.* (First printed 1979) Graz: Styria Verlag.

Reiter, M. (1995) ' "In unser aller Herzen brennt dieses Urteil": Der Bad Ischler "Milch-Prozeß" von 1947 vor dem amerikanischen Militärgericht'. In M. Gehler and H. Sickinger (eds), *Politische Affären und Skandale in Österreich: Von Mayerling bis Waldheim.* Wien: Kulturverlag, pp. 323–45.

Rosenthal, G. (1995) *Erlebte und erzählte Lebensgeschichte: Gestalt und Struktur biographischer Selbstbeschreibung.* Frankfurt am Main: Campus Verlag.

Samuel, R. and Thompson, P. (eds) (1990) *The Myths We Live By.* London: Routledge.

Sandgruber, R. (1985a) 'Der Lebensstandard in der ersten Nachkriegszeit'. In S. Karner (ed.), *Das Burgenland im Jahr 1945. Beiträge zur Landessonderausstellung 1985.* Eisenstadt: Amt der Burgenländischen Landesregierung.

Sandgruber, R. (1985b) 'Vom Hunger zum Massenkonsum'. In G. Jagschitz and K.-D. Mulley (eds), *Die "wilden" fünfziger Jahre. Gesellschaft, Formen und Gefühle eines Jahrzehnts in Österreich.* St Pölten: Niederösterreichisches Pressehaus.

Steinbauer, J. (1997) *Land der Hymnen: Eine Geschichte der Bundeshymnen Österreichs.* Wien: Sonderzahl.

Thurner, E. (1995) 'Die stabile Innenseite der Politik: Geschlechterbeziehungen und Rollenverhalten'. In T. Albrich *et al.* (eds), *Österreich in den Fünfzigern* (Innsbrucker Forschungen zur Zeitgeschichte, vol. 11). Innsbruck: Studienverlag, pp. 53–66.

WOMEN, POLITICS, FEMINISM

7 Italian Women Enter Politics

Anna Rossi-Doria

My aim in this chapter is to outline the main issues in the political history of Italian women in the short but crucial period between the Resistance (1943–45) and the Constituent Assembly (1946–47): years full of legacies from the past and potential for the future. What features of the difficult relationship between women and politics emerged during this transition from the Fascist to the Republican era?

Some preliminary remarks are required. First, contemporary Italian historiography is beginning to integrate women, but so far only in the history of everyday life. Italian women still have no place in political history, yet women's history is crucial for any in-depth exploration of the main issues of Italian contemporary history in its three periods – the Liberal (1861–1922), the Fascist (1922–1945), and the Republican (since 1946). Women were in fact central to the great processes of modernization and 'nationalisation of the masses' (Mosse, 1974), to the relationship between State intervention and the development of civil society, and to the mix of elements of change and continuity between the Fascist era and the social and political order under the Republic.

Second, in this as in other fields of study, there are features specific to the 'Italian case' which may appear as contradictions. In the Liberal period for instance, Catholic culture and rural society identified women strictly with the family and the private sphere; yet at the same time, Italian women, although still deprived of political rights, could be deeply involved in politics. At the turn of the century, many young women, especially elementary school-teachers (the *maestre*), in whose training and employment the State played a major role (Soldani, 1993), were active members of the Socialist Party, the Catholic movement and the trade unions. In the early twentieth century, the national secretary of the biggest union, the Federterra, was a woman, Argentia Altobelli (Beato, 1989; Casalini, n.d.).

Third, Fascist policy towards women also left a complex and contradictory legacy. On the one hand, women were limited to the role of procreation, seen as a biological function, yet on the other, motherhood received great social recognition: Fascist (like Nazi) strategy aimed to give mothers not a private but a public function (Koonz, 1987). Furthermore, the Fascist laws against women's employment[1] were not always implemented, so that in spite of the law women were not in fact confined to the private sphere. And the new women's mass organizations under Fascism gave them a specific form of political participation without citizenship (De Grazia, 1992). It is against this background that the changes brought about by World War Two must be viewed.

World War Two: women's political invisibility in the Resistance

The Fascist regime collapsed as a direct result of Italy's participation in the war. Italian soldiers saw action in Greece, Africa and on the Eastern Front, but without any success. Discontent with the regime provoked strikes in northern Italy in 1943, and after the Allied landing in Sicily in July, the king dismissed Mussolini. When the armistice with the Allies was announced in September 1943, most Italian soldiers left their barracks despite German reprisals. From then until spring 1945, the front line of the war gradually moved up the length of Italy, with the Allies in the south and a repressive German Occupation in the north. During this period, the Italian Resistance consisted largely of groups known as partisans, of varying politics but temporarily united by their anti-fascism and anti-Nazism. Full Liberation (and the death of Mussolini, who had made a brief return as a German puppet) came in May 1945, followed by an unsettled provisional regime under the monarchy. In June 1946, the first free elections were held in which all adult Italians, both men and women, voted. A simultaneous referendum resulted in the establishment of the Republic.

For many years women have been all but invisible in records of the Resistance. One anecdote about Liberation celebrations, told by a Communist woman partisan, is a sobering reminder that this might result from neglect, censorship and even self-censorship:

> We went to Turin. I could not take part in the march of the partisans because the comrades wouldn't let me participate. No woman partisan of the Garibaldi brigades took part. But the men were right! I remember that I shouted 'I am going to get right in amongst you all at the height of the demonstration, and we'll see if you dare throw me out!' They replied 'No you won't, we'll kick you out if you do. People don't know what you were doing alongside us, and we must show them that we are an extremely serious group.' And so, during the march, I watched from the sidelines, clapping. I saw my commander go by; I saw Mauri, the commander of the monarchist brigade and all his platoons – and they had women with them. Those women, they were there! Good gracious, how lucky it was I hadn't marched as well! Everybody said that they were prostitutes. (Bruzzone and Farina, 1976: 160)

Here was a woman who literally became invisible, with her own consent. How could this happen?

During the war, the majority of women became responsible for the survival not only of their own family but also of the community, and thus were already tending to become the centre of social, public life. A minority, in central and northern Italy, made the unprecedented moral and often military choice to work in the Resistance, a decision which drew them into political life. The history of this minority has until recently been neglected or distorted (while the history of the majority has not yet been written). 'Women of the Resistance were always mothers and wives, who performed a double workload, a double duty, and if nobody spoke of a double death, it was only because in this world, even women only die once', as the pioneer of Italian women's history put it, arguing that both witnesses and historians had erased the political character of women's presence in the Resistance (Pieroni Bortolotti, 1978: 9–10).[2]

Today, the false impression that women were absent is being deconstructed by many oral history studies of women partisans, changing both the general definition of the Resistance itself, and the boundaries of women's actions within it

(Bruzzone and Farina, 1976; Guidetti Serra, 1977; Anni *et al.*, 1990; Fraser, 1994; Provincia di Massa Carrara, 1994; Gagliani *et al.*, 1995). These new studies demonstrate first of all that the customary sharp distinction between private and public spheres must be revised. The concept of 'civilian Resistance' helps to show that family and kinship networks played a key role in the Resistance, as has also been found in similar research on women in the French and Dutch Resistance (Schwartz, 1987; Kaizer, 1995; Sémelin, 1989). When women hid people or arms or documents in their houses, they were playing a role in public political life – while remaining, to all intents and purposes, in the home.

Women often became involved in the Resistance for the first time by protecting runaway soldiers when the Italian army disintegrated on 8 September 1943: 'a sort of mass "mothering", which was a choice as politically decisive at the time as it was politically meaningless later on' (Bravo, 1991: 110). As a woman partisan from Bologna, Vittorina Tarozzi, testifies:

> We were able to organize the escape … of almost 3,000 soldiers, bringing them civilian clothes. You know what this means? That every family gave their last piece of clothing. But this way, a solidarity, a conscience, was established which could be used later to build Women's Defence Groups [Resistance units], because the person who is available to give clothing is also available to take leaflets or give something else for the Resistance movement. (Verzelli, 1989: 77)

Even when recorded, women's participation in the Resistance has traditionally been described as apolitical. When the wives, sisters, daughters or sweethearts of partisans joined the Resistance, either to be with their man, or because he had been killed, their decision has been considered purely emotional with no political meaning. It is in fact impossible to distinguish between emotional and political reasons for these women's choices. A leading woman partisan, Ada Gobetti, a member of the Partito d'Azione (Action Party) in the Resistance Front, wrote of this time that many women 'were actually drawn in by a transport of love, but in the course of the struggle their consciousness became clearer … their beloved's battle became *their* battle' (Marchesini Gobetti, 1961: 248).

Women could move from feelings of sympathy to group solidarity, leading to political and military commitment. The fact that contemporaries at the time, and historians since, have ignored or undervalued this process stems from long-standing and deep-rooted stereotypes about maternal instinct and the notion that women's moral choices have more to do with sensibility than with sense. Such stereotypes may have provided an underlying reason for women's exclusion from the political sphere – first literal exclusion, and later symbolic exclusion (still with us today to some extent): the idea that 'maternal' and 'sentimental' behaviour is alien to, or even incompatible with, politics and political ability.

What was the political legacy of the Resistance years for women? The demand for equal rights which women obtained when democracy returned was combined with an emphasis on gender difference, as expressed in specific political proposals after the war. These ideas were already to be found in leaflets produced by the Women's Defence Groups, linking the partisans' struggle with the future of women's political rights:

> [Italian] society holds that 'It is absurd for women to attend to politics: politics is for men'. But war, with its horrors, slaughter and ruin, has succeeded in shaking women, in waking them up. A woman can now see that as long as politics is determined by

men, she too suffers the consequences, and maybe worse ones … Women demand
the right to dispose of their own fate … Women should all join our Groups, because
we all share a common interest: the right, when the war is over, to decide the destiny
of a country which is our country too.[3]

This interlinking of the ideas of equality and difference also meant that during
the Resistance there was already a twofold aim: that women should enter politics
and that politics should be redefined by women. In the first editorial of their
clandestine journal, the women of the Partito d'Azione declared:

Having been deprived for centuries from fulfilling any public activity, women have to
face this task today with technically less preparation than men. But precisely for that
reason, they are free from preconceptions and prejudices, and have all their reserves
of energy, feelings and spirit of enterprise still intact. These months of clandestine
struggle have shown what women can do when political imperatives coincide with
their emotional demands … We positively believe that … the mass of Italian women
will be able … to give an essentially womanly life and warmth to businesses,
organisations, and reforms, which until now have been created by men's minds and
wishes alone.[4]

An important part of the wartime legacy recalled by women partisans in their
testimonies and life histories is the bitter disappointment they felt at the end of
the war. This disappointment calls for analysis. It seems to arise less from the
disparity between the imagined world and the real world after Liberation, than
from lack of acknowledgement of the work accomplished by women partisans
(Anni *et al.*, 1990). This was later translated into a silent retreat from politics, but in
the first post-war years, it was often expressed clearly and resentfully. An article in
the magazine of the principal women's organization the Unione Donne Italiane
(UDI: Italian Women's Association), explained how women felt:

'It isn't fair! Nobody remembers us! We are not even on the committees of the
partisan associations!' How many times have we heard words like these from women
who participated in the war of Liberation? How many of them are there? Thousands,
certainly. (Ascoli, 1977; Michetti *et al.*, 1984)[5]

Redefining politics: local government and welfare work

In Italy, as elsewhere, social welfare had always been considered women's work.
Early Italian feminists had centred their strategy on bringing women's private
sense of virtue into the public sphere in order to transform the basis of social
reform. Feminists had also sought to transfer this strategy from the social to the
political arena through the concept of 'social motherhood', current during and
after World War One. After that war, involvement in welfare work was 'conceived
by women as fully political, as a different way of being in politics, and consciously
supported as such' (Gaiotti, 1989: 73).

During and after World War Two, women were once more deeply involved in
welfare work, not only within the partisan groups but for the general population
as well. This work was political as well as philanthropic:

It was women who gave back to the people in the liberated areas a sense of
institutional life, but with different institutions from the traditional ones … They tried
first of all to organize aid, to provide for the needs of the community … Nobody in

1944 was debating women's suffrage … but women were solving the problem for themselves, taking part in public life, 'politicizing' the people as we used to say. Women began to talk to people who used the soup kitchens, the first-aid stations, the nursery schools, the improvised hospitals, and to explain their reasons for being in the Resistance. (Pieroni Bortolotti, 1978: 72)

The women appointed to the governments of the partisan Republics (liberated and for a short while self-governed areas) were asked to handle welfare work.[6] Immediately after the war, widespread women's networks of welfare work developed throughout the country, partly spontaneously and partly on the initiative of the major women's organizations, the UDI and the Centro Italiano Femminile (CIF: Italian Women's Centre) (Dau Novelli, 1995). Both these organizations were created in 1944. The UDI was attached to the Partito Comunista (Communist Party) and the CIF to the Azione Cattolica (Catholic Action) with the aim of encouraging women's support in the light of the imminent granting of the vote (Casella, 1984).

The UDI brought together Communist, Socialist and other left-wing women. It tried to attract Christian Democratic women too, but they did not stay long and soon created their own organization, the CIF. The CIF could tap into the powerful network of the parishes which in many villages, especially in the south, were the only centres of social life for women. The fact that both major women's organizations were set up on political grounds does not mean that they offered no scope for women's autonomy: on the contrary, autonomy developed precisely in the field of welfare work, something given priority by women because men considered it politically unimportant. The UDI and the CIF, although in competition with each other, were united in pursuing political legitimacy for themselves and for women in general. Their unity was strongest in the first months after the war, when there was significant mobilization: women helped survivors, the young, the elderly, the sick, the homeless; they opened nursery schools, collected medicines, money, food and clothes; they prepared meals and parcels. In their work for children, Catholic women equipped holiday camps, while Communist women organized a 'major initiative of popular solidarity, the most important, original and complex one our country has ever seen' (Mafai, 1979: 137). Four thousand children from the severely bombed area of Cassino (between Rome and Naples) and then about 10,000 from Naples were given hospitality during the winter of 1945–46 by 'red' families of Emilia, a wealthy region of northern Italy with a strong Socialist and Communist tradition (with the Communist Party taking the lead, for propaganda purposes).

Women's attempts to give political meaning to welfare work could easily be undermined if this work was viewed simply as part of a traditionally feminine role. Their political involvement was clearer in their participation in local government and the control of food rationing. It was in local government, where various forms of direct democracy were practised just after the war, that women sought to assert a new kind of politics. These attempts were short-lived, both because women gradually returned to 'normal' domestic life, and because of growing conflict between the Catholic and Communist women's organizations. Anna Garofalo, speaking in radio broadcasts for women at that time, sensed the change of climate very early on: 'Many men are still away from home, but when they come back, everything will change' (Garofalo, 1956: 16).

The UDI used the example of women's role in local government in northern Italy to legitimize full access to national politics: 'The experience that our friends in the North are gaining ... must be used by all Italian women to assert their rights and their power.'[7] But by the end of 1945, it was already clear that women's political self-assertion would not emerge automatically from their involvement in social assistance and local government, and that the process would be slower and more difficult than it had seemed at Liberation. The Christian Democrat leader Angela Cingolani protested against this situation at a highly symbolic moment: during her maiden speech in the Consulta (Consultative Assembly)[8] – the first in Italian history to be made by a woman in a representative assembly:

> Colleagues, in your applause, I acknowledge your greeting to the first woman to speak in this hall. It is not applause for me personally, but for me as representative of Italian women, who are taking part in the political life of this country for the first time ... We have heard many kind words addressed to us, but there is little evidence of trust in us through appointments to public office. And yet in the fields of employment, social security, maternity and childcare, and social welfare, especially in the aftermath of the war, our maturity and abilities could so easily have been demonstrated.[9]

This public protest corresponded to the inner sense of disappointment felt, as has been noted, by many women from the Resistance. One of them, Maria Angelini, wrote to a left-wing magazine six months after Liberation that groups of women partisans from the province of Piacenza were returning to their everyday lives, disheartened at 'the uncertainty and injustice that prevail, [and at] the ignorance in which it seems they are deliberately kept'.[10]

Women discover politics: the vote

On 1 February 1945, a Cabinet decree granted 'the extension of voting rights to women'. So, while the war was not yet over in the north, the second Bonomi government in liberated Italy implemented a decision which had already been taken in the summer of 1944 by the Christian Democrats and the Communists, and approved soon afterwards by the Socialists. All three parties aimed to establish a new democracy through mass consent, for which women's suffrage appeared essential. By contrast, the small parties from the liberal and radical tradition, the Partito Liberale (Liberal Party) and the Partito d'Azione could not openly oppose women's suffrage but they distrusted it for fear of being crushed by the mass parties.

Women's suffrage was the result of initiatives taken not only by political parties, but also by a cross-party group of women activists, who overcame their political differences in order to achieve this aim. The campaign was limited in time (lasting only a few months) and in the numbers involved, but it was important as the first *women's* campaign for rights in the new democracy. The initiative was launched by the UDI which, although it made no mention of women's suffrage in its founding manifesto (15 September 1944), sent Prime Minister Bonomi a memorandum on the subject on 7 October, which was also signed by two pre-Fascism feminist associations – the Alleanza femminile pro-suffragio (Pro-suffrage Women's Alliance) and the Federazione Italiana Laureate e Diplomate Istituti Superiori (FILDIS: Federation of Women Graduates). In a meeting convened by the UDI in Rome on 25 October 1944, where women of all political parties and both feminist associations were represented, a committee was established, the *Comitato Pro-voto* (Pro-suffrage Committee). It published a pamphlet on women's right to vote, sent memoranda to the government pressing for a statement 'on an issue which concerns half the thinking population of the country',[11] and organized a petition on the same issue which was signed by some thousands of women.[12]

Older feminists played a crucial role in this campaign. Marisa Rodano, at that time a young leading member of a small party of the Christian Left, remembered them:

> I looked at these women, whose hair was grey and who were so combative, with admiration and with astonishment. They were older, more skilful, perhaps keener than we were to achieve the right to vote. To me at that time – but maybe I was naive – it seemed quite obvious that once democracy had been restored women would automatically gain the right to vote.[13]

These women may indeed have helped to overcome the remaining obstacles to full political rights for women, one of which was eligibility.

Women's right to vote, when decreed in February 1945, was received by the press in near-total silence. In France too women's suffrage had been established by a decree issued by de Gaulle's provisional government on 21 April 1944 'in a hurry, on the quiet' (du Roy, 1994: 14). The lack of political debate and public attention over such a crucial event is partly explained by the fact that at the time the war was still going on and that no representative assembly was in session. But this does not explain why, both in contemporary sources and in later histories, this event became literally a non-event. What explains such silence?

It was in fact a double silence, not just about the present but also about the past. The vote had been fought for before and after World War One and the Italian parliament had almost passed it. But the memory of women's past battles for the vote had been lost because of hostility to feminism from both Left and Right. Fascist propaganda in the 1930s had depicted feminism as old-fashioned and foreign to Italian tradition; Communist ideology, whose influence was significant in the Resistance and after the war, continued to condemn 'bourgeois feminism' in terms established by the Third International in 1920. Most Italian women in the immediate post-war years were largely ignorant of past battles for the vote.

If the decree granting the vote was received with apparent indifference, that may have masked the fears that this new measure aroused. Officially declared to be absolutely necessary in the new democracy, votes for women stirred both conscious and unconscious anxiety and distrust. This is already evident from the text of the decree, which failed to mention women's eligibility for office, a question only settled by another decree a year later on 10 March 1946, just before the first post-war elections – no oversight this, but a symptom of the deep uncertainties still surrounding this issue.

Party leaders might have committed themselves to women's suffrage, but ordinary party members remained suspicious. Communist and Socialist activists feared the influence of the Church on women – a fear based partly in reality but partly resulting from nineteenth-century stereotyping. The same activists continued to attribute the Christian Democrats' victory in the 1946 and 1948 elections to women's votes. But Christian Democrats too were worried, for all their electoral confidence and despite the fact that the Catholic Partito Popolare had been the first party to include women's suffrage in its programme in 1919. They were concerned by the threat of what women's suffrage could mean for family unity. Pope Puis XII, however, in speeches on 15 August and 21 October 1945, described women's suffrage as not only legitimate but a duty: 'Your hour has struck, Catholic women and girls. Public life needs you. To everyone, we can say: this concerns you!'[14]

The general indifference towards women's new right to vote was, oddly enough, shared by women partisans, that is by women closely involved in politics. They tended to register news of the decree as no more than they expected. Ada Gobetti recalled in 1961:

> The news that in liberated Italy women had been granted the vote did not raise any special new enthusiasm: it was something natural, self-evident. It was essential that women have the vote after the experience of the war, which had swept away … so many absurdities and outdated customs. (Marchesini Gobetti, 1961: 249)

Another woman partisan, Marisa Ombra, interviewed in 1986, said: 'I have been rather baffled by the fact that I do not remember any special enthusiasm [for the vote]. In fact, for such a fundamental conquest, I hardly reacted at all … We felt that the vote was something self-evident' (Ombra, 1987: 77).

This indifference contrasts sharply with expectations raised among 'ordinary' women by the prospect of voting, and the emotion they experienced on voting for the first time. As Christian Democratic leader Maria Federici, president of the CIF and a member of the Constituent Assembly, recalled:

> We experienced the vote as payment for all the human suffering of the war; in that torment, long-received wisdoms about women simply melted away … Women seemed to clutch at this right as a weapon of vindication or even revenge … In the market-place, women irritated by high prices and shoddy goods, said 'The first time we go and vote, you'll see', threatening a supreme and invisible power with their shopping baskets. (Federici Agamben, 1956: 31–2)

Many women recalled the emotion they felt on first going to vote: for them, becoming citizens meant becoming individuals. This emotion was deeply rooted in history. Citizenship and individuality had been closely linked since the French Revolution, and the exclusion of women from citizenship had long been motivated by the wish to maintain their exclusion from individuality (Rossi-Doria, 1996). The secret ballot was thus crucial for women's new sense of independence. 'The ballot is secret. Women said this at home, too, to their husbands … For the first time, men felt uneasy, and the uneasiness had a name: its name was loss of control over women's behaviour in the family' (Ombra, 1987: 7). Such feelings were not confined only to middle-class women. An anthropological study on women peasants in the post-war period pointed out that

> the right/duty to vote made explicit the existence of women's individuality, because it assigned to women as individuals regular responsibility for formally-defined and guaranteed behaviour. It expressly drew attention to a woman's independence and autonomy of action, in clear opposition to her traditionally-defined role as subordinate to her husband. (Signorelli, 1991: 635)

Sometimes individual emotion was connected to ideas of collective redemption, as a partisan from Bologna, Zelinda Resca, suggested:

At last we could vote. It was revenge, revenge for women who had never been allowed to do anything. For our mothers who had never been able to say a single word, this was a real opportunity … Quite honestly, I am still moved today when I go and vote, imagine what it felt like at the time! I think my hands trembled.[15]

Women writers too, when interviewed on the events of that unforgettable year 1946, have testified that their hands trembled. They singled out as their most important memory the date of the first general elections to the Constituent Assembly on 2 June, when they also had to choose between the Monarchy and the Republic in a referendum.[16] Anna Banti wrote:

What did I see and feel was important in 1946? What else but that day, 2 June, when as I went into the polling-booth my heart was in my mouth and I was afraid of making a mistake between the mark for the Republic and for the Monarchy. Maybe only women will understand me – and illiterate men. It was a wonderful day … When I feel depressed, I remember that day and I have hope.[17]

Another writer, Maria Bellonci, said:

It was an intimate event for me, that 2 June, when in the evening, in a flimsy wooden polling-booth and holding a pencil and two ballot papers, I suddenly came face to face with myself, a citizen. I confess that my heart failed and I felt an impulse to run away … I felt that I had suddenly seen the truth.[18]

The subjective importance of the vote for women was paralleled by the objective importance of their electoral turnout. On 2 June 1946, a very high percentage of women electors turned out to vote, almost exactly the same percentage as men (89 per cent and 89.2 per cent) (Ghini, 1976: 33).

Women's representation

Even today, in most democratic countries, the most difficult issue for women's progress towards a new politics is that of representation. Italian women did better in those first post-war elections than in subsequent elections; the hopes raised by the new democracy and women's rights found strongest expression in the early days. In the first regular legislature of 1948, there were forty-one women Deputies (7.8 per cent), a number falling to thirty-six in 1953 and dropping further to seventeen in 1968.[19]

In the very first polls, more women were elected than expected. In the local elections of spring 1946, over 2000 women were elected to local councils, and on 2 June 1946, twenty-one women were elected to the Constituent Assembly out of a total of 556.[20] Of these, nine were Christian Democrats, nine Communists, two Socialists, and one from the right-wing party L'Uomo Qualunque (Ordinary Man). They represented only 3.7 per cent of the total, but since only 6.5 per cent of the candidates of the three mass parties had been women, over half the women candidates were in fact elected (Spano and Camarlinghi, 1972: 152–3; Fanella Marcucci, 1987: 180). In an article published in the Christian Democrat Party (DC) women's magazine, protesting that the party had put only one woman's name on each constituency list, one activist observed that men are 'always ready, by ancient custom, to open the door for a woman, but would like to give up this habit when it comes to the door of the Montecitorio'.[21]

The UDI, which had urged women to vote for women, had eleven members elected. Giving a hearty welcome to all the twenty-one women Deputies, it called them 'representatives of Italian women',[22] the very words used by Angela Cingolani, cited above, and widely repeated by women Deputies in the Constituent Assembly.

In 1946, then, the two main problems of women's representation were already in evidence: the small number of women elected and the ambiguity over whether women were elected to represent their party or to represent women. Women's new potential for political intervention had tried to find expression in social assistance networks and in women's participation in the various forms of direct democracy that flourished at the end of the war (local Liberation committees, people's councils, committees responsible for housing and food rationing) but they quickly lost any power and influence. The transition from direct to representative democracy was difficult for women who could draw on long-standing family and community traditions at local level, but who had no tradition at all to invoke as Deputies, at national level. The contrast between local and national politics was very clear in the way people reacted to women politicians. In regions where the Resistance had been strong, women elected to local office were received both solemnly and joyfully; in national politics, they were often ignored or looked down on. It was as if 'small-time' politics could accept women, while 'big-time' politics could not.

Two examples show the symbolic significance of this difference. Elda Magagnoli, the first woman elected to the local council in Bologna recalled her first entry into the council chamber:

> When I entered, there was the valet, I don't know his name, the head of the door-keepers, in full uniform with his baton, and he announced the name and the political party of each person who entered, and then he pointed to the highbacked chair where you had to sit. When I arrived, he announced my name, saying that I was the first woman to set foot in the local council of Bologna, and outside in the square there was an ovation ... I will never forget the emotion, just seeing all the men who were already there standing, and the whole square applauding, because there was a loudspeaker which connected the hall (which was full, and everyone clapping) with the square outside. It was really an event, the first woman, one of the main events. (Verzelli, 1989: 53-4)

The second example, revealing prejudices at national level, comes from the reaction to the first speech made in the Chamber of Deputies by a woman who was not speaking about a so-called 'women's issue':

> A woman, Marisa Cinciari Rodano of the PCI took the floor in a foreign policy debate, the first time a woman had done this since women have been in parliament ... Among journalists, there was an impulse that might be labelled 'pre-emptive distrust' ... they were overcome by a compelling need to go for a coffee or a smoke in the lobby, reappearing now and then to exchange muttered witticisms about the pots the speaker had neglected to put on the stove and the socks that she was no doubt incapable of darning. (Garofalo, 1956: 105)

Despite these obstacles, women Deputies in the Constituent Assembly (except the member of the Uomo Qualunque) worked together effectively to insert women's rights into the text of the Constitution. In this sense, they did indeed operate as 'representatives of Italian women' and succeeded in establishing principles on which women would later obtain equal civil rights which, in Italy, followed but did not accompany the granting of political rights. Later on, for instance, legislation admitted women to the Court of Assizes in 1956, closed brothels in 1958, stated that women should have equal access to all careers, including the Bench, abolished marriage as grounds for dismissing women in 1963, allowed divorce in 1970. New family laws came in in 1975, new laws on equality in the workplace in 1977 and on abortion in 1978.

In the almost spontaneous work that the women Deputies of the Constituent Assembly did together concerning women's rights issues, something of the old feminism came back, although most of the women had not been involved in pre-war feminist associations. One of the few who remembered the past actions was Maria Federici:

> Had it not been for women in the Constituent Assembly, women would not enjoy the status they now have ... Women Deputies had more influence than before, but they faced a very difficult task, with few allies in the Chamber and with impatient expectations from the world of women. It was in the Constituent Assembly, therefore, that the final stage of Italian feminism, action led by women on behalf of women, was enacted. (Federici, 1969: 202–3)

The 'impatient expectations' concerned the protection of motherhood guaranteed by Article 37 of the Constitution and equal rights. In this field, women Deputies obtained the insertion of the words 'without discrimination of sex' into Article 3 on the equality of citizens (proposed by the Socialist Lina Merlin). They also succeeded in changing Article 48 (at that time 51) on equal access to public office from 'according to their aptitude' to 'according to the qualifications demanded by law', proposed by Maria Federici.

The complex relations between public and private would continue to mark Italian women's political history, as major changes in their lives took place in the post-war world. Women's emancipation began silently in the 1950s, was furthered by educational expansion and modernization in the 1960s, and then by the second wave feminism of the 1970s. The foundations of many of these changes had been laid by women in the short post-war period we have examined here.

Notes

1. Women could not be head teachers (1923), or teach history, philosophy or economics in secondary schools (1926); they could be legally excluded from posts in the civil service or there could be quotas limiting the number of women able to enter the 'open' (*sic*) competitions for these posts (1934); in 1938 – in the least observed law – the number of women employed in white collar jobs either by the State or by the private sector was limited to 10 per cent.

2. The word 'participation' ought to be avoided as it 'presents women as casual guests in a history which is not theirs, where the norm and normality is the action of men' (Bravo, 1991: v-vi).

3. Leaflet of the Women's Defence Groups, Provincial Committee of Cuneo, entitled 'Why women must be involved in politics,' in the Archives of the Italian Communist Party, Fondazione Istituto Gramsci, Rome. Section 'Lavoro femminile 1944–1945,' Box III, sheet 0242 0144.

4. Editorial, *La Nuova Realtà*, journal of the Movimento femminile Giustizia e Libertà (Women's Movement for Justice and Liberty) No. 1, p. 1, 27 February 1945.

5. 'Onore alle donne della Resistenza!' *Noi Donne*, 15–30 April 1947.

6. Women still did not have the vote, leading to the paradoxical situation where it was easier for women to govern than to choose their governors.

7. 'In tutta l'Italia ormai libera le masse femminilie sono unite,' *Noi Donne*, 31 May, 1945.

8. As in France, a consultative assembly was set up in Italy before the first elections, to oversee the return to democracy, with members nominated by the provisional government in consultation with political parties and trades unions.

9. Speech in Consulta Nazionale, 1 October 1945. *Atti delle Consulta Nazionale. Discussioni dal 25 settembre 1945 al 9 marzo 1946.* Roma, Tipografia della Camera dei Deputati, p. 121.

10. 'Rispondiamo ai nostri lettori', *Il Politecnico*, No. 8, 17 November 1945.

11. Published in *Noi Donne*, 15 November 1944.

12. 142 copies of the petition, either printed or typed, with hundreds of signatures of Roman women, are kept in the National Archive in Rome (Archivio Centrale dello Stato, ACS). 'Presidenza del Consiglio dei Ministri. Gabinetto'. Dossier 1.6.1, Number 26716.

13. Marisa Rodano, speaking at the Conference 'Il voto alle donne cinquant'anni dopo' held in the Capitol in Rome on 6–7 March 1995, on the 50th anniversary of women's suffrage.

14. See L. Giordani (ed.) *Le encicliche sociali dei papi da Pio IX a Pio XII*, Roma, Editrice Studium, 1945, p. 779. These strong words from 21 October 1945 must be placed in the context of the anti-communist campaign he was leading in the post-war years and of the long-lasting Catholic strategy of penetrating into civil society.

15. This woman was interviewed by Laura Mariani in the course of the group research cited in the references under D. Gagliani *et al.*, 1995.

16. After the Liberation, it had been decided that the Constituent Assembly would choose between Monarchy and Republic, guaranteeing the victory of the Republic. But, under pressure from the Christian Democrats, who aimed to garner both Monarchist and Republican votes, and of the Allies, who did not want the Constituent Assembly to have too much power, it was decided (16 March 1946) that the choice would be made by referendum.

17. 'Il 1946 di Anna Banti,' *Mercurio* III 27–28. November–December 1946, p. 174.

18. 'Il 1946 di Maria Bellonci', *ibid.* p. 172.

19. This happened in France too, where the number of women Deputies fell from thirty-nine in 1946 to eight in 1968 (Brimo, 1975: 86–7).

20. The electoral system was a type of proportional representation, with constituencies based on the district, so that each district had a minimum of seven Deputies and a maximum of thirty-six. Political parties had freedom in compiling the lists of candidates (Piretti, 1995: 320–41).

21. Clelia D'Inzillo 'Precisiamo la nostra posizione'. *Azione femminile* II, 14, 2 June 1946. The Palace of Montecitorio is the seat of the Chamber of Deputies.

22. 'Messaggio dell'UDI eletta alle Constituente'. *L'Unità*, 30 June 1946.

References

Anni, R., Lusiardi, D., Sciola, G. and Zamboni, M. R. (1990) *I gesti e i sentimenti: le donne nella Resistenza bresciana: Percorsi di lettura.* Brescia: Comune di Brescia: Assessorato alla Cultura.

Ascoli, G. (1977) 'L'UDI tra emancipazione e liberazione (1943–1964)'. In *La questione femminile in Italia dal '900 ad oggi.* Milano: Franco Angeli.

Beato, F. (ed.) (1989) *Il riformismo nelle campagne: Da Argentina Altobelli all'Agronica.* Venezia: Marsilio.

Bravo, A. (1991) 'Simboli del materno'. In A. Bravo (ed.), *Donne e uomini nelle guerre mondiali.* Roma-Bari: Laterza.

Brimo, A. (1975) *Les femmes françaises face au pouvoir politique.* Paris: Editions Montchrestien.

Bruzzone, A. M. and Farina, R. (eds) (1976) *La Resistenza taciuta: Dodici vite di partigiane piemontesi.* Milano: La Pietra.

Buttafuoco, A. (1988) 'La filantropia come politica: Esperienze dell'emancipazionismo italiano nel Novocento'. In L. Ferrante, M. Palazzi and G. Pomato (eds), *Ragnatele di rapporti: Patronage e reti di relazione nella storia delle donne.* Torino: Rosenberg e Sellier.

Casalini, M. (n.d.) *Argentina Altobelli: Episodi di vita di una donna battagliera.* Forli: Editrice Socialista Romagnola.

Casella, M. (1984) *L'Azione Cattolica alla caduta del fascismo: Attività e progetti per il dopoguerra (1943–45).* Roma: Edizioni Studium.

Dau Novelli, C. (1995) *Donne del nostro tempo: Il Centro Italiano Femminile (1945–1995).* Roma: Edizioni Studium.

De Grazia, V. (1992) *How Fascism Ruled Women: Italy, 1922–1945.* Berkeley: University of California Press.

Elshtain, J. B. (1987) *Women and War.* New York: Basic Books.

Fanello Marcucci, G. (1987) *Donne in Parlamento: I conti che non tornano.* Roma: Bagatto Libri.

Federici Agamben, M. (1956) *Il cesto di lana.* Roma: S.A.L.E.S.

Federici, M. (1969) 'L'evoluzione socio-giuridica della donna alla Costituente'. In *Studi per il ventesimo anniversario dell'Assemblea Costituente, Vol. 2. Le libertà civili e politiche.* Firenze: Vallecchi.

Fiorino, V. (1993) 'Essere cittadine francesi: Una riflessione sui principi dell'89'. In G. Bonacchi and A. Groppi (eds), *Il dilemma della cittadinanza. Diritti e doveri delle donne.* Roma-Bari: Laterza.

Fraser, M. (1994) 'Tra la pentola e il parabello: considerazioni sui rapporti tra privato e pubblico nella Resistenza attraverso le testimonianze di quaranta donne di sinistra'. *Venetica: Annuario di storia delle Venezie in età contemporanea,* 11(3), 189–228.

Fraisse, G. (1994) 'Quand gouverner n'est pas représenter'. *Esprit,* March–April, 103–14.

Gagliani, D., Guerra, E., Mariani, L. and Tarozzi, F. (1995) 'Donne della Resistenza: una ricerca in corso'. *Italia Contemporanea,* 200, 477–98.

Gaiotti, P. (1989) 'L'accesso alla cittadinanza, il voto e la Costituzione'. In Camera dei deputati, *Le donne e la Costituzione: Atti del Convegno promosso dalla Associazione degli ex-parlamentari (Roma, 22–23 marzo, 1988).* Roma: Camera dei deputati.

Garofalo, A. (1956) *L'Italiana in Italia.* Bari: Laterza.

Ghini, C. (1976) *L'Italia che cambia: Il voto degli italiani 1946–1976.* Roma: L'Unità-Editori Riuniti.

Guidetti Serra, B. (1977) *Compagne* 2 vols. Torino: Einaudi.

Kaizer, M. de (1995) 'La "resistenza civile": Note su donne e seconda guerra mondiale'. *Italia contemporanea,* 200, 467–76.

Koonz, C. (1987) *Mothers in the Fatherland: Women, the Family and Nazi Politics.* New York: St. Martin's Press.

Mafai, M. (1979) *L'apprendistato della politica: Le donne italiane nel dopoguerra.* Roma: Editori Riuniti.

Marchesini Gobetti, A. (1961) 'Perché erano tante nella Resistenza'. *Rinascita,* March.

Michetti, M., Repetto, M. and Viviani, L. (1984). *Udi: Laboratorio di politica delle donne.* Roma: Cooperativa Libera Stampa.

Mosse, G. (1974) *The Nationalisation of the Masses: Political Symbolism and Mass Movements in Germany from the Napoleonic Wars through the Third Reich.* New York: Howard Fertig.

Ombra, M. (1987) 'Una fonte per lo studio del comportamento elettorale delle donne: l'archivio dell'Unione Donne Italiane'. In Istituto storico della Resistenza in Piemonte, *Dalla Liberazione alla Repubblica: I nuovi ceti dirigenti in Piemonte.* Milano: Franco Angeli/Regione Piemonte.

Pieroni Bortolotti, F. (1978) *Le donne della Resistenza antifascista e la questione femminile in Emilia (1943–1945)* (Volume 2 of the series *Donne e Resistenza in Emilia-Romagna*). Milano: Vangelista.

Piretti, M. (1995) *Le elezioni politiche in Italia dal 1848 a oggi.* Roma-Bari: Laterza.

Provincia di Massa-Carrara, Comitato provinciale per le celebrazioni del cinquantenario della Resistenza and Commissione provinciale pari opportunità (1994) *A piazza della Erbe! L'amore, la forza, il coraggio delle donne di Massa Carrara.* Massa: Provincia di Massa-Carrara.

Rokkan, S. (1970) *Citizens, Elections, Parties.* Oslo: Universitetsforlaget.

Rossi-Doria, A. (1996) *Diventare cittadine: Il voto alle donne in Italia.* Firenze: Giunti.

Roy, A. du and Roy, N. du (1994) *Citoyennes! Il y a 50 ans, le vote des femmes.* Paris: Flammarion.

Schwartz, P. (1987) 'Redefining resistance: women's activism in wartime France'. In M. Higonnet *et al.* (eds), *Behind the Lines: Gender and the Two World Wars.* New Haven: Yale University Press, pp. 141–53.

Sémelin, J. (1989) *Sans armes face à Hitler.* Paris: Editions Payot.

Signorelli, A. (1991) 'Il pragmatismo delle donne: La condizione femminile nella trasformazione della campagne'. In P. Bevilacqua (ed.), *Storia dell'agricoltura italiana in età contemporanea.* Vol. 2, *Uomini e classi.* Venezia: Marsilio.

Soldani, S. (1993) 'Nascita della maestra elementare'. In S. Soldani and G. Turi (eds), *Fare gli italiani: Scuola e cultura nell'Italia contemporanea.* Vol. 1. Bologna: il Mulino.

Spano, N. and Camarlinghi, F. (1972) *La questione femminile nella politica del PCI.* Roma: Edizioni Donne e politica.

Verzelli, A. (ed.) (1989) *Il voto alle donne: Testimonianze delle donne elette nel Consiglio comunale a Bologna dal governo CLN ad oggi.* Bologna: Comune di Bologna.

8 The Adventure of Women's Suffrage in Greece

Tasoula Vervenioti

In Greece, the right to vote has been a constitutional right since the National Revolution of 1821, which led to the country's Independence. According to successive Constitutions 'all Greek citizens are equal before the law'. Theoretically, according to Greek grammar, 'Greek citizens' included both men and women, but in practice this equality was often hard to find.

A confusing picture emerges when we consider the history of women's suffrage in Greece, one that reflects social attitudes, political structures and ideological divisions, and the vagaries of war. Partial suffrage was first given to women in 1930; during World War Two, the Resistance movement granted women the right to vote in local elections and later in general elections. In 1952, the post-war government decreed that women could vote but, for technical and logistical reasons, it was not until 1956 that women could in fact go to the polls on equal terms with men. This chapter will try to unravel the complex adventures of women's suffrage in Greece.

In the 1920s, one hundred years after Greece had become an independent nation, many women's organizations began to demand women's right to vote. In this struggle, the primary role was played by the League of Women's Rights, a liberal, feminist association (Avdela and Phara, 1985; Varika, 1987; Xiridaki, 1988). In 1930, the government granted the right to vote in local council elections to those women over 30 who knew how to read and write. These two conditions seriously restricted women's voting rights: according to the 1928 census, 57.9 per cent of Greek women were illiterate, whereas this percentage rose to 65 per cent for women over 30. It is estimated that, in the local elections of 1934, about 10 per cent of those eligible voted (Papadopoulou, 1981: 14, 16). The feminists, discouraged, concluded that 'the majority of Greek women were not interested, for the time being, in the exercise of their political rights'.[1]

To understand why the vote was not widely demanded by women, we have to consider that a demand of this kind is never based on practical political considerations alone, but depends on certain preconditions: for instance, the existence of a certain social structure, which in its turn shapes people's way of thinking and acting; the internalization of the ideas of the Enlightenment and of the rising bourgeoisie – confidence in the individual, in rationalism, in linear progress and society's improvement through science and technology (Rowbotham, 1973, Greek edn 1980: 31). In Greece, parliamentary institutions were introduced and integrated into civil society through traditional interpersonal relations – networks of patrons and clients. During the interwar period, clientelism and the system of buying votes dominated political life; patron–client relations were used to keep people away from active politics or to permit them to participate only in a 'safe' way (Legg, 1977; Mouzelis, 1979). In the countryside, where two-thirds of the population lived, people defined themselves in terms of the group (family, village, nation) to which they belonged, rather than in terms of their individual identity (Pollis, 1965: 32). As a consequence, women's suffrage was demanded only by urban women organized in small associations.

In 1936, the dictatorship of Ioannis Metaxas was established and the progressive women's associations were disbanded. The war (1940–41), the triple Occupation (German, Italian and Bulgarian) and the Resistance radicalized large sectors of society and created the certainty that 'something' had to be changed. Expectations were high that after the war a 'better' and more just society would be created. Especially for women, these expectations went along with the change in their social status. Expressions such as 'People's Democracy' and 'women's equality' could be found in the programmes of the left-wing National Liberation Front (EAM) as well as the right-wing Greek National Republican League (EDES).[2]

Women's suffrage and the Resistance

During the Occupation (1941–44), the Resistance movement pronounced itself in favour of women's right to vote in the local elections which took place in the liberated area (Free Greece), as well as in the general elections for its parliament, the National Council.[3] The process of this legislation is a characteristic example of how a human right operated in rural people's consciousness, and how rural women were involved with politics and with the vote. It began slowly. In this early phase, in the regions that were freed by the partisans of the EAM military organization ELAS (National People's Liberation Army), women did not vote, nor did they seem to take part in meetings – nor is there any evidence that they wanted to do so. However, they intervened in the decisions of the Committees, which ran the villages, when these decisions affected their own sphere of responsibilities.[4]

The spring of 1943 was a turning point for the Greek Resistance and especially for women's participation in it. In Free Greece, ELAS badly needed women's participation and, in the summer of 1943, three separate documents from three different authors in different areas all granted women the right to vote.[5] In the autumn, the Resistance movement made efforts to persuade women to vote. Articles in Resistance newspapers, many written by women, called on other women not only to vote, but also to stand as candidates. Politically organized women promised other women that if they voted, men would consider them as 'human beings' and would no longer dare to tell them 'You women had better be good cooks, because these things [politics] are not for you'. A Circular (23 February 1944) of the ELAS General Headquarters addressed to men, urged them to stop having 'rusty' ideas and 'prejudices' and to send their mothers and sisters to vote. Wives could only be the 'true companion' of men's lives (so the text ran) if they had equal political and social rights. Yet the tasks reserved for women in the Resistance, according to the same text, were limited to traditional 'female' activities, such as social welfare, food and schools. A forceful argument, offered in order to change the mind of any Communist who continued to believe that women should not be involved in politics, was put forward by the Thessalian Bureau of the Communist Party of Greece (KKE): 'We won the self-government [local council] elections in some villages because of women, and men who had been won over by EDES came back to EAM.'[6]

In the local council elections, which took place in the areas controlled by ELAS (the major part of Free Greece), EAM/KKE recognized that the participation of women 'gave a special flavour' to the elections. According to the evidence available in Resistance newspapers, almost 50 per cent of women went to the polls. However, women who thus formed 25 per cent of the electors, represented not more than 5 per cent of the elected. The remarkable thing is that in isolated and 'backward' villages, such as Dermati, 'built on a rocky mountain top like an eagle's nest', three women, all members of EPON (the EAM/KKE youth organization), were elected.[7] In small villages, women were also elected as members of the People's Court. On the other hand, in the city of Grevena, no women were elected to the eleven-member Town Council, although in the election of 19 March 1944, the number of women voters had tripled since the first elections of 1943.[8]

One explanation for these facts has to do with women's important place in rural production, which made them feel more like participants in social life than the women who lived in the cities (Dubish, 1986; Friedl, 1965). In addition, their participation in the Resistance, even if it was through their traditional role (such as washing and cooking for the partisans), gave them the possibility of entering the public sphere. They participated and debated in public meetings. They felt that their opinions about the immediate problems of their village had some value. On the other hand, their co-villagers elected them because they recognized and accepted their abilities to accommodate not only family life, but also community life. It is no accident that most women partisans were from small mountain villages (Vervenioti, 1994; Van Boeschoten, 1997). In the cities, the distinction between public and private was clearer. Moreover, there were broader party political interests at stake in the cities, and those things, it was said, were not for women.

In the spring of 1944, the EAM Resistance movement founded the Political Committee of National Liberation (PEEA), which in April announced elections all over Greece (Free and Occupied) for the National Council. It would be the first time that women could vote in a general election. The women's vote obviously increased the number of electors in comparison with the pre-war period. This could be useful as a bargaining chip in the EAM/KKE bid for power, as liberation was 'ante portas'. The Minister of Internal Affairs and Secretary of the KKE explained in his manifesto that PEEA had granted women the right to vote and to be elected because 'the women of Greece participated so actively in the struggle against fascism, and so by their own efforts they won the right to debate and manage communal affairs'.[9] It is not, of course, the only text where women's right to vote was presented as a gift in exchange for their contribution to the 'national liberation struggle'.

Women of the Resistance who were educated and went into the mountains from the cities had a different perspective from their comrades. Maria Svolou, a pre-war feminist and later a Communist, said in her speech to the National Council: 'We are not asking [for women's suffrage] as a price for our struggle. We are claiming it on behalf of half the population of this country.'[10] And a woman teacher wrote: 'And who are the people? Is it not all of us, men and women, who live in the villages all over Greece? Should not all of us be consulted? How can one half of the people, men only, be asked to take part in the government? And what about us, the other half, the women, should we not be asked to take part? Of course, that cannot be.'[11]

Five women were elected to the National Council. In spite of the massive presence of women in Resistance organizations, they made up only about 3 per cent of the National Council.[12] Two of them came from the countryside: Mahi Mavroidi and Fotini Filipidi. Three were elected in Athens: Maria Svolou, Kaiti Zevgou, member of the Central Committee of the KKE and Chryssa Chatzivasi-leiou, member of the KKE Politburo.

Of the five women elected to the National Council, only three attended its sessions, which were held at a mountain village in Central Greece. The Secretary of the KKE City Committee of Athens did not permit Kaiti Zevgou to attend meetings, because her Party duties in occupied Athens were considered more important.[13] Mahi Mavroidi could not go because her child was sick and later died.[14] She made a personal choice between taking care of her sick baby and politics. However, the case of Zevgou is a marked example of the Party's attitude towards women's vote. The KKE was not formally against women's equality, although it did not support the struggle of the women's associations for the vote, and even considered feminists as 'reactionaries' – 'voting is not the ideal for the working-class woman. It does not symbolise her liberation. The main problem for her … is "the whole social problem".'[15]

In their oral testimonies, some Resistance women did not remember whether or not they had voted. 'I do not remember if I voted. It may have happened, without giving us [the Party] any details. It may have happened!' said a woman worker from Athens.[16] Most women do remember that they voted, but not how. Exceptions were women living in areas where the elections took on a festive tone, and women activists. Many young women did not know that in the past women had not had the right to vote. One university student said: 'I did not even know then that women could not vote. I thought it was something really natural, once we had guns, we were fighting, we went on demonstrations, we lived on a fully clandestine basis … Why should we not vote?'[17] The majority faced it as one of the Party's duties which was not of great importance. 'Anything that came "from above" was welcomed. As for me, I did not understand what difference it made to vote or not.'[18] In fact, in the everyday struggle full of anxiety and danger, the ballot represented a mere moment. 'When you had spent two weeks travelling on foot, listening to machine guns behind you, who cared if you went to vote! You could shout your political opinion in the town square. It didn't seem very significant.'[19] Women who had joined the underground, travelled alone during the night in the mountains, participated in battles, have more to remember than the vote.

Furthermore, these women had learned to function in groups, such as the family or the Party, where personal desire and personal interest came second. They accepted the subjection of their will to the broader 'good' of the national liberation struggle very easily and voted not as individuals but as members of the organizations of EAM/KKE. Moreover, the Resistance gave them the chance to enter the political game. They gained self-respect and self-confidence. Their place in the organizations of EAM/KKE was more equal than in the rest of the society and so they accepted all the terms of the game, even the KKE views on women's suffrage. This does not mean that they did not want to vote or that they could not understand that the vote secured their place in the political arena, but that in practice they had gained much more than suffrage.

Women's massive participation in the Resistance did not grant them political rights immediately after the war as was the case in Italy and France (Sineau, 1992; Rosanvallon, 1993; Footitt, 1995; Rossi-Doria, 1996). After the war, the 'new' society, People's Democracy, which was expected by EAM/KKE members and supporters, did not become a reality. Liberation was followed by a bloody Civil War in two stages – first, between the Communist-dominated EAM/ELAS and the conservative Greek government supported by British troops in the Battle of Athens (December 1944). The surrender of ELAS (February 1945) was followed by the so-called period of 'white terror'. Followers of the EAM Resistance were persecuted, imprisoned, exiled, murdered or took to the mountains again. A new armed conflict began in 1946 and ended in 1949, when the Democratic Army of Greece/KKE was defeated by the Government Army supported this time by the USA.

During the Resistance, the vote was given to women as a gift in exchange for their participation in the national liberation struggle. It was given for purposes of expediency as well as in order to keep pace with social change, and with changing attitudes towards gender roles in the public and private spheres. In the post-war period, it was also given as a gift but first the women had to prove that they were 'good' (that is, traditional) women; they had to look after their homes and children. They were called to the polls as 'pure' women, not as citizens. The winner of the 1956 elections, the leader of the Conservative Party (ERE), characterized them as 'a new factor … free from the old hatred and passion',[20] apparently assuming that women had not lived through a World War and a Civil War.

Communism and feminism

The KKE sought to create a 'women's movement' which it would control through its women members. During the Occupation, it had achieved something similar among the young with the establishment of the United Panhellenic Organization of Youth (EPON). However, in the women's sector things were not so easy for the KKE. The pre-war feminist groups were active and there were no women's organizations controlled by KKE. As well, relations between feminists and Communists were antagonistic; women Communists regarded the feminists as 'bourgeois'; feminists were suspicious of the Communist women's party member-ship. At the ideological level, the debate focused on the question of whether the 'women's movement' should be linked to the 'popular movement' or deal only with women's issues, to be 'independent of and beyond political parties'. The first position was defended by Chryssa Chatzivasileiou, head of the 'Women's Department' of the CC of the KKE and the second by Avra Theodoropoulou, the President of the League of Women's Rights.[21]

In spite of the disagreements, the cooperation between feminists and Communists was valuable for both sides. On the one hand, the feminists found a massive audience of women who, during the Resistance, had 'discovered' that they could do things as well as men. These women provided fertile ground for the creation of women's associations and a lobby for women's rights. However, these women had close links with the KKE, even if they were not members. On the other hand, this cooperation was valuable for KKE, as it could control all the women's associations which had no Communist 'stigma' attached. These associations elaborated a framework of demands which included equality and parity (the feminist view) and the defence against Fascism and right-wing terror (the Communist view).

In the spring of 1945, the Panhellenic Union of Women (PEG) was established by KKE women members and supporters. In November of the same year, a delegation of the PEG took part in the founding conference of the Fédération Démocratique Internationale des Femmes (FDIF: International Democratic Federation of Women) in Paris, and Fani Simiti (mother of the present Prime Minister of Greece) was elected to its presiding board. Women's groups mushroomed all over Greece. The main demand was the right to vote. They organized mass meetings and gathered thousands of signatures in favour of women's suffrage. In their struggle, they had the support of several men. In the summer of 1945, the Town Councillor of Athens, Yiannis Koutsoheras, proposed to the City Council that all women should be allowed to vote in the local council elections. His proposal was rejected (Koutsoheras, 1945). The government did not mention the pre-war law; neither did the women's groups, because of its high age limit and its literacy clause. They argued instead that during the Occupation women had had the right to vote. Moreover, Greece had recently signed the United Nations Charter on the equality of gender, which had theoretically become Greek law.

The establishment of PEG in 1945 was KKE's first step to dominate the women's sector, functioning as a counterbalance to non-Communist feminist associations. The next step was the establishment of the Panhellenic Federation of Women (POG) in February 1946, in order to coordinate the actions of women's associations. The President of POG was Avra Theodoropoulou, a feminist and President of the League of Women's Rights; its secretary was Roza Imvrioti, cadre of KKE.

In the minutes of POG there is a marked difference in the positions defended by Communists and feminists. In the Foundation Act (8 February 1946), the Federation's goals were formulated in the following order: 'a) the protection of mother and child, b) the political, social and economic equality of women and c) the defence against fascism and the consolidation of peace'. This order meant that the majority of the women's associations' representatives on the Executive Committee of POG were controlled by KKE. Ten days later (18 February 1946), Avra Theodoropoulou proposed to change the order and give priority to the goal of 'equality'. It was not accepted. However, women Communists badly needed her as President of POG, so they decided that she, as President of the 'historic' League of Women's Rights, should have four 'honorary' votes. The majority was still theirs.[22]

In spite of the conflicts, the cooperation continued and in May 1946 the First Panhellenic Conference of Women was organized in Athens. Six hundred and seventy-one delegates took part, representing 120,000 women from all over Greece. In her opening speech Avra Theodoropoulou considered women's suffrage as a 'peaceful weapon', which would help women 'express their will as free people, as citizens'. She continued, saying that women had gained the right to vote through their struggle, their sacrifices, and their productive and voluntary work during the war and the Occupation. This first conference of Greek women became the 'swan-song' of the massive women's movement.

Women's suffrage and the Civil War

In March 1946, the first general elections after the war were held. The KKE and the other parties of the centre and left decided to boycott the elections. They believed that the Greek people could not express their free will in the ballot box because of the 'white terror'; gangs, especially in rural areas, were persecuting everyone involved in the Resistance, considering them to be Communists. The poll results legitimized the state and, without opposition from the centre-left, the Greek Parliament was now free to vote 'emergency measures' mainly directed against the Communists.

The civil conflict sharpened and politicized the women's associations and the question of the women's vote. Some women now believed that they should not 'yet' have the right to vote. One of them openly expressed her fear about women's vote in the press: 'The political ideas of our people, especially during Occupation … were in chaos. This chaos would cause greater political problems if Greek women had the right to vote just now.'[23] In a similar vein, during a tempestuous meeting in 1946, the Union of Greek Women Scientists adopted the view that women should not be given the right to vote immediately 'due to reasons of high national interest'.[24]

In the civil conflict, the nation was the 'apple of discord' for Left and Right. The persecuted members of EAM/KKE argued that during the Occupation they had struggled and sacrificed themselves for the liberation of the nation. Those who continued the struggle in the post-war period believed that they were fighting against the 'new occupiers', the British and Americans, who supported the 'monarchic-fascist' government. Their political opponents considered all members and followers of EAM as Communists and therefore non-Greeks and enemies of the Greek nation. They accused them of wanting to surrender part of Greek territory to Bulgaria, the long-standing enemy of Greece. They called them 'Bulgarians' or 'EAMobulgarians'. The state asked EAM/KKE members to sign a 'repentance declaration' denouncing both their Resistance actions and the KKE, thus giving proof of their 'sound national feelings' or *ethnikofrosini* (loyalty towards the nation). *Ethnikofrosini* did not refer only to the defence of the homeland, but also to the defence of traditional Greek values (Alivizatos, 1981). For women it implied a return to domestic tasks and submission to the rules of the patriarchal family. EAM/KKE women were not only called 'Bulgarians' but also 'whores'.

The presence of women on the political scene undermined the ideological structure of *ethnikofrosini*. Those men and women who believed in *ethniko-frosini* were afraid not only that women would vote for the Left, but that women's suffrage would dissolve the unity of the family, which constituted the cell of the community. The women members of EAM/KKE, since they were not restricted to the private sphere and related to men outside the family, were called 'prostitutes', 'dishonoured' and 'immoral'; they would be a 'bad' example for the 'other' women. The EAM/KKE women believed that in post-war society they should have a more equal place and they were demanding the right to vote. This was considered as the key which would open the door to the public sphere for all women. And this door had to be kept closed.

The effort to push Resistance women back to their 'traditional duties' was carried out not only through propaganda, but also through raw violence. Women had to endure a medieval form of punishment for prostitutes: tonsure and public ridicule. During the Resistance, women who had had sexual relationships with the Occupier were punished by ELAS with a 'haircut' (see Chapter 17, for similar punishment in France). After the war, different women – women of the Resistance – were considered as 'prostitutes'. Their torturers acted out their sexual fantasies on women's powerless bodies. The right-wing terrorist gangs, the police and the army raped women of the Resistance because they saw them as 'dishonoured' women, as whores.

In this political climate, the activities of the group members of POG were gradually weakened. Resistance women faced a sharp dilemma: the vision of social change was fading away; should they continue to act in the public sphere or accept the 'traditional values' and become 'good housewives'? In acute circumstances, choices are made under the pressure of necessity. Besides, these women often had no choice, because they were persecuted anyway. While many of their sisters were facing the firing squad, the struggle for the vote looked like a luxury. On the other hand, some feminists debated that, in fact, the KKE did not want women to vote because it believed that more women would vote for the right than for the left, as had happened in France. The POG Executive Committee, in its final meetings, did not discuss the vote at all. Their main concern was to stop the right-wing violence and to that end they sent delegations to official authorities, such as the Archbishop and the Head of the Police.[25] Finally, towards the end of 1947, the women's associations (PEG, POG) were dissolved as 'followers' of EAM/KKE, which was outlawed.

During the Civil War, the vote was not a matter of major concern. In September 1947, two committees of Greek women participated in an international congress on 'Women and Peace' in Paris. They were obviously hostile. The right-wing group was led by Lina Tsaldari, widow of Prime Minister Panagis Tsaldaris, leader of the Conservative Party in the pre-war period. The Communist women were represented by the writer Melpo Axioti who, at that time, lived in Paris. They accused the Greek government of persecuting and imprisoning women, while Lina Tsaldari defended the government.[26]

In 1948, Greece was deeply divided because of the Civil War; there were two governments and two armies. In the Democratic Army of Greece (DSE), dominated by KKE, women made up about 30 per cent of the fighters. In 1948, the newspaper *Machitria* (Woman Fighter) began publication and the Panhellenic Democratic Union of Women (PDEG) was established by women fighters of the DSE, as the Greek branch of the FDIF. In 1949, PDEG arranged its first Panhellenic Conference at Vitsi Mountain. Slavomacedonian women, who lived in DSE territory, had their own organization, the Antifascist Front Zena (Zena Woman) (AFZ), established in 1945.

During the armed conflict (1946–49), the headquarters of the Democratic Army/KKE had enacted the right to vote for those women who lived in the villages it controlled. Women fighters did not vote; they did not seem to need equality through the vote. They were armed and participating in battles. According to the newspaper *Exormisi* (HQ of DSE, 1 January 1948) the number of women voters was only slightly lower than that of men. Of 2540 voters from eight villages, 1140 were women and 1400 men. In some of these villages the number of women voters exceeded that of men, a fact that could be explained by the absence of men in the battles of the Civil War. However, out of ninety-two elected representatives of twenty-three villages, only twenty were women (*Exormisi*, 1 February 1948). In the same newspaper, according to a report from the Conference of People's Committees, a woman said: 'In our village, there are only women. We do all kinds of work. So, it is proven that we can govern our village better than anybody.'

The slow road to women's suffrage in post-war Greece

The official successive governments in Athens, however, resisted the pressure to grant women's rights. They faced two kinds of pressures to inscribe women's equality in law and especially to grant women the right to vote: from the international organizations, especially the UN, and from the Women's Committee, a committee of seven, mostly right-wing, co-ordinating women's associations. In many of the UN meetings, the Greek government was accused of torture, of executions and of transgressing human rights; the vote was also a human right. Despite their international commitments and the pressure of the Women's Committee, the Greek governments were hesitant and granted the vote only partially. The Law of 29 April 1949, which gave women the right to vote in local council elections, was ratified by parliament only two years later, in 1951.

The Women's Committee consisted of the pre-war women's associations: the National Council of Greek Women and the Lyceum of Greek Women (which had 'survived' during the Metaxas dictatorship), the Christian Union of Young Girls, the League of Greek Women Scientists, as well as the League of Women's Rights (in the front line of the struggle for women's suffrage since the 1920s). In the Women's Committee could also be found the Greek Federation of Women's Unions (the Greek branch of the American General Federation of Women's Unions) founded in 1948; its President was Lina Tsaldari. The Women's Committee was also founded in 1948, when Greece was asked by the UN to participate in the Third Session of the Committee on the Status of Women. The Greek government's delegate was Lina Tsaldari. Before leaving for the UN, she sent a letter to her nephew, Konstantinos Tsaldaris, who was Minister of External Affairs. She asked him to brief her about the decisions of the government concerning the women's vote, 'so that the people, who are disgracing Greece [i. e. the Communists], will stop taking advantage of this issue'.[27]

The methods of struggle used by the Women's Committee were quite different from those used in the 1945–46 period: members of the Committee spoke on the radio to convince public opinion that women should have the right to vote and gathered statistical material to persuade the Ministers; they also cooperated with the Ministry's clients to get women's names on the electoral register. The arguments were also a little different. Lina Tsaldari wrote in the newspaper *Ethnos,* 12 February 1949: 'Our historical tradition and the progress of Greek women in recent years, their actions during the war, the Occupation and the defence against Communism gives them the right to equality.'

In the first post-war elections in which women exercised the right to vote (the local council elections of 16 April 1951), two major restrictions were imposed: women could not be elected as mayors or presidents of the village council; and women under the age of 25 were not allowed to vote – they were not 'mature' enough. This exclusion was in fact because of the really impressive participation of young girls (14 to 18) in the EAM Resistance. These girls had had no time to assimilate traditional gender roles. The radical spirit of the Resistance and the difficulties of the struggle gave them opportunities for initiatives and activities outside fixed gender frames and they could therefore offer stronger resistance than older women to their post-war 'domestication' and their restriction to the private sphere. At any rate, the polling results of the local elections 'dissolved' the fears of the state and the parties about women's voting behaviour: the majority of women voted conservative.

The new Constitution was adopted on 1 January 1952. It gave the right to vote to all citizens, women and men alike. However, the relevant article, Article 70, was interpreted in such a way as to suggest that parliament had to pass a law to determine the exact parameters of women's vote, including the date when they could vote for the first time. The Women's Committee protested and finally parliament granted women the right to vote on 30 May 1952 (Law 2159). The Centre Party was in power, led by Nikolaos Plastiras. On 24 June 1952, the League of Women's Rights celebrated the granting of the vote and its own thirty-second anniversary. High government officials, including the Prime Minister Nikolaos Plastiras, the government's vice-president Sofoklis Venizelos and ex-Prime Minister Panayiotis Kanellopoulos, were members of the Honorary Committee for this event. At this occasion, Roza Imvrioti, KKE's cadre and Secretary of the dissolved POG who was in exile, noted that Avra Theodoropoulou, the ex-President of POG, did not even mention the massive women's movement of 1945–46.

Furthermore the cautious attitude of the League of Women's Rights proved to be of no avail as, once again, legislation on women's suffrage was delayed. The government had to issue a decree in order for women to vote. The decree was published in the government newspaper on 13 August 1952 as was a Circular defining the details. But on 28 August, the Minister of Internal Affairs stated to the newspapers' reporters that women could not vote because all women's names were not yet on the electoral register. The Women's Committee objected that this was unfair and anti-constitutional. However, the new electoral law, passed by the parliament at that time, included an amendment saying that women could not vote until the next elections, which were held on 16 November 1952 (Tsaldari, 1967: 264–57; Thanopoulou, 1957).

At the beginning of 1953, a by-election took place in Thessaloniki. Women could vote and also stand as candidates. There were three candidates. The candidates of the Right and the Centre were women, but the Left did not honour women; its candidate was a man. Thus, while a woman (Heleni Skoura) was elected, she was paradoxically right-wing and during the Civil War had supported the postponement of women's suffrage.[28]

In the general election of 19 February 1956, Greek women finally participated on equal terms with men. There were two main parties: the Democratic Union

(DE), which included the centre and left-wing parties, and the National Radical Union (ERE), the right-wing party. Among the 300 members elected to the Parliament, there were only two women, both from Athens. One was a candidate of the Democratic Union (Vasso Thanasekou, left-wing) and the other was elected for ERE (Lina Tsaldari). The Democratic Union had founded a 'Women's Committee for Electoral Struggle'. In its Declaration, the women's vote was related to 'the life of the nation'; it ended: 'Life comes from us, women. The life of our country will also depend on us, on our vote.'[29] ERE had founded a Women's Electoral Centre in Athens. At its opening, Lina Tsaldari said: 'The first duty of the Greek women is to vote for the protection of mother, child and family.'[30] She came first out of all the ERE candidates and became the first woman to hold a cabinet post, serving as Minister of Social Welfare.

Left-wing men insisted that without the women's vote the Democratic Union would have won the elections. They said that women had voted for the right-wing party, ERE, because its leader was young and handsome. In fact the women's vote made a difference only in urban areas. In the countryside it did not bring any change. Political scientists insist that women voted in the same way as the men in their family, and so the parties just doubled their votes (Nikolakopoulos, 1988: 225–7). In practice, the husband–father used to give a marked ballot paper to his wife or daughter; in most cases he asked them to bring back the other ballot papers, so that he could be sure that the women of the family had voted for the 'right' party. Moreover, in Greveniti, a small remote village, there were even more women than men among the left-wing voters. The explanation given is that many 'single' women lived in this village; the men had been killed during the Civil War or were political refugees (Damianakos, 1981).

In the cities, however, there was a marked difference between men's and women's votes. The most significant was in Athens, where 13 per cent more women than men voted for ERE. The official *Statistics of the Parliamentary Elections of 19th February 1956* does not distinguish between male and female voters. The only available information about gendered voting comes from newspapers. According to them, 126,788 men and 77,156 women voted in Athens: only 59.2 per cent of eligible women voted (Nikolakopoulos, 1988). We do not know how exactly the other 40.8 per cent would have voted. What we do know is that they did not make any effort to get their electoral booklet in order to vote, even though they were entitled to vote.

Conclusion

There was never a massive suffragist movement in Greece. All men had had the right to vote since the establishment of the Greek State. As far as women were concerned, it seems that they did not want to vote, that most, consciously or not, were apathetic about suffrage and about politics in general. In 1934, only a few women voted. The Resistance movement (1943–44), by giving them the vote for reasons of political expediency as well as for their participation in the national liberation struggle, tried to persuade them to vote, but even those who did, did not consider it to be significant. In 1956, when they were granted universal and constitutional suffrage, 40 per cent did not participate in the elections. What really happened? Were women not 'politically mature'? Were they indifferent to what happened outside the walls of their homes? Their participation in the Resistance movement contradicts this suggestion. During the Occupation too, women in rural Greece not only voted but also undertook social and political responsibilities. In the first post-war period (1945–46), 120,000 women were organized in women's associations.

However, I think it is fair to say that most Greek women functioned in the framework of the family, especially when their action could not change the reality that oppressed them. It was easy for them to say 'My husband votes. Why should I?' when this referred to the government, because the Greek State was never a welfare state and was not interested in 'women's' problems. However, when they believed that their participation, for instance in the Resistance, would make their social and personal life better, they did not hesitate. They were active not only in the civilian but also in the military organizations of the left-wing National Liberation Front. In other words, when women perceived that their interests were at stake, they could be as politically active as men.

Moreover, we have to make a distinction between women leaders and women followers. The leadership of women's organizations, left-wing as well as right-wing, had close connections with the political parties; these women had accepted the terms of the political game, even their practices. Left-wing women demonstrated and gathered signatures and right-wing women used their personal contacts to achieve their goals. The Civil War that followed World War Two divided Greek society and the women's organizations with it. The League of Women's Rights, the only self-defined feminist organization, cooperated with the left in 1945–46, and after the defeat of the left (1949), with the right.

As far as the 'other' women were concerned, the 'immature' (the 'chickens' as they used to be called in Greece), after the end of the Civil War they had other things to do: build a house, raise and educate their children, and make sure that their suffering of recent years would not be repeated.

Notes

1. 'I Efthyni mas' in *O Agonas tis Gynaikas*. no. 162, December 1932. Syndesmos gia ta Dikaiomata tis Gynaikas.

2. From 1941 to 1944, Greece was occupied. While Germany dictated the terms, most of Greece was under Italian Occupation, with Bulgarians in the northeast of the country. Germany occupied the port of Piraeus and the major town of Thessaloniki. After 1943, the Italians were removed and Germans occupied the entire country. The main Resistance organizations were EAM and EDES, which were in opposition to each other. The most radical and the larger of the two was EAM. It was formed by a coalition of many political parties, in which the Communist Party of Greece (KKE) played the dominant role. EDES was Republican, anti-Communist and was supported by the British.

3. 'Free Greece' refers to areas, mostly mountainous, where, following the withdrawal of the Italian occupiers, Greeks took charge of governing their own villages. In Free Greece, claims were made in favour of social revolution, and popular institutions such as People's Courts were established. See Mark Mazower (1993) *Inside Hitler's Greece*, New Haven: Yale University Press.

4. As well as housework and childcare, rural women had to bake, sew clothes

and blankets, etc. They also worked in the fields with men. They were responsible for the animals of the house – chicken and pigs – and for cultivating vegetables.

5. The three texts were: the 'Sterea Code', approved by the delegates of the KKE 'first conference for representatives of self-government'; the second was known as 'Decision No. 6' emanating from the Joint Guerilla Headquarters of ELAS and EDES, written by an army officer, Lieutenant Konstantinos Gikopoulos (at that time a member of EDES); the third was the EAM 'Circular of the Panthessalian Committee'.

6. *Leninistis*, KKE newspaper, November 1943.

7. *Communistiki Epitheorissi*, April 1944.

8. Information from the EAM resistance newspapers in Macedonia, April–May 1944.

9. Minutes of the first meeting of the National Council (14-27 May 1944). The same argument was used by leaders of the French Communist Party (PCF). See Jenson, 1987.

10. EAM newspaper from Thessali, 9 July 1944.

11. EAM newspaper from Macedonia, 12 April 1944.

12. Women were under-represented everywhere: for instance, in Thessali two EAM conferences were held. At the first one, in the summer of 1943, 15 per cent of the 4000 delegates were women whereas they formed 20 per cent of the EAM membership at that time. At the second, in the summer of 1944, 7 per cent of the 175 delegates were women, who by then comprised 40 per cent of EAM members. (Information from EAM resistance newspapers in Thessali, June–July 1943, 1944.)

13. Zevgou believed that there were other unstated reasons for the decision not to let her go (Zevgou, 1980: 279).

14. Interview Titsa Stulianea, 17 February 1987.

15. In the 1930s, women Communists had cooperated with the feminists of the League of Women's Rights, in line with the Kominform's Decision for Popular Fronts. For the KKE policy on women's suffrage, see: KKE, *Official Records 1918–1924* pp. 356, 543; *Official Records 1929–1933* pp. 18-23, 205, 543; *Official Records 1934–1940* pp. 53, 183, 238, 251, 396.

16. Interview, Violeta Lalopoulou, 1 September 1989.

17. Interview, Sasa Tsakiri, 10 March 1988.

18. Interview, Mina Giannou, 22 December 1995.

19. Interview, Heleni Kamoulakou, 18 June 1987.

20. In his final speech before the elections, *Kathimerini* (newspaper) 17 February 1956.

21. See Avra Theodoropoulou's opening speech at the First Panhellenic Conference of POG (the Panhellenic Organization of Women), May 1946 (Roza Imvrioti archive, which belongs to the Federation of Greek Women (OGE)); see also Chatzivasileiou (1946).

22. Roza Imvrioti archive; some of the material has been published (OGE, 1985). The women's journal *Ellenides*, published by PEG, and KKE texts are also useful for analysing this period.

23. Roula Papadimitriou, *Nea Alitheia*, 19 August 1946.

24. *Sygchronoi Provlimatismoi tu Gynaikeiou Kinimatos* (1979). Movement of Democratic Women, pp. 56-7. See also Maria Thanopoulou (1957, and Phara (1988).

25. Roza Imvrioti archive.

26. See Tsaldari's report to the Ministry of the Interior in *Ethikai, Koinonikai, Politikai Prospatheiai*, self-published, Athens, 1967, Volume A, pp. 155-9; see also *Rizospastis*, KKE newspaper, 17 October 1947.

27. 'Epitropi Thesseos Gynaikon', United Nations, Beirut, 1949, in Tsaldari, n. 26, pp. 164-71.

28. In the same year, discrimination against women in law was ended, and in 1954 and 1955 all obstacles blocking women's entry into all aspects of public life were removed.

29. Helen Bambouki, personal archive.

30. In *Kathimerini*, 12 February 1956.

References

Archives

Roza Imvrioti, Federation of Greek Women (OGE), unclassified.
Helen Bambouki, Personal archive.

General newspapers

Kathimerini, 12 and 17 February 1956.
Rizospastis, KKE's CC, 17 October 1947.

Resistance newspapers

Apeleftherotis, CC of EAM (National Liberation Front), Athens 19 April 1944.
Eleftheri Macedonia, EAM, 1 May 1944.
Leninistis, KKE Thessalia, November 1943.
Rigas, EAM Thessali, 9 July 1944.
Synagonistria, EAM Macedonia, 12 April 1944

Books, chapters, articles

Alivizatos, Nickos (1981) 'Kathestos "ektaktis anagis" kai politikes eleftheries, 1946-1949'. In John O. Iatrides (ed.), *Greece during 1940-1950: A Nation in Crisis*. Hanover: University Press of New England (Greek edn: 1984, Athens: Themelio), pp. 383-98, Greek edn.

Avdela, Efi and Pharra, Aggelika (1985) *O Feminismos stin Ellada tou Mesopolemou*. Athens: Gnosi.

Chatzivasileiou, Chryssa (1946) *To Communistiko Komma Ellados kai to Gynaikeio zitima*. Athens: Edition of the KKE CC.

Damianakos, Stathis (1981) 'Les fiefs électoraux en Epire: une analyse quantitative des élections dans le département de Jannina entre 1956 et 1964'. *Epitheorissi Koinonikon Erevnon*, Numéro Spécial, 49-92.

Dubish, Jill (ed.) (1986) *Gender and Power in Rural Greece*. Princeton: Princeton University Press.

Editorial (1932) 'I Efthyni mas'. *O Agonas tis Gynaikas: Syndesmos gia ta Dikaiomata tis Gynaikas*, no. 162, December.

Ellinides, monthly publication of the Panhellenic Union of Women (PEG), 1945–1947.

Ethniko Symvoulio: Praktika tis Protis Synedriassis (14–17 May 1944) (1992) Self-publication of the Koryschades Community.

Fédération Démocratique Internationale des Femmes (1949) *IIe Congrès International des Femmes*. Paris: FDIF.

Footitt, Hilary (1995) 'The first women Députés: "les 33 glorieuses"?' In H. R. Kedward and Nancy Wood (eds), *The Liberation of France: Image and Event*. Oxford: Berg, pp. 129–41.

Friedl, Ernestine (1962) *Vasilika, a Village in Modern Greece*. New York: Holt, Rinehart and Winston.

'I Aftodiikissi stin Eleftheri Ellada', *Communistiki Epitheorissi*. Central Committee of the KKE, April 1944.

Jenson, Jane (1987) 'The Liberation and new rights for French women'. In Margaret R. Higonnet, Jane Jenson, Sonya Michel and Margaret C. Weitz (eds), *Behind the Lines: Gender and the Two World Wars*. New Haven: Yale University Press, pp. 272–84.

KKE (1974) *Epissima Keimena 1918–1924*. Athens: Sygchroni Epochi.

KKE (1975) *Epissima Keimena 1929–1933*. Athens: Sygchroni Epochi.

KKE (1975) *Epissima Keimena 1934–1940*. Athens: Sygchroni Epochi.

Koutsoheras, I. P. (1945) *I Gynaikeia Psifos*. Athens: Aetos A.E.

Legg, Keith (1977) 'The nature of the modern Greek state'. In John T. A. Koumoulides (ed.), *Greece in Transition: Essays in the History of Modern Greece 1821–1974*. London: Zeno, pp. 285–95.

Mazower, Mark (1993) *Inside Hitler's Greece: The Experience of Occupation, 1941–1944*. New Haven: Yale University Press (Greek edn: 1994, Athens: Alexandria).

Mouzelis, Nicos (1979) *Modern Greece: Facets of Underdevelopment*. London: Macmillan.

Nikolakopoulos, Ilias (1988) *Kommata kai Vouleftikes Ekloges stin Ellada 1946–1964*. Athens: National Centre for Social Research.

OGE. (1985) *A' Panelladiko Synedrio Gynaikon: Dokumenta apo to Archeio tis Rosas Imvrioti*. Athens: Edition of the Federation of Greek Women (OGE).

Papadimitriou, Roula (19 August 1946) *Nea Alitheia, I Archaioteri Efimerida tis Voreias Ellados, apo to 1903*.

Papadopoulou, Koula (1981) *Agones kai Nikes tis Ellinidas*. 5th edn. Athens: Pyli.

Phara, Aggelika (1988) 'Chroniko mias metavassis 1934–1948'. *Diavazo*, 198, 29–36.

Pollis, Adamantia (1965) 'Political implications of the Modern Greek concept of self'. *British Journal of Sociology*, 26, 149–59.

Rowbotham, Sheila (1973) *Hidden from History: 300 Years of Women's Oppression and the Struggle Against It*. London: Pluto Press (Greek edn, 1980, Athens: Editorial Group of Women).

Rosanvallon, Pierre (1993) 'L'histoire du vote des femmes: réflexions sur l'exception française'. In Georges Duby and Michelle Perrot (eds), *Femmes et Histoire*. Paris: Plon (Greek edn, 1995, Athens: Ellinika Grammata), pp. 87–93, Greek edn).

Rossi-Doria, Anna (1996) *Diventare cittadine: il voto alle donne in Italia.* Firenze: Guinti.

Seminar of the Democratic Women's Movement (1979) *Sygchronoi Provlimatismoi tou Gynaikeiou Kinimatos.* Athens: Edition of the Democratic Women's Movement.

Sineau, Mariette (1992) 'Droit et démocratie'. In G. Duby and M. Perrot (eds), *Histoire des femmes: Le XXe Siècle.* Paris: Plon, pp. 471–97.

Thanopoulou, Maria (1957) *Neos Dromos*, 1 December.

Tsaldari, Lina (1967) *Ethikai: Koinonikai, Politikai Prospatheiai,* vol. A. Athens: The author.

Van Boeschoten, Riki (1997) *Anapoda Chronia: Syllogiki Mnimi kai Istoria sto Ziaka Grevenon (1900–1950).* Athens: Plethron.

Varika, Heleni (1987) *I exegersi ton Kirion.* Athens: Idrima Erevnas kai Paideias tis Emporikis Trapezas tis Ellados.

Vervenioti, Tasoula (1994) *I Gynaika tis Antistasis: I Eisodos ton Gynaikon stin Politiki.* Athens: Odysseas.

Xiradaki, Koula (1988) *To Feministiko Kinima stin Ellada.* Athens: Glaros.

Zevgou, Kaiti (1980) *Me to Yianni Zevgo sto epanastatiko kinima.* Athens: Okeanida.

9 Communist Women in Finland, 1944–1948: Olga Virtanen's Story

Elina Katainen

Finland's history has been strongly marked by its proximity to Russia and, in the twentieth century, by the influence of Communism. In the years immediately following World War Two, the relationship between Finland and the Soviet Union was filled with tension. Historians researching the 1940s in Finland have often called the period 1944 to 1948 the 'Years of Danger', referring to the fear of a Communist coup (Hyvämäki, 1954; Haataja, 1988; Beyer-Thoma, 1990) but for Finnish Communists, the period was one of optimism. From 1945 until as late as the 1970s, 20 to 25 per cent of Finns voted for the Finnish Communist Party (FCP) in parliamentary elections – its support was comparable to that of the Social Democratic Party (SDP) and the Agrarian Party. The 'Big Three', as they were called, formed a coalition government between 1945 and 1948. After 1948, the FCP was in opposition, although remaining an important party (see, for instance Rentola, 1994, 1997; Leppänen, 1994).

The two issues which have dominated the historiography of the period are first, why Finland was the only Western neighbour of the Soviet Union which did not become a 'people's democracy', and second, the question of 'Finlandization' (the situation whereby a small nation is obliged to adapt its politics to accord with the interests of a Great Power). The history of Finnish Communism has been interpreted in this context too (Vihavainen, 1991; Nevakivi, 1996; Rentola, 1997).

In this chapter, I will consider the history of Finnish Communism from a different perspective. The life story of Olga Virtanen, one of the FCP's women cadres, a district organizer and a Member of Parliament in 1945, is used as a focus for a discussion of women's political activism in Finland in the post-war years, and of the contradictions women experienced in the Communist movement – in spite of its ideology of gender equality, influenced by the Bolshevik vision of the socialization of family life (see Goldman, 1993: 12, 48-58, 96-100, 254-7). I hope to show some of the complexities of the choices they had to make and the often difficult relationship between personal life and political ideology. I also want to show that the Communists were neither heartless conspirators nor selfless utopians (as they have often been described), but ordinary men and women: their lives and decisions could, like everyone else's, be based on emotions and irrationality, although their private lives have often been erased from their memoirs (Kaihovaara, 1997).[1]

Olga Virtanen and the generation of 'Red Orphans'

When, in the 1980s, Olga looked back on her life, she began with something her father had impressed upon her when she was young: 'Whatever you do, never side with "the butchers".'[2] This refers to the Finnish Civil War of 1918, the founding event of the Finnish Communist movement (Rentola, 1992: 77). There were two sides in the war, Whites (mainly the bourgeoisie and well-to-do farmers) and Reds (industrial and farm workers as well as tenant farmers). The victorious Whites ('the butchers') executed more than 5000 Reds and interned 80,000 more in prison camps, where 12,000 died of hunger and disease (Paavolainen, 1974; Alapuro, 1988: 176–7).[3] More than 10,000 Reds fled to Russia (Saarela, 1996: 27). All these men and women – killed, imprisoned or in exile – had families, relatives and friends. Bearing in mind that there were only about 3.1 million people in Finland in those days, the war touched virtually all working-class families in one way or another.

A chasm developed, not only between the Whites and the Reds but also inside the workers' movement. The Social Democratic Party (SDP) split, as did socialist parties all over Europe. In the 1920s there were two legal working-class parties in Finland, the SDP and the Socialist Party which was connected to the illegal FCP, founded by Finnish refugees in Moscow in 1918. In the 1930s, the whole movement to the left of the Social Democrats was made illegal and had to operate underground. By 1932 there were barely 2000 FCP members in Finland, about one fifth of them women (Rentola, 1994: 80).

After the events of World War Two, during which the Party remained illegal (see below), the Finnish Communist organization was transformed from a small, underground cadre party into a mass movement of tens of thousands of people under an umbrella organization, the Finnish People's Democratic League (FPDL), in which the FCP was in practice the leading force. The leadership of the movement remained, however, in the hands of the comrades who had learned their ways of thinking and acting in the clandestine pre-war organization.

In this process of change, gender took on new meanings. After the war there were many women in the 'inner circle' of the FCP, something exceptional in the Finnish political parties of those years. During the first legislative period (1945–48) almost a fifth of the Communist Members of Parliament were women, and in 1948 Hertta Kuusinen was appointed Minister without Portfolio for some months.[4] But a separate organization for women, the Finnish Women's Democratic League (FWDL), was also founded on 3 December 1944. Its function, as party leaders saw it, was to mobilize women to vote for the Communists in the first elections (Katainen, 1994).[5]

Olga belonged to what has been called 'the generation of Red Orphans' which formed 'the hard core of Finnish Bolshevism' and took over the leadership of the FCP after 1944. They were not all actual orphans but they shared the same experience. Taught at home (as Olga's father taught his children) to distinguish between 'them' and 'us', this generation 'trusted only those who had passed through the same mill; they stuck together, married each other and made judgements in a Manichean way: it was always either/or. They learned to be so loyal that they never wavered, even when their relatives were taken in purges while they were in prison in Finland' (Rentola, 1992: 82–6).

This characterization is accurate in many respects and the picture one gets from Olga's memoirs is often similar to that given by Rentola. But Olga, like many others (including men) did waver, and wavered for reasons connected with her private life.

Olga's journey to the Communist movement

Olga Virtanen was born in a rural district in south-western Finland in 1910, one of eight children of tenant farmers. After four years of elementary school and some years as a dressmaker, she left her birthplace and in 1929 moved to Lahti, a small town in southern Finland. Having joined a leftist sports club and an association for aid to political prisoners,[6] in the spring of 1932 she started to date a young man already involved with the Communist movement, Väinö Sievänen. He invited Olga to join the illegal district committee of the FCP.[7]

Between 1918 and 1944, there were thousands of political prisoners in Finland (Aho, 1981; Peltonen, 1989). The secret police, the Detective Central Police (DCP), was organized soon after 1918 to counter threats to the Republic from various dissidents.[8] The DCP soon had Olga on file among thousands of other Finns suspected of being 'Communist-minded' and therefore endangering national security. She was detained for some months in 1932–33 and given a suspended eight-month sentence. In September 1933 she left for the Soviet Union to study in a Party school in Leningrad.[9] Almost all the leading cadres of the post-war years spent some time in the Soviet Union in the 1920s or 1930s.

Olga's three years in Leningrad were rich in experience for a small-town girl. The splendour of the Czarist era was still there and the atmosphere of the Communist boarding school was international. Everyday life was simple but eventful and the subjects studied ranged from natural sciences to languages, by way of Marxist philosophy and the science of warfare.[10]

Sexual morality was relatively free in Communist circles in those days; men and women could live together without marriage and the so-called 'Soviet marriage' meant hardly more than moving in together. Abortion was free until 1936.[11] According to the DCP, Olga had at least two relationships during her stay in Leningrad: the second led to a pregnancy in the summer of 1936, by which time abortion was no longer available.[12]

Things had changed in other ways, as well. Finnish Communists – as well as many other national minorities – who lived in the Soviet Union faced harsh treatment. It has been estimated that some 20,000 Finns were killed in the purges of the Stalinist era, 1937–38 being the worst years of persecution. This number parallels the number of Reds killed in the Finnish Civil War, and the number of Finns killed in the Winter War of 1939-40 (Rentola, 1994: 23–74). The school was closed in June 1936 and for that reason, or perhaps because she was pregnant, Olga was sent back to Finland in October to join the underground.[13] But as soon as she crossed the border, she was arrested for treason and in January 1937, sentenced to four years in prison.[14] The baby was born soon afterwards and spent the first two years in Hämeenlinna prison with her. In 1939 her old friend Väinö arranged foster parents for the child, on the understanding that Olga would take her son back on her release.[15]

But at the end of November 1939 the so-called Winter War between the Soviet Union and Finland began. The Soviet attack was based on the Nazi-Soviet pact, whereby smaller neighbouring countries were divided between these two powers. The war came as a shock to Finnish Communists: many abandoned their faith; some went to the front to fight against the Socialist Fatherland, and the secretary-general of the FCP, Arvo Poika Tuominen, left the Party (Rentola, 1994: 10). In 1940, Finland was defeated but not occupied.

Olga was released in autumn 1940 but ordered to stay in Helsinki. Her son was in Lahti and she could see him only occasionally.[16] Although many Communists were bewildered by the Winter War, many others remained loyal. The latter organized a new movement, the Society for Peace and Friendship between Finland and the Soviet Union. Before long, it had some 40,000 members and Olga became involved. After the Winter War, the Finnish government moved gradually closer to Germany and in the summer of 1941 it backed the Nazis when they invaded the Soviet Union. Before the attack, many Communists had already been arrested, and during the Continuation War (as it has been called in Finnish historiography[17]) almost all the well-known party cadres were either convicted or in prison without trial. Olga was arrested again in October 1941 and sentenced to eight years for treason.[18]

The Communist legacy

An armistice was concluded in September 1944. Finland had lost the war, and ceded Karelia and other areas to the Soviet Union. Eleven per cent of its population was forced to move, and an Allied Control Commission (in this case a Soviet Control Commission) was set up in Helsinki in September–October 1944. Under the terms of the peace treaty, political prisoners were released immediately, while rightist organizations, like the powerful Civil Guard, were suppressed. Olga and her comrades were set free soon after the armistice, and could celebrate and make plans for the future. There were 'glorious opportunities' to be realized, a 'new mood' among the workers.

According to the memoirs of one Finnish woman cadre, Lydia Arppe, the autumn of 1944 and the following year were 'the period of new, strong and forward-looking action – the battlefronts were silent, prison bars had been broken and a movement forced into inactivity for fifteen years was looking for a channel through which it could break out. There was an atmosphere of enthusiasm.'[19] Olga wrote to her friend Lydia in January 1945, that 'the sea of life roars stronger than ever – and we, who have been put in the bows of the ship must endure'.[20] On the other hand, a few lines in the same letter sound more wistful: 'I think it would do both of us (and, perhaps, many others …) good to spend a moment on a desert island. I think we are a little tired, mentally and physically, if we are honest with ourselves.'

A new Communist identity had to be assembled out of rather conflicting elements. In singling out Olga's story to outline that identity, I may be distorting the picture. Perhaps most Communists really were strong and purposeful. But several of the leading women cadres were less sure of themselves, as appears from the letters they wrote to each other when working as local organizers after the war. In these letters, they vividly described their political work, such as the 'agitation tours' to villages in the middle of nowhere. But they also told each other about their feelings and everyday concerns. Only a few of Olga's letters have survived, but they are emotionally very similar to letters written by other women in the same position.[21]

Olga was still a loyal Communist. The basic component of her identity was hatred for the Whites, the 'butchers' of the Civil War and the 'ohranas' (secret police), the visible enemy of the 1920s and 1930s. It was time to make up for what the Communists had suffered, and Olga was proud to be firmly on the anti-fascist side. But memories that were partly painful and partly puzzling began to emerge from behind the enthusiasm and the relief of getting out of prison.

The most problematic question for the Communists was the almost total destruction of the FCP in the Soviet Union. During her three years in Leningrad, Olga must have known many of those who were later killed in the purges, including the father of her child. By 1944, that part of the movement hardly existed: a few hundred emigrants returned to Finland, but only a few achieved any position in the post-war Party. The Communists in Finland were aware of what had happened across the border but there was almost no reaction. Kimmo Rentola has used the analogy of incest: the purges were something that had happened 'in the family circle', were never mentioned afterwards but left a permanent mark (Rentola, 1994: 73). The events were never analysed. Some former Communists – Arvo Poika Tuominen, in particular – wrote about the purges after the war but they were simply considered 'doomed defectors'. The question must in any case have been sensitive for everyone.

Besides the problematic legacy of the movement, Communist women (and men in their own way) now faced the physical and mental consequences of the years in prison. They had to reassess their attitude to family and parenthood, and they had to decide what the place of women in the Communist mass movement ought to be.

'I just want to stay in bed all day …'

Soon after her return to Helsinki in September 1944, Olga was sent as a Party agent to a small town in western Finland, some 40 kilometres from the home village she had left seventeen years earlier. She was in charge of mobilizing people to political action. As a revolutionary by profession, she knew the ideology by heart, was trained in shooting and conspiracy, knew how to use codes and keep secrets – but she knew almost nothing about organizing the masses or making public speeches. Nor, after all the years abroad and in prison, was she familiar with the everyday life of Finnish working women or their political traditions. Having learned to obey Party directives, she tried to do her best. But she was exhausted and the dark Finnish winter was approaching.

In her new station, Olga was lonely. The people she knew best in the world were the women with whom she had spent years in prison. Only to them could she tell her innermost feelings and they were now scattered throughout the country. So she wrote them letters. 'You can tell the boys everything I've said above [a detailed account of the local political situation]', she wrote to a friend working in the Party bureau – 'the boys' meaning the leading cadres there – 'but not the rest. It probably would not even interest them.'[22] 'The rest' meant subjects that could be discussed only among women, that is, matters dealing with the emotions and the body.

Some of these women were shy and wrote only about their political work. But those who revealed their weaknesses to each other felt relief: they were not the only insecure cadres amid the strong-minded. 'Dear Lyyli. You will never know how happy I am to receive your letter. Not happy because you are having inward struggles, but because you told me your worries. I felt at least someone needed me', Olga wrote to Lydia Arppe in January 1945. (Lydia's 'worries' probably referred to the fact that her brother and his wife had been killed in the Soviet Union.) In the same letter, she commented on the narrow 'Communist' range of emotions. Party cadres did not have the right to be fallible and weak. Olga did not know how to comfort her distressed friend and wrote: 'I have always felt awkward in such situations and now I feel – to my horror – that all the words of comfort have disappeared.'[23]

Physical problems caused by the bad sanitation and poor food in prison (Peltonen, 1989) were also a subject one could take up only with one's closest friends. Olga was in poor health throughout the winter of 1944-45. In her letters she wrote about her insomnia and her wish to do nothing but lie in bed. She had influenza, prolonged fever and diarrhoea, and trouble with her eyes. She went to see the doctor because of her heart and was told to rest. Resting might help with the heart trouble, she complained to Kaisa Junttila, another FCP cadre, but 'there is also the liver, the stomach and the vagina'.[24] But you could not tell 'the boys' this kind of thing, nor could you admit you were too sick to work.

The Party and private life

For the members of the FCP, the line between private and public was problematic. Sometimes private life seemed to be irreconcilable with political loyalty. In the middle of a personal crisis, it was hard to relate clearly to the duties of a Communist cadre.

Olga's most personal concern was her child. Late in 1944, she was trying to decide whether to ask for her son back or let his foster parents raise him. In mid-December she wrote to Kaisa Junttila that she had 'decided to fight'. The couple asked Olga's old friend Väinö (by now a prominent cadre) to persuade her to give up her claims, arguing that the boy had become estranged from his mother. Väinö wrote telling Olga to listen to reason, not to emotion.[25]

'Until now I have tried to be reasonable,' Olga wrote to Kaisa Junttila, 'I have suppressed my feelings, and tried to do what would be best for the cause and the child. I have been patient, hoping that when times changed, I would get him back. Kaisu, you can hardly imagine what he means to me. Or maybe you can because you know the circumstances in which we lived.' And then Olga added, feeling guilty: 'You may find it selfish talking like this at a moment when such big and new issues concerning the whole human race are at stake. Tomorrow I will not cry. Tomorrow I will think of other matters, our great cause, my work.'[26]

Olga was not alone with these problems. Many women in prison had children; the youngest (up to two years old) usually lived in prison with their mothers, older ones with relatives or foster parents. The husbands of married women were often in prison too.[27] Some women had left children in Finland when they went to the USSR, others, like Hertta Kuusinen, had left children in the Soviet Union when they returned to Finland and might never see them again.

Duties in the movement

Olga's weariness and uncertainties affected her political work and she became self-critical, writing to her friends that she felt unable to get anything done. Yet, as well as the general FCP action in the district, she was responsible both for organizing women (towards the end of 1944) and for the 1945 election campaign.

In 1945 Olga wrote that she was not interested in women – the 'petticoat battalion' – and their problems. She had accepted the view that men and women were similar, and had little enthusiasm for organizing women separately.[28] Her first contact with women's activities came when she tried to start a local section of the FWDL, without immediate success. To Kaisa Junttila, she poured out all the annoyances she had had with women: 'The founding of our women's section has been postponed until the week between Christmas and the New Year. To my surprise – and this will surprise you too – in this place one must pay attention to such matters as Christmas preparations. When we discussed it with the women and I suggested next Sunday or the week before Christmas, the others said it was no use even trying, as people were busy with all the Christmas bustle.' The revolution would have to wait. But she added: 'You cannot even imagine all the snags and obstacles before you encounter them yourself. Landing up here has been instructive in many ways. You learn to see things from the peasants' point of view.'[29]

The women's branch was founded in the end, and became one of the largest and most active local organizations of the FWDL. Members arranged entertainment to raise money both for the branch and for the whole movement, and to strengthen the Communist (or 'people's democratic') identity of the members. Outsiders flocked to the branch's dance evenings. Women visited local authority homes for the elderly and the mentally ill, for whom they collected food. Olga did not at first have much time for the branch but she did act as a speaker on various occasions.[30]

In the March 1945 elections, Olga was nominated as a candidate. She was reluctant and accepted only out of Party loyalty. The nomination, as she explained to her friends, meant making numerous public speeches at electoral meetings, something she hated. She wrote that she felt sick and wanted to vomit every time she had to take the floor. Two weeks before the election she was predicting: 'Hopefully – and very likely – I will not become a Member of Parliament'.[31]

Her wish was not granted. The FPDL was successful at the polls and Olga Virtanen was one of the six women elected from its list. A promising political career seemed to lie ahead and the political future for the whole movement appeared bright. With 23.5 per cent of the vote, the Party now participated in a coalition government with the Social Democrats and the Agrarian Party.

At this stage, however, Olga's private life intervened. She had just reached another turning point in her life, one that proved in the long run more permanent than the political change, or rather helped to change her political orientation. During the dark midwinter days when Olga had reflected on her past and future, her fellow-worker in the local bureau had been a man with whom she had much in common. They had been in the Soviet Union at the same time, had both spent years in prison and had now been sent to the same district. Olga mentions the man in her letters but gives no hint of deeper feelings. The relationship was, however, established and soon after the election Olga found that she was pregnant. They married in the summer, and in December 1945 the baby was born.[32]

The political agenda of women

Olga's children (two others were born later) were part of the post-war baby boom.[33] This, together with the other social consequences of the war, changed women's political agendas. Many women working outside the home or working in social and political groups now had small children. Poverty was widespread and especially difficult for families with several children. Problems such as illegal abortions and venereal and other diseases increased (Katainen, 1994: 249–257, 279–84).

In 1947–48 one of several committees on women's status reported on the problems of wage-earning mothers. Its signatories included Communist and Social Democratic women. The report illustrates the debates of the time: should women stay home or should there be public services enabling women – particularly mothers of small children – to work outside the home? According to the report, ideally all children should be raised at home. But the need to develop the public day-care system was also stressed (Satka 1993: 68–71; Katainen, 1994: 271–315; Kuusipalo, 1994: 170–2).

These questions also concerned the women in Parliament and the women's section of the Finnish Confederation of Trade Unions. Communist women proposed bills on maternity care, the improvement of conditions in day-care centres, the provision of nine years compulsory education for all children and reform of the poor law. During her years in Parliament (1945–48), Olga concerned herself with the problems of women's waged work. The FWDL also took an active interest in these questions and from the start backed public services like communal day-care centres and homes for the elderly. Its position on abortion was cautious, but it considered social grounds as well as medical grounds to be valid, whereas the prevalent opinion and law accepted only medical grounds (Katainen, 1994: 279–84).

Local activists were prompted to action by the problems they saw in their everyday lives. In the branches, initial enthusiasm and activity were fairly soon directed into routine work and the need to relieve the shortages and ease the daily life of working-class families. 'Democratic women' held meetings in private homes where they talked about childbirth and the prices in the cooperative stores. This had a contributory influence on drawing FWDL leaders' attention to social questions. Another motive was competition with other political groups, especially the Social Democratic women (Katainen, 1994: 165–266).

Olga Virtanen and the women's movement

The 1948 election was a setback for the Communists. Although they won 20 per cent of the votes they were ousted from government. The Soviet Control Commission left the country and a people's democracy was never established.[34] Little remained of the political optimism of the winter of 1944–45.

How did Olga's career develop in the new situation? By the end of the 1940s, she was working in the local FWDL branch in Pori on the west coast. Looking at these years may shed light on the grass-roots nature of the Communist movement. After being a cadre in an illegal party and a Member of Parliament, Olga Virtanen was now a wife and mother in a small town. By 1945, she had given up hope of getting her first child back but the new babies occupied her days. She now had a new focus for her political action, too. She was primarily responsible for the work among women, though with a third pregnancy her activity was limited. By this time she had developed more sympathy for the world of rural women and the problems they faced in their everyday lives and in political participation. In her letters to the secretary of the women's league, Helvi Laine, Olga now repeatedly argued against the directives sent to local branches. The proposed timing of meetings for instance was insensitive. May was out of the question, because women were busy with their farm work: 'When the cattle are out to grass, then they will have time – before haymaking.'[35]

Women's sections around the country had to schedule their action bearing in mind women's everyday routines and seasonal work. In a poor country like Finland, the season for picking berries or gathering mushrooms was no good for organizing women's courses or meetings. In March 1949, Olga asked Helvi Laine to arrange for someone else to take over her duties in the district because she could no longer manage: 'I can see clearly what should be done – but my time is limited when the family has had its share. My room for manoeuvre is even more limited. And besides my health is not that good.'

Gradually, women like Olga began to question the suitability of the Party's policy for women whose family duties set their daily time-table, limited their freedom to move and determined their social life. The Party leaders, on the other hand, began to express doubts about the seriousness of the women's organization. According to them, women could not see the really important things and their political action was often called 'tinkering' (Kataineu, 1994: 78–80).

In the long run, however, the concerns raised by the women's organization did bear fruit. The FWDL became a relatively independent organization, pursuing its objectives both through major campaigns and through the continuous 'tinkering' process in the local branches which were, in fact, laying a foundation for the policy of the Communist Women's League and for the participation of women in politics. At the end of the 1960s, the Communists returned to the government and at the same time, such important measures as a new abortion law, reform of the day-care system[36] and of elementary schools were planned and carried out. It is not easy to estimate the exact contribution of Communist women, but they were certainly involved in all these reforms. They also had more influence in politics, through ministers such as the Minister of Social Affairs and Health, Anna-Liisa Tiekso, and Members of Parliament: after the 1970 elections, almost 28 per cent of the Communist parliamentary group were women (Katainen, 1994: 129).

The groundwork for this had been laid by women political activists in the immediate post-war years, by women like Olga. And yet her political work, and the work of women like her, has been totally undervalued, or even forgotten. Their attempts to make the Party rethink its policy in line with women's own preoccupations failed at the time; their own uncertainties about how to fulfil both their role as Party cadres and their lives as 'ordinary' women were hidden. In the history of the Finnish Communist Party, Olga is remembered as the wife of a District Secretary, and not for the work she accomplished in her own right.

Acknowledgements

I would like to thank Pirjo Kaihovaara, Joni Krekola, Tauno Saarela and all the members of the study circle for gender and labour history who have commented on this paper. I have also had inspiring conversations with Riitta Oittinen about biographies of women.

Notes

1. For a history of the Communist women's organization in Finland, see my book on the Finnish Women's Democratic League (FWDL) (Katainen, 1994).

2. Collection of memoirs: Olga Terho (OT), 1982, 1, People's Archives (PA), Helsinki. Olga's 'memoirs' are in fact an interview conducted by a PA employee. Olga's maiden name was Virtanen, but she married in 1945.

3. The Reds also executed about 600 Whites; several thousand men and some women died in battle on both sides.

4. In the Party management (consisting of twelve plus six cadres) Hertta Kuusinen and Aili Mäkinen were permanent members, Tyyne Tuominen and Kaisu-Mirjam Rydberg substitutes. Tuominen was also the secretary-general of the FPDL. Mäkinen was responsible for the educational section of the Party, and Kuusinen was the leader of the FPDL parliamentary group. She was often depicted in political cartoons as a symbol of the whole movement. Other women such as Inkeri Lehtinen (who returned from the Soviet Union after the war) also held these positions. In 1945 women had six of the FPDL's forty-nine parliamentary seats. In 1948 there were nine women in the group, a larger percentage (18 per cent) than in any other party (FCP Annual Reports 1945–48, 5; Katainen, 1994: 59-62, 126-7).

5. There had been a women's organization in the working-class movement since 1900. When the Communists tried to suppress it in the 1920s, many had opposed the decision (Katainen, 1994: 21-2; Lähteenmäki, 1995: 180-91; Saarela, 1996: 330-4).

6. OT memoirs, PA.

7. OT memoirs, PA; personal papers of Väinö Sievänen: memoirs, 153-4, PA; Finnish Secret Police collection (SP): OT file, National Archives (NA), Helsinki.

8. SP collection: index, NA.

9. SP collection: OT file, NA.

10. See, for example, personal papers of Jaakko Lehtoranta: memoirs, 142-6, PA; see also SP collection: file 680 (information about the University for the National Minorities of the West), NA.

11. Arvo Poika Tuominen has written in his memoirs about the courtship and abortion practices among the Finnish students in the Moscow Lenin-School (Tuominen, 1957: 68-70).

12. SP collection: OT file, NA.

13. SP collection: OT file, NA; collection of memoirs: Väinö Sievänen, 192, 200, 202, PA.

14. Going to the Party school was interpreted as a treasonable act. Collection of SP: OT file, NA.

15. Personal papers of Väinö Sievänen: memoirs, 200 and 202, PA.

16. SP collection: OT file, NA.

17. The war was perceived as a continuation of the Winter War because the intention (from the point of view of many Finns) was to win back the area of Karelia annexed in the peace treaty (a large region where about 10 per cent of the Finns had lived).

18. SP collection: OT file, NA.

19. Personal papers of Lydia Arppe (LA): memoirs, PA.

20. Olga Virtanen's (OV) letter to LA, 19.1.1945, personal papers of LA, PA.

21. In the People's Archives there are some fairly large collections of letters, the most interesting being those of Lydia Arppe, Elina Hämäläinen, Kaisa Junttila (KJ) and Hertta Kuusinen.

22. OV's letter to KJ, 16.11.1944, personal papers of KJ, PA.

23. OV's letter to LA, 19.1.1945, personal papers of LA, PA.

24. OV's letters to KJ, 14.12.1944, 30.12.1944 and 22.2.1945, personal papers of KJ; see also OV's letter to LA, 1.3.1945, personal papers of LA, PA.

25. See OV's letters to KJ, 16.11. and 30.12.1944, personal papers of KJ, PA.

26. OV's letter to KJ, 16.11.1944, personal papers of KJ, PA.

27. See, for example, the personal papers of Elli Mänttäri in PA. Her letters and a memoir have also been published in Peltonen, 1989.

28. OV's letter to KJ 22.2.1945, personal papers of KJ, PA.

29. OV's letter to KJ 14.12.1944, personal papers of KJ, PA.

30. Annual report 1945, Papers of the Democratic Women's branch in Pori, PA.

31. OV's letters to KJ, 14.12.1944 and 22.2.1945, personal papers of KJ; OV's letter to LA, 19.1. and 1.3.1945, personal papers of LA, PA.

32. OT's letter to KJ, 21.11.1945, personal papers of KJ; correspondence of the FPDL's parliamentary group, 18 December 1945; records of the FPDL's parliamentary group, 21.12.1945, PA.

33. In 1939 – the last 'normal' year before the war broke out – there were just under 80,000 births; in 1947 the highest ever total in Finland was reached, about 110,000. *Statistical Yearbook of Finland 1958*, 54.

34. The fact that Finnish territory was never occupied was, according to Finnish historians, one of the reasons keeping the country out of the Soviet camp during the Cold War. There was also a large and independent Social Democratic Party as a counterforce for the Communists (Laulajainen, 1984; Rentola, 1997). Besides, in spite of its large support, the FCP was, in fact, weak. During the war, there had been no resistance movement in Finland which might have given the Communists a leading role in post-war politics (Jussila, 1990: 253-4). And all the charismatic leaders of the Party were dead except Otto-Wille Kuusinen who never received permission to return to Finland; his daughter Hertta Kuusinen was witty and popular, but had one defect – she was a woman.

35. These letters are in the collection of the FWDL, correspondence from the districts, Satakunta 1948-49, PA.

36. Today the law guarantees communal day-care for all pre-school children.

130   *Elina Katainen*

References

Aho, Timo (1981) 'Vankiluvun kehitykseen vuosina 1881–1978 vaikuttaneista tekijöistä'. *Suomen vankeinhoidon historia*, osa 1, Toim, Helsinki; Elina Suominen.

Alapuro, Risto (1988) *State and Revolution in Finland*. Berkeley: University of California Press.

Beyer-Thoma, Hermann (1990) *Vasemmisto ja vaaran vuodet*. Helsinki: Kirjayhtymä. (An abridged version of Beyer-Thoma's dissertation 'Kommunisten und Sozialdemokraten in Finnland 1944–1948', Veröffentlichungen des Osteuropa-Institutes München, Reihe Geschichte.)

Goldman, Wendy Z. (1993) *Women, the State and Revolution: Soviet Family Policy and Social Life, 1917–1936*. Cambridge: Cambridge University Press.

Haataja, Lauri (1988) *Demokratian opissa: SKP, vaaran vuodet ja Neuvostoliitto*. Helsinki: Tammi.

Hyvämäki, Lauri (1954) *Vaaran vuodet 1944–48*. Helsinki: Otava.

Jussila, Osmo (1990) *Suomen tie 1944–48: Miksi siitä ei tullut kansandemokratiaa, Juva*. Porvoo: Werner Söderström.

Kaihovaara, Pirjo (1997) 'Missä paikkasi, tiedätkö sen? Kommunistisen puolueen kaaderien elämäkerrat – poliittiset valinnat, kulttuuri, kertomus'. Unpublished licentiate's dissertation (sociology), University of Helsinki.

Kalela, Jorma (1996) 'Suomalaisten historiakuva huolestuttaa'. *Helsingin Sanomat*, 18 August.

Kataineu, Elina (1994) *Akkain aherrusta aatteen hyväksi: Suomen Naisten Demokraattinen Liitto 1944–1990*. Helsinki: KSL.

Kuusipalo, Jaana (1994) 'Emännät ja työläisnaiset 1930-1950 – lukujen politiikassa – oppaina Tyyne Leivo-Larsson ja Vieno Simonen'. In Anneli Anttonen, Lea Henriksson and Ritva Nätkin (eds), *Naisten hyvinvointivaltio*. Tampere: Vastapaino, pp. 170–2.

Laulajainen, Pertti (1984) 'The Communist defeat in the 1948 Finnish election: notes on the impact of organization'. *Scandinavian Political Studies*, 1, 39–53.

Leppänen, Veli-Pekka (1994) *SKP: Ohranasta oppositioon. Kommunistit Helsingissä 1944–1951*. Helsinki: KSL.

Lähteenmäki, Maria (1995) *Mahdollisuuksien aika: Työläisnaiset ja yhteiskunnallinen muutos 1910–30 luvun Suomessa*. Bibliotheca Historica 2, Helsinki: SHS.

Mikkeli, Heikki (1996) 'Älymystö, valta ja suomettuminen', *Helsingin Sanomat*, 18 September.

Nevakivi, Jukka (1995) *Zdanov Suomessa: Miksi meitä ei neuvostoliittolaistettu?* Helsinki: Otava.

Nevakivi, Jukka (1996) *Miten Kekkonen pääsi valtaan ja Suomi suomettui*. Helsinki: Otava.

Paavolainen, Jaakko (1974) *Suomen kansallinen murhenäytelmä: Punainen ja valkoinen terrori ja vankileirit v. 1918*. Helsinki: Tammi.

Peltonen, Ulla-Maija (1989) *Naisia turvasäilössä: Poliittisena naisvankina Suomessa 1930–1944*. Helsinki: Arthouse.

Rentola, Kimmo (1992) 'Kommunismin kahdeksan kohorttia'. In Mikko Majander (ed.), *Ajankohta: Poliittisen historian vuosikirja 1992*. Helsinki: Tutkijaliitto.

Rentola, Kimmo (1994) *Kenen joukoissa seisot? Suomalainen kommunismi ja sota 1937–1945*. Helsinki: WSOY.

Rentola, Kimmo (1997) *Niin kylmää että polttaa. Kommunistit, Kekkonen ja Kreml 1947–58*. Helsinki: Otava.

Saarela, Tauno (1996) *Suomalaisen kommunismin synty 1918–1923*. Helsinki: KSL.

Satka, Mirja (1993) 'Sota-aika perhekäsitysten ja sukupuolten suhteiden murroksena'. In Pertti Haapala (ed.), *Hyvinvointivaltio ja historian oikut*. Väki voimakas 6. Tampere: Työväen historian ja perinteen tutkimuksen seura, pp. 68–71.

Tuominen, Arvo (1957) *Kremlin kellot: Muistelmia vuosilta 1933–39*. Helsinki: Tammi.

Vihavainen, Timo (1991) *Kansakunta rähmällään: Suomettumisen lyhyt historia*. Helsinki: Otava.

10 Women's Associations in Hungary: Demobilization and Remobilization, 1945-1951

Andrea Petõ

Hungary had been in an uneasy alliance with Germany during much of World War Two, joining Hitler in his invasion of the Soviet Union in June 1941 and entering the war against the Allies later that year. In the face of Hungary's increasing reluctance to participate fully in the Axis alliance, the Nazis occupied the country in March 1944. After the invasion by the Soviet Union in September 1944, the Hungarian Regent Miklós Horthy signed an armistice with the USSR which was then abrogated and a Fascist government installed. Hungary became a battlefield between the retreating Germans and the advancing Soviet Red Army, which left it in a state of physical and material devastation and political chaos.

When the war was over, the previous 'evil enemy', the Soviet Union, stationed troops on Hungarian soil. The pre-war political elite was totally discredited and Hungarian society as a whole was faced with the moral and political consequences of Hungary's wartime alliance with the Nazis. The Hungarian Communist Party (HCP), benefiting from the military, financial and moral support of the Soviet Army, and using the available democratic parliamentary methods as well as illegal extra-parliamentary measures, gained power by 1948.

The history of the immediate post-war years in Hungary is the history of the Communist takeover. On Stalin's instructions, this was intended to be a gradual process rather than another version of the rapid takeovers in other parts of East Central Europe (Poland, Romania, Bulgaria and the Soviet Zone of Germany). However, unexpected setbacks in the 1945 elections – in which the conservative Smallholders Party won an overall majority – pushed the HCP to speed up its bid for control. Forming an alliance with the Social Democratic Party and the National Peasant Party, the HCP gained control of several key offices including the Ministry of the Interior. The Party used what became known as 'salami tactics' to strengthen its control in coalition governments, gradually ousting rival parties from government and discrediting their leaders as 'antidemocratic'. By the end of 1947, the takeover was complete.

The role of social movements – trade unions, youth groups and women's groups – was always recognized by Communist parties as crucial for reaching, recruiting and controlling the 'masses'. Control of these groups was thus always a key feature of Communist strategy. Hungary was no exception. The history of Hungarian women's associations as a part of the broad spectrum of social movements reveals a forgotten chart of our post-1945 history. In this chapter, I will look at this forgotten part of the history of social movements in order to tell the untold story of Hungarian women's associations and to illustrate the process of the political demobilization and then remobilization of Hungarian women by the Communist Party.

Once the Communist Party had gained total control over civil society, the archives and documentation of different associations were taken by the police in boxes to an unknown destination. After 1990, when research opportunities opened up, I discovered the lost, boxed world of Hungarian women's groups in the archive of the Ministry of the Interior. This chapter is based on documents of Hungarian women's associations and the women's sections of different political parties in the early post-war years. I will focus first on the responses of women's associations to the war and then on the new elements of political life which changed the environment in which these women's associations operated.[1]

Hungarian women's associations' experience of World War Two

The Hungarian women's associations were required to submit a report to the Ministry of the Interior on their wartime activity. Their activities can be defined in three ways: apolitical system conformity, political resistance and feminist resistance.

Before 1 September 1939, there were two main types of women's association. The first believed in women's equality with men. These associations included the liberal Feminist Association (founded in 1904) and women in the labour movement. The second type believed in emphasizing women's difference and tried to improve women's status in society using the available cultural and charitable means. These associations (charities, religious groups, artistic and scientific groups, women alumni) tended to have small local memberships; they supported families in need and individuals such as women artists. These activities were not generally construed as being political: the definition of politics for many women's groups was activity in political parties. In their reports, the women's associations pointed out proudly that they had nothing to say about their political activity: they were never involved in 'politics' because their members were mostly women. During the war, they organized charity balls and ice-cream afternoons, and, when the front was approaching, 'silent balls' to express their sympathy with those who were suffering.

The generally complicated picture of Hungarian resistance is complicated further if we look at how some of the women's associations resisted official war aims.[2] The political resistance of women's associations to government war efforts began with offering shelter for Poles who used Hungary as a transit point. Since the Hungarian government, although officially in alliance with Germany, unofficially supported this Polish evacuation, this did not represent a high risk activity. This changed dramatically after anti-Jewish legislation was introduced in 1938. Only those women's associations which owned shelters, homes and dormitories were in a position to become involved in helping Jews, which became increasingly risky. According to their reports, some of both the Catholic and the Protestant women's associations helped Jews. Several associations pointed out that their form of resistance was deliberately to ignore the official anti-Jewish legislation which excluded Jews from public life in 1938, by allowing Jews to remain as officers of the association. The official political anti-Semitism pulled together different groups of women's associations into a quasi-coalition for cooperation based on humanitarian values. This form of cooperation was supported by religious associations which, ignoring the anxious politics of the clerical hierarchy, tried to save lives in the name of Christian values. The Social Missionary Society, the first women's charity order founded in 1908 by the first woman MP of the Hungarian Parliament, Margit Slachta, used all available resources to save lives. Margit Slachta declared a struggle against two types of materialism, Bolshevism and Nazism. She believed that: 'The Cross stands in the middle. People's opinions are like a pendulum; shifting from left to right and back again, they will eventually stop in the middle.'[3] Belief in the universal Christian cohesion force of the Cross motivated her to play an active role in the Polish rescue operation, and when the first deportations started, she raised her voice against them.[4] Margit Slachta organized shelters for Jews in fifteen Hungarian cities and distributed forged baptism certificates. Her society lost one of its main activists in the struggle, Sára Salkaházi, who was not only a talented journalist and theoretician of Christian feminism but also a fighter for humankind. She was taken by members of the Hungarian Fascist organization, the Arrow Cross, and killed on the bank of the Danube together with those Jews to whom she had offered shelter.

The third type of resistance was feminist resistance. The Feminist Association was the only liberal feminist women's organization which declared its independence from political parties. Informal and family ties bound its members to the few Hungarian liberal parties, but these parties became less and less visible as Hungary was subordinated to German war aims. The Feminist Association continued to hold meetings, ignoring the fact that it threatened their lives – indeed, the leader of the Feminist Association, Mrs Meller, was arrested during one of those illegal meetings in 1944. She and other Jewish members of the Feminist Association were murdered at Auschwitz. Mrs Meller was awarded the Silver Liberty medal posthumously in 1946 for her role in the Hungarian national resistance, but during the 'canonization' process, her role as a feminist was forgotten.

Cooperation between different women's organizations during the harsh circumstances of the war proved to be short-lived. Resistance based on purely general humanitarian principles was overtaken by a monolithic view of political resistance represented by the anti-fascist tradition of the Communist movement. The redefinition of meanings of resistance gave a powerful weapon to the Hungarian Communist Party, and they did not hesitate to use it during the revolutionary transformation process.

Continuity and change in the life of Hungarian women's associations after 1945

After the war, the political context of social movements changed. The main question for all social movements in 1945 was of continuity or discontinuity with their pre-war activity. In 1945, women were forced to face a new set of challenges.

In 150 towns and villages, 243 women's associations were formed and they all continued the activities which they had abandoned before 1945, in particular their charity work.[5] They missed the opportunity to redefine their position in Hungarian society, given the changes in the political environment. This is clearly shown by the fact that they filed totally unamended deeds of association in their petition for re-activation after the war – documents prepared in the last decade of the nineteenth and the first of the twentieth century, which was the founding period for Hungarian feminist associations. The members could not see any reason to modify the often century-old documents. They considered neither their goals nor their internal structure as in need of alteration. Leaders of the women's associations believed that their tea parties, charity performances and lectures continued to serve their aims effectively: believing in women's difference, their goal was to help women perform their roles better. The change also brought a generational problem to the surface: the leaders of the women's associations belonged to the middle and older generation. This was the great generation of the women's movement, who had personally experienced World War One, the rise of Fascism and victorious Bolshevism on the one hand, and the revolutionary expansion in women's rights, and educational and labour opportunities on the other.

However, certain changes were unavoidable. First because in the election of 1945 universal suffrage was introduced in Hungary for the first time. To the surprise of the Communist Party, women voted for the Smallholders' Party, which represented traditional values, and was strongly supported by the religious institutions and associations. The election of 1945 was the first and only one in Hungary when men and women voted with ballot papers of different colours. The Communist Party received 15 per cent, Social Democrats 17 per cent, Peasant Party 6 per cent and the Smallholders' 60 per cent of women's votes.[6] As the first results of the election became known, the Communist Party began working on the mobilization of Hungarian women for its own political aims. Between 1945 and the next election, in 1947, Hungarian women were labelled with the scarlet letter of backwardness by the increasingly strong Communist Party. Prominent leaders of the Communist Party's Women's Section – usually wives of Party leaders or members of the former illegal Communist resistance in Hungary, France or Moscow – pointed out that women had to be educated.[7] The Secretariat responsible for women's issues declared after the first round of the 1945 elections: 'Women have not reached the proper political level, they have not realised who is responsible for the present situation. The voters did not know what they were doing. We have to regain women's support. Women should raise the political awareness of the other women.'[8] It is not surprising that many women felt inferior; massive Communist propaganda blamed them for the victory of the Smallholder's Party, suggesting that their vote was based either on the fact that they were easily deceived or that they were simply ignorant. This same Communist Party promised them a shining path paved with opportunities leading to the promised land, the New Democratic Hungary.

The second important factor of change was in the general framework of Hungarian democratization between 1945 and 1947. The Hungarian Parliament passed bills and laws in unprecedented number which had been on the agenda of women's associations for decades. Principles of women's emancipation were discussed in the general framework of basic human rights. Opening up higher education without any restriction (1946. XXII Act), the reform of family law (1945.

6800 decree of the Ministry of Education), pension and childcare benefit (1945. decree of the Minister of Welfare 10350.), elimination of sex segregation in professions such as the police (1945. decree of the Minister of the Interior 45703.12) were important steps towards equality. Only two professions, the army and the church, remained closed to women.[9] As the leader of the Feminist Association, Mrs Szirmaine, put it: 'as far as our goals are concerned, we have to declare that in a certain way, we have achieved them. The intellectual foundations of democracy have brought the full emancipation of women in politics, in social and scientific life.'[10] The number of women MPs increased from one or two in the pre-war parliament up to fourteen in 1945 and to twenty-two in 1947.[11] The Communist Party systematically put women forward for parliamentary office to demonstrate the importance of 'women's issues' in its politics, but the main decisions were taken in the Party hierarchy where there were no women at all. Speeches in parliament mostly remained on the ideological level, articulating one of two points of view: labour party politicians (Hungarian Communist Party and Social Democratic Party) argued for equality between men and women, since women had already proved that they could do what men could do. The second group, the MPs of bourgeois parties, who were annually declining in number, put the emphasis on the biological and social differences between men and women.

Searching the archives of women's sections of different political parties we do not find any evidence of lobbying for women's special interests. Nor do we find women MPs fighting specifically for women. Although the general social climate created a favourable situation for emancipatory legislation, several discriminatory provisions were still exercised such as citizenship – married women were automatically deprived of their original citizenship. Protection of women's rights within the framework of human rights did not lead even to the shadow of emancipation.

Regulation of Hungarian women's associations

Learning from the results of the election of 1945 and following the Soviet example, the Hungarian Communist Party first had to gain control of the existing women's associations in order to achieve the mobilization of Hungarian women for its political ends.

The legal framework for associative life after 1945 was regulated by the decree of the Prime Minister No. 529/1945, which dissolved all Fascist military and political organizations on 26 February 1945. In accordance with the Armistice and the 1947 Peace Treaty, the enforcement of this decree was reported to the Peace Commission. Freedom of association was a delicate problem which could have international implications. Hungarian regulations show that within the framework of basic law, the state regarded the spontaneous organization of citizens with cautious suspicion.

Act No. I. of 1946 recognizes freedom of association as the inalienable right of citizens and Act No. X. of 1946 recommended five years' imprisonment for the infringement of human rights, including the right of association. In fact, the Ministry of the Interior gradually extended its jurisdiction to cover all aspects of associative life: in addition to licensing, it supervised financing as well. The issuing of the decree of the Minister of the Interior (No. 20.165/1945) on who would oversee the associations provoked an internal power struggle which ended with the full victory of the Ministry of the Interior, controlled by the Communist Party.[12]

From the summer of 1945 onwards, citizens could exercise the right of association as regulated by law and officers could apply for their licensing and approval. However these laws on the day-to-day operation of associations soon became incomprehensible; they seemed to change daily. A poorly run bureaucracy, along with increasing coercion to come under state control, made the activities of the associations impossible.[13] (During the administrative procedure of registration, it happened fairly often that the amended deed of association was submitted on the same day that the resolution on the dissolution of the very same association was issued by the Ministry. The ultimatum declaring re-activation submitted by the subprefect simply never arrived at the relevant department of the Ministry of the Interior.)[14]

The elimination of financial support, the impoverishment of members of the middle class or the loss of their assets did not lead directly to the termination of these associations. Other factors played their part. The changing and inconsistent administration by the Ministry of the Interior often evaluated the same phenomena, people or organizations in various ways at different times, causing a high degree of uncertainty in the civil organizations. The organizations' spontaneity did not match the centralizing policy of the Communist Party, which was determined to control social movements. Also, the threat of possible police atrocities decreased the willingness of Hungarian citizens to form and to take an active part in social movements.

Beginning in 1945, the leaders of the associations found themselves dealing with frequent bureaucratic requirements. Both the Department of Associations of the Ministry of the Interior and the relevant department of the local authorities bombarded them ceaselessly with requirements for different reports and standardized forms. Despite the legal hierarchy between the Ministry of the Interior and the local authorities, memoranda from the Ministry were sent directly to the associations and to the local authorities at the same time. It happened several times that the same organization which received moral and legal support from the local authority was dissolved by the Ministry a month later.[15]

Special police methods were always involved in the communication between the women's associations and the authorities. As soon as the documents arrived at the Ministry of the Interior, the Department of Associations gave the data to the State Defence Department (Államvédelmi Osztály (ÁVO), later called Államvédelmi Hatóság (ÁVH)), in effect the Security Police, for supervision. The State Defence Department of the local police supervised the submitted files and checked the list of the officers to see if they were on a censored list. If the police found no problems, the Ministry of the Interior approved its re-activation and ordered the association to hold a general meeting and to file a list of the elected officers. If there were any names on this list which were not considered by the supervising body to be compatible with the new democratic values, the authorities ordered suspension of approval until the censored names were deleted.

A person could be listed in police records for two reasons. One was financial abuse, which often happened with the treasurers of the associations. The other was political. There were hardly any names on the re-activation petitions which could ever be found in the history books. After 1945, the history of women's associations is the history of anonymous citizens. Celebrities, members of aristocratic families, famous public figures of the previous political regime who had lent prestige to women's organizations were out of public sight after 1945. Nonentities remained in the leadership of the associations. The gulf between the influence of social movements, including women's associations, and political parties increased.

At first, even when leaders of the women's associations were arrested for political reasons, they were generally released and their case never reached court. However, after 1948, when the official politics became openly hostile towards associations, it was enough for the supervising body if the leader had a non-desirable party membership or if the spouse had such a membership. If this was the case, the report of the Security Police labelled her an extremely dangerous individual jeopardizing democracy. From that point on, no one urged the associations to expel its leaders as the licensing laws required, since by that time the real aim was the termination of the associations. The only exceptions were those women's associations whose scope of activities were well-defined and which were difficult to replace immediately.

The process of regulation was based on different sorts of information sources. The responsible local authorities were generally satisfied with papers submitted by the associations themselves, whereas the Department of Associations in the Ministry of the Interior accepted all the information submitted to them without any doubts about its origin. The Security Police was in a key position, for it was authorized and able to obtain necessary information about the women's associations to which no one else had access. This information, however, reveals the perspective from which these data were evaluated during investigation.[16]

In the first investigation, the leaders of the associations were screened and their papers were collected and checked. In the second or third investigation – after the dissolution of the association – there were only on-the-spot inquiries. These inquiries were carried out by Security Police clerks, who interrogated the leading members of the association. In some cases they sought the opinion of the local democratic parties or that of the local representatives of the Magyar Nők Demokratikus Szövetsége (MNDSZ) (Democratic Association of Hungarian Women), the Communist Party's women's organization. These reports were a relatively decisive factor in the fate of the associations – Departments of Associations quoted them word-for-word in their resolutions on dissolution. Obviously, the investigators used covert informers as well. The commissioner of all investigations was the Ministry of the Interior, so the point of view of the Ministry was decisive.[17]

Elimination and dissolution of women's associations

The first wave of dissolutions of women's associations was caused by the implementation of the Armistice in 1945. Immediate dissolution orders were issued to the most significant women's associations of the previous regime, for example the Magyar Asszonyok Nemzeti Szövetsége (MANSZ) (National Alliance of Hungarian Women).[18] Enforcement of this order took place quite slowly in the local branches. Local MANSZ associations were still submitting applications for re-activation even in 1946. Although the dissolving order had been published in the Official Gazette, it could hardly have reached everyone in the turmoil after the war.

The other group of associations targeted were those women's associations which did not comply with the obligation to re-register. This mainly meant the 152 associations under the umbrella of the Alliance of the Jewish Women's Associations, out of which only sixteen exercised their right of appeal. These associations would in fact have had a good chance of approval during the re-activation period of 1946–47, when Hungarian society was trying to atone for its guilt at the extermination of most of Hungary's Jews.

A motion for dissolution could be suggested by the local National Commission, the appropriate local authorities, the Department of Associations of the Ministry of the Interior, and the Security Police. All these authorities employed clerks who notoriously asked for dissolution no matter which association was mentioned. The most significant opinion was that of the Security Police. Should the Security Police call for dissolution, not even the Department of Associations could object, however exclusive its jurisdiction over the dissolution process might have been. They could only delay the service of the dissolution order until all documents had come to the Ministry. The changed political environment could be felt in the second wave of dissolution. No one challenged the grounds on which the associations were dissolved or why their assets were seized. The illusion of the rule of law had faded away by 1947.

Here is a typical example of how these associations were dissolved:

> After 10 p.m. on 27 January, 1947, a man appeared at the site of the National Alliance of Catholic Working Women and Girls, in Budapest, No. 4. Rákóczi street. He presented no identity card. He had an allegedly official document in his hands which he neither read out loud nor handed over. He asked why the association was still working despite having been dissolved … The man was interested in the whereabouts of the cash and the balance sheets of the association. As soon as he understood that no money had left the building, he said he would take the necessary measures and telephone the Minister to seal the office of the Alliance.

Indeed, on 29 January a representative of the authorities appeared and sealed the office. Paradoxically enough, the Alliance really had been dissolved before, on 19 July 1946. The association had appealed, however, but received no answer and thus continued to function. But the leaders of this prestigious women's association acknowledged the inevitable – dissolution.[19]

The formal argument for dissolution was often that the aims of the association had already been fulfilled by others, often by the MNDSZ.

> I believe that an association whose object is to give aid to the poor is not needed. The major aim of our peoples' democracy is to give assistance to all working people. For this exact reason, it has established social institutions which undertake these tasks.[20]

The dissolution order of the Feminist Association on 19 October 1949 includes the following ruling:

> Its purpose as described in the deed of association, i.e. to emancipate women in all areas of society and to safeguard women's employment, has already been guaranteed to all women in the Constitution. It does not have the required accounting and the

financial means necessary to achieve the goals of the association. Its objects are achieved by the MNDSZ.[21]

These are arguments and slogans of high politics and certainly had little to do with reality. As a result, religious associations were absorbed by the churches, institutions run by women's associations (nurseries, homes for the elderly) were taken over by the state, interest groups merged into trade unions, and other associations disappeared with no trace at all.

The third investigation was much less important if a women's association was to be dissolved, for it was merely an attempt to account for the assets of the organization after its dissolution. An investigator was sent from the Security Police only if the assets were presumed to be valuable, otherwise police constables or clerks from the criminal department were sent. However, even the Security Police was not at the peak of its effectiveness. Often a long time elapsed – 3 to 4 months – between the order of investigation and its accomplishment. The inquiry itself took only one day as is clear from the police reports. The investigation of the associations imposed quite a burden on an otherwise fairly busy office. In many cases no investigator was sent to the spot, not even after the third notice to the Department of Associations in the Ministry, and so most cases were not closed officially. Probably this was a decisive factor in the decision of the Security Police in 1948, when it ordered the dissolution of all women's associations, without investigation.

The assets of the associations

The race for the assets of associations started straight after dissolution. It was clear to the dissolving authorities that the only immediate inheritor of these assets could be the MNDSZ.[22] Therefore the assets of MANSZ were transferred to the newly-formed MNDSZ in February 1945. Should the MNDSZ fail in or neglect the maintenance of the newly-formed institutes, creches, kindergartens, schools, hospitals, shelters or colleges, the assets were to be assigned to the appropriate Ministry or to the local authorities. The MNDSZ considered it important to maintain creches and kindergartens in order to support women's employment. Although there had been some financial problems in the MNDSZ early on, ultimately it was able to avoid losing these institutions to the municipal authorities. 'The property [of the dissolved associations] belongs to the local community in the relevant region', as was described by the official regulation. The only exceptions were extremely valuable property or the assets of those associations whose activities spread over various regions; these were handled separately.

The inventories of the associations prepared during the dissolution give quite a clear picture of their financial situations. Liquid assets hardly ever exceeded HUF 1,000.00. On the other hand, for the associations whose main object was to hold tea-parties or charity performances, the inventories usually consisted of glasses, bottles of brandy, chairs, props and decorations. After the dissolution, everything – from the coffee cups to cloud decorations – was inherited by the MNDSZ.[23] Nevertheless, in some cases the MNDSZ itself did not even wait for the dissolution order and simply walked into the offices of other women's associations and confiscated their possessions. As they paid no rent to begin with, these poor women's associations were deprived of their most important revenue resources.

The assets of women's associations which had been seized could be returned only by order of the Ministry of the Interior. Even the personal effects of the people living there could not be saved if they failed to prove their ownership of the property. There was no exception made whatsoever, not even when the later nationalized property turned out to be the lifelong work of some individual, such as in the case of the Sancta Maria Women's Home Society; here a lonely woman sacrificed all her wealth and life's work for the operation of the home. Even Father Balogh[24] attempted to intervene personally by contacting János Kádár, who was at that time the Communist Minister of the Interior. This was in vain, as the Ministry of the Interior awarded the personal belongings only to the applicant. Valuable property easily found new owners.

The charity function of women's associations was taken over by state institutions, religious women's associations were absorbed by their church, and political mobilization was undertaken exclusively by the MNDSZ. In the time after 1945, state involvement in social welfare increased in Western Europe and there were tendencies towards centralization everywhere. The tragedy of the Hungarian women's associations was that this centralization was carried out by a Stalinist regime which did not tolerate dissent.

Political mobilization by a new women's association

The political mobilization of women by the HCP meant the foundation of a new mass organization, the MNDSZ. After 1945 a new option was opened for women's political activity, because the MANSZ, the prominent mass organization of the previous regime, was banned. The women's associations were too weak to use this moment to renew their activity. The place of the MANSZ was filled by the Communist mass organization MNDSZ. This new women's association was founded in January 1945 and succeeded in mobilizing those layers of Hungarian society which had remained untouched before the war.

Political parties which had existed before 1945 continued their women's politics along the same lines and with the same organizational structure as in the pre-war years. The Communist Party, as a new party in the legal world, also organized a Women's Section but kept the key to women's mobilization in their own hands. The MNDSZ was organized in such a way as to avoid the image that it was simply a branch of the Communist Party. Activists were warned not to use the rooms of the Communist Party for meetings but try to get a 'room of their own'.[25] They were not allowed to wear the badge of the Communist Party but only the MNDSZ badge which was typically 'nice and pretty'. Communist activists were also warned not to leak information before it had been officially given to them by the MNDSZ. The MNDSZ did not have to struggle with financial problems like the other women's associations because they were among the first to receive serious support from the state. They were also the inheritors of the remaining wealth of the women's associations. From teacups to pictures of Stalin with kids, everything was donated to the MNDSZ, together with the most desirable assets, the buildings.

The new element in the profile of the MNDSZ was that their task was explicitly to mobilize women for political purposes. The definition of politics was given by the Communist Party: gaining the electoral support of women for the election of 1947. The MNDSZ called women to the streets in order to protest against high prices in 1946. They were given instructions such as 'There will be no singing during the march', and 'According to the previously distributed materials, slogans and short poems should be read out'. The unified, mobilized masses of women fitted into the concept of the Hungarian Communist Party. As Mihály Farkas,[26] the notorious Minister of Defence, said in his speech at a great Budapest women's mass rally in 1947 just before the election: 'Generally my opinion is that if women had more space and if they played a more important role in political life today, then there would be more order.' But it was surely a certain kind of order.

Conclusion

The network of women's associations in Hungary survived the war, but failed adequately to confront the war experience. In this essay I have explored how the altered political context of the immediate post-war years affected women's associations; how, like other social movements, women's groups were oppressed, eliminated or reactivated in a shape and form acceptable to the Communist Party, with their aims subordinated to the aims of the Party. However Act No. XLIII. issued on 26 November 1948, declared the emancipatory rights of women and the Constitution of 1949 recognized the equal rights of association for all workers. All women's associations – including the most significant one, the women's division of the Social Democratic Party – had by this time already merged into the MNDSZ. The world of the Hungarian women's associations was lost until the revival of 1990 when, once again, political upheaval brought new possibilities for social movements.

Notes

1. On the Hungarian women's movement in the interwar period, see Mária M. Kovács (1994) 'The politics of emancipation in Hungary' in Andrea Petõ (ed.), *Women in History: Women's History*, CEU History Department Working Paper Series, No. 1, pp. 81–91; and Andrea Petõ (forthcoming) 'Continuity and change in the Hungarian women's movements in the interwar period' in Ute Gerhard (ed.), *Feminism and Democracy: On the Significance of the Women's Movements for the Process of Democratization in European States after the First World War*, Frankfurt: Campus Verlag (in German).

2. See István Deák (1995) 'Fatal compromise? The debate over collaboration and resistance in Hungary'. *East European Politics and Society*, 9(2), 209–34.

3. Quoted in Ilona Móna (1991) 'Slachta Margit közéleti tevékenysége' in Margit Beke and István Bárdos (eds), *Egyházak a változó világban*, p. 569 (Esztergom).

4. Tamás Majsai, 'Egy epizód az erdélyio zsidóság második világháború alatti történetéből. Slachta Margit fellépese a Csikszeredáról kiutasított zsidók érdekében.' *Medvetánc* 1988/4–1989/1, pp. 4–35.

5. For further information, see Andrea Petõ (1995) 'As the storm approached: the last years of the Hungarian women's movements before the Stalinist takeover', in *CEU History Department Yearbook 1994–1995*, Budapest: CEU, pp. 181–207.

6. Sándor Balogh (1984) *Válsztások Magyarországon, 1945: A fővárosi törvényhatósági és a nemzetgyülési választások.* Budapest: Kossuth, p. 157.

7. PIA 276.f.19.cs.1.öe. p. 81. Minutes of the Women's Section of the Hungarian Communist Party, October 1945. For the speech by Rákosi, see p. 100.

8. Politikatörténeti Intézet Archivuma (Archive of the Institute of Political History), 274.f.19.cs.1.80pp.

9. See Mária Palasik (1990) 'Nők és nőkrol a koaliciós Paramentben'. *Ring* 13, 4–5.

10. Magyar Országos Levéltár továbbiakban MOL P 999 1.cs. 17pp. Minutes of the Feminist Association Annual General Meeting, 27 December 1948.

11. See Károly Jonas (1990) *Pártpanoptikon 1948–1990.* Budapest: Adams.

12. In the debate relating to who had the final word for approving the registration of associations, we find the following proposed amendment: 'All final decisions must be made by the Ministry of the Interior. The National Commission [the autonomously founded local municipal authorities] and the local authority may make only recommendations, taking into account the need for uniformity and the political interests related to the overseeing of associations.' ÚMK XIX-B-1-c.6.d.22.

13. 'The file is lost.' Charity Women's Association of Mór, 29 January 1948. ÚMK XIX-B-1-h, 5638.403.

14. Association of Women Graduates. ÚMK XIX-B-1-h,5638.190.

15. For example, the Annual General Meeting of the Jewish Women's Association of Székesfehérvár on 30 December 1949 established a cultural section; the Association had however already been dissolved on 9 December. The formal merger with MNDSZ was declared on 3 February 1950. ÚMKXIX-B-1-h. 168.d.5638.68.

16. As Ferenc Schliffblatt, a retired prison warder, demonstrated in his report on the Association of Hungarian Unitarian Women, 20 December 1948: 'The leadership is composed of non-Party members; some of the leaders' husbands are members of the Communist Party. Almost all of them, originally from Transylvania, have a petit-bourgeois attitude … There is no positive evidence of proper policy-making in the Association, but the way in which it delays the merger and cooperation with the MNDSZ, plus the fact that it has organised only one language course – which is a course in English – and the interviews with the leaders, all show that the Association is not in line with democratic development.' ÚMK XIX-B-1-h.195.d.5639.336.

17. The Ministry considered 'whether the safety measures and other measures relating to state defence and security requirements had been taken concerning conduct of the leadership; whether the resources of the Association were used properly; whether the membership acted properly; whether the requirements for the achievements of the Association's goals were relevent and proper.' Ministry of the Interior, memo issued in 1949. ÚMK XIX-B-1-h.

18. Petition by Mrs Sándor Török of MANSZ for the reactivation licence on 24 August 1945: 'The Association has nothing whatsoever to do with politics. Our main goal was to assist the children of the people. We would certainly work hard to adapt to new circumstances. The MANSZ itself has always been democratic, because its membership was recruited not only from the middle class but from all sections of society.' ÚMK XIX-B-1-.18.d.5632.784.

19. 'We duly notify our dear fellow members at this general meeting, that we

have received a notice from the Ministry of the Interior forbidding this meeting and referring to its order of 20 October 1949, in which it prescribed the merger of our Association [with the MNDSZ]'. Minutes of the Annual General Meeting of the Feminist Association, 22 November 1949, p. 578. In a letter from Mrs Oskár Szirmai, president of the Association, to Noémi Kóbor, she wrote: 'Well, such is our life, we have to give up, there is nothing else we can do … my dear sister, we expected this, but it is still a sad surprise.' MOL P 999 1.cs.p580.

20. Desző Tóth, Mayor's report, 27 March 1950, concerning the St Elisabeth Society of the Iron Factory in Diósgyõr. ÚMK XIX-B-1-h. 164.d.5638.20.

21. ÚMK XIX-B-1-h,5639.105.

22. Cf report by Mrs Albert Szegedi, 3 December 1949, prior to the dissolution of the Lutheran Women's Association in Békéscsaba: 'We believe that the local MNDSZ … would serve the interests of democracy and work for the goals of democracy with the same enthusiasm as the Lutheran Women's Association. Should those town women who are being cared for by the Association so request, they could be looked after in the social shelter in Békéscsaba.' ÚMK XIX-B-1-h.166.d.5638.30.

23. In the inventory of assets prepared for the dissolution process by the Society for St Vincent's Sisters of Mercy from Gyöngyös, there were posters of Rákosi, Szakasits, Lenin and Stalin with children. 29 December 1949. ÚMK XIX-B-1-h.164.d.563.

24. István Balogh (1894–1976), Catholic priest and an influential politician of the Smallholders' Party. He was later a founder of the Independent Hungarian Democratic Party and in 1949 joined the Popular Front (an umbrella organization which was formed as all political parties were forced to join together).

25. PIA 274.f.19.cs.1.öe.p.12.

26. Mihály Farkas (1904-1965) began his political career in interwar Czechoslovakia and then emigrated to the Soviet Union. He returned to Hungary in 1945 and worked in the Politburo of the Hungarian Communist Party.

References

Balogh, Sándor (1984) *Válsztások Magyarországon, 1945: A fövárosi törvényhatósági és a nemzetgyülési választások.* Budapest: Kossuth, p. 157.

Deák, István (1995) 'Fatal compromise? The debate over collaboration and resistance in Hungary'. *East European Politics and Society*, 9(2), 209–34.

Jonas, Károly (1990) *Pártpanoptikon 1948–1990.* Budapest: Adams.

Kovács, Maria M. (1994) 'The politics of emancipation in Hungary'. In *Women in History: Women's History.* CEU History Department Working Paper Series, No. 1, ed. Andrea Petõ, pp. 81–9.

Majsai, Tamás (1988–89) 'Egy epizód az erdélyio zsidóság második világháború alatti történetéböl. Slachta Margit fellépese a Csikszeredáról kiutasított zsidók érdekében.' (A part of the history of Jewry in Northern Transylvania; the activity of Margit Slachta.) *Medvetánc* 1988/4–1989/1, pp. 4–35.

Móna, Ilona (1991) 'Slachta Margit közéleti tevékenysége' (The public activity of Margit Slachta). In Margit Beke and István Bárdos (eds), *Egyházak a változó világban.* Esztergom, p. 569.

Palasik, Mária (1990) 'Nók és nókrol a koaliciós Paramentben'. *Ring*, 13, 4–5.

Petõ, Andrea (forthcoming) 'Continuity and change in the Hungarian women's movements in the interwar period'. In Ute Gerhard (ed.), *Feminism and Democracy: On the Significance of the Women's Movements for the Process of Democratization in European States after the First World War*. Frankfurt: Campus Verlag (in German).

Petõ, Andrea (1995) 'As the storm approached: the last years of the Hungarian women's movements before the Stalinist takeover'. In *CEU History Department Yearbook 1994–1995*, Budapest: CEU, pp. 181–207.

Petõ, Andrea (1998) *Nöhistóriák: A politizáló magyar nök története, 1945–1951* (Women's Stories: History of Hungarian Women in Politics 1945–1951). Budapest: Seneca.

Petõ, Andrea (1999) 'Memory unchanged: redefinition of identities in post WWII Hungary'. In *CEU History Department Yearbook,1997–98*. Budapest: CEU, pp. 135–53.

11 'Feminism is dead. Long live feminism!' The Women's Movement in France at the Liberation, 1944–1946

Sylvie Chaperon
Translated by Claire Duchen

In France, the history of women and of feminism during the immediate post-war period is relatively new. The first historians dealing with the period treated it with some disdain, presenting these years as of little feminist activity and of serious decline, dominated by a rather ladylike and much weakened reformism. More recent historiography, motivated by the intense feminist activism of the 1970s, first paid attention to periods of radicalism, which seemed more relevant to the present. However, a new generation of historians, less concerned with the post-1968 blaze of activity, have cast a fresh eye over the reformist decades, and recent work has thrown into question many preconceived ideas about the post-war years (Chaperon, 1996; Duchen, 1993, 1994, 1995; Guéraiche, 1992; Montreynaud, 1989; Thébaud, 1992; Van der Casteele Schweitzer and Voldman, 1985). When studied more closely, the period can be seen to be rich in events, ideas and paradoxes. These were particularly abundant in the years immediately following the war (summer 1944 to the end of 1946) which deserve to have an entire study devoted to them. During these months, France gained a new Republic which included women citizens, developed a comprehensive welfare state, and saw its political life significantly renewed. How did women participate in all these changes? Did they manage to influence the shape of reforms in the post-war period?

The idea that achievement of women's suffrage in 1944 put a definitive end to the suffragist movement has been firmly planted. For the historian Jean Rabaut, and for many others after him, 'the historic women's organisations were fundamentally undermined by winning the right to vote' (Rabaut, 1978: 322; see also Albistur and Armogathe, 1978; Bouchardeau, 1977). Did this mean that the women's movement disappeared at the Liberation? If the women's movement is defined as encompassing the associations and activists who, whatever their philosophy, fought to improve women's lives, then the movement was alive and even booming during these years. However, it is true that its feminist component (that is, self-defined as such) was declining and was marginalized in relation to new groups.

Two major features characterize this women's movement understood in the broadest sense: its institutional fragmentation and its global dynamism. The fragmentation of associative life came partly from the renewal of women's elites brought about by the Resistance. Diverse new organizations emerged and rubbed shoulders with the older ones. However, these new groups rarely managed to last. The fragmentation of the women's movement can mostly be attributed to the politicization of women since gaining political rights: once they were able to vote, women were courted by all the political parties active at the Liberation. However, the dispersal of all these groups was countered by an increasing polarization of the groups between those influenced by Communism and those closer to Catholicism.

The fragmentation and polarization of the women's movement

Several component parts of the women's movement at the Liberation must first be identified. There were the old associations of the first feminist wave, which kept going determinedly. The groups emerging from the Resistance, on the other hand, were short-lived. Both old and new were however overtaken numerically by Catholic and Communist groups. Yet these divisions should not hide a certain common ground. The activists knew each other, saw each other socially; many of them were active in more than one group and met together in the numerous joint activities undertaken during the consensual and reformist phase which followed the Liberation. Later on, the mounting tension leading to the Cold War made any agreement increasingly unlikely.

What happened to the suffragists?

The verdict of the death of suffragism must be seriously rethought. The old feminist organizations were re-formed at the end of the war with the clear intention of continuing their struggle. In spite of the interruption caused by the war, significant continuity between pre-war and post-war can be observed in the political paths followed by the activists and in the composition of this part of the women's movement. It is, however, true that they suffered a real loss of influence: the 1930s and World War Two had greatly diminished their strength. They carried little weight in the new political context (Bard, 1995).

The entire range of reformist feminist groups were reactivated after the war with the same women involved and the same ideas expressed. The four most important organizations of the pre-war movement, at the head of liberal feminism – the Ligue Français pour le Droit des Femmes (LFDF) (French League of Women's Rights), the Union Française pour le Suffrage des Femmes (UFSF) (French Union for Women's Suffrage), the Conseil National des Femmes Françaises (CNFF) (National Council of French Women) and the Union Nationale pour le Vote des Femmes (UNVF) (National Union for Women's Vote) – carried on in the same way as before.

The LFDF, mixed, secular and free-thinking, had been founded in 1870 by Léon Richer and Maria Deraismes, both Freemasons. At the Liberation, Andrée Lehmann (1893–1971), a former Vice-President of the League, took over its presidency. She was 52 and had been a barrister at the Paris Court of Appeals since 1921. She was not afraid of making a spectacle of herself and had been arrested three times in front of the Senate, going as far as flying over the building and dropping political tracts to make her feminist position public (Bard, 1995: 333). As before, the League prided itself on its strong, independent feminism; it demanded equality of the sexes and maintained a strict policy of political independence.

The UFSF, founded in 1909, was one of the major suffragist groups in France. Cécile Brunschvicg (1877–1946) presided over it from 1924 to 1946. She was a member of the centrist Radical Party and had been one of the first three women cabinet members (Under-Secretary of State for Education) during the left-wing Popular Front government of 1936, alongside Suzanne Lacore and Irène Joliot-Curie. At the Liberation, she was back at the helm for the last two years of her life. Following her death, her former vice-president Germaine Malaterre-Sellier took over. This progressive Catholic was active in the League of Nations and in other international women's organizations. Odette Simon-Bidaux, Doctor of Law and barrister, member of the Radical Party and long-standing UFSF member, became its secretary. In 1947, the Union was renamed the French Union of Women Voters (UFE). The UFE remained close to the by this time rather lacklustre Radical Party.

The CNFF, founded 18 April 1901, represented the respectable and moderate Republican female élite. Marguerite Pichon-Landry (1877–1972) led the Council in the 1930s and then again after the war, right up until 1955. The Council kept its pre-war structure, operating as an umbrella group for a number of women's associations, each of which was represented by two delegates. The particular shape probably explains the slow reorganization of the Council after the war (all its affiliated groups had to be reconstituted first).

The UNVF, founded in 1920, was Catholic and on the right of the feminist spectrum. Renamed the National Union of Women, its President remained the Duchesse Edmée de La Rochefoucauld (1895–1991), close to conservative political groups, seconded as before by Marie-Thérèse Moreau (barrister, Knight of the Legion of Honour), Suzanne Desternes (graduate of the prestigious Institute of Political Science) and the younger Mariel Brunhes-Delamarre, a geographer.

These groups, at the heart of the old feminist movement (and indeed calling themselves feminist), were surrounded by other groups with more limited objectives: women doctors, women lawyers, women graduates, business women, all had their own associations, and the Soroptimists sought to gather together the 'best' of each profession. All these groups of the first feminist wave stayed true to their history and their struggles; the bleak war years, dangerous as they were, hardly seemed to make any difference to them.

At the end of the 1930s, as the threat of war increased, these feminist groups put their feminism to one side and put themselves to work for the 'fatherland in danger'. The great majority of them were disbanded following the defeat of France in 1940. The patriotism displayed by most of their leaders explains their refusal to request from the German authorities the now necessary permission to publish. Feminist militants ran clear risks by openly carrying on their activities. This was obviously the case for Jewish women: Andrée Lehmann of the LFDF, Marcelle Kraemer-Bach, Suzanne Schreiber-Crémieux and Cécile Brunschvicg, longstanding activists in the UFSF, the radical feminist Yvonne Netter – all these women went underground in the southern so-called 'free' zone of France, some of them joining the Resistance. Women Freemasons were also subjected to innumerable persecutions (Brault, 1953). Even the simple fact of being a feminist aroused suspicion: the word itself was banned from the Press Guide, which decided criteria for censorship under Vichy (Bertin, 1993).

Once the groups had broken up and their archives had been destroyed or hidden, the women nonetheless stayed active. There were many women Resisters, even though the information we have about them is too patchy for any statistical assessment to be made. Feminist and women's networks more generally seemed to serve as stepping stones towards Resistance activity, making use of their long-standing political practice and political consciousness, and their many contacts. The leaders of the Association des Femmes Françaises Diplômées de l'Université (AFFDU) (French Association of University Women Graduates), for instance, used their contacts with their American counterparts. Marie-Louise Puech, who presided over the Association's foreign affairs committee and Madame Cazamian, the Association's president, took over AFFDU during the war. Thanks to their *News-letter*, they managed to keep in touch with their members in the unoccupied southern zone until 1942. They organized a solidarity network for British, Belgian, Polish, Czech and Jewish refugees. Some were hidden, others evacuated with financial help from the USA. Marie-Louise Puech, based in the south, was sent significant sums of money by the Quakers and by the American Unitarian Church which she distributed to the most needy. Madame Cazamian, who remained in Paris, took care of many intellectuals who were interned in camps in the Paris area and throughout France.[1] During the war, women often kept on with their prior activities; for instance Lucie Chevalley, member of UFSF and CNFF, founded and presided over the Social Aid Service for Emigrants, which offered support for families from allied countries (whose menfolk had been interned) and for Jewish families.

At the Liberation, the newsletters of these associations praised their members for their Resistance activities. For instance, to cite only the most well-known cases: Marcelle Kraemer-Bach, who under the name Jeanne de Kergaradec was part of an information network; Suzanne Schreiber-Crémieux was in the Resistance in the south; Jeanne Chaton of AFFDU participated in several networks before joining the University National Front Resistance network. Germaine Poinso-Chapuis (1901–1981), active in the UFCS (Women's Civic and Social Union) as well as in the CNFF and the LFDF, was decorated with the Medal of the Resistance,[2] as was Marguerite Pichon-Landry of the CNFF. Germaine Peyroles (1902–1979), member of the UFCS, was also in the Resistance. This period spent in the Resistance does not however seem to have inspired new practices or ideas after the war; the paths followed by groups and individuals display, rather, great continuity with their pre-war activities.

All these suffragist groups had to confront the difficulties of the Liberation and the dispersal of their members throughout France. But the commonly held idea that achievement of the right to vote demobilized or even ended the women's movement seems to go against the evidence. Suffragist groups, indeed, did everything they could in order to use this historic moment to benefit from the political context and make national decision-making favourable to women. For suffragists, the right to vote was not a goal in itself but the means by which other reforms, already waiting in the wings (some for a long time) could be achieved. The LFDF stated this very clearly when it started up again. Its membership form stated that 'the League considers that the vote is not a goal, but the means which will allow women to fulfil their duties'. The League then set out the reforms which it was consistently to demand over the next two decades: full civil rights for married women, equal parental rights, reform of the legal status of illegitimate children, equal pay for equal work, opening of all professions to women, the abolition of regulated prostitution.[3]

Yet, in spite of their dynamism – and, in some cases, their heroism during the war – the suffragists were out of the spotlight. In the months following the Liberation, it was women Resisters who were the incarnation of all the virtues in female form.

The unsung legacy of women's Resistance

While it was omnipresent in political discourse at the time and in the collective memory of the French since the war, the Resistance – and particularly the women in the Resistance – faded very fast from the institutional landscape of the Liberation. The indifference of masculine party hierarchies towards women was added to internal divisions and to the hostilities of political parties which were not enthusiastic about the Resistance's conversion to peacetime and electoral campaigns. With the notable exception of the Communist Party, the different Resistance groups did not seek to develop women's sections which amounted to anything more than token gestures.

As they settled into peacetime structures, the various Resistance groups produced a number of women's organizations at national level, apart from the Union des Femmes Françaises (UFF: Union of French Women), which will be examined below. They tended to be shortlived and lack any specific goal apart from opposing the Communist UFF. On the left were women from the Femmes de Libération Nationale (FLN: National Liberation Women). The well-known Resister Lucie Aubrac was brought in at its head without asking or wanting to be its leader, and distanced herself quite quickly from it.[4] However, FLN groups developed spontaneously throughout France 'on the initiative of an active comrade rather than through a central national directive', and this movement 'born quite spontaneously, expressing the deep need felt by women to form groups to work together to aid the reconstruction of their country'[5] set up its own organization and its own journal *La Femme* (Woman). In the centre was the Organization Civile et Militaire (OCM: Civil and Military Organisation) which did not adopt any formal structures, but did involve well-known personalities, in particular Marie-Hélène Lefaucheux (1904–1964) who was a member of the Provisional Consultative Assembly.[6] On the right, the group called Les Françaises Libres, or the Free Frenchwomen, was not a direct outcome of the Resistance, even though its leaders included Hélène de Suzannet, who had been in the Resistance, alongside Irène de Lipkowski and Marcelle Devaud, both from prominent political families of the upper-middle class, and both of whom went on to be Gaullist members of parliament. Once again, the desire not to give Communist women free reign was the thinking behind the action taken by the three founders. The first congress saw several thousand women meeting in February 1945 in the Salle Wagram in Paris and the congress declared that it wanted to represent 'the union of all French people of moderate opinion' (quoted in Dore-Audibert and Morzelle, 1988: 151) – in other words, it was right wing but nobody at the time used the word. Finally, Christian Democrat women in the Resistance (Germaine Peyroles and Solange Lamblin, who were MRP (Mouvement Républicain Populaire) members of the Constituent Assemblies)[7] founded a new women's magazine, *Marie-France*. The title indicates their goal – to be a sort of patriotic *Marie-Claire*. The magazine quickly abandoned any political content and became a very traditional women's magazine.

All these initiatives failed. The political parties either born or reborn after the war gave them no support. All the parties started their own women's sections: the 'Women's Team' in the MRP; the Socialist Party (SFIO) 'National Women's Committee'; the Communist Party (PCF) 'Work Amongst Women Committee'; the 'Women's Committee' of the Rally of the Republican Left (RGR); the 'Republican Women' of the Radical Party and so on. They all attempted to attract women voters. Each party sought to put one or two well-known women (preferably former Resisters themselves or widows of Resisters) in the limelight, and each one published pamphlets targeting 'ordinary' women. However, most of these women's sections played a barely noticeable role and few were developed by their party in any way (Guéraiche, 1997).

However, this rapid decline of Resistance groups didn't necessarily mean that they completely disappeared. The spirit of the Resistance, often reduced to simple patriotism in the discourses of the time, spread through civil society as its former activists went back to their peacetime lives. The historian Olivier Wieviorka (1989) has suggested that there was a 'Resistance generation' which was effective in spite of being dispersed. This description fits many women Resisters, who continued to make a difference for women but were not active in political parties. Evelyne Sullerot and Marie-Hélène Lefaucheux, for instance, both very active during the war, failed to be integrated into the MRP afterwards. The former, disgusted by political manoeuvring, devoted herself to family life before launching into the battle to liberalize contraception in the 1950s. The latter, although elected to the first Constituent Assembly where she tried in vain to create an interparty women's group (Guéraiche, 1992: 190–1), did not stand for election again and turned towards less directly political interventions: she presided over the CNFF and over the Women's Committee of the United Nations. Lucie Aubrac rejected a political career in favour of her former profession as a teacher. Célia Bertin and Marie-Jo Chombart de Lauwe, both young Resisters, worked on women's issues in their respective careers as journalist and sociologist. Ménie Grégoire moved from print to radio journalism as an 'agony aunt' (her programme was the first call-in programme for women). And so the list goes on. There were many women in the Resistance who, while rejecting political careers at the Liberation, continued their battle for women's rights throughout the 1950s and 1960s; for instance, they were all, or nearly all, involved in the battle for legal contraception (see Duchen, 1994; MFPF, 1982). Yet in the immediate aftermath of the Liberation, the Resistance seemed to quickly vanish or melt into the political divisions that reappeared.

The heavy hitters: Communists and Catholics

It might seem paradoxical to put these two irreconcilable enemies together: Catholic (and more generally Christian Democratic) women's organizations on the one hand and Communists on the other. They seem to be complete opposites in every way – in their wartime experiences (supporters of the Vichy regime's

family policy, mostly, for the former, Resisters for the latter); in their organizational structures (dispersed, centralized); and of course in their ideologies. But it
is precisely because the political conflicts at the Liberation were centred around
these two poles that it seems appropriate to discuss them together. Furthermore,
they had other things in common, especially the fact that Catholics and
Communists were the only ones to really go after the vote for women and to
try to mobilize women politically – no doubt because each offered women a very
different vision of the future.

During the war, Catholic women's organizations were very clearly seduced by
the sirens of the Vichy government's so-called 'National Revolution'. The UFCS,
founded in 1925 by Andrée Butillard (1881–1955) who remained its president
until her death, was very close to the familialism of the Pétain regime: pronatalism,
restoration of the traditional family, renewed value placed on Catholic education,
new moral values for France, the culture of the 'eternal feminine' and sacrifice, the
glorification of motherhood (Muel-Dreyfus, 1995). The observation by historian
Etienne Fouilloux seems apposite: 'French Catholicism didn't … really believe that
it had supported Vichy; but rather was most satisfied to see public authority
acknowledge the pertinence of Catholicism's positions and ideas after so much
secular straying' (Fouilloux, quoted in Buton and Guillon, 1994: 121). So unlike
the suffragist groups, Catholic women's organizations were not disbanded at the
defeat in 1940 and the UFCS continued its activities and its publications.

On the whole, Vichy policies largely pleased the UFCS although it is impossible
to say to what extent they derived directly from it.[8] The UFCS approved of all the
Vichy family legislation: the law restricting divorce (2 April 1941), the law
increasing the penalty against abortion (15 February 1942) and the law penalizing
abandonment of the family (23 July 1942). Only on the acknowledgement of
adulterous children were there any divergences (Vichy partly accepted that they
should be acknowledged). On divorce, the UFCS would have liked the legislation
to be even more restrictive.[9]

The first years of the Vichy regime were a sort of golden age for the UFCS and
for its offshoot, the Ligue de la Mère au Foyer (the League of the Mother at
Home). Francine Muel-Dreyfus has pointed out the extraordinary vitality of these
associations. One hundred and fifteen UFCS members became local councillors
(after 16 November 1940, town councils had to appoint one 'qualified woman' to
take care of social work and other good works). All the UFCS national leaders
were appointed to the Consultative Committee on the Family.[10] The League and
the UFCS held conference after conference, recruited heavily and organized new
sections throughout France. The confusion of many mothers left alone after the
war helps to explain their success (Muel-Dreyfus, 1995: 186–7).

In spite of UFCS close affinities with the National Revolution's familialist
ideology, there was opposition to some aspects of the Vichy regime within the
UFCS and the difficulties grew as living conditions became harder. Faced with
increased shortages and especially with the introduction of the Service du Travail
Obligatoire (STO: forced labour service), sending French nationals to work in
Germany, the UFCS pressed the Church to stress its independence from and its
disagreement with Vichy.[11] Indeed, several UFCS leaders went into the
Resistance: Eve Baudoin, who received the Medal of the Resistance posthumously; Daisy Georges-Martin, arrested in March 1944, tortured, and killed during
the Saint Genis-Laval massacre;[12] Yvonne Pagniez, a political deportee who

managed to escape (Paigniez, 1947) and many more. Many Catholic women were in the Resistance and participated in the founding of the MRP after the war.

At the Liberation, nobody tried to hide the collaboration between the UFCS and Vichy. Andrée Butillard mentioned it quite naturally in her numerous articles. The UFCS in fact protested against the post-war modification of the Vichy law on divorce. At the Liberation, the UFCS did not suffer in any way because of its recent past – it never had difficulty in obtaining paper, for instance, which is quite surprising given the draconian conditions of the time.

Communist women took a totally different path. When the French Communist Party (PCF) was banned after the signature of the Nazi–Soviet pact in 1939 and several leaders were arrested, the Party was re-formed in secret and relied heavily on its women activists who could operate more anonymously than men. Organizations for women and young girls associated with the PCF also played an important role, and their leaders set up a specifically female and working-class form of resistance. These organizations emerged mainly from two pre-war groups. From the Communist – and non-feminist – Union des Jeunes Filles de France (UJFF- Union of Young French Women) came Danielle Casanova, its founder and general-secretary, Claudine Chomat, Josette Dumeix and Marie-Claude Vaillant-Couturier. From the French branch of the World Committee of Women Against War and Fascism (part of the Communist International, suffragist and closely linked to feminist organizations) came Maria Rabaté and Simone Bertrand. All these women, or almost all of them, were card-carrying members of the PCF, but the women's and working class committees that they set up were open to everybody. Together they worked in these frequently informal and dispersed groups, a difficult and dangerous task: Danielle Casanova, for instance, was deported for her activities and died at Auschwitz.

These committees organized protests in markets, in factories and during strike actions to emphasize women's immediate demands: the return of prisoners, increased rations and military benefits, price controls and so on. The best known of these demonstrations took place in Paris, at the Rue Daguerre and the Rue de Buci in 1942, where the leaders paid for their actions with deportation (London, 1995; Schwartz, 1995). But there were countless less spectacular actions, using more traditionally 'female' skills. Danielle Tartakowski has counted 239 house-wives' demonstrations between November 1940 and March 1942 (quoted by François Rouquet, 1997: 676). At the Liberation, Yvonne Dumont counted 4405 local committees in 87 Departments of France (Bourderon, 1977). These diverse groups, initially isolated and with no links, prepared handwritten or typed newsletters: *Femmes d'Ivry, Femmes de Belleville, Femmes d'Orly* and so on. In June 1944 they joined together and held a national meeting to plan the armed uprising against the Nazis in Paris and in other parts of France, and to consider how women Resisters would be represented in the new post-war power structures. The fusion between the north (Femmes Françaises) and the south (Union des Femmes de France) took place on 1 October 1944 and adopted the name Union des Femmes Françaises (UFF). The UFF included women of all ages and political profiles, but the leadership fell to pre-war Communist activists who had not necessarily been Resisters (such as Jeannette Vermeersch, companion of Maurice Thorez, PCF general secretary, who had spent the war years in the USSR). The association was faithful to the Party.

In spite of their very different wartime trajectories, Catholic and Communist women's organizations both experienced a remarkable boom at the Liberation. Both undoubtedly knew how to channel the growth of attention to women's citizenship of those years to their benefit. Together, the Communists and Christian Democrats had played key roles in the decision to grant women political rights, and both the Catholic and Communist press at the Liberation were vociferous in their support for women's entry into politics (see Rudelle, 1994; Guéraiche, 1995a, b). Both knew how to attract these new voters. Pope Pius XII, on 21 October 1945 to an audience of hundreds of representatives of Italian Catholic women's associations, presented women's participation in political life as a serious Christian duty: 'Every woman, without exception, has the duty, the strict duty of conscience, not to remain absent, to take action to contain those trends which threaten the family, to contain the doctrines which undermine its foundations' (quoted by Cecilia Dau Novelli, 1988: 340). With this speech, the Church broke with its previous discourse in which women were presented as apolitical, and exhorted women to be full and active citizens. The UFCS led this political mobilization and its membership leapt from 12,000 to 70,000 from 1945 to 1947 (Doneaud, 1991: 27). In its wake followed other smaller groups such as women in the Catholic trade union confederation (CFTC) leadership, the UNF and the CNFF. The MRP Women's Team, led by Simone Rollin, would provide the linking point between all these organizations.

The PCF, following the Moscow line, obviously wanted to attract the largest possible number of women, indispensable for the building of a mass party. The UFF was the focal point for this and claimed to have over half a million members at the end of 1945, nearly double that a year later, and produced 100,000 copies of its weekly journal *Femmes Françaises*. The UFF was a proselytizing organization and spread its influence beyond the traditional spheres of the PCF. Its national executive cleverly mixed Communists and non-Communists, involving particularly Catholics, to whom the hand of friendship was constantly extended. *Femmes Françaises* published the work of diverse talents such as the writers Edith Thomas, Clara Malraux, Françoise D'Eaubonne and Marguerite Grépon, and the doctors Françoise Dolto and Jenny Roudinesco. The women leaders of the Communist trade union confederation (CGT) and the secular feminists of the UFE and the LFDF joined in several of the Communist actions.

The dynamism of the women's movement

The months immediately following the Liberation of France were marked by contradictory trends. On the one hand, the leading officers were replaced and a clean break with the past made via the strong but very short-lived influence of Resisters. On the other, the many fears provoked by so many rapid changes fed the significant return of conservatism of all kinds and a virulent anti-Communism which prefigured the Cold War. In this way the doors which had begun to open for women were slammed shut. Even so, women activists of all shades managed to achieve some impressive victories.

Women's organizations used the spirit of the Liberation to their advantage. The desire for renewal and for social justice, the rejection of traditional hostilities and political manoeuvring made women, new to politics and long devoted to good works, ideal candidates to carry forward the values of the Resistance. Women activists throughout the spectrum recalled women's new spirit, their sense of the concrete, their pragmatism. Through the discourses of the associations, a syncretism between the women's groups represented and dominant at the Liberation can be seen. The housewife and mother go hand in hand with the Resister to incarnate the ideals of justice, democracy and national renewal. The imagery of France and the Republic blend with the imagery of Woman and Resister to paint the portrait of the ideal citizen. Women's Resistance becomes an allegory of female grandeur and worth:

> What an immense task for women just as they enter the world of politics. The return of our dear ones, a more humane and equitable France to create, a France attentive to reality but dreaming of ideals, a proud, dignified and tender France ... The profile of the Republic, [Marianne] ... should look just like the faces of our Resistance girls. (*La Femme*, no. 2, 31 March 1945)

In fact, while women's participation in the new political structures of the Liberation was modest, it reached levels regained only recently. Lucie Aubrac, asked by Emmanuel d'Astier de la Vigerie (Commissioner in charge of Internal Affairs for the Provisional Government) to supervise the Departmental Liberation Committees (the provisional local authorities prior to the first elections), struggled to get them to admit women (Guéraiche, 1992: 173). Women formed between 7.5 and 10 per cent of the members of these committees. There were sixteen women, either former Resisters or widows of Resisters, in the Provisional Consultative Assembly when it returned to Paris from Algiers in the winter of 1944. In the first elected assemblies of liberated France (the two Constituent Assemblies and the first Legislature of late 1946), between thirty and thirty-five women took their seats in the National Assembly. There were far more women representatives from the PCF and the MRP than from the other parties (between seventeen and twenty-three for the PCF, eight or nine for the MRP). There is evidence that there were women-only lists for the municipal elections of April–May 1945 and for the legislative elections of October 1946.[13] These lists, about which there is little information, were the initiative of women who were poorly integrated into the political world. There were no significant results, but the lists bear witness to women's stubborn desire to hold public office.

There were very clear specifically 'women's' demands at the time, which show a certain radicalism, even if the term 'feminist' was only used by the former suffragists. The most radical groups were the former suffragists (the LFDF and the UFE), and the Communist UFF, demanding as they did equality in every domain including in family law:

> To sum up, we want the [Civil] Code to be revised so that the husband and wife are considered to be two associates in law and that any action involving family life should be agreed upon by the two spouses (*Le droit des femmes*, March–April 1946)

said the League. The UFF prioritized the right to work and its first National Congress in June 1945 'having acknowledged the need for work' wanted 'to transform this need into law, the guarantee of the independence and the dignity of women and mothers' (*Femmes Françaises*, no. 41, 5 July 1945). Following the Pope's injunction, Catholic women mobilized in defence of the Christian hierarchical and indissoluble family: the mother's place was at home and the husband's authority was unquestioned. The Catholic influence could be felt, to a lesser degree, in the UNF and the CNFF. However, all these groups actively demanded women's participation in all levels of political life. Brochures were published and meetings were held to ensure that women voters, conscious of their duty, would go well-informed into the polling booth. Indeed, the UFCS asked (unsuccessfully) for the vote to be made mandatory.

The impossible union of women's groups

Immediately after the war there was a real gender solidarity between women activists of all kinds: the older suffragists rubbed shoulders with the younger Resisters, Communists worked with Catholics. Together they achieved several victories; once political rights had been won, women pushed for further reforms, often in the first few weeks after the Liberation. For instance Marianne Verger, a Resister associated with feminists in the Radical Socialist Party got all the twelve women at that time in the Consultative Assembly to sign a proposal to open the magistrature to women. This was achieved by the law of 11 April 1946. The Communist syndicalist Marie Couette led the struggle for equal pay, a cause then taken up by Jeannette Vermeersch. When the Communist Ambroise Croizat became Minister of Labour, this battle speeded up and the ministerial order of 30 July 1946 rendered illegal the 20 per cent disparity between men's and women's pay for equal work, in spite of opposition from within the government (Liszek, 1997). Marthe Richard, a local councillor in Paris is well-known for the law bearing her name which closed brothels and criminalized pimping.

Finally, women representatives and women's associations participated in the preparation of a new Constitution for France. The debates leading up to the drafting of the Constitution are interesting for they reveal the points which united and divided the women's groups. There were initially two clear camps. On the one hand, those who believed that sexual equality should be clearly inscribed in the Constitution included suffragist organizations (especially the LFDF and the UFE) and the Communists. On the other were the Catholics who demanded protection of the mother and the family. The final version was a compromise solution which satisfied everyone. Article 1, a masterpiece of its kind with its concise formulation and its generalization, satisfied partisans of equality: 'The law guarantees to women, in every domain, equal rights with men.' However, this Article is totally contradicted by Article 24:

> The Nation guarantees for the family the conditions necessary for its free development. Equally, it protects all mothers and all children by appropriate social institutions and legislation. It guarantees to women the exercise of their functions as citizen and worker, in conditions which allow them to fulfil their role as mothers and their social mission. (Godechot, 1970: 374).

The most interesting thing is that nobody complained, and both the UFF and the LFDF congratulated themselves that the rights of both women and mothers were safe. This mixture of women's rights and mothers' protection was not unique to France; the Italian Constitution, drafted in 1947, contains very similar stipulations (Mafai, 1979: 415–56). Even for the most radical women, women's rights and mothers' duties were not in contradiction. Egalitarianism flourished in the public and legal spheres, but barely touched private life, so that an egalitarian rhetoric for women, citizens and workers was juxtaposed with far more traditional words about the function and duties of mothers. This is especially true for Communist women, who switched easily between the two as necessary.

This first Constitution was rejected by the French people when put to them for ratification by referendum, with more women than men voting against it. In the second version, the passage on mothers and families was modified. It became: 'the Nation guarantees for the individual and the family the conditions necessary for their development'. And later, 'It guarantees for all, especially children, mothers and older workers, protection of their health, material security, rest and leisure.' This second draft was more coherent than the first. Imperceptibly, however, the unity which had prevailed during the war disintegrated under the weight of accumulated disagreements, and, after 1946, any progress in the field of women's rights slowed down to a snail's pace. For example, the reform of the marriage law was not discussed in Parliament until 1959, although feminist associations had constantly tried to put it forward and had supported many parliamentary bills proposed in the intervening years.

With the development of the Cold War and the removal of Communists from government in 1947, the UFF fell permanently into a discourse which was familialist and defended mother's rights. It was as if they had fallen in with the slogans of their Catholic competitors, who greatly benefited from the virulent anti-Communism of the time. With the disappearance of the women's Resistance groups and the new moderation of the Communists, the suffragist groups found themselves practically alone in the fight for the legislative reform of women's rights.

Many factors contributed to the disintegration of women's groups and feminist groups. The unity of the Resistance against a common enemy was short-lived once the war had ended. It carried on until the first elections, after which political life was once more organized around the parties, which took control and imposed their own discipline on women representatives and delegates. Women's suffrage (which doubled the electoral body) had contradictory effects: on the one hand, it sparked joint actions calling for the civic education of the new women voters; on the other, it led to competition for this massive influx of electors. Finally, differences over foreign policy (Indochina, Greece, Eastern Europe, American aid) and domestic policy (education, the Constitution) hardened existent oppositions and made activists turn towards other issues.

The Cold War thus opened a new, very different, period. Political struggles were accompanied by a conservative familialism, pronatalism was triumphant, and shortages followed by the beginning of the 'thirty glorious years' of economic expansion combined to present the exclusive image of woman as housewife, the mistress of her home and a clever consumer. In this hostile climate, the older feminists struggled to keep the flame alight, while progressively the newer activists put their efforts together to fight for legal contraception and natural childbirth. Slowly, the personal became political.

Notes

1. AFFDU brochure, 'Historique 1920–1950', Cahors, 1950, 12pp. See also *Many a Good Crusade: Memoirs of Virginia Crocheron Gildersleeve*, New York: Macmillan, 1954, which describes the wartime roles of Mme Monod and Mme Puech.

2. She was Minister of National Health in 1947–48, the first woman to hold a full ministerial position in France.

3. Andrée Lehmann Archive at the Bibliothèque Marguerite Durand, Paris.

4. See her interview in *Clio* no. 1, 1995 'Résistances et Libérations France 1940–1945'.

5. Speech by Mme Girard during the FLN study days 6–8 September 1945; published in *La Femme* 15 September 1945.

6. At the end of the war, a Provisional government under de Gaulle was established. The role of its appointed members was to oversee the smooth return to representative democracy and electoral politics, in particular the election of a new Assembly which would draft a new Constitution for France.

7. The Constituent Assembly was the first elected assembly in France after the war; its function was to draft a new Constitution (see note 8). As the first Constitution – drawn up by an assembly that was mainly socialist and communist – was rejected by the French people when put to the vote, a second Constituent Assembly was elected in which the Christian Democrats were the dominant party, ensuring the drafting of a more moderate Constitution which this time was accepted.

8. Henri Rollet implied in his book *Andrée Butillard et le féminisme chrétien*, (Paris: SPES, 1960) that Vichy legislation was directly taken from the UFCS .

9. 'Un frein au divorce' in *La Femme dans la vie sociale* no. 138, May 1948, quoted in Francine Muel-Dreyfus, op. cit., p. 201.

10. Created under the Vichy government, this Committee included representatives of family associations and its role was to give advice on family policy initiatives.

11. Letter from the UFCS to Cardinal Suhard (1943) quoted in *Recherches sur l'UFCS et son histoire à partir des archives du mouvement*, Amicale UFCS, November 1988, roneotyped.

12. This massacre refers to the occasion when prisoners from Montluc prison were shot and then burned.

13. In the local elections of April 1945, there was a women-only party list (the system was one of proportional representation) in Frasnes (Doubs) and two in Paris. After much hesitation UFCS members in Paris did not participate. In Angoulême, Mathilde Mir led a women-only list for the October 1946 legislative elections. No women were elected from these lists. Details of local electoral initiatives come from *La femme dans la vie sociale*, no. 176, May 1945; *UNF revue des électrices*, no. 1, May 1945; William Guéraiche, 1992, op. cit., p. 193; and Duchen, 1994, op. cit, note 36, p. 218.

References

Albistur, M. and Armogathe, D. (1978) *Histoire du féminisme français* (2 vols). Paris: Éditions des Femmes.

Bard, C. (1995) *Les filles de Marianne: histoire des féminismes 1914–1940*. Paris: Fayard.

Bertin, C. (1993) *Femmes sous l'Occupation*. Paris: Stock.

Bourderon, R. (1977) 'Le premier congrès de l'UFF: un bilan d'action'. In *Les femmes dans la Résistance*. Actes du colloque UFF. Paris: Editions du Rocher.

Bouchardeau, H. (1977) *Pas d'histoire les femmes: 50 ans d'histoire de femmes*. Paris: Syros.

Brault, E. (1953) *La franc-maçonnerie et l'émancipation des femmes*. Paris: Dervy.

Buton, P. and Guillon, J.-M. (eds) (1994) *Les pouvoirs en France à la Libération*. Paris: Belin.

Chaperon, S. (1996) 'Le creux de la vague, mouvements féminins et féminismes 1945–1970'. Unpublished doctoral thesis, Instut Europeèn Universitaire, Florence. Published as *Les années Beauvoir, 1945–1970*. Paris: Foyard, 2000.

Chaperon, S. (1998) '1945-1970, reprendre l'histoire du féminisme'. In A.-M. Sohn and F. Thélamon (eds), *L'histoire sans les femmes est-elle possible?* Paris: Perrin.

Dau Novelli, C. (1988) 'Il movimento della cristiana dal 1944 al 1964'. In F. Malgeri (ed.), *Storia della democrazia cristiana*, vol. 3, 1955–1968. Roma: Cinque Lune.

Doneaud, T. (1991) 'Des femmes, un mouvement féminin: une expérience de 35 ans de pratique de l'UFCS 1948-1983'. Unpublished diploma dissertation, Université de la Sorbonne Nouvelle, Paris III.

Dore-Audibert, A. and Morzelle, A. (1988) *Irène de Lipkowski: Le combat humaniste d'une Française du XXe siècle*. Laval: Siloë.

Duchen, C. (1993) '1944-1946: women's liberation?' In D. Berry and A. Hargreaves (eds), *Women in 20th century French History and Culture*. Loughborough: Loughborough University, European Research Centre, pp. 49-64.

Duchen, C. (1994) *Women's Rights and Women's Lives in France 1944-1968*. London: Routledge.

Duchen, C. (1995) 'Une femme nouvelle pour une France nouvelle ?' *Clio*, no. 1. pp. 151-64.

Godechot, J. (ed.) (1970) *Les Constitutions de la France depuis 1789*. Paris: Garnier Flammarion.

Gaiotti de Biase, P. (1980) 'Il voto alle donne'. In G. Rossini (ed.), *Democrazia cristiana e costituente*. Roma: Cinque Lune, pp. 415-56.

Guéraiche, W. (1992) 'Les femmes de la vie politique française de la Libération aux années 1970: essai sur la répartition du pouvoir politique.' Unpublished doctoral thesis, Université de Toulouse Le Mirail. Published as *Les femmes et la République*. Paris: Editions de l'Atelier, 1999.

Guéraiche, W. (1995a) 'Les femmes politiques de 1944 à 1947: quelle libération?' *Clio*, no. 1, pp. 165-86.

Guéraiche, W. (1995b) 'L'octroi des droits civiques et l'entrée des Françaises en politique'. *Espoir*, Special Issue '1945-1995: De Gaulle et la réforme de l'Etat', 103, July, 24-34.

Guéraiche, W. (1997) 'La question "femmes" dans les partis (1946-1962)'. *Historiens et géographes*, 358, July–August, 235-48.

Liszek, S. (1997) *La CGT et la défense des femmes salariées de 1944 à 1968*. DEA, University of Paris VII-Denis Diderot.

London, L. (1995) *La mégère de la rue Daguerre: Souvenirs de la Résistance*. Paris: Le Seuil.

Mafai, M. (1979) *L'apprendistato della politica: Le donne italiane nel dopoguerra*. Roma: Editori Riuniti.

Montreynaud, F. (1989) *Le vingtième siècle des femmes*. Paris: Nathan.

Mouvement Français pour le Planning Familial (MFPF) (1982) *D'une révolte à une lutte: 25 ans de planning familial*. Paris: Tierce.

Muel-Dreyfus, F. (1995) *Vichy et l'éternel féminin*. Paris: Le Seuil.

Pagniez, Y. (1947) *Scènes de la vie du bagne*. Paris: Flammarion.

Rabaut, J. (1978) *Histoire des féminismes français*. Paris: Stock.

Rollet, H. (1960) *Andrée Butillard et le féminisme chrétien*. Paris: SPES.

Rossi-Doria, A. (1996) *Diventare cittadine: Il voto alle donne in Italia*. Firenze: Giunti.

Rouquet, F. (1997) 'Dans la France du Maréchal'. In C. Fauré (ed.), *Encyclopédie politique et historique des femmes*. Paris: PUF, pp. 663–84.

Rudelle, O. (1994) 'Le vote des femmes et la fin de l'exception française'. *Vingtième siècle*, April–June.

Schwartz, P. (1995) 'La répression des femmes communistes (1940–1944)'. In F. Rouquet and D. Voldman (eds) 'Identités féminines et violences politiques, 1936–1946'. Special issue, *Les cahiers de l'IHTP*, 24–37.

Thébaud, F. (ed.) (1992) 'Le XXe siècle.' vol. 5 of G. Duby and M. Perrot (eds), *Histoire des femmes dans l'Occident*. Paris: Plon.

Thébaud, F. (ed.) (1995) *Clio*, no. 1. Special Issue: 'Résistances et Libérations France 1940–1945'.

Van der Casteele Schweitzer, S. and Voldman, D. (1985) 'Le mouvement féministe après la seconde guerre mondiale'. *Matériaux pour l'histoire de notre temps*, no. 1.

Wieviorka, O. (1989) 'La génération de la Résistance'. *Vingtième siècle*, no. 22.

12 'Anything but a suffragette!' Women's Politics in Germany after 1945: A Movement of Women?[1]

Ute Gerhard
Translated by Tobe Levin

Research in the history of women during the German post-war period is not only of historical but also of contemporary relevance. As in other eras, a particular woman-conscious historical perspective was needed before any attention could be paid to women's special role in the early years of the Federal Republic. And particularly because the following reflections deal with the immediate past and with the complex histories of that generation which form a part of the post-war generation's own stories. These studies and analyses have as much to do with contemporary feminism and its political aims and hopes as they do with those of the generation before us.

Whereas several sociohistorical, biographical and political science studies held that, at least for the years after 1945, 'a woman's political breakthrough' could be discerned (cf. Kuhn, 1986: 12–38), other researchers came to the sobering conclusion that after 1945 women had missed their opportunity to influence politics (Möding, 1988: 619–47), or that they had been barred from their share of political power by the usual patriarchal means (Schubert, 1984: 15). Yet others try to do justice to the fact that for women, after they had shovelled the 'rubble' and exhausted themselves with 'survival labour', nothing was left but to remain the principal agents of family life. Some, for example Ute Frevert, criticize this as a reconsignment to domesticity (Frevert, 1990: 119; Moeller, 1993), while feminists such as Sigrid Metz-Göckel (1987: 25–57) argue that the 'women's emergency communities' held the potential for politicizing the daughters.

This chapter attempts to describe and reflect on the meaning of West German women's political initiatives during the immediate post-war years. My purpose is to explore the significance of this era for the history of the West German women's movement, to discover whether there are lines of continuity or whether the difficulties posed by the war and the undigested catastrophes of National Socialism (NS) have meant that a radical break between 'waves' of women's movements occurred.

The women's movement: a period of stagnation
or a time for building bridges?

Because the very concept of 'movement' had been exploited and discredited by the National Socialists, it is no wonder that women after 1945 had problems fitting into a 'movement'.[2] To be sure, the first women's movement before 1933 had been denounced by the Nazis as intellectual, feminist and Jewish (Siber von Groote, 1933), but at the same time, the term was also used by the NS women's organizations, for instance in the motto: 'The programme of our German women's movement can be contained in a single word "child"' (Hitler, 1941: 13). As a result, women who took on women's issues after the war avoided at all costs any association with the National Socialist movement. In their first attempts at mobilizing, they spoke about the need 'to found a powerful women's organization' (*Frankfurter Frauenausschuß*, 1946: 5) emphasizing a new beginning. Nonetheless, we have evidence that although some women understood themselves to be heirs to the older women's movement, they still wanted 'to give birth to a new women's movement' (Mayer-Katz, 1981: 132). Yet from today's perspective, we might wonder if there was any women's movement at all in the post-war years.

To evaluate the specifics of the 'German problem' (Arendt, 1986: 23), the break with cultural tradition and the consequent loss of a coherent history of the women's movement, it is exciting to draw comparisons with other women's movements. For instance, Leila J. Rupp and Verta Taylor have examined the American movement between 1945 and 1960, calling the situation 'Survival in the Doldrums' (1990). Behind this transparent metaphor is the image of social movements as agents of social change which can be envisioned in 'long waves'. That is, social movements don't simply run their course through various phases of mobilization ending in institutionalization (Rammstedt, 1978; Raschke, 1985); rather, in their ebb and flow, they might adopt 'different structural forms and strategies at various periods in [their] history' (Rupp and Taylor, 1990: 9). Stages of increased activity and effectiveness can be countered by periods of stasis or even reaction. So the question remains: what are the specific social and political configurations which offer options as well as the experience of contradiction between norm and reality which thereby lead to mobilization (Bock, 1988; Marx-Ferree and Hess, 1985; Buechler, 1990).

As surprising as it may seem, the starting point for women in both the victorious USA and the defeated Germany is structurally the same: a basic contradiction between constitutional equality in a society calling itself a democracy and actual inequality between individuals and particularly between the sexes. American women who understood themselves to be political missionaries educating Germans in democracy had nonetheless had problems in their own country ever since the unsuccessful attempts of the 1920s to use the hard-won vote to achieve equality in all other areas of law by passing an equal rights amendment (ERA). Rupp and Taylor, too, in their initial analysis of the 'doldrums' between 1945 and 1960 considered that this period represented a transitional stage decisive in binding the older movement to the younger. Because it was a small cohort who understood themselves as engaged in the women's movement, 'mostly survivors of the suffrage struggle who maintained their commitment in a period inhospitable to feminism' (Rupp and Taylor, 1990:

7-8), they created a network of personal, professional and political interests and brought with them their aims, their lobbying, their organizational experience, their individual careers and, above all, a historical tradition of women's struggle and political ideas which helped pave the way for a new feminism.

As this analysis reveals, unequal relationships and a collective awareness of injustice are insufficient to power a movement. Other structural preconditions, 'political opportunity structures' (Katzenstein and Mueller, 1987), must exist, including access to social resources, education and the professions. A change in the economics and demography that cause contradictions in the balance of power are necessary in order to give a movement the impetus and effectiveness it needs. This comparison has been introduced to sharpen our attention to the options of a women's movement and women's politics in Germany, where the world lay covered in rubble and there were no recipes for a new beginning.

Motives and activists in the movement: the 'Old Guard'

'Women have begun to join in the moulding of German life. With womanly strength they want to help, to ensure not only that something new, but that something better results, and they have found an organizational form to extend female influence in public life' said the *Rheinische Post* on 20 April 1946 (Kuhn and Schubert, 1981: 25-6). Motives for women's involvement were the same everywhere: 'twelve years of dictatorship and denial of civil rights ... especially for women' (*Frankfurter Frauenausschuß*, 1946: 5); 'the failure of masculinist politics; a new self-consciousness drawn from the emergency and women's sole responsibility for survival' (Haag, 1945, quoted in Hauser, 1984: 59). Actually, these arguments were based on an understanding of sex roles ascribing to women a special talent for giving the world a more human face. Finally, women were the majority of the population – and it seems that this so often cited demographic factor (females represented 60 per cent of the population) was the most convincing argument put to contemporaries to justify their democratic participation. There were, in addition, moral appeals, calls to action, discourses urging shared responsibility for the past and the future, references to 'women's duties' as well as rights, and attempts to define and reform politics as a whole.

After the end of the war, Germany was occupied by the four Allies and divided into four zones, controlled by the Americans, the British, the Russians and the French respectively. Whereas in the West the military governments, especially the British and the American, soon worked together, the division between East and West hardened with the beginnings of the Cold War. This development finally led to the founding of two separate German states in 1949, the Federal Republic of Germany (FRG) in the West and the German Democratic Republic (GDR) in the East. Immediately after 1945, women's first initiatives were the same everywhere: in all four occupied zones, in nearly all large and small cities, so-called women's committees took the building of democracy from below into their hands with energy and with the aim, 'in the short run to relieve economic and social suffering in large parts of the population; in the long run to assure the re-establishment of a peace-loving, democratic social order and to ensure passage of the constitutional guarantee of equality between the sexes in economic, social and political realms' (Kolossa, 1990: 207).

In 1945, the first leaders of the post-war women's movement were the same women who had been activists in the pre-war women's movement, or politicians espousing feminism from before 1933. They also included women from the labour movement, the Sozialdemokratische Partei Deutschlands (SPD) (German Social Democratic Party), and Kommunistische Partei Deutschlands (KPD) (German Communist Party), parties which had suffered persecution in concentration camps.

Among the first group of activists was Agnes von Zahn-Harnack, the last chair of the Bund Deutscher Frauenvereine (BDF, Federation of German Women's Associations), which had cleverly avoided forced Nazification by dissolving itself (Gerhard, 1990: 373). With her political integrity intact, having resisted Nazism, recognized as an academic and journalist prominent in the women's movement, biographer of her father, the Protestant theologian Adolf von Harnack (Zahn-Harnack, 1936), she was the first after 1945 whom the four occupying powers in Berlin held to be worthy of representing German women or a women's movement, officially inviting her to a women's meeting in England in 1946. At the end of 1945 Zahn-Harnack had already founded the Berlin Women's Association 'to raise in women a new consciousness and will to action' (Zahn-Harnack, 1951: 61).

Sister campaigners like Dorothee von Velsen, Emmy Beckmann, Marie-Elisabeth Lüders, but also Gertrud Bäumer or the somewhat younger Else Ulrich-Beil also tried to link their common pre-history, political tradition and personal relationships to the pre-war movement. They were quickly in touch with one another, lectured in devastated cities and zones, met for instance in Stuttgart's Peace Circle around Freda Wuesthoff (see Hauser, 1996) or at the First Inter-zonal Women's Meeting in 1947 in Bad Boll. Here, as chronicler Dorothee von Velsen noted with surprise, 'parliamentary opponents from before the war, Dr. Lüders and Kathinka von Kardorff fell into … each other's arms … [while] Agnes von Zahn-Harnack found the right words for our destiny, our guilt and our tasks' (von Velsen, 1956: 372).

A few of the old companions landed up in the East and were excluded from Western historiography: Else Lüders for instance, who created one of the rare radical classics for the older movement with her text *The 'Left Wing'* (Lüders, 1904). A politician concerned with social welfare, she had held high office as a ministry official (*Oberregierungsrätin*) in the Reich's Labour Ministry during the Weimar Republic. Another of this cohort was Frieda Radel, well known as a campaigner in the suffrage movement (see Radel, 1910). Following World War Two, both were named honorary presidents of the Demokratischer Frauenbund Deutschlands (DFD) (German Democratic Women's Union), an umbrella organization of East German women's groups. Else Lüders, as 'elder stateswoman', opened the founding conference of the DFD in March 1947 in Berlin with 'heart-stirring' words and not long afterward tried again to mediate increasing East–West tensions, writing in the journal *Der Silberstreifen* (The Silver Stripe) that the organization represented an 'independent democratic women's movement' (Lüders, 1947: 5; on women's politics in Berlin, see Genth *et al.*, 1996).

By this time, however, some of the emigrants – left-wingers, pacifists and radicals from the earlier era, for instance Helene Stöcker, Anita Augspurg and Lida Gustava Heymann – had died or were no longer active. For Lida G. Heymann who, like her friend Anita Augspurg, died in exile in Switzerland, a memorial ceremony was held in 1946 by the 'Internationale Frauenliga für Frieden und Freiheit' (IFFF) (International Women's League for Peace and Freedom), one of the few women's organizations in continual existence since 1919. Magda Hoppstock-Huth, who had led the Hamburg IFFF group since 1928 and who had survived persecution, concentration camps and a death sentence, kept the flame of remembrance for the association's founders burning.

The older generation shared a conviction, accepted by the younger ones only with reservations, that women had to struggle for rights. In her report of the Inter-zonal meeting 20–23 May 1947 in Bad Boll, Lisbet Pfeiffer noted 'that the [mature generation's] tone ... became, from time to time, somewhat belligerent and hostile to men'. But she mentioned that 'a few in particular gave remarkable performances and made admirable speeches' (Pfeiffer, 1947: 6). In 1948, however, when a second Inter-zonal conference in Frankfurt's Paul's Church took place (Henicz and Hirschfeld, 1986: 127–37), it became clear that although admired and honoured by the larger number of younger participants, the older generation had begun to experience a friendly distancing. Although in her speech Helli Knoll, chair of the Frankfurt Women's Committee, gave an extensive survey of the women's movement and regarded it an honour to be called a 'suffragette', the secretary Lisbet Pfeiffer wanted to avoid at all costs the impression that 'an eccentric Suffragism was being revived' (Pfeiffer, 1948: 5).

The 'new' women

The 'new' woman alongside this old guard formed a leadership cadre whom Gabriele Strecker, in her self-description, portrayed as 'previously unknown women who now felt that they were called on by the times to do something' (Strecker, 1951: 34). Strecker belonged to this group and played a leading ideological role as head of Women's Radio (*Frauenfunk*) for the Hesse station and supporter of the Frankfurt Women's Committee. She also emerged as one of the few chroniclers of the era (Strecker, 1965).

More than a few of these 'new' women had already been active or experienced their political socialization before 1933 but the majority represented a new generation. They were middle-aged, politically 'clean' (checked out and supported by the occupying nations) and were either already members of political parties or were soon to join. In contrast to the older women, they were sober and pragmatic, ready to work, clever and industrious as well as willing to compromise, in particular with regard to men and the question of working together with them. 'Straight-forward, practical, skilled, and humane' – these were the official characteristics expected of women by 'reconstruction society' (Möding, 1988: 636), qualities that underwrote confidence and an ability to persevere. Charged with responsibilities that ensured their personal and political growth, these 'new' women took inspiration from the older women's movement while at the same time clearly distancing themselves from it. 'I am not a suffragette' was the slogan guiding Theanolte Bähnisch (later Hanover county president) to solve women's everyday problems, treating as 'political issues' 'the housing shortage', 'cookery, nourishing the family' and 'the education of children, including consideration of their future job prospects' (Bähnisch, 1948, quoted in

Kuhn, 1986: 226). For as Bähnisch saw it, 'we would rather not ... become factors of power in public life but rather become "factors of order"' (Kuhn, 1986: 222).

The activists in the post-war movement thus very consciously linked themselves to the traditional women's movement but the inheritance remained incomplete, administered and handed down in a one-sided manner. In West Germany, only the moderate bourgeois and conservative women's politics from the Weimar period had survived.[3] Thus, an image of women was adopted which accepted traditional roles and emphasized a harmonious complementarity between the sexes, even in politics. Lost and devalued were the exciting discussions about what might lie beyond male norms and the goals of equal rights. Forgotten were the battles already fought on the question of how not only women but rather gender relations and social conditions could be changed and what female specificity and cultural achievement could mean with regard to self-determination and sexuality, peace and welfare politics. The loss of history concerned not only these ideas but also and above all what would follow from the debates and what the future might learn from them. One example is the discussion of sexuality and sexual reform, whose enlightenment potential was smothered throughout the 1950s and into the 1960s by petit-bourgeois sexual morality and prudishness.

An additional example is the peace movement: certainly the longing of all people for peace was never greater, but after World War Two, women in particular were prepared to act, convinced that they must do their part to ensure a better, more tranquil world. Numerous peace initiatives and congresses in East and West, the speedy re-organization of the 'Internationale Frauenliga für Frieden und Freiheit' (IFFF), as well as the world movement of mothers which formulated in 1947 the 'Mothers' Charter'; and finally the World Organization of Mothers of All Nations (W.O.M.A.N.) founded by American journalist Dorothy Thompson, all appear to suggest how broad was public support for a specifically female pacifism (Kuhn, 1986: 176 and 25). Nonetheless, the radical pacifist tradition of movement activity failed to garner any respect. On the contrary, pacifists, especially those from the IFFF such as Magda Hoppstock-Huth (former IFFF chair) were soon thrown out, accused of collaboration with the Communists (Strecker, 1951: 68). Other cases included that of Anna Haag, the new chair of the IFFF in Stuttgart and of peace activist and professor of education Klara Marie Faßbinder, who signed the 'Mothers' Charter' (Kuhn, 1986: 177) in 1947 and who, despite being barred since 1953 from exercising her profession, played a leading role in the West German women's peace movement (WFFB) (see Hervé, 1979: 181). 'The word "peace",' wrote Leonore Mayer-Katz, initiator of a women's discussion circle in Baden-Baden and later founder of the German 'Women's Circle' in the state of Baden, 'had become a term camouflaging communism' (Mayer-Katz, 1981: 136).

Politics: new and old

Clearly noticeable is the fact that the composition and political direction of the women's committees depended on which groups of activists were most heavily represented. The Women's Committee in Bremen, for instance, consisted mainly of members with extensive experience in politics, especially across a broad left-wing spectrum: founder Irmgard Enderle of the labour movement returned to Bremen from exile in Sweden. Social Democrat Anna Stiegler, Liberals Elisabeth Lürßen and Agnes Heineken (the latter already active in the women's movement before World War One) as well as Communist Käthe Popall, the first woman in Bremen elected Senator in 1945 (Popall, 1985) and Anna Klara Fischer from the Temperance Movement were also key members. The history of these women clearly influenced the anti-fascist, anti-militarist direction of the Bremen Committee. In comparison to other Women's Committees, the Bremen group succeeded in working effectively and significantly in the community through multi-partisan cooperation, despite individual party ties, dealing with topics ranging from management of food and domestic space, to the realization of equal opportunity in education, to prostitution and the founding of a school for mothers – even though, to hold women together, certain basic political questions increasingly often went unasked. With hesitation, then, the Bremen group joined the umbrella organization for West German Women's associations, the Deutsche Frauenring (German Women's Circle) in July 1950 (Hoecker and Meyer-Braun, 1988: 107).

In contrast, the Frankfurt Women's Committee may serve as the prototype for a changing of the guard and adoption of a 'new' women's politics. The group not only paved the way for founding other women's committees but already in 1947 had taken the first step toward becoming a registered umbrella organization covering the city of Frankfurt as well as the state of Hesse, thus pioneering what would appear at the end of the 1940s as a politics of women's associations. Certain characteristics fell into place early on, including working methods and structure, the importance of sub-committees and expert groups, and citizenship training as the central task. Many participants, and especially the leaders, experienced this work in women's committees as a way-station en route to other social and political engagements, for example in political parties and the Church. And not least significant was the protection – and that meant financial support, as well as influence on personnel recruitment and political direction – of the occupying US power. This support played a powerful part, especially in the American sector, in stabilizing this particular organizational model.

The political aims of the Frankfurt Women's Committee were formulated objectively and pragmatically in the 'call to women' issued by the founders. This document contains the entire programme which remained the order of the day into the 1950s. The Committee demanded realization of equality in all areas of life, but especially in family law; the right to work; an increase in the number of positions open in the social sector and education; and a 'higher value placed on housework' (*Frankfurter Rundschau*, 25 December 1946; see Schüller, 1993: 98). This was the programme. Nothing revolutionary, no soul, no world-view, but the left-overs from equal opportunity efforts since 1919, now to be implemented as step-by-step reforms. The necessary pragmatism plus a new sobriety and self-consciousness expressed themselves in the fact that these women wanted to do it differently and better than their forebears: '[The Frankfurt Women's Committee] distinguished itself from the older women's organizations ... above all because the distinction between the bourgeois and the socialist women's movements had been abandoned in favour of a classless representation of women's issues. Here an effort was made to forge a women's movement in line with the times' (Strecker, 1951: 35).

Nonetheless, this commentary by Gabriele Strecker also contains certain problems. The principle of nonpartisanship, the opening toward the labour party, the SPD and later the KPD would soon be made obsolete by the new confrontation with the so-called 'real existing socialism' in East Germany. This nonpartisanship experienced an abrupt end when the Hesse Women's Associations voted in 1950 an incompatibility clause which led to expulsion of KPD and DFD women. Put so much on the defensive, nonpartisan politics was reduced to civil rights education. Truly 'political' work – according to Elisabeth Selbert, deeply concerned in 1949 with women's equal rights in the *Parlamentarischer Rat* (Constituent Assembly) – was to be possible only within political parties, with which the very idea of political work had become identified.

Continuity or change? Difficulties in 'overcoming' the past

Attempts to live with and work through the Nazi past differed greatly from one women's group to another. The topic was present in the earliest press releases which clearly posed the particular need for women's political intervention, given their ambivalent role in the Nazi state; and an effort was made to overcome the evident disgust with politics on the part of the younger, disappointed 'sceptical' generation.

'Hanging over all of us is the *mea culpa, mea maxima culpa*, the bitter awareness of the guilt of the German people who failed all along the way' – wrote journalist Mila Ketterer, member of the IFFF in Stuttgart, in *Der Silberstreifen* (1946: 2, 20). She was joined by Helli Knoll, who before 1933 together with Doctor of Jurisprudence Elisabeth Schwarzhaupt (in 1961 the first West German woman minister), had already 'run a hearty media and speech campaign' [against National Socialism]. And Knoll remained very convincing as she argued: 'We'll show the world how capable and determined we are to atone for our guilt, and to do our part in securing the future welfare of all peoples' (*Frankfurter Rundschau*, 6 October 1945; see Wischerman, 1993).

Yet, the increasing silence and repression of the past indicate a change in generations. Certain exclusions were already foreshadowed: distancing from the left, alienation of Communist women and ultimately also removal of the pacifists, at the latest by the beginning of the 1950s with Chancellor Adenauer's politics of rearmament. And the 'new' women were therefore enabled to be involved in politics because they could be certified 'innocent', not weighted down by the past. What then accounts for their failure? Should they have denounced the older generation that had been involved?

For instance, the fascinating Marie-Elisabeth Lüders who at that time clearly exercised considerable political influence on the younger generation of women – as a representative to the Reichstag for the Deutsche Demokratische Partei (DDP) (German Democratic Party) and a board member of the Organization of Bund Deutscher Frauenvereine (BDF), she had earned her stripes in the National Women's Service, organized by the women's movement during World War One. And she was one of the few in the early years of the Federal Republic who not only made a come-back as a parliamentarian for the Free Democratic Party and as past president in the Bundestag but managed a successful political career. Her powerful autobiography *Never Be Afraid!*

(Lüders, 1963) which filled a gap in historical knowledge of readers at that time, nonetheless suppressed mention of her publications from the Nazi era. Her book *The Unknown Army* (Lüders, 1936) is irritating today not only because it ennobled war work and the patriotic services of women in World War One but, with its introduction by the Reich's Minister of War, it clearly supported National Socialist propaganda.

After the war, there were also the increasingly embarrassing appearances of Gertrud Bäumer against whom voices were raised from many directions (Kuhn, 1986: 21ff, 164ff). The objections are not insignificant particularly when we consider Bäumer's decisive role in Germany's political history and in the reception of the new women's movement. While it is beyond the scope of this chapter, a systematic analysis would be valuable in order to follow the trail of Germany's 'inability to mourn' (Alexander and Margarete Mitscherlich's term and the title of their 1967 book). Nonetheless, inescapable in any evaluation of women's politics in the post-war era is the question of how her contemporaries dealt with Bäumer's political history: M. E. von Zahn-Harnack, von Velsen and Lüders (Lüders, 1963: 141) had disapproved and advised Bäumer against continuing publication of the journal *Die Frau* (The Woman), calling-card of the bourgeois women's movement under the Nazi government. Bäumer's counter-argument against accusations of collaboration after 1945 was noticeably weak, wrapped in an obfuscating language meant to suggest depth of thought and the highest educational level but which remains incomprehensible due to the abstract style. Her defence, published in 1946, contains among other things an attempt to whitewash most of the guilt from sight:

> It really doesn't pay to renew the intellectual struggle against National Socialism. Of course, you won't want to avoid it if you run across someone still defending it, and the need to confront it will be felt by the young in any case. As for the rest of us: Guarda e passa! [Take a look and move on!] (Bäumer, 1946: 28, 42–3).

We cannot assume that because contemporaries said nothing they felt that these remarks, though abstruse, didn't call for comment, but it seems that a public debate was lacking. And little by little the Cold War began to influence dealing with the Nazi past even among politically organized women. Like the word 'Peace', concepts like anti-fascism, anti-militarism or the 'singular war guilt of Germany' became signposts of totalitarianism and Communist propaganda (Lüders, *c.* 1952).

The German Women's Circle: 'An upper class society game'?

Criticism of the 'West German Restoration' (Huster *et al.*, 1979) including its women's politics was expressed most sternly from the start by anti-fascists, the Left and representatives from East Germany. This meant, however, that their arguments were discredited in the West: they were considered to be suspect and specious, the increasingly ossifying result of the Iron Curtain, which existed even in women's minds. An example of the East's criticism of the West, which also demonstrates the difficulty of communicating with and understanding each other, comes from a representative from the East at an inter-zonal meeting in 1947 in Bad Boll. A press release states:

> Problems are handled in the old style. Nothing positive has been said either about German unity or denazification, about punishment of war criminals or land reform ... The congress maintained a high level. Nonetheless, a women's meeting which was to have represented the German people should have been composed differently. Neither working women nor employees nor typical housewives and farmers were present. (Frauenkonferenz, 1947: 2)

Much of this critique hits the mark: the 1949 founding of the Deutscher Frauenring (DFR) (German Women's Circle) signalled the uniting of West German bourgeois women's organizations and determined the direction the movement would take over the next few decades: the work of the associations would be accomplished without the masses of women. The DFR understood itself to be following in the footsteps of the BDF (Strecker, 1970: 15) and yet this label is inappropriate. Structured to work on municipal, state and federal levels with a federal board, the DFR worked as a corporate body covering an increasing number of women's organizations. This sufficed, however, to at least garner recognition as a representative of West German women's organizations and led, for instance, to a 1951 invitation to join the International Council of Women (ICW).

According to their many statutes, two of the DFR objectives should be underscored. First, leadership training. Work in the women's associations was considered as a preschool or 'training area' for those 'who dared enter into public life in any way' (Strecker, 1981: 74). This training involved participating in diverse committees, editing position statements and submission of draft bills to parliament, attending professional conferences, and maintaining contact with politicians and parliamentary outer offices – honourable enough activities in themselves, but they reduced the activists to the role of lobbyist.

The second aim of the DFR was 'citizenship education' for all women. Assuming that women were not able to participate in politics at all, political education was a cautious and harmless strategy of intervention. Who would have thought of training male citizens before gracing them with political rights and posts, no matter how well they fulfilled their duties? A major element in this citizenship training, at least in the first years of the Republic, was the message of anti-communism. By the mid-1960s, only elderly members remained in the DFR. Younger women stayed away. The practice of modest demands, which constantly emphasized transcendence of 'hostility to men', hadn't even ensured its own descendants.

Conclusions: doldrums, or bridge to the new women's movement?

Even a critical summary of women's politics in the post-war years is not meant to imply that the period from 1945 to 1955 (actually, up until the mid-1960s, if we talk about 'long waves') was without significance or even that it should have a negative connotation in emancipation history. On the contrary, as time distances us from events, it becomes easier to recognize what was preserved and won, what survived the setbacks. Preserved was the concern with 'the woman question', which is why the issue of gender is still discussed today. Stubbornly and with great precision, experts, lawyers, labour unionists and bureaucrats in all the women's associations posed the woman question in the post-war years as a civil rights issue, keeping it on the 'back burner' warmed and ready to be dealt with by the courts when legal improvements were fought for. At least the as yet unrealized equality prescribed in Article 3 of West German Basic Law remained in the public eye, making it possible to notice the ever-increasing discrepancy between legal norms and real inequalities. The virulence of this problem was, for instance, the trigger for the writing of the first *Report of the Federal Government on the Situation of Women in Professions, Family and Society* in 1966, whose conclusions offered the basis and legitimation for numerous attempts at reform (Gerhard, 1992: 17–41).

The background for this success was a network of individuals, experts, chairs of associations and organizations as well as the exceptional and token women in higher education, economics and politics, who discovered each other through publications, meetings and committee work, particularly because there were so few of them. And they both supported and competed with each other. For this reason you find the same important names again and again in schedules of speeches, lists of seminars and association colloquia among members of the DFR, known to the younger women only through books, politics and academia. An important link of impressive continuity and solidarity is the periodical *Informationen für die Frau* (Information for Women) which currently documents more than forty years of West German women's associations' work. Nonetheless, the style and form of bourgeois civic training attracted almost no one. The prescribed form of activity, somewhere between an instructional seminar and a *kaffee klatsch*, had to be deliberately disrupted by loud protests, participation 'from the grassroots', consciousness-raising and so forth in order to be replaced and allow us to talk about a new 'movement'.

At the beginning of the 1970s, the gulf between established women's associations and the new feminism was so wide we may wonder whether a particular political culture was in fact handed down from one wave of the movement to the next. In the process of repressing the German past, the oppositional history especially of women had been muted. Resistance, critique, admission of political guilt were considered destructive, even sacrilegious, in a society in reconstruction. The unacknowledged inferior position of women in German society continues however in the fact that to be successful, the legacy of the mother is still frequently rejected by the daughter. Does this happen with the legacy of feminists too? Our foremothers fought for suffrage and suffrage is therefore no longer our problem. And yet, in a 1992 issue of *Informationen für die Frau*, a 15-year-old's future is described. Her mother and grandmother both called themselves feminists. The headline read: 'Anything but a women's libber!' (March 1992: 21).

Notes

1. This chapter is the revised English version of an article that is part of a project and a book by Ulla Wischermann, Elke Schüller and Ute Gerhard (eds) (1993), *Staatsbürgerinnen zwischen Partei und Bewegung: Frauenpolitik in Hessen 1945 bis 1955* (*Women's Citizenship between Political Parties and Social Movements: Women's Politics in Hesse, 1945–1955*), Frankfurt: Helmer.

2. From the end of the nineteenth century to 1933, when all the organizations of the German women's movement were dissolved by the Nazi regime, the

movement consisted of three wings: the mainstream and majority were liberal moderates, with a membership of about one million women from charitable, professional, confessional and party-political associations. They were united under the umbrella organization the Federation of German Women's Associations (BDF) (see p. 164) As such, they were represented in the International Council of Women (ICW). The second wing was composed of so-called radical liberals, who constituted a small but very effective minority at around the turn of the century, demanding women's suffrage, sexual reform and legal rights within marriage. After 1914, the Radicals were committed pacifists engaged in the International League for Peace and Freedom. The third wing consisted of the women's organizations of the labour movement, allied to and supported by a strong German labour movement and by the SPD. From the 1920s onwards, this wing was mostly Communist and was under the leadersip of Clara Zetkin.

References

Arendt, Hannah (1986) *Zur Zeit: Politische Essays.* Berlin: Rotbuch.

Baum, Marie (1956) *Des Lebens wie der Liebe Band: Briefe von Gertrud Bäumer.* Tübingen: Wunderlich.

Bäumer, Gertrud (1946) *Der neue Weg der deutschen Frau.* Stuttgart: Deutsche Verlags-Anstalt.

Bock, Ulla (1988) *Androgynie und Feminismus: Frauenbewegung zwischen Institution und Utopie.* Weinheim: Beltz.

Buechler, Steven M. (1990) *Women's Movements in the United States.* New Brunswick, NJ: Rutgers University Press.

Frankfurter Frauenausschuß (1946) 'Ruf an die Frauen!' *Frankfurter Rundschau,* 7, 5.

Frauenkonferenz in Bad Boll (1947) *Frankfurter Rundschau, 64,* 2.

Frevert, Ute (1990) 'Frauen auf dem Weg zur Gleichberechtigung: Hindernisse, Umleitungen, Einbahnstraßen'. In Martin Broszat (ed.), *Zäsuren nach 1945.* München: Oldenbourg, pp. 113–30.

Genth, Renate, Jäkl, Reingard, Pawlowski, Rita, Schmidt-Harzbach, Ingrid and Stoehr, Irene (1996) *Frauenpolitik und politisches Wirken von Frauen im Berlin der Nachkriegszeit: 1945–1949.* Berlin: Trafo-Verlag.

Gerhard, Ute (1990) *Unerhört: Die Geschichte der deutschen Frauenbewegung.* Reinbek: Rowohlt.

Gerhard, Ute (1992) 'Frauenleitbilder und Etappen bundesrepublikanischer Frauenpolitik'. In Mechthild Veil, Karin Prinz and Ute Gerhard (eds), *Am modernen Frauenleben vorbei. Verliererinnen und Gewinnerinnen der Rentenreform 1992.* Berlin: Edition sigma, pp. 17–41.

Gerhard, Ute (1993) ' "Fern von jedem Suffragettentum": Frauenpolitik nach 1945, eine Bewegung der Frauen?' In Ulla Wischermann, Elke Schüller and Ute Gerhard (eds), *Staatsbürgerinnen zwischen Partei und Bewegung: Frauenpolitik in Hessen 1945 bis 1955.* Frankfurt: Helmer, pp. 9–40.

Gravenhorst, Lerke (1990) 'Nehmen wir Nationalsozialismus und Auschwitz ausreichend als unser negatives Eigentum wahr?' In Lerke Gravenhorst and Carmen Tatschmurat (eds), *Töchter-Fragen.* Freiburg: Kore, pp. 17–37.

Hauser, Andrea (1984) 'Frauenöffentlichkeit in Stuttgart nach 1945: Gegenpol oder hilflos im Abseits?' In Anna-Elisabeth Freier and Annette Kuhn (eds), *Frauen in der Geschichte V, 'Das Schicksal Deutschlands liegt in der Hand seiner Frauen': Frauen in der deutschen Nachkriegsgeschichte*. Düsseldorf: Schwann, pp. 51ff–89.

Hauser, Andrea (1996) *Stuttgarter Frauen für den Frieden: Frauen – Politik – Alltag nach 1945*. Tübingen: Silberburg Verlag (= Frauenstudien Baden-Württemberg, Bd. 7).

Henicz, Barbara and Hirschfeld, Magrit (1986) 'Der Club deutscher Frauen in Hannover'. In Annette Kuhn (ed.), *Frauen in der deutschen Nachkriegszeit*. Vol 2, *Frauenpolitik 1945–1949*. Düsseldorf: Schwann, pp. 127–37.

Hervé, Florence (ed.) (1979) *Brot und Rosen: Geschichte und Perspektive der demokratischen Frauenbewegung*. Frankfurt: Marxistische Blätter.

Hitler, Adolf (1941) 'Die völkische Sendung der Frau'. In N.S. Frauenschaft (ed.), *N.S. Frauenbuch*. Leipzig: Lehmanns, pp. 9–14.

Hoecker, Beate and Meyer-Braun, Renate (1988) *Bremerinnen bewältigen die Nachkriegszeit: Frauenarbeit, Frauenalltag, Frauenpolitik*. Bremen: Steintor.

Huster, Ernst Ulrich, Kraiker, Gerhard, Scherer, Burkhard, Schlotmann, Friedrich-Karl and Welteke, Marianne (1979) *Determinanten der westdeutschen Restauration 1945–1949*. Frankfurt: Suhrkamp.

Informationen für die Frau (1992) ed. by Deutscher Frauenrat – Lobby der Frauen – Bundesvereinigung von Frauenverbänden und Frauengruppen gemischter Verbände in Deutschland e.V. Bonn

Katzenstein, Mary Fainsod and McClurg Mueller, Carol (eds) (1987) *The Women's Movements of the United States and Western Europe*. Philadelphia: PEN.

Ketterer, Mila (1947) 'Über den sieben Bergen'. *Der Silberstreifen*, 2 (10), p. 36.

Kolossa, Jan (1990) 'Neubeginn oder Restauration? Frauenalltag und Frauenbewegung Hamburgs in den Gründungsjahren der Bundesrepublik Deutschland'. In Karen Hagemann and Jan Kolossa (eds), *Gleiche Rechte – Gleiche Pflichten? Der Frauenkampf für 'staatsbürgerliche' Gleichberechtigung: Ein Bilder-Lese-Buch zur Frauenalltag und Frauenbewegung in Hamburg*. Hamburg: VSA-Verlag.

Kuhn, Annette and Schubert, Doris (1981) *Frauenalltag und Frauenbewegung im 20. Jahrhundert. Materialiensammlung zu der Abteilung 20. Jahrhundert im Historischen Museum Frankfurt. Frauen in der Nachkriegszeit und im Wirtschaftswunder 1945–1960*. Frankfurt: Dezernat für Kultur und Freizeit.

Kuhn, Annette (1986) 'Frauen suchen neue Wege in der Politik'. In Annette Kuhn (ed.), *Frauen in der deutschen Nachkriegszeit*. vol 2, *Frauenpolitik 1945–1949*. Düsseldorf: Schwann-Bagel, pp. 12–38.

Lüders, Else (1904) *Der 'linke' Flügel*. Berlin: Loewenthal.

Lüders, Else (1947) 'Soziale Frauenarbeit in Deutschland'. *Der Silberstreifen*, 2 (10), p. 38.

Lüders, Marie-Elisabeth. (1936) *Das unbekannte Heer: Frauen kämpfen für Deutschland 1914–1918*. Berlin: E.S. Mittler & Sohn.

Lüders, Marie-Elisabeth (c. 1952) *Frauen sichern Stalins Sieg*. ed. by Berliner Frauenbund e.V. (Brochure; place and exact date not known).

Lüders, Marie-Elisabeth (1963) *Fürchte Dich nicht: Persönliches und Politisches aus mehr als 80 Jahren, 1878–1962*. Köln: Barth.

Marx-Ferree, Myra and Hess, Beth B. (1985) *Controversy and Coalition: The New Feminist Movement*. Boston: Twayne.

Mayer-Katz, Leonore (1981) *Sie haben zwei Minuten Zeit: Nachkriegsimpulse aus*

Baden. Freiburg: Herder.

Metz-Göckel, Sigrid (1987) 'Die zwei (un)geliebten Schwestern: Zum Verhältnis von Frauenbewegung und Frauenforschung im Diskurs der neuen sozialen Bewegungen'. In Ursula Beer (ed.), *Klasse Geschlecht: Feministische Gesellschaftsanalyse und Wissenschaftskritik*. Bielefeld: ASZ-Verlag, pp. 25–57.

Mitscherlich, Alexander and Mitscherlich, Margarethe (1967) *Die Unfähigkeit zu trauern: Grundlagen kollektiven Verhaltens*. Frankfurt am Main.

Möding, Nori (1988) 'Die Stunde der Frauen? Frauen und Frauenorganisationen des bürgerlichen Lagers'. In Martin Broszat (ed.), *Von Stalingrad zur Währungsreform. Zur Sozialgeschichte des Umbruchs in Deutschland*. München: Oldenbourg, pp. 619–47.

Moeller, Robert G. (1993) *Protecting Motherhood: Women and the Family in the Politics of Post-war West Germany*. Berkeley: University of California Press.

Peyser, Dora (1958) *Alice Salomon: Die Begründerin des sozialen Frauenberufs in Deutschland*. Köln and Berlin: Heymanns.

Pfeiffer, Lisbet (1947) 'Frauen am Scheideweg. Bericht über das Interzonale Frauentreffen in Bad Boll'. In *Welt der Frau*, no. 1, p. 6.

Pfeiffer, Lisbet (1948) 'Frauen zur Demokratie'. *Welt der Frau*, no. 8, p. 5.

Popall, Käthe (1985) *Ein schwieriges politisches Leben*. Fischerhude: Atelier im Bauernhaus.

Radel, Frieda (1910) *Warum fordern wir das Frauenstimmrecht?* Leipzig: Dietrich.

Rammstedt, Ottheim (1978) *Soziale Bewegung*. Frankfurt: Suhrkamp.

Raschke, Joachim (1985) *Soziale Bewegungen: Ein historisch-systematischer Grundriß*. Frankfurt: Campus.

Reese, Dagmar and Sachse, Carola (1990) 'Frauenforschung zum Nationalsozialismus: Eine Bilanz'. In Lerke Gravenhorst and Carmen Tatschmurat (eds), *Töchter-Fragen*. Freiburg: Kore, pp. 73–106.

Rupp, Leila J. and Taylor, Verta (1990) *Survival in the Doldrums: The American Women's Rights Movement, 1945 to the 1960s*. New York: Ohio State University Press.

Schubert, Doris (1984) 'Einführung'. In Doris Schubert (ed.), *Frauen in der deutschen Nachkriegszeit*. vol. 1. *Frauenarbeit 1945–1949*. Düsseldorf: Schwann-Bagel, pp. 25–117.

Schüller, Elke (1993) 'Keine Frau darf fehlen! Frauen und Kommunalpolitik im ersten Nachkriegsjahrzehnt in Hessen'. In Ulla Wischermann, Elke Schüller and Ute Gerhard (eds), *Staatsbürgerinnen zwischen Partei und Bewegung. Frauenpolitik in Hessen 1945 bis 1955*. Frankfurt: Helmer, pp. 88–149.

Siber von Groote, Paula (1933) *Die Frauenfrage und ihre Lösung durch den Nationalsozialismus*. Berlin: Kallmeyer.

Strecker, Gabriele (1970) *Gesellschaftspolitische Frauenarbeit in Deutschland. 20 Jahre deutscher Frauenring*. Opladen: Leske.

Strecker, Gabriele (1951) *100 Jahre Frauenbewegung in Deutschland*. Wiesbaden: Arbeitsgemeinschaft 'wir alle'.

Strecker, Gabriele (1965) *Frausein Heute*. Weilheim: Barth.

Strecker, Gabriele (1981) *Überleben ist nicht genug: Frauen 1945–1950*. Freiburg: Herder.

von Velsen, Dorothee (1956) *Im Alter die Fülle. Erinnerungen*. Tübingen: Wunderlich.

Windaus-Walser, Karin (1988) 'Gnade der weiblichen Geburt? Zum Umgang der

Frauenforschung mit dem Nationalsozialismus und Antifeminismus'. *Feministische Studien,* no. 1, 102–15.

Wischermann, Ulla (1993) 'Frauen und Politik in der hessischen Tagespresse 1945–1950'. In Ulla Wischermann, Elke Schüller and Ute Gerhard (eds), *Staatsbürgerinnen zwischen Partei und Bewegung. Frauenpolitik in Hessen 1945 bis 1955.* Frankfurt: Helmer, pp. 41–87.

Zahn-Harnack, Agnes von (1928) *Die Frauenbewegung: Geschichte, Probleme, Ziele.* Berlin: Deutsche Buch-Gemeinschaft.

Zahn-Harnack, Agnes von (1936) *Adolph von Harnack.* Berlin: Hans Bott Verlag.

Zahn-Harnack, Agnes von (1951) *Wandlungen des Frauenlebens. Vom 18. Jahrhundert bis zur Gegenwart.* Berlin: Pädagogischer Verlag.

Zahn-Harnack, Agnes von (1964) *Schriften und Reden 1914 bis 1950.* Tübingen: Hopfer.

RECONSTRUCTING COMMUNITIES: EXILE, RETURN, BELONGING AND BETRAYAL

13 'A howl unheard': Women Shoah Survivors Dis-placed and Re-silenced

Ronit Lentin

> I came back from the dead
> and believed
> this gave me the right
> to speak to others
> but when I found myself face to face with them
> I had nothing to say
> because
> I learned
> over there
> that you cannot speak to others.
>
> Charlotte Delbo, *Auschwitz and After*

The Nazis aimed not only to annihilate Europe's Jews (and also Roma and Sinti, homosexuals and other 'a-socials'), but to wipe their memory off the face of the earth. After the Shoah[1], most survivors balanced precariously on the edge of an enforced silence. Having suffered the unthinkable, their senses numbed and their emotions silenced, many now did not want or know how to tell of their experiences. They were dis-placed. Most were unable or unwilling to return to their countries of origin – their homes had been destroyed or confiscated. And they were also re-silenced, because no one was there to listen to their horrific experiences.

The Shoah is remembered, commemorated and 'memorized' differently in every culture, but everywhere, as with other catastrophes, there is a 'memory gap' between the experience and its memorized representation, an inability to remember and talk about the experience, in some instances even now, more than fifty years after the war.

Women Shoah survivors, many of whom found it difficult to rebuild their lives after the Shoah, were particularly prone to silence. Questions such as 'What did you do in order to survive?' made women more reluctant to tell their stories, as some were branded as having allegedly traded their sexuality for the chance of survival. Only in recent years have an increasing number of feminist scholars (e.g. Laska, 1983; Lentin, 1996, forthcoming; Linden, 1993; Milton, 1984; Ringelheim, 1985, 1993, 1997; Rittner and Roth, 1993; Ofer and Weitzman, 1998; Baumel, 1998;

Fuchs, 1999) incorporated gender into the study of the Shoah. Their scholarship is helpful in seeking to break the conspiracy of silence which enveloped displaced women Shoah survivors.

This chapter examines the accounts of women Shoah survivors (in testimony, poetry and fiction), the signs of their faith in the possibility of life after survival. It explores the possibility of constructing new discourses which enabled women survivors to relocate after the trauma of their Shoah experiences. It also draws on interviews I conducted with Israeli daughters of Shoah survivors who tell of their mothers' silencing.

Shoah survivors between language and silence

After Michal Klepfisz's death during the Warsaw Ghetto uprising, his widow, poet Irena Klepfisz's mother, Rose, 'at one time expected to live, not survive' (Klepfisz, 1990a: 35). Instead, she survived. Survival included motherhood, 'passing' as a gentile Polish woman, because of her blonde hair and blue eyes, on the ghetto's Aryan side; it included widowhood, and finally New York, where she became a dressmaker. Irena Klepfisz's extraordinary poems about women and the Shoah illuminate the gap between surviving and living, highlighting, according to American poet Adrienne Rich, not only survivor experiences, but also 'what happens after survival: the life that seems to go on, but cannot persevere; the life that does go on, struggling with a vast alienation' (Rich, 1990: 19).

Rosa, scavenger and madwoman in Cynthia Ozick's story of that name, is also surviving rather than living. Rosa had carried her baby daughter, Magda, murdered by a concentration camp guard, in a shawl during the long death march. Rosa runs a store in New York and one day she decides to give it up – she smashes it up herself – and moves to Miami, where she becomes a dependent. Her niece in New York sends her money and she lives among the elderly, in a dark hole of a 'hotel' room. She says to Mr Persky whom she meets in a Miami laundromat, 'Without a life, a person lives where they can. If all they got is thoughts, that's where they live' (Ozick, 1991: 34). Rosa's Shoah experiences are her 'real' life; she spends her days, lonely, writing letters to her dead daughter Magda and to her one remaining relative, her cold-hearted niece, Stella, who was in the camp with her, and who, Rosa believes, should have died instead of her beloved baby.

There is a gap between simply surviving – when traumatic memories prevent you from relating to your present surroundings – and living to the full. This gap between surviving and living parallels the gap between Shoah experiences and the language available to express those experiences. The memory of the past needs to be mediated by a fully experienced present to be capable of being articulated. A 'memory gap' separates the material, bodily, immediate knowledge of the traumatic experiences of the Shoah and the discursive, mediated memories that followed (Grunfeld, 1995).

The search for a discourse for telling the Shoah required establishing a delicate balance between silence and the duty to tell: remembering and telling about the Shoah must always include the temptation to succumb to silence, or avoidance. The debate about the balance between language and silence in relation to the Shoah began with Theodore Adorno's often-cited claim (1949: 362) that 'after

Auschwitz, it is no longer possible to write poems'. In 1962 Adorno recanted, admitting that surrender to silence would be surrender to cynicism and to the very forces that created Auschwitz (Adorno, 1962: 313).

Survivors often stayed alive precisely so that they could tell their stories; many needed to tell their story in order to survive. According to American psycho-analyst Dori Laub, what made a 'Holocaust' out of the event is the unique way in which, during its historical occurrence, the event produced no witnesses. Not only did the Nazis try to exterminate the physical witnesses of their crime; but the inherently incomprehensible and deceptive psychological structure of the event – not being told where you were going, being deliberately given hope against hope by the Nazis, intent on ensuring the docile cooperation of their victims – precluded its own witnessing, even by the Shoah's very victims (Felman and Laub, 1992: 80).[2] Many survivors speak of not being able to remember, not being able to take in the horror; of being able to actually remember only when their grandchildren asked, forty, fifty years after the event.

Telling or writing about the Shoah must involve a certain degree of silence. The imperative to tell the story of the Shoah is inhabited by the impossibility of telling and, therefore, silence prevails: the 'not telling' of the story serves as a perpetuation of its tyranny and the longer the story remains untold the more distorted it becomes in the survivor's conception of it (Felman and Laub, 1992: 79). Irena Klepfisz, herself a child survivor, hidden during the Shoah by nuns, had lost all her family bar her mother. In contrast with the claim by the Czernowitz-born poet and survivor of the Transnistria camp Paul Celan, that language, in spite of everything, survived the events 'and came to light again, "enriched" by it all' (Celan, 1968: 128-9), Klepfisz writes that 'silence had become and remains a central theme in my writing' (Klepfisz, 1990b: 168).

Silence was forced upon Shoah survivors who often did not want or know how to tell their experiences. Because the Shoah, the greatest Jewish tragedy of the twentieth century,[3] signified its own death and reduction to silence its survival in historical memory inevitably implied the presence of an informal discourse, a degree of unconscious witnessing that could not find its voice during the event itself. Diaries were written and hidden, pictures were taken in secret, but all those attempts were doomed to failure. The events were not transmittable at the time – victims were numbed by humiliation and death. The French (non-Jewish) Resistance activist and writer Charlotte Delbo suggests this numbness began for her when a truck full of women passed where she and other Auschwitz inmates were labouring:

> The women pass by near us. They are shouting. They shout and we do not hear anything. This cold, dry air should be conducive in an ordinary human environment. They shout in our direction without a sound reaching us. Their mouths shout, their arms stretched out towards us shout, everything about them is shouting. Each body is a shout. All of them torches flaming with cries of terror, cries that have assumed female bodies. Each one is a materialized cry, a howl – unheard. (Delbo, 1995: 33)

After the war, telling, for most survivors, seemed impossible.[4] Psychologist Nadine Fresco describes the silence that swallows up survivors' past: 'to speak up and thus to realise the grip of death, which was the grip of silence, seems to have represented for these [survivor] parents too grave a danger for such an action to seem possible' (Fresco, 1984: 417-27). Psychoanalyst Dinora Pines speaks of the lack of public recognition for Shoah survivors in Britain, where 'many remained hidden in the population, and were silent'. She documents a 'disavowal' state of mind, which Freud (1925) described as the 'blindness of the seeing eye in which one knows and does not know a thing at the same time', reported by many women survivors whom she works with in her London clinic (Pines, 1993: 207). For Pines, this is the survivor's dilemma, a dilemma revisited upon their children, for many of whom their parents' inability to tell resulted in a state of 'knowing and not knowing' about the Shoah, also reported by Israeli daughters of survivors in my own study (Lentin, forthcoming).

Not only did survivors find it hard to tell. In many cases there was no one listening. Israeli writer Ruth Bondi who survived Theresienstadt and Auschwitz writes:

> No one wanted to listen ... the listeners lowered their eyes, as if they were told things which were too personal, not fit for public memory. We learnt very quickly to be Israelis outside and survivors at home. Not even at home – why burden your loved ones – only in your heart. (Bondi, 1972: 20)

Women and the Shoah: different voices

It seems odd to claim that the Shoah was surrounded by silence in view of the plethora of books and films about it. But for survivors the silence was real. Many claim they belong to a 'secret order' that is sworn to silence. As 'subhumans,' a position they have internalized and assumed as their identity, they feel they have no right to speak (Felman and Laub, 1992: 82).

An even more deafening silence envelops the link between gender and genocide in relation to the Shoah. Although it is asserted that 'the greatest atrocities in Auschwitz were committed against Jewish women and children' (Ainsztein, 1974: 788), gender-specific experiences tend to be overlooked in Shoah literature, especially when written by men. Women's experiences tend to be neutralized into a so-called 'human' perspective, which, on examination, turns out to be masculine. Though rape, abortion and prostitution in the ghettos and camps happened to women, we hear how these affected men in works by writers such as Tadeus Borowski (1976), Azriel Eisenberg (1981), Bruno Bettelheim (1970) and others. Alvin Rosenfeld, for instance, writing about *Sophie's Choice* (Styron, 1979), where the choice a mother had to make between her two children was undoubtedly a gendered experience, says: 'one of the characteristics of Holocaust writing at their most authentic, is that they are peculiarly and predominantly sexless' (Rosenfeld, 1980: 164).

The Nazi genocide was, however, not gender-neutral. Gender was a factor in the destruction of the Jewish populations. Jewish women, linked to the race struggle of National Socialism because they carried the next generation of Jews, were killed not simply as Jews but as Jewish women, sexually and maternally targeted. A further reason for killing women rather than men was that men's labour was valued more highly than women's; when Jews and others remained alive, it was often because they could be put to work in Nazi war industries.

Nazi sexism encouraged Aryan women, the 'mothers of the race,' through nationalistic emotional blackmail and financial incentives and by outlawing abortions and sterilizations, to increase the numbers of so-called German 'children of confidence,' allegedly showing the 'confidence of the [German] people in its Reich, its Führer, its future' (Burgdörfer, 1942, quoted in Bock, 1993: 168). At the same time, Nazi racist and sexist ideology was directed at Jewish (and other 'racially inferior') women, guilty of 'racial degeneration', through prohibition of motherhood and forced abortions and sterilizations which began as early as January 1934. To prevent the birth of the 'racially undesirable', the surest method of birth control was death, and Jewish women were targeted accordingly (as were Roma and Sinti and other 'racial degenerates') (Bock, 1993: 161–86).

The Washington-based historian Joan Ringelheim, a pioneer researcher into Shoah and gender, found it necessary to analyse the death statistics to determine the gender proportion of deportation and death. Camp figures are not useful in analysing death rates, as only those who entered alive were recorded – only some ten per cent of those who were deported to Auschwitz became members of the camp population, for instance (all others were killed on arrival). Analysing earlier killing operations (such as those of the *Einsatzgruppen*[5]) and population and deportation records of the various ghettos, Ringelheim concludes that more Jewish women were deported than men and that women may have been murdered in greater numbers than men in the killing centres. 'Women and children [were] among the least valuable to keep alive even for a little while. Whatever skills women might have, their "biological skills" could never be useful for the Nazis' (Ringelheim, 1993: 393–5).

The Israeli historian Hanna Yablonka reports that at the end of 1945 there were some 90,500 Jewish refugees in Germany, Austria and Italy. By 1947 their number increased to 245,000 (Yablonka, 1994: 3). According to Ringelheim, women survivors remember clearly that in the displaced persons' camps there were more men than women, although UN Relief and Rehabilitation Agency (UNRRA) figures do not confirm the wide disparity of the anecdotal evidence. Jewish population records in the displaced persons' camps in 1946 show that 40 per cent of the population was female, 60 per cent male; in 1947, 44 per cent was female, 56 per cent male (UNRRA archives, 1947). Yablonka confirms this gender survival gap. More men than women survivors arrived in Palestine. In post-Shoah Poland male numerical superiority was maintained even in later years. This was, Yablonka argues, a consequence of the extermination process. Furthermore, over 80 per cent of the survivor families who settled in Palestine either had no children at all or had only one child: 'after the war many women survivors were too old ... many younger women who had experienced medical experimentation during the war, were left sterile' (Yablonka, 1994: 11).

That women's Shoah experiences were different from those of men is evident to anyone who has worked with survivors' testimonies. Women, targeted by the extermination machine as mothers and sexual objects, suffered greater sexual vulnerability. They were robbed of their femininity; stripped naked in full view of male camp guards and fellow prisoners; vaginally examined in full view of male Nazi officers; shaved all over, often in a sexual stance, straddling two stools. They were vulnerable to rape, murder of themselves and their children, to the necessity of killing their own and other women's babies lest a baby's cry jeopardize the lives of others, to forced abortions, and to other forms of sexual exploitation, in the ghettos, in resistance groups, in hiding and passing, and in the camps (Ringelheim, 1993: 375).

Many women survivors who became mothers at a very young age in the displaced persons' camps had often experienced sexual humiliation which made talking about their experiences doubly hard. Israeli psychotherapist Dina Wardi (1990), who works with children of survivors, argues that in order to understand how women survivors functioned as mothers, we have to examine how they re-constructed their feminine identity after the war. This depended upon being able to overcome dependence upon their own murdered mothers. Many women survivors, Wardi argues, experienced a post-Shoah conflict between the wish to preserve the defences built during the war, which protected them from complete destruction, the need to re-establish the link with lost relatives, and the necessity to reconstruct their own identity and sense of belonging (Wardi, 1990: 50).

Wardi lists three categories of women survivors. The first consists of women who were young girls during the Shoah and who, separated from their loved ones, had to fight for survival alone. These women, often sexually abused, matured before their time and the traumas left indelible scars upon their self-image. Many had to witness their mothers being humiliated and they often battled between anger at their parents for failing them and a need to idealize their memory. After the Shoah these women repressed their anger, replacing it with 'survivor's guilt'. Lonely and depressed, these survivors often married hurriedly, projecting their dependence upon the first man who showed them any kindness. Many became pregnant immediately after the war; they felt a desperate need to have a child, yet were fearful about the damage they might inflict upon it, perpetuating their own stigma. Many had nightmares about their baby's health and miscarriages were common (Wardi, 1990: 51-55).

The second group were women survivors who had already formulated their feminine identity during the Shoah. Often exposed to sexual abuse and sometimes employing their sexuality as a survival strategy, these women experienced ambivalence over their sexual identity. Because they had separated from their mothers before the Shoah, they were better able, according to Wardi, to cope with depression and anxiety. However, unresolved conflicts resulted in many of these women becoming obsessively active after the Shoah, often rushing back to work soon after the birth of their children (Wardi, 1990: 55-58).

The third group were women who had reached adulthood or who had already had children before the Shoah. Many had lost their parents, their brothers and sisters, their spouses and, worst of all, their children. The generational chain was severed most cruelly during the Shoah when the mother survived and her children were murdered. The Israeli novelist Aharon Apelfeld describes the feelings of one survivor whose children were torn away from her:

> I lost my children. I did, I thought, all I could, but I lost them. The older was nine and the younger seven. You see: I am alive, I even eat. They did not touch me, I am seemingly made of iron. (Apelfeld, 1983: 70)

The main conflict informing the guilt of a mother who had, supposedly, abandoned her children, is a sense of having lost her maternal instinct. Mothers were utterly powerless to save their children's lives under the Nazis, but they could never get over the terrible guilt of having broken their children's trust. After the Shoah these women lived in a state of chronic mourning, and their new spouses and children have had to live with the knowledge that they could never replace the 'first' children (Wardi, 1990: 59-60).

'I've come back from another world'

Not only did women and men experience the Shoah differently. Women survivors and men survivors also tell their experiences differently, according to Zvi Dror of Kibbutz *Lochamei Hagetaot*. This kibbutz, founded by Shoah survivors many of whom had taken part in the Warsaw Ghetto uprising, is dedicated, via its Shoah Museum, to commemorating the Shoah. Dror collected and edited many volumes of survivors' memoirs (Dror, 1984):

> Judging by the testimonies, women experienced their fate differently than men. Men tend to generalise. Women's testimonies are ... more personal, more concrete, closer to their personal experiences ... When a woman tells of her Shoah experiences, she has a need to expose her inner world. When a woman speaks, her world view is one of sorrow, of images of a hungry child, of illness, of the lack of hygiene. A man says 'if I ate – I lived'. A woman tells how she looked for water in Auschwitz and how she was forced to use the latrine water. (personal communication, December 1992)

Men also often resorted to the factual, the 'heroic'. Israeli writer Nava Semel told me how her father's 'heroic biography' compared with the 'black hole' that was Auschwitz in her mother's biography:

> My father's biography, he brings what I call a 'heroic Shoah biography'. Because he was in the underground, he was a member of the 'Zionist Youth' and he was active during the Shoah. He forged passports, he changed identities, later he travelled to Transnistria, as part of the operation to save the orphans ... My mother, on the other hand, had a black hole in her biography. If she spoke about her childhood, she referred to it up to the age of 18, and if she spoke about her life, she returned to it at the age of 23. That means that five years were missing. (personal communication, December 1992)

Often gendered rites of passage, such as a daughter becoming a mother herself, offer women survivors the possibility of breaking their enforced silence and bringing that 'black hole' back from the depth of memory into words.

Men survivors often seem to find it easier than women survivors to talk of their 'ordinary,' non-heroic Shoah experiences too. Israeli film director Tsipi Reibenbach's film *Choice and Destiny* (Reibenbach, 1993) documents the almost banal life of her Shoah survivor parents. As they shop, clean, prepare and eat food, her father Yitzhak tells his Shoah story. He tells it factually, unemotionally, although the story itself is heartbreaking. All the while Fruma, Reibenbach's mother, continues her domestic chores obsessively, a silent witness. Thirteen minutes before the end of the two-hour film, the mother suddenly speaks, for five whole minutes, while stuffing and shaping soup dumplings, about her unwillingness to remember, her inability to tell:

> What do you think? How can I tell everything? ... I lie down at night and I can't fall asleep ... I see how Heshik carried Getzele. I see everything he told me. I don't sleep. I lie there with my eyes open and I see it. I wasn't there when they shot Avraham Lozer. I imagine how they shot him, how they carried him. I didn't see; they told me, and I can imagine. I lie down for hours and when nobody is at home, sometimes I walk around and I call out loud Sarahle, Shimshele, where are you? Where are you? Where? I don't even have a tombstone for you. I can't even give you a flower. There are so many flowers in this country. What do I have left? A memorial candle to light. That's it.

Tomorrow I can tell you a lot, a lot, a lot. I'll remember again. That's it. (Reibenbach, 1993)

Fruma's outburst is followed by a long silence, as her husband and grandchildren look on. But she knows the value of telling, despite the fact that for years she refused to talk, unable to remember:

Heshik - he didn't live to tell. To get it off his chest. Maybe it would have been easier for him. Maybe he wouldn't have become so sick. He suffered because of it. Maybe it'll be easier for me too. I'd be able to fall asleep at last. I see the picture. [All those years] I didn't want to talk. I didn't want to. I have told you nothing. All these years I didn't want to talk. Leave me alone, let me be. I don't want to remember, I don't want to remember. [But] now, you see I'm talking. I could talk all day long ... so many events! So many! I never talked before and now maybe I'll feel better if I let everything out. (Reibenbach, 1993)

But were women survivors really able to talk? And were they really heard? Did liberation from the camps really bring freedom, when telling was not a possibility? Charlotte Delbo, in *The Measure of Our Days*, the third book of her trilogy *Auschwitz and After*, writes about her camp comrade, Gilberte, who said she 'felt at a loss at once, as soon as I came to Paris'. 'Is this freedom,' Gilberte asks, 'this intolerable solitude, this room, this fatigue?' (Delbo, 1995: 242-4). Solitude, the inability to tell, the fear that no one was listening, and that even if they were, they could not possibly understand, was not freedom. It was the ultimate silencer, as was the double life, the life 'here' - in everyday post-World War Two Europe, or Israel, or the United States,[6] and the life 'there' - that life which is always present, like a dark shadow:

Auschwitz is so deeply etched on my memory, that I cannot forget one moment of it. So you are living with Auschwitz? No, I live next to it. Auschwitz is there, unalterable, precise, but enveloped in the skin of memory, an impenetrable skin that isolates it from my present self. (Delbo, 1995: xi)

And, having 'come from another world', survivor women live with despair, death, memory and the ruins of memory. They live without living, forever tortured by the 'survivor's guilt'. As Mado, another of Delbo's comrades, says: 'I am not alive, I'm imprisoned in memories and repetitions. I sleep badly but insomnia does not weigh on me. At night I have the right not to be alive. I have the right not to pretend. I join the others then. I am among them, one of them' (Delbo, 1995: 261).

'Life' and life story are part of the same fabric, in that life informs and is informed by stories. Life cannot be determined outside of the stories told about it nor can the meaning of stories be determined without reference to human life as it is lived (Widdershoven, 1993: 2-20). But if telling becomes a near impossibility, does this not cast doubts upon memory itself? For many Shoah survivors the fear of losing their memory was the fear of losing their 'selves'. After Auschwitz, Charlotte Delbo always feared losing her memory: 'To lose one's memory is to lose oneself, to no longer be oneself' (Delbo, 1995: 188). Women's memories of sexual abuse and humiliation often result in 'splitting in two'. A similar process happened after the Shoah, as Poupette says:

For twenty years I kept this providential faculty which helped me get out alive from Auschwitz: to split myself in two, not to be there. You know, that's what I used to do in the camp. You say it was impossible to achieve this split in two over there. I did.

Passing by a pile of corpses, I saw it, of course, but I'd quickly look away; you must not look, must not see. And I succeeded in not seeing. (Delbo, 1995: 273)

The silencing was imposed by a post-war society that wanted to rehabilitate, and not be weighed down by the horrible past. Israeli film maker Naomi Ben Natan tells of her mother's first encounter with a sister who had arrived in Palestine before the war, the only time her mother was allowed to 'tell', her tale apparently so threatening that no one ever listened again.

I remember my mother's meeting with her family in Israel, with her sister ... I will never forget the first meeting of the two sisters. They stood and cried for half an hour – a terrible crying – their whole childhood, everything they had lost. It all ended with this hug. I stood by their side in the yard. After this there were no more questions, no more talking. Nothing. For years ... It seems natural to me that if I had a sister I had not seen for years and in the meantime everything that happened happened and their mother had died – and I would not have been able to talk to her – I suppose it would have choked me. But it was a complete refusal to listen by those who were here. (personal communication, December 1992)

Survivors frighten us, we are afraid to truly face the traumas of our own history, and the very life-assertion of the victims constitutes another threat (Felman and Laub, 1992: 74). This inability to listen stemmed from deep discomfort in the face of atrocity and from our inability to ask the right questions, as Delbo writes so achingly:

You'd like to know
ask questions
but you don't know what questions
and you don't know how to ask them
so you inquire
about simple things
hunger
fear
death
and we don't know how to answer
not with the words you use
our own words
you can't understand
so you ask simpler things
tell us for example
how a day was spent
a day goes by so slowly
you'd run out of patience listening
but if we gave you an answer
you still don't know how a day was spent
and assume we don't know how to answer.
(Delbo, 1995: 275)

Researchers too find certain facets of the specificities of women's Shoah experiences particularly difficult to hear. Ringelheim has interviewed a woman survivor she calls Pauline who told her of having been molested while in hiding: 'I can still feel the fear ... Sometimes I think it was equally as frightening as the Germans. It became within me a tremendous ... I don't know how [to deal with it] ... what to do with it. I had nobody to talk about it. Nobody to turn to' (Ringelheim, 1997).

Pauline understandably minimizes the importance of the specifically female aspects of her Shoah experiences by asking 'Is this important?' It is also understandable that researchers are often unable to connect women's sexual experiences to the broader persecution and murder that was the Shoah. Only recently have researchers such as Ringelheim begun to ask questions about women's sexual victimization as a group.

Asking 'Why has there been a split between genocide and gender in the memories of witnesses and the historical reconstruction of research?', Ringelheim argues that this split exists because first, gender is considered irrelevant to the Shoah. This results in 'forgotten' memories. Second, there is a dividing line between what is personal to women and the 'proper' collective memory of the Shoah. This results in 'ignored' memories, which eventually turn into 'forgotten' memories (Ringelheim, 1997). Researchers need to begin giving women survivors an opportunity to talk of their sexual exploitation, a topic shunned by most Shoah historians, despite the acknowledgement that 'the Final Solution was intended by its creators to ensure the annihilation of all Jews ... yet the road to annihilation was marked by events which specifically affected men as men and women as women' (Hilberg, 1992: 126).

Sex and all experiences connected with sex – rape, abortion, sexual abuse, pregnancy – are intimate parts of women's lives and therefore never easy to ask questions about, or to talk about. Facing women survivors' sexual exploitation confronts us with our own sexual vulnerability as women. And for family members,

> the rape of mothers, grandmothers, sisters, friends, or lovers during the Holocaust is difficult to face. The further possibility that mothers or sisters or lovers 'voluntarily' used sex for food or protection is equally difficult to absorb ... but to dismiss situations that relate so specifically to women makes it impossible to begin to understand the victimisation of women. It may even make it impossible to really see Jewish women as victims, or visualise their victimisation. (Ringelheim, 1997: 25)

Some people believe that connecting sexuality with the Shoah, even in fiction, desecrates the memory of both the dead and the surviving, and belittles or even denies the Shoah itself. Many women survivors, although they were sexually exploited, decline to 'name' their abuse as sexual exploitation by men, both Nazis and Jews. The first interview Ringelheim conducted was in 1979, with Susan, who told her about the uses of sex in Theresienstadt where 'you survived as a woman through the male' (Ringelheim, 1997). When Ringelheim visited her again in 1982, Susan told her, almost casually, 'I was raped in Auschwitz.'

Instead of asking her to tell her what happened, Ringelheim found herself counselling Susan. Did Ringelheim, like the people Delbo writes about, not know how to ask? Or did she not want to hear? It took her some years before she returned to Susan to ask. She says that the incident reveals important things about

> how deeply we may not want to hear; and about the ways in which we avoid listening no matter how directly a survivor (male or female) may tell us what happened (e. g. cannibalism, hiding in a latrine, killing newborn babies). Sometimes we avoid because we are afraid; sometimes we avoid because we don't understand the importance of what is being said. (Ringelheim, 1997: 27)

Conclusion: 'Had we returned?'

Most post-Shoah studies cast the survivors as clinical subjects. The 'survivor syndrome' coined by the Norwegian psychiatrist William Niederland (1968) detailed the symptoms all survivors supposedly shared: anxiety, depression, inability to experience pleasure, nightmares, psychosomatic disorders, social withdrawal, irritability and profound alteration of personal identity. These symptoms, Niederland argued, were a consequence both of the traumatic experiences during the Shoah and of the defence mechanisms required to cope with these traumas and survive. For many years psychoanalytical studies were the only available material about survivors, side by side with survivor testimonies, some (Elie Wiesel's and Primo Levi's, for instance) more prominent than others. Testimonies were fragmented, varied, and many did not enjoy a large readership: many were published by *landsmannschaft* associations,[7] whose target audiences were limited.

The tendency to view Jewish survivors as a unitary category and to psycho-pathologize them prevailed despite survivors' highly individual experiences. This ignored the fact that the majority of survivors 'have not sought any form of psychotherapy' (Hass, 1990: 18), perhaps because 'the trust in organised society has been shaken to the extent that survivors avoid seeking the support of social institutions' (Dasburg, 1987: 99). There is also a tendency to forget that in continuing to live and bring up families, many Shoah survivors have achieved remarkable success, probably due to their need for continuity and compensatory life-affirming attitudes.

Survivors are those who were lucky or strong enough to pull through. There is an urgent need to create a forum for those who are still alive, to enable them to speak, to finally tell their story, and be able to sleep at last, as Fruma suggests.[8]

More specifically, going beyond the 'survivor syndrome,' we must make room for women survivors' experiences of sexual exploitation. If not, all we will be left with as documents of women's Shoah experiences would be Anne Frank and *Schindler's List*.[9] The film, a typical Hollywood product, unfortunately the only source of information about the Shoah for countless people, not only exploited gender stereotypes (for instance in the scene of the woman who tarts herself up in order to persuade Schindler to take on her elderly parents; and in the scene between Schindler and the maid of the camp commander Goetz), but also erased the central role played by Oskar Schindler's wife in procuring daily provisions for his workers.

If we learn to listen, new discourses must enable us to understand the gender-specific experiences of women during the Shoah and the nature of their silence. In the face of the use of mass rape as a political instrument by Serbian soldiers in the early 1990s, linking genocide and gender may have implications well beyond the Shoah which was not, as Zygmunt Bauman (1989) reminds us, an aberration of modernity, but its logical consequence.

For Jewish women the Shoah produced experiences which do not necessarily parallel those of men. As Pauline told Ringelheim: 'Everything else is the same. But there are certain things that are different' (Ringelheim, 1997: 32). We must acknowledge, and thereby attempt to heal the 'split memory' of genocide and gender. And, we must ask the question implied so eloquently in Delbo's book: Did anyone really survive the Shoah? To hear the 'howl unheard' we should have promised the survivors 'love' rather than 'roses' as did 'a poet', according to Delbo:

> why roses
> we harboured no such expectations
> love was all we needed
> had we returned
> (Delbo, 1995: 270)

Notes

1. I use the Hebrew word Shoah, meaning 'catastrophe' or 'calamity,' in preference to the English term 'Holocaust,' from the Greek *holokauston*, literally 'burnt offering', which implies a Christian notion of Jewish sacrifice.

2. Anne Karpf (1997: 204) argues that because the Nazis intended the extermination of European Jewry to leave no trace, the massacre made no deep impression on the rest of Europe until relatively recently. Kushner (1994: 114) quotes Himmler as acknowledging that the Nazis intended to leave no witnesses or record of the extermination: 'this is an unwritten and never to be written page of glory in our history'.

3. Although I agree with Zigmunt Bauman (1989) and Joan Ringelheim (1993) that the Shoah must not be marginalized as an exclusive Jewish tragedy, this chapter deals primarily with the fate of Jewish Shoah survivors after the war.

4. In Austria, between 1945 and 1947, silence was apparently not the rule. Anti-fascist groups invited survivors to speak to the public. In 1947 this stopped as political parties tried to re-integrate the Nazis as the Cold War climate set in (personal communication, Irene Bandhauer-Schöffmann).

5. *Einsatzgruppen* were mobile killing units of the SS and SD attached to the *Wehrmacht.* Their official tasks were to wipe out political opponents and seize state documents. They carried out mass murders, primarily of Jews in German-occupied areas in the USSR and Poland (Rittner and Roth, 1993: 428).

6. Naturally, there are differences between women who went to Palestine, those who remained in Europe (very well articulated by Delbo, for instance, 1995), and those who went to the USA. Israeli society, itself, I argue, as a 'daughter of survivors', in its efforts to establish a new society, in contrast with the Diaspora, tended to silence the experiences of survivors as 'unheroic' and passive by comparison with the pre-state Israelis' self image as active and brave (Segev, 1991; Lentin, 1996). In the USA, this dichotomy was seemingly not as paramount.

7. Fellow-countrypeople's associations.

8. There are several projects to video-record survivors' testimonies, the most recent master-minded by Steven Spielberg who has financed the *Survivors of the Shoah Visual History Foundation* with the task of collecting 150,000 testimonies (Leventhal, 1997: 14–15). However, these projects do not appear to specifically target gender issues.

9. It is interesting to note that of the 1200 Jews saved by Oskar Schindler, 1000 were men and 200 were women, a fact not highlighted by the film (Ringelheim, 1993: 399).

References

Adorno, Theodore W. (1949) 'After Auschwitz.' In his *Negative Dialectics*. New York: Continuum (reissued 1973).

Adorno, Theodore W. (1962) 'Commitment'. In A. Arato and E. Gebhardt (eds), *The Essential Frankfurt School Reader*. New York: Continuum (reissued 1982).

Ainsztein, Reuben (1974) *Jewish Resistance in Nazi-Occupied Europe*. London: Elek.

Apelfeld, Aharon (1983) *Hakutonet veHapassim* (*The Shirt and the Stripes*). Tel Aviv: Hakibbutz Hameuchad.

Bauman, Zygmunt (1989) *Modernity and the Holocaust*. Cambridge: Polity Press.

Baumel, Judith T. (1998) *Double Jeopardy: Gender and the Holocaust*. London: Valentine Mitchell.

Bettelheim, Bruno (1970) *The Informed Heart*. London: Paladin.

Bock, Gisela (1993) 'Racism and sexism in Nazi Germany: motherhood, compulsory sterilisation and the state'. In Carol Rittner and John Roth (eds), *Different Voices: Women and the Holocaust*. New York: Paragon House, pp. 161–86.

Bondi, Ruth (1972) *Lefeta Belev Hamizrach* (*Suddenly, at the Heart of the East*). Tel Aviv.

Borowski, Tadeus (1976) *This Way to the Gas, Ladies and Gentlemen*. New York: Penguin.

Burgdörfer, Friedrich (1942) *Kinder des Vertrauens*. Berlin: Eher.

Celan, Paul (1968) *Ausgewählte Gedichte*. Frankfurt am Main: Suhrkamp Verlag.

Dasburg, Haim (1987) 'Hahevra HaIsraelit mul trauma me'urgenet, o: hametapel mul hanitsol (Israeli society confronting organized trauma: the therapist confronting the survivor)'. *Sichot,* 1(2), 98–103.

Delbo, Charlotte (1995) *Auschwitz and After*. New Haven: Yale University Press.

Dror, Zvi (ed.) (1984) *Dapei Edut* (*Testimonies of Survival: 96 Personal Interviews from Members of Kibbutz Lochamei Hagetaot*). Kibbutz Lochamei Hagetaot: Beit Lochamei Hagetaot, Hakibbutz Hameuchad.

Eisenberg, Azriel (ed.) (1981) *Witness to the Holocaust*. New York.

Felman, Shoshana and Laub, Dori (1992) *Testimony: Crises in Witnessing in Literature, Psychoanalysis and Representation*. New York: Routledge.

Fresco, Nadine (1984) 'Remembering the unknown'. *International Review of Psychoanalysis*, no. 11, 417–27.

Freud, Sigmund (1925) 'Negation'. In James Strachey (ed.), *The Standard Edition of the Complete Psychological Works of Sigmund Freud*. London: Hogarth, 1953–73. Vol. 19, 235.

Fuchs, Esther (ed.) (1999) *Women and the Holocaust: Narrative and Representation*. Lanham: University of America Press (vol. 22, *Studies in the Shoah*).

Grunfeld, Uriel (1995) *Holocaust, Movies and Remembrance: The Pedagogical Challenge*. Unpublished paper, Pennsylvania State University.

Hass, Aharon (1990) *In the Shadow of the Holocaust: The Second Generation*. Ithaca: Cornell University Press.

Hilberg, Raul (1992) *Perpetrators and Bystanders: The Jewish Catastrophe 1933–1945*. London: Lime Tree.

Karpf, Anne (1997) *The War After: Living with the Holocaust*. London: Minerva.

Klepfisz, Irena (1990a) 'The widow and daughter'. In her, *A Few Words in the Mother Tongue: Poems Selected and New 1971-1990*. Portland, OR: Eighth Mountain Press, pp. 35-8.

Klepfisz, Irena (1990b) 'Forging a woman's link in *di goldene keyt:* some possibilities for Jewish American poetry'. In her *Dreams of an Insomniac: Jewish Feminist Essays, Speeches and Diatribes.* Portland, OR: Eighth Mountain Press, pp. 167-74.

Kushner, Tony (1994) *The Holocaust and the Liberal Imagination.* Oxford: Blackwell.

Laska, Vera (ed.) (1983) *Women in the Resistance and the Holocaust.* Westport, CT: Greenwood Press.

Lentin, Ronit (1996) 'A *Yiddishe mame* desperately seeking a *mame-loshn:* the feminisation of stigma in the relations between Israelis and Holocaust survivors'. *Women's Studies International Forum*, 19 (1-2), 87-97.

Lentin, Ronit (forthcoming). *Israel and the Daughters of the Shoah: Re-occupying the Territory of Silence.* Oxford: Berghahn Books.

Leventhal, Michael (1997) 'Schindler's sequel'. *Jewish Student,* May, 14-15.

Linden, R. Ruth (1993) *Making Stories, Making Selves: Feminist Reflections on the Holocaust.* Columbus: Ohio University Press.

Milton, Sybil (1984) 'Women and the Holocaust: the case of German and German-Jewish women'. In Renate Bridenthal, Atina Grossman and Marion Kaplan (eds), *When Biology Becomes Destiny: Women in Weimar and Nazi Germany.* New York: Monthly Review Press.

Niederland, William (1968) 'Clinical observations on the "survivor syndrome": symposium on psychic traumatisation through social catastrophe'. *International Journal of Psychoanalysis,* 49, 313-15.

Ofer, Dalia and Lenore J. Weitzman (eds) (1998) *Women in the Holocaust.* New Haven: Yale University Press.

Ozick, Cynthia (1991) *The Shawl.* London: Jonathan Cape.

Pines, Dinora (1993) 'The impact of the Holocaust on the second generation.' In her *A Woman's Unconscious Use of Her Body.* London: Virago, pp. 205-25.

Reibenbach, Tsipi (1993) *Bchira Vegoral (Choice and Destiny).* 16mm film, 118 minutes.

Rich, Adrienne (1990) 'Introduction'. In Irena Klepfisz, *A Few Words in the Mother Tongue: Poems Selected and New 1971-1990.* Portland, OR: Eighth Mountain Press, pp. 13-25.

Ringelheim, Joan Miriam (1985) 'Women and the Holocaust: a reconsideration of research'. *Signs*, 10(4), 741-61.

Ringelheim, Joan Miriam (1993) 'Women and the Holocaust: a reconsideration of research'. In Carol Rittner and John Roth (eds), *Different Voices: Women and the Holocaust.* New York: Paragon House, pp. 373-418.

Ringelheim, Joan Miriam (1997) 'Genocide and gender: a split memory'. In Ronit Lentin (ed.), *Gender and Catastrophe*. London: Zed Books, pp. 18-35.

Rittner, Carol and Roth, John K. (eds) (1993) *Different Voices: Women and the Holocaust.* New York: Paragon House.

Rosenfeld, Alvin (1980) *A Double Dying: Reflections on Holocaust Literature.* Bloomington: Indiana University Press.

Segev, Tom (1991) *Hamillion Hashevi'i: HaIsraelim vehaShoah (The Seventh Million: The Israelis and the Holocaust).* Jerusalem: Keter.

Styron, William (1979) *Sophie's Choice*. New York: Random House.

United Nations Relief and Rehabilitation Agency (1947) UNRRA archives, Pag. 4/ 3.0.11.0.1.1, Box 4. January.

Wardi, Dina (1990) *Nos'ei Hachotam: Dialogue im Bnei Hador Hasheni Lashoah (Memorial Candles)*. Jerusalem: Keter.

Widdershoven, G. A. M. (1993). 'The story of life: hermeneutic perspectives on the relationship between narrative and life history'. In Ruth Josselson and Amia Lieblich (eds), *The Narrative Study of Lives,* vol. 1. Newbury Park: Sage.

Yablonka, Hanna (1994) *Achim Zarim: Nitsolei Hashoah Bimedinat Israel 1948-1952 (Foreign Brethren: Holocaust Survivors in the State of Israel 1948–1952)*. Jerusalem: Yad Yitzhak Ben Zvi Press and Ben-Gurion University of the Negev Press.

14 Unwelcome in Austria: Returnees and Concentration Camp Survivors

Helga Embacher

'There has not been a single day since 1945 on which I haven't thought of Auschwitz' (Dagmar Ostermann, *Standard*, 17 July 1995).

'Victims? There was no such thing! Everyone knew that Austria itself had been Hitler's first victim. Herr Karl, who always found a way to make the best of the situation for himself, under Hitler and afterwards, Herr Karl is everywhere' (Zaloscer, 1988: 178).

In accordance with the Moscow Declaration signed by the Allies (except France) in 1943, Austria had succeeded in portraying itself as the 'first victim of National Socialist Germany' and to thus deny its responsibility for the expulsion and extermination of the Jews (Bischof, 1993). The so-called 'Annexation' by Germany in 1938 had indeed been a violation of international law. However, the Austrian people did not have to be forced to take part in the 'Aryanizations'. during the course of which many of them proved to be even more zealous than the Germans.[1] The vast majority did not feel that their land had been occupied in 1938, and Austrian soldiers (a majority of them even to this day) identified with the German *Wehrmacht*. In the aftermath of bombardment, faced with housing shortages, hunger, cold and the fear of rape, in mourning for dead or missing soldiers, no sympathy could evidently be spared for the suffering of their fellow human beings who had been deported and driven into exile in 1938. No one wanted to confront the past. Everywhere there was 'this I-don't-remember, this glossing over, this playing down, this tendency to move on to matters of everyday life', the art historian Hilde Zaloscer recalled with regret (1988: 117).

Nevertheless, the political leaders involved, as well as the Austrian people, were fully aware that the 'victim theory' was extremely tenuous and rather more along the lines of a 'half-truth'. It was above all the survivors of concentration and extermination camps and the returnees from exile (altogether only a few thousand) who posed the greatest threat to this shaky construction. In *their* recollections, Austrians were not victims but rather enthusiastic Nazis, anti-Semites, 'Aryanizers' and, among other things, concentration camp guards. They remembered with horror how their neighbours had turned into their persecutors. During the war, they had been on the side of the Allies, hoping for the defeat of the German *Wehrmacht*. Their return evoked feelings of guilt, particularly among those with less-than-clear consciences (Embacher, 1995a).

Historical scholarship in Austria has only recently turned its attention to the problematic issue of emigration and exile, or, to formulate it more concretely, the deportation of its Jewish population. Whereas the expulsion of Jewish politicians, scientists and artists has been treated and gradually worked through since the 1980s (such that regret for the losses thereby occasioned for Austria has become an increasingly common sentiment even in the speeches of politicians), the expulsion and murder of Jewish women as well as the chasm produced by the loss of women intellectuals and artists has been paid too little attention up to now. Research on concentration camps has also dealt primarily with men imprisoned for political reasons; the special circumstances of women inmates have been left out of consideration for far too long (Embacher, 1989, 1996; Berger *et al.*, 1987; Milton, 1984). Of those who returned from exile or the camps, few went public with their stories and problems; some did so only after a long delay. We know little of the fate of persecuted Catholic women, strictly Orthodox or Zionist Jewish women, Roma and Sinti women, women members of the Jehovah's Witnesses, women who hid Jews, partisans and deserters, women who aided slave labourers or carried on affairs with them, or women who were sent to concentration camps as so-called malingerers or prostitutes.[2] 'The wars belong to the men; therefore, the memory of war as well. And of course Fascism, regardless of whether one had been for it or against it – strictly a man's business. In any case, women have no past. Or have none to have. It's ill-mannered, almost indecent,' as Ruth Klüger wrote in her widely discussed book *Weiterleben* (*Getting on with Life*) (Klüger, 1992: 10).

Life after survival: the return of concentration camp survivors

Many concentration camp prisoners had no strength left to rejoice in their long-awaited freedom. After their liberation, all they wanted was to eat, to rest and to sleep in a clean bed. A relatively large number of camp prisoners died shortly after the liberation as a consequence of exhaustion or malnutrition. Those who were strong enough to travel wanted to return to Austria as soon as possible to search for friends and relatives.

The Austrian government expended little effort to assist the return of former concentration camp inmates. Women were among those who marched on foot, mostly in groups, often through regions where fighting was still going on. Sometimes a horse-drawn wagon or a crowded train offered the chance to ride a part of the way (Berger *et al.*, 1985: 309). Having survived the murderous SS, women now had to contend with an additional lurking danger. Some were able 'to escape only by the narrowest of margins from being raped by their Russian liberators, while others, it must be concluded, had less good fortune and were forced to undergo, at the end of their concentration camp existence, this one additional trauma,' Ruth Klüger wrote (Klüger, 1992: 189). Even after liberation, the age-old rites of sexuality and war lived on (Embacher, 1996: 162).

The closer they got to home, the more they began to worry about the insecure situation facing them, about potential disillusionment and bad news. Every meeting with old acquaintances meant not only joy but also pain and mourning for the many friends killed by the Nazis. The Socialist Antonia Bruha described in expressive words her arrival in Vienna:

> My heart was pounding as we drove through the Simmeringer Hauptstraße, past the ruins of bombed-out buildings ... I kept my eyes closed, not wishing to see my beloved home town in this state of destruction. I tried to keep my mind off the question of whether I would find my parents, my husband and my child still alive. I trembled with fear and dug my fingernails into the flesh of my palms. (Bruha, 1984: 130)

Following a long separation, Antonia Bruha could once again embrace her husband and child. Her friend Hermine Jursa, though, had already received official notification that she had been divorced by her husband while she was an inmate at Ravensbrück. As a result, she lost her apartment and, upon her return, had to initially seek asylum in emergency quarters set up for returnees (Jursa and Fritz, 1983: 73).

Arriving in Austria following an arduous trek, the concentration camp survivors were quickly brought to the realization that they were despised and unwelcome in their own homeland. The *KZler,* as they were called, were considered criminals by a broad segment of the population. 'They must've been up to something wrong or else they wouldn't have been locked up' (Jursa and Fritz, 1984: 108) was a widely-held opinion. Jews, moreover, continued to encounter the old anti-Semitism. The only thing that was new was the label for them – 'Hitler's unfinished business' (Embacher, 1995a: 102).

Many Jews and Gypsies could certainly have benefited from special care and treatment programmes; however, those persecuted 'on racial grounds only' were initially excluded from the state's victim welfare system[3] (Bailer, 1993). Even the Survivors' Association (*KZ-Verband*), which had already been set up in 1945, refused admission to 'merely' Jews as well as other groups of victims such as Gypsies, homosexuals and women who had come to the aid of slave labourers or had hidden Jews (Embacher, 1995a: 96–107). When the physician Ella Lingens applied for membership in the Association following her return from Auschwitz, she was initially rejected since 'hiding Jews is a private matter and not a form of resistance' (DÖW, 1992: 634). Women who had been sent to the camps as punishment for intimate relationships with 'foreign workers' and, above all, those who survived by becoming prostitutes in the camps were often regarded as morally inferior human beings even among their fellow survivors. No one in post-war society took up their cause and they themselves were extremely reluctant to speak of their experiences (Embacher, 1996: 150).

On the loss of femininity

In the concentration and extermination camps, women were robbed not only of their human dignity but also of their female identity. They repeatedly describe the shock they experienced at the loss of their femininity, as well as the efforts to maintain a female identity under extreme conditions (Embacher, 1996; Milton, 1984). Having their hair shaved off was perceived as particularly humiliating, as a form of de-sexualization. All Jewish women were required to be shaved, but others could keep their hair as long as they did not have lice. 'We looked like monkeys. There were many beautiful women among us; without hair, they looked like wrecks,' wrote Grete Salus (1958: 20).

In Auschwitz/Birkenau, almost all women stopped menstruating though, in spite of the conditions in the camp, this was not unanimously viewed as easing the situation. 'It was painful to no longer experience these days of impurity. One no longer felt like a woman, one was already among the elderly' wrote Fania Fénelon (1981: 108) in her famous book on the girls' orchestra in Auschwitz. Some women reported that their menstruation began again after conditions in the camp improved; in other cases, this occurred on the way home; for still others, it began again only months or even years later. Many suffered for years from gynecological problems such as ovarian cysts, some became permanently infertile (Berger *et al.*, 1985: 312). Their emaciated bodies and the rapid ageing resulting from the extreme conditions constituted a severe burden for many women after their liberation. Simha Nahor, a native of Vienna who emigrated to Israel after the war, became conscious of 'what a frightful sight I must have been, one that must have seemed to a normal person like a being from another world' (Nahor, 1986: 65). Antonia Bruha touchingly described how she was rejected by her own daughter as a result of her appearance.

> 'Look, your mother is back,' said my husband, fighting back his tears. 'No, no,' the child screamed and hid behind her aunt – this was how she referred to her foster mother. Crying, the girl whispered behind her back: 'My mommy is the one in the picture, this ugly woman isn't my mommy!' I always imagined how beautiful it would be, if I survived, how I would embrace my child and hold her close. The actual reunion was absolutely nothing like what I had visualized … What indescribable bliss I felt when, after what seemed like an eternity, my daughter first put her arms around my neck, snuggled up to me and, in a trembling voice, said 'Mommy, I love you!' (1984: 131)

Attempts at coming to terms with the past

Many women married soon after they were liberated from the camps. Their partners had to assume the role of replacement for their murdered family and relatives, certainly an understandable need but one which could not be fulfilled, and so many marriages were doomed to failure. Many women wanted to bear children immediately as proof that their femininity and ability to become a mother had indeed not been taken from them, though also as a sign of victory over the murderous SS.[4] As scholarly studies have shown, not only this second generation but also the next as well were often deeply affected by the concentration camp experiences of their parents and grandparents – despite the fact that these were often kept secret (Hass, 1990; Bar-On, 1997).

The joy experienced upon liberation often lasted only briefly. Life after survival was a learning process. Some attempted to come to grips with what they had experienced by writing stories or essays. But hardly anyone in post-war Austria wanted to be oppressed by these horrible tales – the individual admonishing voices were unheeded (Embacher, 1995a: 96–101). What was especially painful was not only the lack of sympathy shown to individual concentration camp victims but also the doubt expressed about what they described by those who refused to believe the unbelievable. 'Once they were back in Austria, the few who survived might have heard from Austrian bureaucrats: it couldn't have been that bad, or you wouldn't even be here now … Even survival was something that had to be endured' (Jursa and Fritz, 1983: 102).

Surviving the catastrophe also meant suppressing the experience as soon as possible. Even people who were able to found a new family, to pursue a career and in some cases even undertake active political work suffered nightmares – a German shepherd dog or a smoking chimney, post-war symbols of reconstruction, took them back mentally to the concentration camps (Fritz, 1986: 138).

Many women attempted to come to terms with the horrors they had experienced by becoming active in politics. Those who had been politically persecuted (frequently of Jewish descent) found in 'their' party, in the Austrian Communist or Socialist parties, an *ersatz* family, an important social task and a prospect for the future. Apolitical women, so-called 'Pole lovers' (women who had had an affair with a forced labourer from Poland) or women who had been put in a concentration camp for hiding Jews, could often find no explanation for their fate even after their return. They were forced to conclude that the old racism had survived. Some women placed the blame on themselves and kept silent (Maislinger and Riedler, 1986). What remained for many women was their constant fear. 'I'm afraid of people. Nothing scares me as much as people do. How good and how evil they can be – for this, there is no measure, no basis and no protection' (Salus, 1958: 52).

Returnees

In 1938, there were approximately 200,000 Jews living in Austria, representing about 15 per cent of the population of Vienna. After the *Anschluß*, 130,00 were able to flee – many only at the last moment and often by the narrowest of margins; over 65,000 suffered a horrible death in concentration and extermination camps. Approximately 5000 men and women found some way to survive in Austria, mostly in Vienna. After the Shoah, a total of only a few thousand came back to their former homeland (Wilder-Okladek, 1970). There were fewer than 4000 Jews in Vienna at the end of 1945. For Jews, Vienna had become a place haunted by ghosts, a charnel house (Embacher, 1995a). Most of the emigrants considered refusing to return to Austria as a 'matter of character'. Despite the longing felt by many for their former homeland – at least, for their beloved landscapes and familiar *Kultur* – they frequently refused to go there even for a short visit. Others constantly shuttled between disparate existences but could no longer feel at home anywhere: 'Wavering between two worlds, there can be no return' is how the author Maria Berl-Lee ended her poem '*Wandererin zwischen zwei Welten*' (Embacher, 1995a: 113).

Austria showed little interest in the return of those who had been expelled. Aside from a few individual exceptions, no one became actively involved in repatriation efforts. The arrival of the first wave of returning exiles provided a new target for anti-Semitism. Returnees such as concentration camp survivors not only evoked guilty consciences, they were also regarded as competitors in the labour and housing markets. In Vienna, over 60,000 apartments had been 'Aryanized' (see note 1, p. 204) and many new owners were alarmed by the sudden possibility of losing their homes. With the beginning of reparations negotiations in 1952, widespread anti-Semitic prejudices were directed especially at the 'rich emigrants' who, it was said, wanted to drive Austria to the brink of ruin while living there tax-free, and who had lived the good life abroad, safe from the falling bombs, while Austrians were starving (Embacher, 1995a: 77–84). The well-known author Hilde Spiel was greeted with the following words: 'The *Frau Doktor* did the right thing by getting out. The air raids alone, … three times the entire city was ablaze!' (Spiel, 1989: 78). In 1958, the Jewish community complained bitterly that 'the press has recently been conducting a highly diversified smear campaign against emigrants … such that the very word emigrant has become a term of disparagement. The Austrians simply cannot forgive them for not waiting to be sent to the gas chambers and then not apologizing for still being alive' (Embacher, 1995a: 90).

As a broad generalization, the readiness to return from emigration abroad can be traced back, above all, to the hardships of life in the exile countries, to age and illness, to career problems and to the hoped-for return of 'Aryanized' assets. Whereas, for example, only a few (0.2 per cent) of exiles returned from the USA, there was a relatively high rate of return from Shanghai as well as Israel (Wilder-Okladek, 1970, 108).

The Viennese-born Franziska Tausig depicted the arduous life in Shanghai in her biography. Her husband failed totally to adjust to emigrant life; sinking into despair as a result of unemployment, inactivity and helplessness, he was ill from the very beginning. She, however, developed into a self-confident woman – selling homemade Viennese pastries enabled her to survive. Her husband died in Shanghai; she returned to Vienna, where her son, who had survived in England, was waiting for her (Tausig, 1987).

Palestine (after 1948, the State of Israel), shaken by crises and afflicted by wars, proved to be a difficult land of exile. The fate of the famed Viennese actress Stella Kadmon was typical of many German and Austrian Jews in Palestine. Hardly able to speak Hebrew and thus condemned to menial labour, she wanted to return as quickly as possible after the war to work in the theatre again, in her own language. Following her return, she overcame great difficulties to re-establish her own theatre. Whereas most Austrian theatres long continued to boycott controversial dramatists, her *Theater der Courage* was the venue for the Austrian premieres of works by Berthold Brecht and Jean-Paul Sartre (Mandl, 1993).

The return of art historian Hilde Zaloscer proceeded less successfully; she failed to establish herself in a scholarly career in Austria. 'So, I was not shattered by emigration to Africa; although it was often difficult to bear, it was enriching as well. The re-migration to Vienna was what broke my spirit' (Zaloscer, 1987: 636). The author Elisabeth Freundlich also had a hard time re-establishing herself in Vienna. 'If I had known the extent of the difficulties with which I would have to struggle after my return, perhaps I would not have been able to summon the courage to undertake that step' (Freundlich, 1992: 142). Among the things she brought back with her were the novel *Der Seelenvogel* and two short stories. Nevertheless, recognition as a writer in Austria was long denied her, and it was not until 1986, on the occasion of her eightieth birthday, that this novel was published (Freundlich, 1992: 175).

Return for the sake of the husband

Despite all the tragedies, expulsion did help women to achieve a certain level of emancipation. Whereas a man frequently lost his identity as a result of persecution and exclusion from his chosen career, women often proved to be capable of tireless efforts in organizing the departure and negotiating with Nazi officials. In many cases, they made it possible, frequently at the very last minute, for their husbands to escape sentencing to the concentration camps (Blonder and Rattner, 1989). In exile, they readily accepted unskilled jobs and made possible the survival of their families. All of this not infrequently led to a reversal of traditional gender roles – women developed new strengths, whereas their husbands, unemployed and disoriented due to the sudden decline of their social status, could prove to be a difficult burden (Kreis, 1988; Kliner-Fruck, 1994). The Vienna-born Anna Rattner even described the time she spent in Israel as 'the seven years of plenty'. Thanks to her tireless efforts and spirit of inventiveness, she succeeded in opening a boutique in Tel Aviv featuring stylish Viennese fashions. She even experienced a rise in her social status, from lowly salesgirl in Austria to boss in Israel. She returned because her husband, who could find no work in Israel, could not stand this situation. 'It's a big problem when the roles in a marriage are reversed, when the man isn't the boss anymore' (Blonder and Rattner, 1989).

Like Anna Rattner, other women – often counter to their own interests and needs – returned for the sake of their husbands (Embacher, 1995b). One resident of the Jewish Home for the Aged in Vienna described her exile in Shanghai and in the USA, where she had actually been quite happy, whereas her husband, who passionately loved Vienna, wanted to go back. 'I would have gladly stayed in America! But in our marriage, there weren't any debates. That was what my husband wanted, and so we came back right after the end of the war' (*Gemeinde*, 2/1984: 23). F. Fischer had originally emigrated from Poland to Vienna to attend art school. And she had actually felt more comfortable in London. She could not adapt to life in post-war Vienna; it felt eerie to her to live among murderers. She had followed her husband, who was offered his former job as a manager in the public transport system and longed to get back to his former orderly life. 'My husband wanted to return. That's the way it goes when you're married, plus a little bit foolish and you don't put up any resistance … It was very difficult. Despite the fact that we were very happy, it almost ended up in a separation.' She regards her life as a failure and would have accomplished much more if she had not come back. She feels that she was 'defrauded of her life' (*AUF*, Special Edition 1988).

Back to the Party

Jewish Socialists and Communists, many of whom had been summoned by their parties to return and to take part in the reconstruction of a new, democratic and perhaps socialist Austria, constituted a very special group of exiles. Many had already in the 1920s and 1930s exchanged their Jewish identity for a Communist or Socialist one. Faith in their respective political ideologies became a sort of new religion. Even in the aftermath of the Shoah, many resisted the slightest acknowledgment of a Jewish identity. They did not want to be relegated to a Jewish ghetto, but rather to be recognized and accepted as Austrians. Whereas the majority of those who had been driven out or were victims of the concentration camps refused to return to the land which had so brutally expelled them, many of those who had been politically persecuted never lost sight of Austria and refused to accept their expulsion as final. Feelings of political belonging could also constitute an essential factor influencing women to return to Austria (Embacher, 1989, 1995a: 119–23).

Left-wing Jewish men and women frequently describe the year 1934 as the major turning point in their lives. With the establishment of the Austro-Fascist dictatorship and the outlawing of their parties, the Communists (Kommunistische Partei Österreichs, KPÖ) and the Social Democrats (Sozialdemokratische Partei Österreichs, SPÖ), they felt politically homeless. Their hopes for a better future had proved to be illusory. Left-wing intellectuals, especially the Jews among them, were excluded from many professions and careers even before 1938. Women, moreover, were affected by the laws passed in 1933–34, which meant that the wife of a two-income couple lost her job. Many pioneering female students could no longer turn their studies into a profession (Embacher, 1989). Hilde Spiel wrote that she left Austria in 1936 out of disgust for a system she wanted nothing to do with (Spiel, Interview on ORF, 12.10.1989, Ö1, *Im Gespräch*). Women also left Austria to fight against Franco in Spain or to seek a better future in the Soviet Union. Several of them fell victim to the Stalinist purges. Eugenia Quittner, a committed Communist who was unable to find a satisfactory job after completing her studies in constitutional law, emigrated with her husband to the Soviet Union, a move which at the time constituted 'a trip to paradise, to the land of our longings and our dreams'. After the war, she and her child were able to return to Vienna with the help of the KPÖ; her husband had fallen victim to the 'Stalinist purges' (Quittner, 1971; also see Puhm, 1990).

After the war, a few hundred women came back from England, France, Belgium and the Soviet Union, where several Austrian resistance groups had formed. Mostly following the arrest of many male comrades, women had assumed key functions in those countries and campaigned for a 'free Austria'. Above all in England, the Communist-dominated 'Free Austrian Movement' offered exiles a type of 'home away from home'. Political speeches and discussions, as well as Austrian food, Viennese pastries and coffee, and performances of Austrian music helped many to get over homesickness, so that even apolitical individuals developed sympathetic feelings for Communism (Zalud, 1995). In France and Belgium, a group of younger women went about trying to make the acquaintance of members of the *Wehrmacht* in an attempt to win them over to the cause. With the help of these soldiers, anti-Fascist propaganda (handbills and newspapers) was smuggled onto army bases and distributed. In the case of this *Mädelarbeit*,[5] women bore the entire burden of the resistance operation. For many women and girls who were active in the Resistance movement in Belgium and France, these activities ended in betrayal, arrest and imprisonment in concentration camps – torture and death were the consequences (interview with Gundl Herrnstadt, Vienna 1990). As a result of insensitivity or bureaucratic heavy-handedness, all those who had left Austria before 1938, usually due to the anti-Semitic climate or the unpromising outlook for the future, are still denied 'indemnification payments'.

Despite the difficulties, and in contrast to those who had been persecuted because of their Jewish descent alone, these political exiles found acceptance within a community and could re-establish connections in familiar surroundings. For these reasons, they returned above all to 'their' party, to 'Red Vienna', filled with the hope of being able to carry on these personal relationships and the political work in which they had been active prior to 1938 (Reinprecht, 1992).

'Perhaps it was different in my case because I had had a second home in the Party, because Socialism led to the formation of strong fraternal bonds ... One big family gathered together, reminisced, discussed, planned. And I was once again a member of this family' was how the Socialist Stella Klein-Löw described her return. She would have been ashamed to have then 'left Austria and Socialism in the lurch' (1980: 166).

In return, they were prepared to accept numerous contradictions and to shut their eyes to blatant anti-Semitism. Nevertheless, the confrontation with the realities of post-war Austria meant bitter disappointments for resistance fighters and above all for Communists. Austrians did not feel that they had been liberated but rather occupied once again, and by 1948 at the latest, with the beginning of the Cold War, the Austrian Resistance movement was swept under the carpet. In the wake of the first post-war elections, the KPÖ had sunk into political insignificance. In 1968, after the Soviet Union had invaded Czechoslovakia, a majority of the Jewish returnees and concentration camp survivors resigned from the KPÖ or were expelled from the Party.

Even women who had risked their lives abroad or in the Resistance were not rewarded with significant political functions by the SPÖ and the KPÖ after 1945; mostly they accepted being shunted aside to do 'women's work' and assumed responsibility for 'social questions'. But obviously women returned to Austria with far fewer expectations than their male comrades, many of whom hoped to be rewarded for their efforts. Indeed, the long duration of the Nazi domination and the war, along with the additional threat their Jewish descent posed to their existence, forced them to lay aside any hopes for a 'normal woman's life'. Only a very few had children during this period. Plans for the future, including the realization of a portion of their female identity, had to be postponed. Relationships and marriages were torn apart. In many lands of exile, living with small children would have been too dangerous – indeed, almost impossible – and women were forced to postpone starting a family. In England, for example, the KPÖ decreed a ban on children for all active members (Zalud, 1995: 46), although this was certainly not observed in all cases. One woman described how she long harboured a sense of guilt with respect to the Party, since she had given birth during her exile in England. She attempted to clear her conscience by means of a particularly high level of political involvement which, on the other hand, brought forth bitter recriminations from her daughter (interview with F.G., Vienna, 1990).

Female re-emigrants also longed for 'normality,' for a family and children, and among the things they overlooked in the course of this were their own careers. Most women resigned themselves thereby to their traditional role. 'We both wished to study and then to have children. My husband ultimately earned two doctoral degrees, and I raised two children' Gundl Herrnstadt remarked rather cynically in an interview (interview with G.H., Vienna, 1990).

The end of all illusions?

To live as a Jew (or as a non-Jewish victim) in Austria after the Shoah meant looking away, repressing one's own emotions and constructing one's own illusions which, nevertheless, continually threatened to collapse. Even those who actively participated in building a new Austria had to maintain a separation between those who had been expelled and those who had remained. *There's No Going Home* was the title Hilde Zaloscer gave to her autobiography (1988).

Despite their concerted efforts toward assimilation, returnees and camp survivors lived in (often unconscious) isolation from non-Jewish society. Their circle of friends consisted of like-minded individuals, men and women who had shared similar experiences. 'I got together only with our people' said a woman who had returned from exile in Moscow. In response to a specific inquiry about what she meant by 'our', she indicated that she meant not all Communists, but rather Communists of Jewish descent. One of her Party comrades expressed a similar sentiment. In response to the question of whether she had been aware of anti-Semitism in the KPÖ, she answered, 'No, but we were mainly together with those who had returned from England. Almost everyone in our section had come from England' (Embacher, 1995a: 211).

In order to avoid being exposed to anti-Semitism, it was better to steer clear of certain bars, inns and *Heurigen* (wine-taverns, typical of Vienna). As Gertrude Putschin put it, certain feelings of mistrust were raised by contacts with non-Jews. Upon meeting such people for the first time, they were initially subjected to a sort of test. 'Was this one a Nazi or not? What, really, was their attitude: well-meaning, merely tolerant or were they anti-Semites? It was very difficult. One really had to be careful to avoid being caught in some way in an unpleasant bind' (DÖW, 1992: 689).

For many survivors, the bitter confrontation surrounding the presidential election of Kurt Waldheim in 1986 reopened old wounds.[6] An especially tragic situation proved to be that of individuals who had been politically persecuted and, although they had broken with the KPÖ, still believed in a humane form of Communism or Socialism. They suffered at the outbreaks of anti-Semitism which they had prematurely deemed impossible, and were also deeply hurt by the collapse of the political system in Eastern Europe. As one interview partner said: 'I have the feeling that my whole life was in vain, that I fought for the wrong cause' (interview with Hilde Koplenig, Vienna, 1990). Disappointed by political developments in Austria and by the many errors committed by 'their' parties, some re-emigrants consider their return – and even their very lives – to be a failure.

Despite it all, many former exiles stress the fact that they have never regretted their return to Austria and could never imagine another country as their homeland. Especially in old age, life in Vienna seems to many to be more pleasant and above all more secure than in New York or Tel Aviv. Many concentration camp survivors and re-emigrants struggle against being reduced to the role of the eternal victim. As psychologist Dorit Bader-Whiteman has emphasized, a large number of those driven out do indeed feel like society's outsiders; on the other hand, they also refuse to regard themselves as eternal victims. Many display extremely strong feelings of self-worth precisely because of their personal victory over tremendous adversity (Bader-Whiteman, 1993). Elisabeth Freundlich also brought out the positive side of her return. She was proud of the person she had become as a result of her experiences during emigration, and the person she remains to this day – a politically conscious, but also independent-minded, author (Kreis, 1988: 73). As another re-emigrant put it ironically: 'We're grateful to the *Führer*. If we had remained at home, we wouldn't have amounted to anything' (Kannonier, 1989: 74).

Notes

1. 'Aryanization' means that Jews were forced to sell their property, but they were not permitted to take the money out of the bank. In Vienna Jewish people were shocked by 'wild' rampages of the Austrian populace and the vicious 'Aryanizations' which broke out immediately after the *Anschluß*.

2. An explanation for this phenomenon can be found in the fact that feminist scholars have wanted to write a history of women during the time of National Socialism with which they themselves could identify. For far too long they have proceeded from the assumption of German and Austrian woman as eternal victim, so that not only the problematic subject of complicity by women or the phenomenon of female anti-Semitism but also the history of Jewish women, of the 'true' victims, had to be left out of consideration (Baader, 1991).

3. The Austrian State's victim welfare system (*Opferfürsorgegesetz*) was based on the so-called *Opferthese* which regarded Austria as the first victim of Nazi Germany. Therefore Austria refused to pay restitution (*Wiedergutmachung*). In 1945 only politically persecuted victims could benefit from special care and treatment programmes; even Jews had to fight for those benefits.

4. Women with children under age 16 were automatically sent to the gas chambers with their children; giving birth to a child also meant death for both of them.

5. This refers to Austrian women in the French and Belgian Resistance who dated soldiers from the Wehrmacht and tried to win them over to work for the Resistance. It was very dangerous work – the soldiers were more interested in sex than in politics, and some of the women were caught and sent to Auschwitz.

6. During the 1986 presidential election campaign, Kurt Waldheim, the candidate of the Österreichische Volkspartei – ÖVP (People's Party), was charged by the World Jewish Congress with having concealed details of his Nazi past. These attacks from abroad triggered a bitter anti-Semitic reaction in Austria.

References and Further Reading

AUF – Eine Frauenzeitschrift, 'Frauen berichten über ihr Leben in der Zeit von 1934 bis 1945'. Sonderheft zum Bedenkjahr 1988.

Baader, M. (1991) 'Unschuldsrituale in der Frauenforschung zum Nationalsozialismus.' *Babylon* 9, 140–5.

Bader-Whiteman, D. (1993) *The Uprooted: A Hitler Legacy*. New York: Insight Books.

Bailer, B. (1993) *Wiedergutmachung kein Thema: Österreich und die Opfer des Nationalsozialismus*. Wien: Löcker.

Bar-On, D. (1997) '*Da ist etwas kaputtgegangen an den Wurzeln ...*': *Identitätsformation deutscher und israelischer Jugendlicher im Schatten des Holocaust*. Frankfurt am Main: Campus Verlag.

Berger, K. *et al.* (1985) *Der Himmel ist blau. Kann sein: Frauen im Widerstand. Österreich 1938–1945*. Wien: Promedia.

Berger, K. *et al.* (1987) *Ich geb Dir einen Mantel, daß Du ihn noch in Freiheit tragen kannst*. Wien: Promedia.

Bischof, G. (1993) 'Die Instrumentalisierung der Moskauer Erklärung nach dem 2. Weltkrieg'. *Zeitgeschichte*, 11/12, 345–66.

Blonder, L. and Rattner, A. (1989) *1938 – Zuflucht Palästina* Bearbeitet und eingeleitet von Helga Embacher. Wien-Salzburg: Geyer.

Bruha, A. (1984) *Ich war keine Heldin.* Wien-München-Zürich: Europaverlag.

Dokumentationsarchiv des österreichischen Widerstandes (DÖW) (Hed) (1992) *Jüdische Schicksale, Berichte von Verfolgten.* Wien: Österreichischer Bundesverlag.

Embacher, H. (1989) 'Außenseiterinnen: bürgerlich, jüdisch, intellektuell – links'. *L'Homme: Zeitschrift für feministische Geschichtswissenschaft,* 2, 57–76.

Embacher, H. (1995a) *Neubeginn ohne Illusionen: Juden in Österreich nach 1945.* Wien: Picus.

Embacher, H. (1995b) ' "Was. Sie san wieder da? Und mir ham glaubt, Sie san verbrennt wurdn" – Zur Rückkehr von Vertriebenen'. *Aschkenas,* 5, 79–106.

Embacher, H. (1995c) 'Unwillkommen? Zur Rückkehr von Emigrantinnen und Überlebenden aus den Konzentrations- und Vernichtungslagern'. *Frauenleben 1945: Kriegsende in Wien.* Katalog zur 105. Sonderausstellung des Historischen Museums der Stadt Wien: Eigenverlag, pp. 99–114.

Embacher, H. (1996) 'Zur Problematik der weiblichen Häftlingsgesellschaft im KZ'. In Robert Streibel and Hans Schafranek (eds), *Strategie des Überlebens: Häftlingsgesellschaften im KZ und GULAG.* Wien: Picus, pp. 145–67.

Embacher, H. and Margit, R. (1990) 'Partisanin aus christliche Nächstenliebe'. In Rudolf G. Ardelt *et al.* (eds), *Arbeiterschaft und Nationalsozialismus in Österreich.* Wien-Zürich: Europaverlag, pp. 553–79.

Fénelon, F. (1981) *Das Mädchenorchester in Auschwitz.* München: DTV.

Freundlich, E. (1992) *Die fahrenden Jahre: Erinnerungen.* Salzburg: Otto Müller.

Fritz, M. (1986) *Essig gegen den Durst.* Wien: Verlag für Gesellschaftskritik.

Füllberg-Stolberg, C. *et al.* (eds) (1994) *Frauen in Konzentrationslagern: Bergen-Belsen, Ravensbrück.* Bremen: Edition Temmen.

Hass, A. (1990) *In the Shadow of the Holocaust: The Second Generation.* Ithaca: Cornell University Press.

Jursa, H. and Fritz, M. (1984) *Es lebe das Leben: Tage nach Ravensbrück.* Wien: Verlag für Gesellschaftskritik.

Kannonier, W. (1989) *Zwischen Flucht und Selbstbehauptung: Frauen – Leben im Exil.* Linz: Universitätsverlag Rudolf Trauner.

Klein-Löw, S. (1980) *Erinnerungen.* Wien: Jugend und Volk.

Kliner-Fruck, M. (1994) *'Es ging ja ums Überleben': Jüdische Frauen zwischen Nazi-Deutschland, Emigration nach Palästina und ihrer Rückkehr.* Frankfurt: Campus.

Klüger, R. (1992), *Weiter leben. Eine Jugend.* Göttingen: Wallstein.

Kreis, G. (1988) *Frauen im Exil: Dichtung und Wirklichkeit.* Darmstadt: Luchterhand.

Maislinger, A. and Riedler, A. (1986) *Keine gebrochenen Frauen.* Videofilm.

Mandl, H. (1993) *Cabarett und Courage. Stella Kadmon: eine Biographie.* Wien: WUV-Universitätsverlag.

Milton, S. (1984) 'Deutsche und deutsch-jüdische Frauen als Verfolgte des NS-Staates'. *Dachauer Hefte,* 3, 3–20.

Nahor, Simha (1986) *Krankengymnastin in Auschwitz: Aufzeichnungen des Häftlings Nr. 80574.*

Puhm, R. (1990) *Eine Trennung in Gorki.* Wien: Verlag für Gesellschaftskritik.

Quack, S. (1995) *Zuflucht Amerika. Zur Sozialgeschichte der Emigration deutsch-jüdischer Frauen in den USA 1933–1945.* Bonn: Dietz.

Quittner, E. (1971) *Weiter Weg nach Krasnogorsk: Schicksalsbericht einer Frau.* Wien: Europaverlag.

Reinprecht, C. (1992) *Zurückgekehrt: Identität und Bruch in der Biographie österreichischer Juden.* Wien: Braunmüller.

Salus, G. (1958) *Eine Frau erzählt.* Bonn: Schriftenreihe der Bundeszentrale für Heimatdienst.

Spiel, H. (1989) *Rückkehr nach Wien.* Ein Tagebuch. Frankfurt am Main: Ullstein.

Spiel, H. (1990) *Welche Welt ist meine Welt?* Hamburg: Reinbeck.

Tausig, F. (1987) *Shanghai-Passage: Flucht und Exil einer Wienerin.* Wien: Verlag für Gesellschaftskritik.

Whiteman, D. B. (1995) *Die Entwurzelten. Jüdische Lebensgeschichten nach der Flucht 1933 bis heute.* Wien: Böhlau.

Wilder-Okladek, F. (1970) *The Return Movement of Jews to Austria after the Second World War. With Special Considerations of the Return from Israel.* The Hague: Martinus Nijhoff.

Zaloscer, H. (1988) *Eine Heimkehr gibt es nicht: Ein österreichisches curriculum vitae.* Wien: Löcker.

Zaloscer, H. (1987) 'Das dreimalige Exil'. In Friedrich Stadler (ed.), *Vertriebene Vernunft I, Emigration und Exil österreichischer Wissenschaft 1930–1940.* Wien: Jugend und Volk, pp. 544–72.

Zalud, J. (1995) *Einem Arbeiter gibt man nicht die Hand: Erinnerungen einer unfreiwilligen Kommunistin.* Wien: Löcker.

Going 'Home'? Politics, Gender and Jewishness in the Return from 'Emigration' to East Germany

Barbara Einhorn

In the early years following the end of World War Two, a substantial number of German Jews returned to Germany from far-flung lands where chance and luck had landed them in their flight from Nazi Germany. This desperate exodus and forced exile is euphemistically but habitually referred to in both individual testimonies and the historiography of the period as 'emigration'. 'Emigration' implies voluntary departure from one's home country, often for economic reasons. The exodus of German Jews from Nazi Germany was a matter of survival. Although they were hounded out by a growing awareness that their lives were at stake for ethnic or, in Nazi eyes, 'racial' reasons, many of the group who returned experienced their expulsion as politically driven - they left as Marxists or Communists.

These returnees represent a distinct category of people. They differed in their determination to return from those thrown up on the shore of their former homeland by the tides of war, or those who came on foot, exhausted and ill from their imprisonment in concentration camps, with - at least in the short run - nowhere else to go. In this sense, the life histories discussed here are diametrically opposed to those of German Jews who returned to West Germany. These were people who made a deliberate decision to come back to Germany from the safe havens - England, the USA, Mexico - where they had established new lives. They came soon after the end of the war, braving hardship and horror in the devastated environment of Berlin. Most of those with whom this chapter is concerned did come to Berlin, whether or not they had come from there originally. They returned by conscious choice, determined to do their bit towards ensuring that Germany should - indeed could - never again become the source of racist persecution, genocide and war. Most of them were Marxists by persuasion, some of them Communist Party members before leaving Germany. Others became politicized during their internment on the Isle of Man (Erika Herzfeld), through classes held at the German Cultural Association in London, via discussion groups in the Free German Youth movement (Ursel Herzberg), or through their professionally linked experiences of social injustice in the USA (Ingeborg Rapoport). Their decision to return was primarily a political one.

My engagement with this topic is far from being driven by dispassionate intellectual curiosity. As the daughter of German Jewish Marxist refugees from

Hitler who chose to stay in their adoptive country, New Zealand, I have a passionate desire to understand what impelled several thousand German Jewish refugees to return, of their own volition, to the country of their persecution and expulsion. Which part of their sense of self was uppermost in the decision at the time, their view of themselves as German, their Jewishness or their political identification with Communism as a liberatory ideology? How do they (re-) interpret that return now? And how far was the experience of the return marked in terms of gender?

This chapter singles out the memories of women from this group of politically motivated German Jewish returnees, who settled in the Soviet Zone of East Berlin which became, after October 1949, the capital of the German Democratic Republic (GDR). The oral testimonies stem from interviews I conducted with several women returnees in Berlin in December 1996 and December 1998.[1] I use them in combination with written testimonies to raise questions about whether the return was experienced in gender-specific ways and to what extent Jewishness played a substantive part in these women's lives. None of the women themselves saw their fate as gendered, even though they would concede that their career opportunities following the return were almost certainly far greater than those available to their peers in West Germany. Yet this favoured position derived in large part from their political status as returned Communists, rather than from post-1949 GDR state socialist policies for women's emancipation.

The chapter is concerned with the intimate interrelationship of the personal and the political in the process of identity formation against the background of the immense and repeated political and social upheavals of mid to late twentieth-century Europe. It looks at the impact of these historical shifts on personal life histories, causing a sense of dislocation, uprooting ('rootlessness'), the experience of 'not belonging' and a simultaneous longing for 'home' (*Heimat*). The group of people with whom the chapter is concerned viewed themselves in terms of a unitary identity, as Marxists or Communists. I am concerned to read the nuances of their self-presentation and to map change over time in order to ground my questions about how, for this group of women, gender articulates with ethnic and political markers of difference. The first section engages with the conceptually difficult categories of gender and Jewishness; the second explores wider issues of memory and history. I examine the life histories of these women in terms of three major turning points: Nazism with its externally imposed categorization as Jews which forced their exile in the 1930s; their identification with Communist aspirations motivating their return in the late 1940s; and the end of state socialism and its aftermath for them in the 1990s. In this way, the chapter illustrates how three major ideologically driven upheavals of twentieth-century European history – fascism, socialism and the end of the Cold War – have influenced the lives of individual women (and men), an impact which in turn subtly shifts and alters personal memories of past lived experiences.

The third section interrogates the women's decision to return, before describing their early impressions of life back in Berlin. The way these women saw things in the period under consideration is contrasted in the conclusion with their post-1990 re-evaluations in the light of the Fall of the Wall and German unification. What is interesting for me as a researcher is that the return exhibits some clearly gendered aspects, yet it was not something which was in the consciousness of the women or indeed in the culture during the early post-war period. Even looking back from the perspective of fifty years after the return and a culture in which gender features much more explicitly, few returnees recognize gender as having coloured their experiences.

Gender and Jewishness as categories of analysis

It is only recently that gender as a category of analysis has featured in studies of the Shoah.[2] Earlier, historians had acted on the assumption that since 'the Final Solution to the Jewish Question' targeted men, women and children for elimination, it was Jewishness rather than other markers of difference such as gender, age, sexual orientation, able-bodiedness, or political affiliation which was the primary identifier. This explains why 'most perspectives on the Holocaust have been gender-neutral', leading the historian Joan Ringelheim (1998: 344; 1997: 20) to remark further that 'a line divides what is considered peculiar or specific to women from what has been designated as the proper collective memory of, or narrative about, the Holocaust', with the result that 'there is a split between genocide and gender in the memories of witnesses and the historical reconstruction of researchers'.

But even Jewishness was not a unitary or simply established category. The Nazis elaborated degrees of Jewishness. For many Jews themselves the issue was and is far from simple, as Erika Herzfeld recalls. On encountering anti-Semitic insults on her very first day at school, she ran to her mother and asked, 'Mummy, what are Jews?' She reflects from the hindsight of 1996 on her mother's attempts to explain this to a 6-year-old: 'It's a very difficult question to answer, even today. If one observes the Jewish religion, then fine, one is Jewish, but if one isn't religious …' Many non-religious German Jews who considered themselves assimilated regarded themselves primarily as Germans, among them those who were politically committed to Marxist values. Thus they felt that their Jewish identity was not self-elected but externally imposed. Volker Dahm writes: 'One was a Jew, whether one liked it or not, one was thrown back onto a form of existence which one hardly knew and indeed had always regarded as very backward' (Dahm, 1993: 78). This involuntary identification with a minority ethnic group selected for extermination made 'emigration' a necessity rather than a matter of choice. Erika Herzfeld recalls: 'So I emigrated to England in 1939. I didn't want to emigrate; I always said, if the Nazis tell me I'm not a German, that makes me even more German … But the pogrom in 1938 made a huge impression on me; that was a dreadful business; I saw terrible things; it was a turning point in my life.'

It was their political rather than ethnic marking as 'Other' which led Communist writers like Anna Seghers to flee in 1933, when her books were being burned. She saw herself as having been forced into exile because of her Communist Party membership, not because she was endangered as being of Jewish origin (Zehl-Romero, 1993). Indeed it was through her political affiliation rather than any cultural, ethnic or imposed 'racial' identity that she defined herself (Einhorn, 1997a, b). This is true for many Marxist German Jews, not only those who returned after the war. They understood themselves as Communist or Marxist first, and as Jewish last if at all, at least until after 1989. Nor would gender have seemed to most of them a primary source of self-definition.

Despite the fact that the Nazis targeted politicals (mainly men) and male Jews first, Joan Ringelheim points out that 'this was one of the rare historical moments when women and children were consciously and explicitly sentenced to death in at least equal measure to men' (Ringelheim, 1997: 21). Moreover, in the later phases of National Socialism, women were targeted specifically in their reproductive role (see Lentin, Chapter 13). For the Nazis, if not for their female victims, gender was significant and thus an important factor in shaping Jewish experiences of the Shoah. My question in this chapter is to what extent gender was also a factor in experiences of that return from exile, specifically in the memories of that return narrated fifty years afterwards.

Memory and history

In exploring the motivations for returning to Germany from 'emigration' and returnees' recollections of and later reflections on this experience, I am relying heavily on the oral testimonies of several women whom I interviewed in Berlin in December 1996 and December 1998. In thus privileging 'women's own accounts of their lives as primary documents' (Lentin, 1997: 5) I am following much earlier feminist scholarship which in my view preceded the establishment of oral history as a discipline. Yet this practice raises questions about the role of memory in retrospective narratives of lived experience. Oral historians are well aware of the way that experience is subjectively coloured in memory. Cathy Gelbin, building on the work of Gabriele Rosenthal, speaks of three levels of life history – of actual past events, of their subjective experiencing and interpretation, of their reworking in retrospect as narrative (Gelbin, 1998: 224–5). The level of narrative reconstruction (in the case of my interviewees from the vantage point of fifty years after the return) is itself further influenced by the presence and input of the interviewer. The question of gender is a case in point, since it is here that a discrepancy emerged between the way my interviewees constructed their past selves and my own interest in the factor of gender as an oral historian from a different era, a different generation and a different culture.

Writing of the historical significance of oral testimonies, Luisa Passerini (1987: 8) pays 'particular attention … not only to the content of their memories but also to the form which those memories take; that is to say, to the cultural and symbolic import of their stories' and asserts that 'to respect memory also means letting it organise the story according to the subject's order of priorities'. In relation to his oral history interrogations of the ANZAC legend in Australia, Alistair Thomson (1994: 5, 8) notes the way 'subjective identification works by linking personal experiences and emotions with public meanings'. He constructs a theory of 'composure' by which people arrange and interpret their memories, on the one hand 'using the public languages and meanings of our culture' and on the other composing 'memories that help us to feel relatively comfortable with our lives and identities'. I would argue that these two processes are inextricably linked, echoing Ronald Fraser's view 'that memory is most reliable when personal and political events overlap in periods of social crisis' (Fraser, quoted in Passerini, 1987: 21).

For the women I interviewed, subsequent historical turning points may well have caused them to reconfigure or 'recompose' their memories of the return in order to be able to continue to function as self-constructed political subjects. In his analysis of the paradox whereby West Germany's 'public memory of the Holocaust' commemorated its Jewish victims, while East Germany constructed an anti-fascist pre-history which excluded public acknowledgement of Jewish, as opposed to Communist, victims of fascism, Jeffrey Herf (1997: 2) writes of 'how past beliefs and contemporaneous political interests' shaped the diametrically opposed narratives of the Nazi past which developed during (and in my view as an integral ingredient in) the Cold War East–West confrontation. For the returnees to East Germany, then, their Jewishness was, during the first post-war decade at least, doubly subordinated: subjectively, through their self-identification with a politically motivated return; and objectively, in the official political discourse of anti-fascism. Gender was even further down the line as a conscious point of identification for the returnees.

If political beliefs shape narratives of the past, conversely lived experience can weaken or dull political ideals. For these women returnees, Stalinist anti-Semitism tarnished (at least as seen from the 1990s, if not as experienced in the 1950s) the idealistic hopes with which they had returned. Thus memory itself may be seen as compromised by, or at risk in, the course of history.[3] The memories of the women I interviewed about their return from exile are very clearly shaped by two cataclysmic and decisive historical turning points: on the one hand, the dual push/ pull of the end of the war in 1945 and the early days of the Cold War in the 1950s which both enabled and constrained their return; on the other, the end of the socialist experiment in 1989 and German unification in 1990 which coloured and helped to 'compose' their narration of this earlier period.

Three decisive historical 'moments' forced fundamental life changes upon these women – the Nazis' programme of exterminating people of Jewish origin, which drove them out of their German homeland in the 1930s; the end of World War Two which motivated their return between 1946 and 1952; the Fall of the Wall in 1989 and unification[4] of Germany in 1990 leading some of them to review their primary political identification. These dramatic upheavals during the trajectory of the women's life histories make their subsequent narrative 'composure' a historically rather than a purely personally driven process, involuntarily necessary rather than necessarily the result of subjective choice. It is noteworthy that although gender appears to me as a researcher to have played a role in their experiences, it remains absent from most of their narratives, in both personal recollections and political evaluations of these historical turning points.

Returning to Berlin: a difficult decision

The motivation behind the decision to return appears at first glance to have been both uniform and uncomplicated in its origins: the German Communist Party in exile (KPD, *Kommunistische Partei Deutschlands*) required this commitment from anti-fascists. Marion Einhorn says: 'My decision to return wasn't taken until the end of 1945 at the earliest. But by the time I was admitted as a member of the KPD in January 1946, the die was cast; a declaration of intent to return was a precondition for Party membership' (Einhorn, in Adam, 1987: 455). Not only the Communist Party, but also the FDJ (*Freie Deutsche Jugend*, Free German Youth) and the German Cultural Association (*Deutscher Kulturbund*) in England 'orientated us for a return. Their thought was: 'How should people who had been infected with fascist ideas be made into anti-fascists without the input of the emigrants?' says Miriam Kölling, adding 'It was considered a commitment'.

The majority of exiled German Jews never did go back to Germany from 'emigration' (Fleischhacker, 1996). But many of those who did return say, even in retrospect, that they never had any doubts about it. Sophie Marum says: 'Where else should we have gone? We left in order to return', even though she qualifies this by speaking of 'the illusion we had, that we could help to build a different Germany. This impulse was understandable, given that I was a teacher' (Marum, in Wroblewsky, 1993: 27). The revered author Anna Seghers ('our Anna' to the GDR regime) was similarly uncompromising, formulating in essays written in Paris during the 1930s a desire to re-educate corrupted and misled German youth (Seghers, 1980). Miriam Kölling states further: 'Actually the response to the question is quite simple: I wanted to come back. In that sense it wasn't a decision as such, but something I took for granted, a clear line.'

On a closer examination of life history accounts, however, it appears that the reasons for return from exile were more various, more tortuous and at times even more arbitrary, than such unquestioning political clarity suggests. And it is women rather than men who appear more able to express, at least in retrospect, the anxiety and dread which accompanied the decision. Marion Einhorn agreed only reluctantly to follow her husband Hans in his unswerving determination to return. She elicited a promise from him that they could leave again at any time the land responsible for her parents' murder and her sister's and grandmother's incarceration in concentration camps.

In some cases, such as that of the Rapoports, return was necessitated by a further political persecution, the McCarthyite hounding of known or suspected Communists in the USA at the beginning of the 1950s. Ingeborg Rapoport found coming back very difficult: she speaks of having felt more 'at home' and more accepted in the USA than she had ever felt in her native Germany. There she had not known of her half-Jewish origins until she was taunted by other children in the street. She describes the feeling of having lost her *Heimat* (homeland, sense of belonging) and her German identity through Nazism. 'Coming back was not coming back to my own country – it was actually a second emigration', in which she 'didn't come back to help Germany, but to help build socialism'. And Berlin, where she ended up, was not 'home' for her or her husband. She came from Hamburg, he from Vienna, towards which she felt he had a 'less broken relationship'. Nor was the return easy. In a macabre repeat of the late 1930s when Jewish Germans seeking sanctuary in their flight from Nazi Germany were refused entry by country after country, once again it was a question of who would have them. For the Rapoports, the return to East Berlin was a fourth choice: the long tentacles of the CIA prevented her husband taking up a position he was offered at Vienna University, no job had been found for them by a colleague of her husband's in England, and the Soviet Union had rejected them as 'Western emigrants', 'which saved our lives at that time' given subsequent revelations about Stalinist purges. Ingeborg Rapoport says she 'had great hesitations about coming back', but the emerging Cold War and her husband's inability to find work elsewhere made the decision for them.

Recent scholarship suggests that women were quicker, because of their everyday involvement in the community, to read the signals of danger posed by

National Socialism's anti-Semitic policies (Kaplan, 1998a, b). On the evidence of memoirs and documents, Marion Kaplan argues that women were often the driving force behind the ultimate decision to 'emigrate'. She cites Wyden (1992: 47) who concludes from his own family experience that 'they seemed to be less rigid, less cautious, more confident of their ability to flourish on new turf' (quoted in Kaplan, 1998b: 45). Conversely, however, when it came to the decision to return to Germany from 'emigration', I argue that women were often more reluctant than men precisely because they failed to subsume the personal under the political in the way many male political returnees succeeded in doing.

When recalling the decision to come back, most women I interviewed spoke in terms of their family situation rather than, or as well as, the political impetus. Erika Herzfeld emigrated alone as an 18-year-old in 1939, and returned in 1947 aged 26. From May 1945 until autumn 1946 she worked for the Jewish Refugee Committee in London, charged with the unenviable task of telling people about the murder of their relatives in extermination camps. From this committee she heard that her parents and younger twin sisters had been deported from Berlin to the Litzmannstadt (Lódz) ghetto in January 1941, that one of her grandmothers had died in a cattle wagon bound for Riga in January 1942, and that the other was murdered in a Breslau (Wroclaw) old people's home at the age of 95. She still feels the agony she experienced then: 'Deciding to go back wasn't easy at all, for I had every reason to assume that all of my family ... had been gruesomely murdered by the Nazis ... I had to consider the fact that I might have to deal with people in Germany who had played a part in this' (Herzfeld, in Adam 1987: 479–80). Ahead of her lay uncertainty and dread, added to which she found it hard to leave her life in England behind.

> For a long time I didn't want to go back – I had felt good about living in England, had good contacts with English people and spoke good English ... but the thing is: I grew up in Germany, with Goethe, Schiller and Lessing, the German landscape – I must tell you, when I got back to Germany and saw my first fir trees, that's when I felt I was somehow back home, I had missed the forests (of course I had been in Yorkshire, where there is very little forest). But what tipped the balance was that I wanted to help ensure that it never happened again ... and that a more just society was constructed here, that's what I wanted to do my bit towards – but I found it *extremely* hard to decide.

It is noteworthy how many returnees speak, as Erika Herzfeld does, of *Heimat*, of homesickness for the landscape and culture of Germany as a factor in their return.

Nevertheless women's accounts betray far more explicit acknowledgement of the emotionally complicated nature of the decision. Men both at the time and in retrospect seem to subsume the personal to the political, partly because in the context of the GDR (even after its demise), they perceived the political as legitimating their life's endeavours. Sonja Miltenberger cites the example of Julius G., who in his testimony constructs a purely political autobiography. He almost omits to mention that his entire family was murdered by the Nazis (Miltenberger, 1998; see also Günter Eiche, in Gelbin, 1998).

Similarly, men's accounts of life in the early days after the return focus on the political and professional almost to the exclusion of the personal and familial. They manage to overlook the devastation and deprivation, focusing on the challenges of work responsibilities rather than the difficulties of finding food or the inadequate housing. Hans Lichtenstein recalls that 'in those early years of antifascist-democratic reconstruction, I was so bursting with the revolutionary fervour that inspired me every single day, and so busy with the interesting challenges I was asked to meet that in contrast external living conditions took a back seat for me, at least they weren't decisive' (Lichtenstein in Adam, 1987: 458). One can only wonder whether his wife shared this view, struggling with four small children in the grim conditions of post-war Berlin.

Many women returned only at the instigation of their husbands, overcoming considerable inner reluctance and fear to face the perpetrators of the murder of their family members. Hilde Eisler says of the return: '[At the end of the war] I heard about the concentration camps. My parents and my sister were killed there, and many of my relatives … It was very difficult [then] for me to go back … I had no choice. I had no choice because, first, I was married and my husband definitely wanted to return – he was a politician' (Eisler, in Borneman and Peck, 1995: 88, 93). The fact that the Party required it seems to have made the men feel there was no question but that they would return. But for the women, the political mission just about tipped the balance, outweighing the personal only through the gendered mediation of their subordinate role in decision-making within their relationships or, in the case of women who returned alone, through the moral support of and sense of solidarity with their surrogate family of other FDJ or Communist Party members.

Early days in Berlin, 1946–1953

The first large wave of politically organized German returnees arrived in Berlin in September 1946. The writer Anna Seghers arrived in October 1947 after seven years in France and seven years in Mexico. She speaks of encountering people 'internally as devastated as their cities were reduced to rubble externally' and of her revulsion at their excuses, every one of them proffering 'an alibi in his outstretched hand' (interview with Delbert Clark of the *New York Times*, April 1947, in Seghers and Herzfelde, 1985: 11). No one, they implied, had wanted what happened, nor had they known about it at the time. Coming back left Seghers feeling, as she wrote to her old friend Georg Lukacs in 1948, that she had 'arrived back in the Ice Age'; to someone coming from exile, far from a return 'home', 'Germany often appears more foreign than do foreign countries' (Seghers quoted in Wagner *et al.*, 1994: 67, 169).

Ingeborg Rapoport, who had begun her training as a doctor in Hamburg before emigrating to the USA, gives a graphic description of arriving at Friedrichstraße Station in February 1952 with four children, suitcases and a husband who is stunned at the news that he is to be Director of the Institute for Physical Chemistry at the Humboldt University, rather than Head of a Blood Research Institute as he had been led to expect (Rapoport, 1997: 263). Hans Einhorn too describes his determination to become a teacher being thwarted by the Party, which had greater need of the legal training he had acquired in the Weimar Republic and hence made him Director of the Office for Labour and Wages in the Berlin City Administration. From 1948 after the formal split between the two Berlins until 1952 when he was summarily dismissed (ostensibly because of his 'Western emigration') he was President of the East Berlin Labour Court (Einhorn, in Adam, 1987: 455-6).

Dr Rapoport, like Hans Lichtenstein a parent of four children, evokes the harsh conditions of their first family accommodation back in Berlin: a fourth-floor room in the one still-standing wing of the previously prestigious Hotel Adlon, where the wind whistled through the windows and there was no hot water for washing nappies. She describes the perilous logistics of taking four small children out for a walk twice a day without a lift. She took one under each arm and ran down four floors, accompanied by the ear-piercing screams of the two left at the top; then put down the first two and went back up to fetch the others, with the loud cries now coming from the bottom of the stairs rather than the top. Her husband seemed at first oblivious to these daily difficulties, absorbed as he was in his responsibilities of creating a new institute from rubble, without resources (Rapoport, 1997: 264–7).

Trude Worner writes of the difficulty of getting hold of food in the early days (in Adam, 1987: 459–60). She found that political work at the local level helped to overcome her fears in relation to the local population. Ingeborg Rapoport's participation through the Party in building a children's playground helped overcome the resistance of the local community to the influx of political returnees in the suburb to which she later moved (Rapoport, 1997: 275). It does not seem to have been the case that women returnees wanted to settle down and become full-time mothers, or indeed that they were pushed out of the workforce, as in many Western European countries at the end of the war. My interviewees seemed either to have had children already and to want to work as well, to put career first and not, ultimately, to become mothers, or to have children somewhere along the way but not to highlight this in their narratives, suggesting that they saw motherhood as an integral part of life but not its central fulfilment. Work and political commitment feature high on their list.

Many of the returnees were young and hence relatively optimistic. In addition, there was a sense in which the return paradoxically gave them the opportunity to regain their former class position. Returning emigrées, or 're-emigrants'[5] were seen as welcome additions to the new state's efforts to replace Nazis in leading positions as teachers and lawyers by recruiting rapidly educated and trained former workers and farm labourers via the ABF (*Arbeiter- und Bauernfakultät*, Workers' and Peasants' University). Education and (political) re-education were given a high priority in what was perceived as the urgent necessity of trying to shift the pernicious and perverted effects of Nazi ideology from people's consciousness. Several of the women I interviewed who as young women had gained their entry permits to England as domestics and factory workers, now were given the opportunity to study.

Marion Einhorn and Erika Herzfeld studied history at the Humboldt University from 1947. Miriam Kölling, who returned in 1949 with a BA in history from Sheffield University, joined them in 1952 in their doctoral studies. Later, these three women were among the group delegated to set up the Museum for German History in East Berlin; Erika Herzfeld was departmental head until 1956. All three later became research historians in the East Berlin Academy of Sciences. Ursel Herzberg became a judge. Ingeborg Rapoport was a renowned and respected paediatrician in the GDR. These women reached prominent positions in careers which might not have been open to them as women either in their exile 'homes' or in West Germany.

Not all activity on return was deadly earnest, politically or professionally driven. On 4 October 1947, Marion Grau and Hans Einhorn were married. The photo of them dancing at their wedding shows that there was room for celebration amidst the privations of those early years. Erika Herzfeld, a former schoolmate of Marion's, had just arrived back in East Berlin from England and inadvertently gatecrashed their wedding celebrations on a quest for information about how to gain entry to university study.

Several of the women remember the fun and exuberance of early efforts for the new country. Friendships formed in 'emigration' or during those years of study became lifelong relationships, often replacing in their closeness the families lost through war and Nazism. Not only friendships but also the Party centrally provided the 'home' which Germany no longer represented. Ingeborg Rapoport says she never became really German again after the return. 'I always said socialism is my home now'. But even with this surrogate *Heimat*, many continued to feel outsiders. Ruth Benario says that her feeling on returning from Moscow to East Berlin in 1954 that 'I don't feel like I am home at all' has persisted 'up until today. [I cannot] call Germany home [*Heimat*], I don't have a home [*Heimat*]. I am home everywhere I go ... the most important thing is that I help wherever I can' (Benario, in Borneman and Peck, 1995: 48–9).

Marion Einhorn recalled her ambivalent feelings on arrival in September 1946. On the one hand were the positive feelings of enthusiasm and solidarity with which her generation of young returnees set about building a new Germany. At the same time, she suffered dreadful fears: 'I had problems at the beginning meeting strangers on the street or on public transport. I used to ask myself whether one of them might not be the murderer of my parents – that was a feeling which made me hallucinate with visions of SA and SS hordes. The only place I felt safe and "at home" was together with Party comrades' (Marion Einhorn, in Adam, 1987: 455–7). Having dreamed of escaping the ghetto of Jewishness into the liberatory and universalist ideology of socialism, these women were consigned through forced exile and return to a Germany still dominated by fascist mentality to membership of a new but still resented minority group.

The end of the socialist 'homeland'

It is clear from the interviews that women returnees' memories have been overlaid and reshaped by the Fall of the Wall in 1989 and events since German unification in 1990. Outbreaks of neo-Nazi racist attacks, anti-Semitic abuse and the desecration of Jewish cemeteries have led many to rethink the return, have facilitated their acknowledgement of latent anti-Semitism and hence of their own Jewishness in pre-1989 East Germany. Gender perspectives too changed in the wake of German unification. Women were the first to be made redundant in the economic transformation process in East Germany and have constituted the majority of the unemployed there ever since (Einhorn, 1993, 1994, 1997c). Two social policy models collided – the GDR model of women as (full-time) workers *and* mothers being subsumed under the West German male breadwinner model (Chamberlayne, 1995; Marx Ferree, 1997).

The decision to return, made in terms of a commitment to Communism, or more simply to build a new Germany from which fascism could never again arise, has inevitably been challenged by the end of the state socialist dream in 1989. This historical turning point forced returnees to question their very sense of identity, cast in terms of an ideological rather than a national 'home', and a political and social rather than ethnic or religious belonging. Cast out of Germany in the 1930s as Jews who saw themselves as Germans committed to a world without prejudice and social injustice, they returned to East Berlin in the late 1940s as Communists intent on constructing a fairer society which would never allow persecution on grounds of imposed 'otherness'.

Several now question the decision to return, and their relationship to Germany as homeland. There is a shift in their sense of identity: even though most still identify as socialists or Communists first, several now say that they feel more Jewish again. Erika Herzfeld says 'the few Jews who remained in the GDR were in the main not religious', and 'I thought of myself very clearly primarily as a Communist. That remains true today'. For most returnees, the ideological home had replaced national belonging. Fascism shattered their sense of *Heimat* and also rendered it suspect. Ruth Benario says 'I don't feel German – I feel Jewish. I am not a German. I don't have anything in common with the whole German people. Granted, I was born here. I lived here for a long time – twenty-two years. I also came back here very consciously, but not to my homeland. I don't call anywhere my homeland. I am at home where I have people with whom I can get on' (Benario, in Borneman and Peck, 1995: 59).

For some of the women, their renewed sense of Jewishness is connected with reawakened fears of anti-Semitic persecution. Once again, it is the women who seem more likely to express these fears. Marion Einhorn found herself turning superstitiously each time she left her apartment building to see whether there were anti-Semitic graffiti painted on the wall. 'Lucky that Hans [her husband, my uncle, who died in December 1992, BE] never lived to see this,' she said. Sometimes she dreamed of, or dreaded [before her death in January 1998] a third 'emigration'. 'I'm afraid here, absolutely afraid. I couldn't deal with that again. I've told your mother [in New Zealand] about this several times; I hope it doesn't reach the point where she has an emigrant knocking on her door.' Ursel Herzberg says, 'If anywhere felt like "home" it was England,' adding in a published interview: 'Had I known how this experiment would turn out, I would probably never have come back to Germany' (Herzberg, 1996: 106). It is interesting to raise the question as to whether the memories of 'emigration' and the adoptive 'homeland' have grown rose-tinted with time and especially in the harsh light of renewed racist outbreaks. It is, further, a question suggesting further research as to whether there is a gender difference in the extent to which past memories are 're-touched' or 're-composed' in the light of subsequent historical turning points.

Certainly it is women who seem more prepared than men to look back through the lens of the rise of the neo-Nazi and radical political right in united Germany and ask themselves: Was it all worth it? Several expressed feelings similar to an Austrian Jewish woman quoted in Chapter 14 by Helga Embacher who says: 'I have the feeling my whole life was in vain, that I fought for the wrong cause'. Ingeborg Rapoport said of her return to Germany in February 1952: 'I had great hesitation in coming back, except that the GDR was of course much more attractive to me; I would never have gone to West Germany … Now I *am* there … that's what has happened to all those people who came back to the GDR from 'emigration' – they landed up where they never wanted to be'.

Cast out twice in one lifespan – driven out of their homeland in the 1930s and thrown out of their jobs and sometimes the Party in the early 1950s as a result of their 'Western emigration' – these people were and are reluctant to give up on the socialist dream which was, at the personal level, a dream of reintegration, of transcending the outsider position. It is therefore particularly painful, indeed in some cases tragic, for them to stand, after the third major disruption to their lives in 1989, with the remains of that dream in shattered fragments around their feet. Small wonder then, that many of them begin, at this late stage of their lives, to reconsider their Jewishness and to re-live the fear of and anxieties aroused by the anti-Semitism which recurs at each of these turning points. What is surprising perhaps is that although many say they feel more Jewish than they once did, none of them sees this as the primary point of identification. Despite their disillusionment with the particular form which socialism took in the GDR, all of them remain socialists, committed to a society characterized by social justice and a lack of persecution. And as far as gender is concerned, only one of them, Ingeborg Rapoport, was explicitly active during her working life in the promotion of women's rights, but she denies being a feminist, seeing that as anti-men.

Conclusion

The question remains as to whether there *is* a gendered reaction to historical turning points and social crisis: do women find it easier to re-evaluate their past lives? Are they more willing to express (or even to acknowledge) ambivalence, fear and anxiety in relation to situations of political transformation and social insecurity? It is women, apparently, who were the first to understand the necessity of flight from Nazi Germany. And it is women (Ursel Herzberg and Marion Einhorn), who spoke to me of the urge to 'emigrate' again, for the third time, in the context of German unification and the re-emergence of the far right and neo-fascist groups wreaking terror on other immigrants and asylum seekers. It is striking that while most of the women returnees emphasize, as do their male counterparts, the political motivation for returning, unlike the men they give almost equal weight to their personal reasons – *Heimat, Heimweh* – tempered by their hesitation or reservations about doing so: fear of anti-Semitism, personal loss and mourning for lost family.

Although women returnees too tend, even now, to define their sense of identity and belonging in terms of the ideology and the community of socialist values, they do not silence either personal hopes and fears for the future or the traumas and regrets of the past in the name of this commitment. In their narratives, personal biography carries equal weight to political allegiance. This would appear to illustrate a clear gender difference in both the experience of return and its re-working in the telling. In giving equal significance to the personal and the political, women failed to create a hierarchy of value, as men did, between the actively sought and passively suffered elements of their life story. At the end of life histories characterized by the major political struggles and historical upheavals of the twentieth century, the question of identity remains ambivalent and painful, but seemingly more so for women than for men. We can say, finally, that in these life histories of return from exile to East Germany, gender and ethnicity reassert themselves almost involuntarily over deliberately chosen political identities.

Acknowledgements

I am extremely grateful to Claire Duchen for her loving friendship, enduring support and encouragement as well as her incisive editorial assistance. For their helpful comments on draft versions, I wish to thank Simon Evans, Sander L. Gilman, Diane Neumaier, Glenda Sluga, and Gavin Williams. Finally, my thanks are due to my interviewees: Marion Einhorn, Ursel Herzberg, Erika Herzfeld, Miriam Kölling, and Ingeborg Rapoport, who were all generous with their time and in sharing their lives with me.

Notes

1. All translations from the taped interviews as well as from oral testimonies published in German are mine. Where no source is indicated, the quotes are taken from the taped interviews rather than published sources.

2. For a summary of the debate about whether the Holocaust or the Shoah is the most appropriate term, see Lentin (1997: 14, note 1).

3. I am indebted for this insight to Diane Neumaier.

4. In the interests of historical accuracy I prefer the term 'unification' to the more commonly used 'reunification'. Germany in its current borders did not exist before World War Two and the subsequent division of the country.

5. I take this term from Wolfgang Herzberg, author of a forthcoming study under this title.

References

Adam, Ursula (1987) 'Rückkehr nach Berlin: Aus dem britischen Exil zur Teilnahme am antifaschistisch-demokratischen Neuaufbau'. *Jahrbuch für Geschichte*, 35, 427-85.

Borneman, John and Peck, Jeffrey M. (1995) *Sojourners: The Return of German Jews and the Question of Identity*. Lincoln: University of Nebraska Press.

Chamberlayne, Prue (1995) 'Gender and the private sphere: a touchstone of misunderstanding between Eastern and Western Germany?' *Social Politics*, spring, 25-36.

Dahm, Volker (1993) 'Jüdische oder deutsche Kultur: die Suche nach Identität'. In Wolfgang Benz (ed.), *Die Juden in Deutschland 1933-1945: Leben unter nationalsozialistischer Herrschaft*. München: Beck, pp. 75-82.

Einhorn, Barbara (1993) *Cinderella Goes to Market: Citizenship, Gender and Women's Movements in East Central Europe*. London: Verso.

Einhorn, Barbara (1994) 'Women in the New Federal States after the *Wende*: the impact of unification on women's employment opportunities'. In Elizabeth Boa and Janet Wharton (eds), W*omen and the Wende: Social Effects and Cultural Reflections of the German Unification Process*. Amsterdam: Rodopi, pp. 18-29.

Einhorn, Barbara (1997a) '1947: Anna Seghers returns to Germany from exile and makes her home in East Berlin'. In Sandra L. Gilman and Jack Zipes (eds), *The Yale Companion to Jewish Writing and Thought in German Culture 1096-1996*. New Haven: Yale University Press, pp. 662-70.

Einhorn, Barbara (1997b) 'Jüdische Identität und Frauenfragen im Werk von Anna Seghers'. *Argonautenschiff: Jahrbuch der Anna Seghers Gesellschaft*, 6: 290–306.

Einhorn, Barbara (1997c) 'The impact of the transition from centrally planned to market-based economies on women's employment in East Central Europe'. In Eugenia Date-Bah (ed.), *Promoting Gender Equality at Work: Turning Vision into Reality*. London: Zed Books, pp. 59–84.

Ferree, Myra Marx (1997) 'German unification and feminist identity'. In: Joan W. Scott *et al.* (eds), *Transitions, Environments, Translations: Feminisms in International Politics*. New York: Routledge, pp. 46–55.

Fleischhacker, Alfred (ed.) (1996) *Das war unser Leben: Erinnerungen und Dokumente zur Geschichte der Freien Deutschen Jugend in Grossbritannien 1939–1946*. Berlin: Verlag Neues Leben.

Gelbin, Cathy (1998) 'Die NS-"Vergangenheitsbewältigung" in der DDR und ihre Widerspiegelung im narrativen Prozess'. In Julius H. Schoeps, Karl E. Grozinger and Gert Mattenklott (eds), *Menora: Jahrbuch fur deutsch-jüdische Geschichte*. Berlin: Philo, pp. 224–44.

Herf, Jeffrey (1997) *Divided Memory: The Nazi Past in the Two Germanys*. Cambridge, MA: Harvard University Press.

Herzberg, Ursel (1996) 'Es war nichts umsonst'. In A. Fleischhacker (ed.), *Das war unser Leben: Erinnerungen und Dokumente zur Geschichte der Freien Deutschen Jugend in Großbritannien 1939–1946*. Berlin: Verlag Neues Leben, pp. 98–107.

Herzberg, Wolfgang (1990) *Überleben heisst Erinnern: Lebensgeschichten deutscher Juden*. Berlin: Aufbau-Verlag.

Kaplan, Marion A. (1998a), *Between Dignity and Despair: Jewish Life in Nazi Germany*. New York: Oxford University Press.

Kaplan, Marion A. (1998b) 'Keeping calm and weathering the storm: Jewish women's responses to daily life in Nazi Germany 1933–1939'. In Dalia Ofer and Lenore J. Weitzman (eds), *Women in the Holocaust*. New Haven: Yale University Press, pp. 39–54.

Lentin, Ronit (1997) *Gender and Catastrophe*. London: Zed Books.

Miltenberger, Sonja (1998) 'Kommunist – Deutscher – Jude: Eine politische Biographie'. In Cathy Gelbin *et al.* (eds), *Archiv der Erinnerung: Interviews mit Überlebenden der Shoah*, Bd. 1: *Videographierte Lebenserzählungen und ihre Interpretationen* (*Archive of Memory: Interviews with Survivors of the Shoah*, vol. 1: *Videoed Life Histories and Their Interpretation*). Potsdam: Verlag für Berlin-Brandenburg, pp. 231–64.

Passerini, Luisa (1984/1987 in English) *Fascism in Popular Memory: The Cultural Experience of the Turin Working Class*. Cambridge: Cambridge University Press.

Rapoport, Ingeborg (1997) *Meine ersten drei Leben*. Berlin: Edition Ost.

Ringelheim, Joan (1997) 'Genocide and gender: a split memory'. In Ronit Lentin (ed.), *Gender and Catastrophe*. London: Zed Books, pp. 18–35.

Ringelheim, Joan (1998) 'The split between gender and the Holocaust'. In Dalia Ofer and Lenore J. Weitzman (eds), *Women in the Holocaust*. New Haven: Yale University Press, pp. 340–50.

Rosenthal, Gabriele (1995) *Erlebte und erzählte Lebensgeschichte: Gestalt und Struktur biographischer Selbstbeschreibungen*. Frankfurt am Main: Campus.

Seghers, Anna (1980) 'Vaterlandsliebe' (1935); 'Deutschland und Wir' (1941); 'Volk und Schriftsteller' (1942); 'Fürst Andrej und Raskolnikow' (1944). All in Seghers, *Essays*, 2 vols. Berlin: Aufbau-Verlag.

Seghers, Anna and Herzfelde, Wieland (1985) *Ein Briefwechsel 1939–1946*, ed. by Ursula Emmerich and Erika Pick. Berlin: Aufbau-Verlag.

Thomson, Alistair (1995) *Anzac Memories: Living with the Legend.* Melbourne: Oxford University Press.

Wagner, Frank, Emmerich, Ursula and Radvanyi, Ruth (1994) *Anna Seghers: Eine Biographie in Bildern.* Berlin: Aufbau-Verlag.

Wroblewsky, Vincent von (ed.) (1993) *Zwischen Thora und Trabant: Juden in der DDR.* Berlin: Aufbau Taschenbuch Verlag.

Wyden, P. (1992) *Stella: One Woman's True Tale of Evil, Betrayal and Survival in Hitler's Germany.* New York: Simon and Schuster.

Zehl-Romero, Christiane (1993) *Anna Seghers.* Hamburg: Rowohlt Verlag.

16 'The GI Bride': On the (De)Construction of an Austrian Post-war Stereotype[1]

Ingrid Bauer

Austria, a nation whose territory had been physically annexed by Nazi Germany in the Anschluß of 1938 and whose population had also been absorbed into the Third Reich by means of an internal mental annexation, was liberated and occupied by the Allies in 1945. For the next ten years, American, British, French and Soviet troops were stationed there. Close relationships between Occupation soldiers and the Austrian population, women in particular, were initially discouraged through highly diverse regulations instituted in the various Occupation zones (Pelz, 1996). At first, there were no restrictions on Soviet soldiers; it was not until 1947 that a general ban was placed on marriages to Austrian women. Anglo-American headquarters issued a decree forbidding fraternization on 13 May 1945; marriage was regarded as the most grievous possible violation of this regulation 'since it represents the most intimate and extreme type of fraternization and would be the most dangerous from a security standpoint.'[2] No ban on fraternization applied to the French; in contrast to the American and British authorities, they considered Austria a 'liberated' and not a 'defeated' nation. But even in the American Zone, in the everyday life of real GIs, the non-fraternization policy was frequently evaded – and, indeed, was evaded from the very start.

Multifaceted life style choices versus a one-dimensional construct

My treatment of the previously taboo historical subject of the relationships between Austrian women and Occupation soldiers begins with a flashback – directly into the experiential horizon of the year 1945: 'It was May 4th; the bombs had stopped falling, the motors were still.' As in so many other interviews conducted for the project 'Living with the Liberators: A History of the Genders in the Occupation Era,'[3] Ingeborg S. depicted the vacuum at the end of National Socialism and the war with an image of 'eerie silence.' Contained within it – unspoken – are the anxieties and hopes, fear and joy occasioned by this first major watershed, which the entry of the victorious Allied troops represented in the post-war lives of Austrian women (Berger and Holler, 1994: 174). 'And then I was struck by the fact that olive brown uniforms suddenly began to appear in place of the grey ones. They marched into our town, the Americans. And I was standing in front of our house, just curious, and all of a sudden a soldier comes up to me.'

What transpired in many memories of the initial confrontation with American GIs[4] was the lightning-fast recall – not unlike the projection of an internal film – of those stereotypical images of the enemy which Nazi propaganda had obviously deeply rooted in the subconscious minds of the populace. 'Man, they look just like us,' is how Elisabeth C. recalled her first impression. In searching for a reason for this sense of amazement, she stated 'I have no idea what kind of preconceptions I had.' Other interviewees were able to cite their biases in more concrete terms – those of an America overrun by Jews and Negroes, of man-eating Blacks, of a strange, non-Germanic world. But no matter how much 'foreignness' had been linked during the Nazi era to that which one detested, it now assumed the image of the victors and became that for which one longed. In both cases, the feelings triggered by this foreignness are 'never only "real" in the sense that they exclusively focus upon things as they are.' 'The other' remains a surface for projections: that which is conjured up in dreams is set in place of actualities, mundane realities or necessities (Petschar and Schmid, 1990: 109). In Ingeborg S.'s recollection, the 'foreign Occupation soldier' as an object of fascination assumes the proportions of an otherworldly freeze-frame image. 'He was so fine, so totally different,' was how she described her intense though short-lived post-war romance with an American GI. It began immediately after the end of the war – despite the ban on fraternization decreed by the US Army – as the then 22-year-old girl first encountered the soldier in a foreign uniform. 'I was immediately swept off my feet. I have to tell you, he was like a god. You probably can't even conceive of what I'm saying to you. But I fell in love with him because he was so handsome. He had lips like cherries, brown skin and blue-black hair.'

Subjective perception could hardly provide a more dramatic contrast to the rubble-strewn scenes of war-ravaged Austria. This suggests what the 'GI bride' life style had also been, particularly in the immediate post-war years: one of many individual endeavours to make up for the shortages, deprivation, losses and oppressive demands of wartime, and to establish a new existence – psychically, materially and with respect to one's world view – in the chaos of the post-war era (Bauer 1995, 1996a).

There were contacts, acquaintanceships and relationships between Austrian women and Occupation soldiers in all four Occupation zones.[5] According to reports in Swiss newspapers, it was particularly the dark-skinned soldiers in the Moroccan units that initially made up the majority of the French contingent who were said to have been 'the object of a certain preference' (Eisterer, 1993) on the part of the female population. Was this a case of the exoticism of that which is foreign being linked to a more or less conscious opposition to the racial teachings of National Socialism? A research project on 'Women in Post-war Vienna' also documents a phenomenon which had previously been accorded scant attention – the 'attraction which Soviet officers could exert upon women from "leftist circles"' (Bandhauer-Schöffmann and Hornung, 1991: 103). Dichotomous stereo-types such as those of 'Red Army soldiers chasing after women' versus 'the GI surrounded by *Fräuleins*', in which not only the ideological traditions of National Socialism as well as the nascent Cold War were key determinants, have masked these nuances of post-war history[6] (Baumgartner, 1993).

Nevertheless, I have developed my considerations in this chapter using above all the example of the so-called 'GI bride' because, alongside other factors, the occurrence of 'Occupation relationships' was much more common in the

American zone. The American Occupation troops were obviously capable of mobilizing fantasies and illusions to an especially high degree and, in contrast to the French, British or Soviet troops, had at their disposal much more than the image of the victor alone. They came 'with the "myth of America" in their baggage' (Wagnleitner, 1991) whose radiant power also inspired the dreams and wishes of a second generation of GI brides. These women had just entered their teens at the end of the war. They were characterized by youthful openness to the world, a mood of awakening, of a new orientation and a purposefulness which desired more than the hard-earned survival which was their lot in Austria even in the early 1950s (Bauer, 1996b). Naturally, the chief feature they associated with the 'land of unlimited possibilities' was its material prosperity, and the local ambassadors of this land, the American soldiers, were tangible embodiments of this sumptuousness.

But the GIs and their life style were also associated with other options, such as an awareness of the freedom life offered, of individuality, naturalness and informality beyond authoritative collectives and structures.

> They had something easy-going and happy about them, even in their walk. They even had different shoes than our soldiers, much lighter. Really, they radiated what you might call gaiety and a certain naiveté, not like the seriousness of our guys, who were just coming back from the war – emaciated, completely exhausted. And these others, despite the fact that they were soldiers, they were almost like boys

recalled Irmgard W. She was 14 years old at the end of the war.

Austrian women entered into a wide spectrum of erotic liaisons with American Occupation soldiers, extending from flirtations to relationships of varying lengths – short-term, for a summer, for the duration of the GI's tour of duty – to several thousand marriages (Bauer, 1996; Pelz, 1996). And there was also every possible variety of professional and semiprofessional prostitution, a thinly veiled fact of life in any army and, in particular, a part of the repertoire of the victor (Sander and Johr, 1992). This fundamental hierarchy defining the relationship between (male) liberators–occupiers and (female) liberated–occupied made a woman's establishment of contact with a GI into a balancing act between the hoped-for autonomy and the actual subjugation. The existence of thousands of children, whose American fathers soon beat a hasty retreat, is an indicator of this fact. The considerable material asymmetries separating US soldiers and Austrian women place these Occupation era contacts in a structural context within which the boundaries separating the voluntary from the forced cannot always be so clearly drawn. The historians Irene Bandhauer-Schöffmann and Ela Hornung (1991: 103) wrote that 'hunger revised social relationships' in order to concretely describe the norms and arrangements which characterized the 'Austrian post-war period', including 'prostitution in order to survive', obtaining foodstuffs by means of sexual contact. Oral history interviews show, indeed, that the boundaries between the hunger for calories and the hunger for living are highly porous.

As far as the individual women in question are concerned, their relationships to American soldiers were above all a matter of a completely personal decision based upon individual feelings, needs and interests. None of the interview subjects, each with her own individual life story, wants to be reduced to the common denominator 'GI bride'. In any case, this label which has endured with such persistence from the post-war era is less a metaphor carrying with it the realities of individual lives and more a discriminatory stereotype.

As numerous sources dealing with the history of everyday life clearly show, the GI brides were a central conversational topic in Austria, above all in the early post-war years. The highly emotionally charged nature of these discussions has not subsided. Reminiscences related by the majority of post-war Austrians – men as well as women – are also characterized by actual events being tightly interwoven with social interpretation. Women who carried on relationships with Occupation soldiers were obviously a multifaceted projection surface. And it is this aspect – the cliché and not the actual life style choice of the GI brides – that I wish to address here, beginning with the conditions from which it emerged and analysing its development in step-by-step fashion. An approach such as this enables us to attain two fundamental insights and to go far beyond a social history of women in the post-war era.

On the one hand, by analysing the excited, often irrational discussions and discourses that raged about these women, we can gain an idea of the mental structures and unconscious fears of Austrian society following the end of National Socialism and World War Two. At the same time, by examining this concrete historical scenario, we are also confronted by the principal rules of the game of the culturally imagined system of gender roles, in which 'the woman' is conceived as 'the other' and is thereby made into a receptive field for the psychic processes of displacement and projection (Bovenschen, 1980). According to my thesis, the GI brides were in an extraordinary way predestined to be receptors of such collective distortions of perception.

The social-psychological underpinnings of an aggressive critique

The next step in the process of deconstructing the cliché GI bride is to investigate two concrete historical questions: In the framework of which discourse, with which images and phantasms was this stereotype produced? Which fears and conflicts can be articulated by this construction?

The central metaphor used in connection with the GI brides is the whore who sold herself for a piece of chocolate. Derogatory labels such as 'dollar floozies', 'gold diggers', 'choco-ladies', 'Yankee tarts', 'Salzburg geishas', 'girls and women of a certain sort' and the like are merely variations on this principal attribution, which was applied regardless of the actual nature of the relationship involving a woman in post-war Austria and an American soldier. And this stigmatization of the perception and remembrance of the events of everyday life have occasionally even been reinforced by the efforts undertaken subsequently by modern historians to come to terms with it. For example, the completely unthinking, moralistic and insinuating formulation of Klaus-Jörg Ruhl in *The Occupiers and the Germans* (1980: 97): 'These were mostly shiftless women and young girls, flotsam of the age, thrown off track by the war and the post-war confusion.'

In the following section, I would like to take a look behind the facade of this one-dimensional polemic at the social-psychological underpinnings of this aggressive critique. In this process, I will point out highly distinctive patterns and lines of argumentation and treat the principal structural methods and mechanisms of this form of discrimination, which was by no means limited to verbal abuse alone. The range and the extent of validity which these private and public discourses and exclusionary practices ultimately reached, however, can be precisely defined only with great difficulty.

'The returning veterans were seething with anger …'

The discussions surrounding the GI brides were driven forward most intently by returning World War Two veterans. In the raging debates which were carried on over the course of months in the letters-to-the-editor columns of various post-war newspapers and magazines, they expressed their infuriated, shocked and bewildered opinions (Mattl, 1985). As social-historical scholarship and biographical research on post-war Austria has convincingly shown, the military defeat had a direct impact on the feelings of self-worth and the sense of male identity of many former soldiers, and left a deep and lasting impression on their patterns of perception (Mattl, 1992: 18; Bandhauer-Schöffmann and Hornung, 1990: 111). This induced them to interpret the existence of GI brides as a destruction of their last remaining position of power, as the loss of their hereditary property rights to 'their women'. And in this interpretational horizon, the Occupation had not only a military–political dimension, but a threatening sexual one as well.[7]

'The Yanks had an easy time of it,' recalled one veteran in an oral history interview. Josef W. had survived Stalingrad severely wounded. 'Even as men, they were far superior to our soldiers returning hungry and emaciated from POW camps.' His recourse to a Darwinian explanatory pattern – 'Of course, that's the way it is in nature too. When the bucks fight it out, the doe goes to the winner.' – permitted him to remain pragmatic in this competitive struggle. Embedding one's own traumatic experiences within a scenario seemingly governed by natural laws imbued them (despite the associated shock and distress) with some sort of sense. In many letters to the editor, though, raw aggression and threats of physical violence were repeatedly articulated, such as the demand for 'corporal punishment for these good-for-nothing broads' or for 'forced labour camps' for GI brides (*Pinzgauer und Pongauer Zeitung*, 2 February, 1946, p. 5). 'Such women of the streets should not be permitted to run around loose and drag the good name of our women into the dirt,' noted the *Pinzgauer und Pongauer Zeitung* of 1 June, 1946. The disparagement of the woman as a whore made bearable the personal threat which they felt as men confronted by the overpowering sexual competition from US Occupation soldiers.

The following excerpt from the novel *Marsch zwischen Hölle und Himmel* (*March between Hell and Heaven*) (author unknown), which was serialized in a weekly newspaper in the Province of Upper Austria, reflects an additional facet of the distraught mental processes of many men. The protagonist, an 'Austrian' soldier captured by the Americans, observes in the POW camp the following scene involving an American guard and an Austrian woman:

> Could that girl possibly be from here? She just keeps panting 'Johnny,' and again 'Johnny' … After all is said and done, y' know, we were out there fighting for you too, lying in the mud somewhere between Rostov and the Crimea, between Volchov and Lake Ilmen, between the Dnestr and the Danube. For you too! And nobody can take that away from us. (*Welser Zeitung*, 6 June 1950, p. 11)

This almost imploring 'And nobody can take that away from us' suggests that contacts between Austrian women and Occupation soldiers also touched upon a model of repression toward which the psychic balance of many returned veterans was oriented and upon which it relied. The actions of the GI brides – and this, of course, is equally applicable to Occupation brides in the other zones – threatened to relativize the immunizing effects of that 'morass of Austrian phraseology' (Hanisch, 1994: 437) in which participation in the Nazis' aggressive warfare had been mystified as a manly deed, as the defence of the homeland women and children. The threatened collapse of this foreground rationalization for an individual's own wartime military service inexorably confronted that man with the true dimensions of that action, with the horrors of the war and thus with the 'question of meaning' as well. As the explanatory potential of psychoanalytic understanding suggests,[8] one may, however, avoid the potentially explosive confrontation with one's self as long as one projects one's own abyss outward (Laplanche and Pontalis, 1980: 309). After 1945, such projections seem to have also been directed at the GI brides.

The constantly repeated refrain of the day was that the 'Americans' whores' were dragging Austria's 'honour' into the dirt. Attributions of this kind were not only functional in connection with injured national-patriarchal property rights in the competitive relations between returning veterans and Occupation troops. Whoever sought in this way to delegate responsibility for 'Austria's honour' – and thus the honour of Austrian men and women – to women alone, sought to rid himself of his entire share of dishonour. And potentially this had an enormous exonerative function, in light of the massive entanglement in the violence which had not only been suffered but had also been abetted by active complicity in the Nazis' reign of terror and war, though the loss of Austrian honour in this respect was rarely discussed then. The linguistic invention 'peace criminal' as an accusatory label for those 'who passively look on at the carryings-on of these fallen women' (*Pinzgauer und Pongauer Zeitung*, 5 January, 1946, p. 2) is just one additional detail in this process of playing down and eliminating the dark side of the war and *its* crimes.

'They cut the girls' braids off ...'

Not only the long-term mental consequences of the war, but also the internalized fundamental attitudes of National Socialism, continued to function below the surface after 1945 in the discourses carried on against the GI brides. This, however, did not prevent some women who had been Nazi Party members from quickly attempting to take up with functionaries of the Occupation powers in order to protect themselves or their families from criminal prosecution.[9] Basically, however, an analysis of the discussions which then took place on the subject of the GI brides makes it clear that they were continually raised to high emotional level along the particularly rigid lines of segmentation dictated by National Socialism, such as 'we and the others' and 'we and the foreigners'.

Thus, on the one hand, racist undertones were often mixed in with the malice directed at the GI brides. As one pamphlet put it: 'but just wait, there'll come a day when even the Negroes will tell you to get lost'.[10] On the other hand, one is struck by the enormity of the effort and the disproportion of the means employed in the reactions against the purportedly 'deviant' behaviour of the GI brides. Among these were anonymous threatening letters, broadsides containing bitter invective posted in public places and the derisive poems which regularly appeared in newspapers. Oral history interviews document the fact that even ancient peasant customs were from time to time converted into rituals of reprimand directed against GI brides, such as the so-called 'threshing dances' following the completion of the harvest, during which the face of a girl with an American boyfriend would be blackened with soot by village youths.

The experience with National Socialism had by no means been accompanied by an increased sensitivity toward stigmatization and ostracism of 'the other'. On the contrary, the discourse of difference continued to function, and even erupted into violent acts directed at the GI brides. Numerous oral history interviewees mention kangaroo courts such as those in Salzburg's Pongau region, although this form of vigilantism occurred only sporadically and spontaneously. It involved cutting off the hair of the GI brides, an age-old sign of disgrace. It is certainly no coincidence that a National Socialist 'model' for this publicly staged expression of abhorrence is documented in historical sources. Thus, the January 1940 Nazi Party bulletin issued by Salzburg district headquarters contained the following report from the Pongau community of St Johann:

> This member of our community … entered into a sexual relationship with a Pole. She has thereby committed an offence against the purity of German blood and the German people. The community has punished her accordingly: her hair was cut off and she was placed in the public pillory.[11]

Extrapolating the National Socialist logic manifested here, in which women were assigned special responsibility for maintenance of 'racial purity', it would also follow that contacts with 'foreign' Occupation soldiers would be interpreted as an act 'harmful to the community'.

'The mighty bulwark of purity completely demolished …'

The discourse and practices of discrimination sketched thus far seem to have been closely connected with the 'community born of necessity during the war and the post-war period' (Hanisch, 1994: 426) which gradually began to break down in 1948. Another line of argument reaches far into the 1950s and develops into one of the theoretical cornerstones of the Austrian reconstruction concept.

'My God, the ease with which these girls are to be had. Barely out of school, they are already running after the Americans. It could almost turn into another Sodom' was a 1945 entry in the parish chronicle of a small village. Similar assertions in sermons, diocesan pastoral letters and the Catholic–conservative press produced a general climate in which an attitude of 'moral panic'[12] can be diagnosed. This did not stop short of the phantasm that, as a result of the war, 'the mighty bulwark of purity' (*Volksbrief der Katholischen Schriftenmission*, no. 24, 1948) had been completely demolished by many women and girls. The interpretational standard by which one presumed to identify such a dramatic violation of accepted norms is an image of Woman in which female sexuality is traditionally located in the conceptual vicinity of obscenity and shamelessness. Such mystifications of femininity ultimately produce a polarization between Madonna and whore. They are obligatory components of a Catholic-conservative critique of contemporary culture and are based upon a model of gender roles which postulates feminine morality as an ennobling countervailing pole to masculine action. In the years following the war, these roles were endowed with a highly specific significance, such as in the rituals staged by the Church as part of the process of coming to terms with the past. In the ceremonies organized in many parishes and communities in conjunction with the return of large numbers of war veterans, female 'figures of light' such as 'white-clad maidens' were part of the symbolic repertoire with conspicuous frequency. Like icons, they functioned as a symbolic representation of angelic innocence, and thus as a contrasting image to the moral anarchy of war. The GI bride stereotype was, so to speak, one of the darker opposites to this figure of light. Throughout the narratives and phantasms produced within this discourse, the connotations of the stereotype were 'Sodom', 'morass' and 'filth'. Thus, in the post-war cleansing process staged by the Church, evil – the excesses of war – also had a symbolic location.

However, in its subsequent forays, the Catholic–conservative campaign against the GI brides also proceeded to focus upon fears of change in the social position of women. For example, a church publication bemoaned the fact that 'Nowadays, many girls take up the search for a man themselves, instead of permitting themselves to be sought.' It went to formulate even more precise views on the subject of the breakdown of traditional hierarchies: 'How many women would still concede to the man the right to have the final word when it comes down to it?' (*Volksbrief der Katholischen Schriftenmission*, 6 June 1947).

It is widely held that the war and the necessity of providing for one's own survival had changed the world of women's experiences in the direction of greater autonomy and independence. The 'Occupation bride' as a social type most openly assumed a position in violation of images of women which were deeply rooted in this culture – that of the women who made their own choices, who *did* select their own partners, even from among the ranks of the former 'enemies'. This broke down a post-war arrangement between the genders (promoted far beyond the context of Catholic–conservative values) in which a patient and selfless Penelope cared for the wounds of her battle-scarred hero.

This relational model constructed upon mythological 'figures personifying the one who returns and the one who waits' (Hornung, 1995) not only accommodated the sentimental-harmonious need for order and respite on the part of Austrian men as well as many women; it was also a central element in the Austrian concept of economic, social and psychic reconstruction. Here, Woman as an element of production was assigned to the 'defensive sector of the ... euphoria of reconstruction' (Kos, 1994: 125), to the management of the private household and the task of cushioning the shocks of the material shortages lasting into the 1950s, on the one hand, and of the post-catastrophe psychic traumas on the other. The aggressive criticism of the GI brides must also be considered in connection with this process of 'post-war normalization'. Among other contributing factors, this normalization was produced, in a mixture of external pressure and a female blockade of their own interests, by means of the renunciation of the occupational, social and erotic emancipation of women.

The behavioural latitude and the freedom to attain self-realization which had been so completely left out of account in the prescribed 'curriculum vitae of a normal woman' re-emerged in the polemic directed at the GI brides, now defamed as the 'greed for living' which knew no bounds. And this was by no means confined to the normative public discourse regarding women; rather, the same applied to the individual reactions of many women themselves. Thus the function of the 'Occupation bride' stereotype as a scapegoat for emotional displacement also becomes clear in the context of post-war female patterns of perception and interpretation.

The step-by-step deconstruction of this stereotype has been carried out using primarily the example of the discourse which unfolded on the subject of the relationships between Austrian women and American soldiers. Simultaneously it has turned out to be an analytical expedition through post-war Austrian society and the ordering models based on gender polarity to which its stabilization mechanisms had recourse.

Notes

1. A preliminary version of this paper entitled 'Austria's Prestige Dragged into the Dirt...? The so-called "GI Brides" and Post-war Austrian Society' was presented at the Nineteenth Annual Conference of the German Studies Association, September 1995, Chicago. The original German version was first published in *L'Homme: Zeitschrift für feministische Geschichtswissenschaft*, 7 (1996), 1, pp. 107–21.

2. SHAEF, Relations with the Civilian Population in Germany, May 1945. In National Archives RG 331 SHAEF G-1 250.1-1 (quoted in Pelz, 1996: 389).

3. For this project, organized by Salzburg's Ludwig Boltzmann Institute for Social and Cultural History, I conducted my research mostly in the former American (Salzburg and Upper Austria) and, for purposes of comparison, French (Tyrol and Vorarlberg) Occupation Zones in Austria. Besides biographical interviews with men and women who lived in post-war Austria, my sources include municipal, police and parish records, daily newspapers, letters to the editor, novels, registry office records, US Army newspapers published for GIs, etc. I also had available to me approximately 60 biographical interviews conducted for the oral history project 'Liberated and Occupied. Salzburg 1945–1955' (headed by Dr. Ingrid Bauer and Univ. Doz. Dr. Reinhold Wagnleitner, commissioned by the Province of Salzburg).

4. GI was originally an abbreviation for government issue and actually referred only to the government-issued uniform worn by members of the US Army. In common parlance, however, 'GI' has become a synonym for an American soldier.

5. Klaus Eisterer (1993) was the first to treat the 'gallant relationships' between Austrian women and French Occupation soldiers in the provinces of Tyrol and Vorarlberg.

6. Also see the research undertaken by Marianne Baumgartner dealing with rape in the Soviet Occupation Zone of Austria and the great extent to which actual events, images, fantasies and ideology became blurred in the 'collective memory'.

7. On this subject, see also Siegfried Mattl's analysis (1985) of the letters to the editor of *Die Frau* and *Stimme der Frau,* the two most important political journals for women in post-war Austria (although a significant number of these letters were written by former soldiers). In preparing this chapter, I investigated the letters to the editor of the regional weekly newspaper *Pinzgauer und Pongauer Zeitung* from 1945 to 1955.

8. I wish to express my thanks to Doris Gödl, a psychoanalyst in Salzburg, for a number of enlightening conversations.

9. References to this occurred repeatedly in the oral history source material gathered by the projects 'Liberated and Occupied' and 'Living with the Liberators: A History of the Genders in the Occupation Era'.

10. This example, however, comes from the French Occupation Zone, and has been quoted from Eisterer (1993: 30).

11. This quotation, translated from the original German, was taken from *Dokumentationsarchiv des österreichischen Widerstandes* (1991: 410).

12. On the subject of the conditions which constitute 'periods of moral panic', see also the work of the Australian historians Kay Saunders and Helen Taylor (1988), research which also focuses on the historical scenarios surrounding World War Two.

References

Bandhauer-Schöffmann, Irene and Hornung, Ela (1990) 'Trümmerfrauen: ein kurzes Heldinnenleben'. In Andrea Graf (ed.), *Zur Politik des Weiblichen. Frauenmacht und –ohnmacht: Beiträge zur Innenwelt und Außenwelt.* Wien: Verlag für Gesellschaftskritik, pp. 93–120.

Bandhauer-Schöffmann, Irene and Hornung, Ela (1991) 'Von der Trümmerfrau auf der Erbse: Ernährungssicherung und Überlebensarbeit in der unmittelbaren Nachkriegszeit in Wien'. *L'Homme: Zeitschrift für Feministische Geschichtswissenschaft*, 2(1), 77–105.

Bauer, Ingrid (1995) ' "Ami-Bräute" – und die österreichische Nachkriegsseele'. In Historisches Museum der Stadt Wien (ed.), *Frauenleben 1945. Kriegsende in Wien.* Katalog zur 205. Sonderausstellung des Historischen Museums der Stadt Wien, Wien: Eigenverlag, pp. 73–83.

Bauer, Ingrid (1996a) ' "USA Bräute". Österreichisch-Amerikanische Eheschließungen auf dem Salzburger Standesamt'. In Erich Marx (ed.), *Befreit und Besetzt. Die Stadt Salzburg 1945–1955.* Salzburg: Anton Pustet, pp. 147–51.

Bauer, Ingrid (1996b) 'Die "Ami-Braut": Platzhalterin für das Abgespaltene? Zur (De-)Konstruktion eines Stereotyps der österreichischen Nachkriegsgeschichte 1945–1955'. *L'Homme: Zeitschrift für feministische Geschichtswissenschaft*, 7(1), 107–21.

Baumgartner, Marianne (1993) 'Zwischen Mythos und Realität: Die Nachkriegsvergewaltigungen im sowjetisch besetzten Mostviertel'. *Unsere Heimat: Zeitschrift für Landeskunde von Niederösterreich*, 2, 73–108.

Berger, Franz Severin and Holler, Christine (1994) *Trümmerfrauen: Alltag zwischen Hamstern und Hoffen.* Wien: Bundesverlag.

Bovenschen, Silvia (1980) *Die imaginierte Weiblichkeit. Exemplarische Untersuchungen zu kulturgeschichtlichen und literarischen Präsentationsformen des Weiblichen.* Frankfurt am Main: Edition Suhrkamp.

Dokumentationsarchiv des österreichischen Widerstandes (DÖW) (ed.) (1991) *Widerstand und Verfolgung in Salzburg 1934–1945, II.* Salzburg: Österreichischer Bundesverlag.

Eisterer, Klaus (1993) 'Fraternisierung 1945.' *Dornbirner Schriften: Beiträge zur Stadtkunde* 14, 21–33.

Hanisch, Ernst (1994) *Der lange Schatten des Staates: Österreichische Gesellschaftsgeschichte im 20. Jahrhundert.* Wien: Ueberreuter.

Hornung, Ela (1995) 'Trennung, Heimkehr und danach: Karls und Melittas Erzählungen zur Kriegs- und Nachkriegszeit'. In Historisches Museum der Stadt Wien (ed.), *Frauenleben 1945: Kriegsende in Wien*. Katalog zur 205. Sonderausstellung des Historischen Museums der Stadt Wien, Wien: Eigenverlag, pp. 133–49.

Kos, Wolfgang (1994) 'Zukunftsfroh und muskelstark: Zum öffentlichen Menschenbild der Wiederaufbaujahre'. In his *Eigenheim Österreich: Zu Politik, Kultur und Alltag nach 1945*. Wien: Sonderzahl, pp. 59–149.

Laplanche, Jean and Pontalis, Jean-Bertrand (1980) *Das Vokabular der Psychoanalyse II*. Frankfurt am Main: Suhrkamp.

Mattl, Siegfried (1985) 'Frauen in Österreich nach 1945'. In Rudolf G. Ardelt *et al.*, *Unterdrückung und Emanzipation*. Wien, Salzburg: Geyer, pp. 101–21.

Mattl, Siegfried (1992) '"Aufbau": eine männliche Chiffre der Nachkriegszeit'. In Irene Bandhauer-Schöffmann and Ela Hornung (eds), *Wiederaufbau Weiblich. Dokumentation der Tagung 'Frauen in der österreichischen und deutschen Nachkriegszeit'*. Salzburg, Wien: Geyer, pp. 15–23.

Pelz, Monika (1996) '"Österreich bedauert, einige seiner schönsten Frauen als Kriegsbräute an Angehörige fremder Militärmächte verloren zu haben …" Heiratsmigrantinnen 1945–1955'. In Traude Horvath and Gerda Neyer (eds), *Auswanderungen aus Österreich: von der Mitte des 19. Jahrhunderts bis zur Gegenwart*. Wien: Böhlau, pp. 569–90.

Petschar, Hans and Schmid, Georg (1990) *Erinnerung und Vision: Die Legitimation Österreichs in Bildern: Eine semiohistorische Analyse der Austria Wochenschau 1949–1960*. Graz: Akademische Druck- und Verlagsanstalt.

Ruhl, Klaus-Jörg (1980) *Die Besatzer und die Deutschen: Amerikanische Zone 1945–1948*. Düsseldorf: Droste.

Sander, Helke and Johr, Barbara (1992) *Befreier und Befreite: Krieg, Vergewaltigung, Kinder*. München: Kunstmann.

Saunders, Kay and Taylor, Helen (1988) 'To combat the plague: the construction of moral alarm and the role of state intervention in Queensland during World War Two'. *Hecate*, 14, 5–30.

Wagnleitner, Reinhold (1991) *Coca-Colonisation und Kalter Krieg. Die Kulturmission der USA in Österreich nach dem Zweiten Weltkrieg*. Wien: Verlag für Gesellschaftskritik.

17 Crime and Punishment in Liberated France: The Case of *les femmes tondues*

Claire Duchen

France was progressively liberated from German Occupation following the landing of the Allied forces in Normandy on 6 June 1944. On 25 August Paris celebrated its liberation and on 26 August General de Gaulle marched triumphantly down the Champs Elysées, welcomed by enthusiastic crowds. France was not yet completely free of the occupiers; the last area, eastern France, was finally liberated by early March 1945.

The Liberation period (spring 1944 to the end of 1946) was a 'complex amalgam of opening and closure' (Kedward and Wood, 1995: 9). Its continued fascination lies in its ambiguity: it was no longer war (although in daily life, wartime conditions still largely obtained) but, without new political institutions fully in place, could not yet be considered as 'normal' peacetime. The Liberation was a key moment of transition, its identity belonging neither to the past nor the future, but implicating both. Suspended between the Occupation of the immediate past and the as yet unknown future, it represented a time when the tensions between the desires for a fresh start and for a return to normality were played out (Duchen, 1993: 50). It was both exhilarating in its celebration and vicious in its recriminations. In the chaos, people wanted order, closure, a clean slate as they entered a new era.

To this end, all those who had been part of the collaborationist government of the Occupation (1940–44) at Vichy had to be purged from public life, punished for their involvement with Nazi Germany. Ordinary people were also targeted: those who had actively collaborated in supporting Nazi or Vichy ideology; those who had made money out of the Occupation, such as industrial manufacturers and owners of large corporations; those who had worked for Vichy or for the Germans; and those who had enjoyed German company, benefiting from material advantages while the rest of the population suffered intense hardship and deprivation.

From 1944 onwards there were extensive purges of the press, the judiciary, the civil service and the media, as well as of politicians and in particular the government around Marshall Philippe Pétain. When compiling figures for the number of individuals involved in the purges, a breakdown by gender was not carried out; researchers are now trying to establish the gendered nature of the purges (Leclerc and Weindling, 1995). Like men, women were shot, imprisoned and suffered national degradation, depriving them of their recently conferred civil rights. Women were accused, often anonymously, of denouncing Resisters,

Communists, Jews. Women were accused of blackmarketeering and of settling personal scores by denunciation to the Gestapo, the militia (a paramilitary police force) or to the police. Women were punished for working for the German authorities or for association with known collaborators. Women were considered guilty by association and were punished for the collaborationist activities of husbands or sons. Unlike men, women were punished for sexual misconduct. They were accused of consorting with the Occupier, flaunting their associations with German soldiers, sleeping with the enemy, sometimes bearing a German's baby.

These forms of so-called 'horizontal' collaboration were not included in definitions of 'national indignity', punishable by national degradation, and usually did not reach the courts. They were nonetheless punished. Before a proper system of tribunals was established, unofficial retribution was widespread[1]. Women were often singled out for a particular kind of punishment – having their heads shaved in public. Theirs is a story told by others, but the main characters remain silent; neither punishers nor punished have wished to speak of the headshavings and their part in them. This silence contrasts strikingly with the apparent ubiquity of photographs of these *femmes tondues* (shorn women), with the widespread knowledge and memory of the events, and with their symbolic significance.

The first part of this chapter will discuss the information and analyses available so far about these headshavings; the second will focus specifically on photographs taken of the scenes. The principal questions addressed in this chapter are: Why did France need to punish women for their wartime sexual conduct? Why have *femmes tondues* come to be emblematic of collaboration and guilt? How do photographs of *femmes tondues* contribute to a gendered analysis of the purges? What function can these photographs have for historians of the Liberation?

First, the facts

The function of the purges was to eliminate, to punish and to cleanse. There was also an undoubted element of revenge. Women who associated with Germans had visibly and publicly enjoyed benefits denied the majority; they were the ones primarily targeted for visible and public revenge. Fabrice Virgili (1992) has carried out research on the press reporting of the public headshaving of women, and this is what he found. The first wave took place in 1944, beginning in the spring before the Allied landings, peaked in June and July, and continued until the autumn. A second wave followed in 1945, after the return of deportees from the concentration camps; it was reported in at least seventy-seven of the then ninety Departments of France.[2] The headshaving took place in towns, villages and rural communities; it was carried out for mostly sexual reasons, but also for denouncing others to the authorities or for 'keeping company' with Germans; a certain amount of score-settling was also undoubtedly involved. The number of women concerned varied widely, from one isolated case to eighty women in the town of Beauvais. Other punishments (stripping, painting swastikas on the body, throwing things at the women or hitting them, jeering, parading them, often naked, through the town, making them sit in a public place with a placard around their neck proclaiming their crime) most usually accompanied the shavings. Women were – although this was rare – shorn before being shot. The women subjected to the headshaving were mostly single (unmarried, divorced, widowed), usually young and poorly educated. They mostly worked for the Germans as cleaners or housekeepers, or had clerical jobs in the local occupying administration. Some had higher level employment, working as translators or secretaries; some were prostitutes. The punishments often occurred at the end of the day, so that people could come and enjoy the sight on their way home from work. They took place at the woman's home or in the street, in a seemingly impromptu fashion; or they became a significant part of local Liberation ritual, taking place in seats of local power – at the town hall, in the town square, outside the main café, in front of the girls' school, at the police station. The headshavings were more or less tolerated by the new Resistance authorities, in spite of official condemnation which formally forbade Resistance involvement in any such event (Virgili, 1992). Anecdotes suggest that Resistance fighters stopped the shaving in some places, turned a blind eye in others and were among the instigators in others – claiming a role as alternative authority as an alternative justice was enacted.

Writing the event

The press was on the whole gleeful in its reporting, although some disapproval was occasionally expressed (Virgili, 1992). Eye witness accounts, reported mainly in memoirs, tend to demonstrate a certain unease. They describe the event generally from the perspective of one who witnessed but did not participate and did not condone what he or she saw (Brossat, 1992, passim).[3] This discomfort is repeated, largely, in the historiography of *les femmes tondues*. Historians have had difficulty in finding an appropriate manner in which to discuss this aspect of the purges, wishing to condone neither the punishers nor the punished, and rejecting the apologetic mode for both sides.[4] Many of the first historians of the Liberation and the purges were reticent about *les femmes tondues*, or tried to excuse the punishers. Peter Novick, for instance, wrote: 'these acts of minor violence corresponded to a population's profound need to give free reign to their emotion, after four years of swallowing their resentment' (Novick, 1968: 78). He notes on the same page that these girls were probably the unsuspecting saviours of those members of the militia and other collaborators who would otherwise have been on the receiving end of the people's wrath. Herbert Lottman wrote that the women were used to 'sop up the anger that would otherwise have ended in bloodshed' (Lottman, 1986: 68). Fred Kupferman mentioned *les femmes tondues* in passing and wrote that 'The chase began. It appeased the hatred and anguish of a starving, humiliated people ... Yes, in 1944, the French were full of hatred' (Kupferman, 1985: 89).[5] It is telling that many historians of the purges restricted themselves to reporting anecdotal evidence and left analysis well alone.[6]

Over the past five years, it has been recognized that the question of *les femmes tondues* is rich in interpretative possibilities. The theoretical insights offered by Michel Foucault (1977) on the public spectacle of punishment, Mikhail Bakhtin (1968) on carnival and René Girard (1982) on the scapegoat have all been valuable. While these works do not themselves pay attention to gender, they can be useful for a gender-based analysis (Brossat, 1992; Kedward and Wood, 1995).

For instance, in *Discipline and Punish* (1977: 49), Michel Foucault suggests that in a public execution, what was at stake was less the re-establishment of justice than the reactivation of power. The purpose was to 'make everybody aware, through the body of the criminal, of the unrestrained presence of the sovereign'. The Liberation, and in particular the purges, can be considered as the ritual of a return to Republican order. *Les femmes tondues* were victims of this process.[7]

The most apposite of these theoretical works comes from René Girard. The 'episode' of *les femmes tondues* is frequently discussed in terms of a scapegoating. Girard has suggested that persecution – a scapegoating, a witchhunt, a lynching – takes place at times of social crisis as a response to a sense of powerlessness. Girard points to the fact that the 'crimes' most frequently evoked during persecution are those which attack the foundations of cultural order, those which are the most taboo and which are often sexual, as tends to be assumed in this case (Girard, 1982, 24–6). These women are targeted because they have allegedly transgressed codes of patriotism and also codes of feminine behaviour. It is this second aspect of their transgression that is highlighted, foregrounded.[8] Women are seen as body, and if women's bodies are the property of men and of the nation, then they must be punished in the body, by the nation. Bauer makes a similar argument to explain the Austrian hatred of the GI bride (Chapter 16).

The women were involved in a public spectacle in which the crowd took revenge, asserting and celebrating its own outraged innocence by designating the few as guilty. In a scapegoating, the weak are targeted as blame is transferred; the finger is pointed at another in order to diminish one's own share of the blame (Douglas, 1995: 195). French society pointed at its Other, thereby making the Self innocent. By means of *les femmes tondues*, French society could reconstitute itself as a coherent whole, as a Resistant whole, morally and politically virtuous.[9] This meshed with the Gaullist construction – that the true, eternal France had never accepted the armistice or the Occupation and had always retained its integrity; and that the people had risen up to liberate their own country. Excise the rotten elements of the nation and the whole may be exonerated, indeed its guilt denied or forgotten.

Feminist approaches to *les femmes tondues* have been slow to gain recognition. Before the mid-1980s, it was never pointed out that there was a specifically gendered dimension to the headshaving scenes – men were doing it to women. It was primarily seen as resisters doing it to collaborators. The first hint of a gendered approach to *les femmes tondues* came from Marie-France Brive in the mid-1980s, at a conference on the Liberation. She suggested that by singling out some women for headshaving, all women were implicitly targeted and therefore there was more at stake than righteous revenge or popular justice. This suggestion was met with anger rather than interest and Brive's contentious argument was dismissed (Brive, 1986: 391).

Since Brive's intervention, however, it has been increasingly hard to ignore or sideline analyses of the events which have gender and sexuality at their core. Both male and female researchers now emphasize the centrality of gender. The metaphoric significance of the headshaving has been privileged over the search for data concerning who did what to whom and why. For instance, a recent reading suggests that the women were scapegoated to compensate for the humiliation of the French male at the hands of the Germans in 1940 (Kelly, 1995). It is possible to read the scene of *les femmes tondues* as a scene of sexual empowerment for men, by which they erase their failure inscribed in the defeat and the Occupation. The metaphor of France as a woman invaded by the Germans while French men were unable to prevent that invasion is too close to the stereotypical image of *les femmes tondues*, women giving themselves to Germans, to be ignored. At some unspoken level, the sight of women voluntarily choosing a German evokes the image of France (so often represented as a woman, Marianne) as a willing partner of Nazi Germany – an image which the French would like to forget. The *tondeurs* (headshavers) take the place of the powerful (and attractive?) male invader in a symbolic re-enactment and reworking of the scene. The French man was masterful once more, the French woman submissive; thus were 'proper' gender roles re-established.

Feminist work on war and nationalism has also proven useful for analysing *les femmes tondues* (Stiglmayer, 1994; Einhorn, 1996; Yuval-Davis, 1997). The headshaving scene can be considered in terms of the sexual violence of war – as one of the final acts of war, a symbolic rape. Rape, sexualized violence, has always been part of war, considered practically a soldier's right. It is about power, humiliation and degradation. The victim's suffering is transformed into the victimizer's display of power. Rape in war is crucial, according to sociologist Ruth Seifert (1996: 41), in that the suffering of the civilian population in war is central to the deconstruction of the culture one wishes to defeat. Symbolically, women represent the nation; literally, in times of war, women hold family and community together. Attack women and you destroy the nation, the community. This also works in reverse. As part of reconstructing a community, some women are defined as outsider/Other. Shorn of their hair, they are raped symbolically by the newly powerful. The identity of outsider, the stigma of unworthiness, is clearly marked on the body.[10] It is marked in discourse too: in narrative accounts, the terms used to describe *les femmes tondues* distinguish between *les femmes à boches* ('Jerry's women') or a *tondue*, and 'real' French women, *les vraies Françaises* (Capdevila, 1995: 70), as if a sexual involvement with a German meant loss of French identity. *Les femmes tondues*, then, had forfeited their right to be called French, and were discursively excised from the nation.

Feminists have long argued that control of women's sexuality was, and is, an integral part of patriarchal societies. Sexuality is political. Dorinda Outram (1989: 126) posits a direct link between sexuality and politics in her work on the body and the French Revolution. She speaks of the 'continuum between virtue as chastity or female fidelity within marriage, and virtue as the upholding of the republic'. The disruptive potential of unrestrained female sexuality endangered the revolutionary republic, because 'any deviation from chastity/virtue involves the collapse of republic/virtue'. The punishment of deviant female sexuality safeguarded the integrity of the new post-war Republic.

If women were punished for transgressing codes of femininity and codes of patriotism, anecdotal evidence and photograph captions suggest that they were judged more for their 'deviant sexuality' rather than for acts of betrayal. Luc Capdevila's research shows that the social profile of the women victims indicated that they were mainly single, employed, sexually active, without children and in control of their own fertility. He, like others, argues that in *les femmes tondues*,

France was punishing those who were perceived as a threat to social and moral order, undermining marriage, family, fertility and the nation (Capdevila, 1995: 81–2; Duchen, 1993; Laurens, 1995). These women seemed to undermine the future of France. The headshaving was clearly not just about punishment; it was also about future agendas. As both Ela Hornung and Ingrid Bauer have suggested in writing about Austria (Chapters 4 and 16), a symbolic reconstruction of the 'family Austria' – or in this case, the 'family France' – was necessary in order to make reconstruction of the nation possible.

Picturing the scene

Les femmes tondues have received significant attention from historians only in recent years. In the popular memory of the Liberation, however, they have been present since the events themselves. They have been evoked mostly via a well-known poem by Paul Eluard ('Comprenne qui pourra'), a well-known song by George Brassens ('La belle qui couchait avec le roi de Prusse'), by Alain Resnais' film *Hiroshima mon amour* and by a few much-circulated photographs by the celebrated photographers Robert Capa and Henri Cartier-Bresson. Photographs of *femmes tondues* have acquired an emblematic status and the same few pictures can be seen repeatedly on magazine and book covers every time an anniversary comes around.[11] The most familiar images show the public humiliation of two women marched through the streets, surrounded by a jeering crowd. (Plates 1, 2).

Plate 1   One of the first pictures of the capture of Chartres (23 August 1944). Two French women collaborators, their hair shaved off, are led back to their home, while the population whistle loudly and jeer after them. Photograph: Robert Capa/Magnum Photos. Courtesy of the Imperial War Museum, London.

Plate 2   One of the first pictures of the capture of Chartres (23 August 1944). Two women collaborators, one holding the child of a German father, are led back to their homes after having their hair shaved off, amid jeers and whistles from the population. Photograph: Robert Capa/Magnum Photos. Courtesy of the Imperial War Museum, London.

They are the most instantly recognizable visual signifiers of the purges and, by extension, of collaboration in France.

How can these photographs serve the historian of *les femmes tondues*? In spite of claims made on its behalf, the photograph is rarely an unambiguous record of a historical moment. It is a complex and unreliable form of testimony on a number of levels. The photograph, by definition the site of a multiple gaze, inevitably resists a single meaning; it is a visual medium but is nonetheless 'invaded by language' (Burgin, 1983: 226). It implies a story but simultaneously withholds that story; without the implicit narrative made explicit 'photographs ... are inexhaustible invitations to deduction, speculation and fantasy' (Sontag, 1973: 23).

The complexity of the photograph as record or testimony is compounded by a number of imponderable aspects: photographic meaning can only too easily be altered, and another meaning imposed, by visual or verbal means (angle, cropping and framing, context, caption);[12] the identity of the photographer cannot always be ascertained.[13] The motivation of the photographers – a particular brief which pushed them towards one set of images or another – is even more elusive; pictures were always subject to censorship but the grounds on which decisions about individual pictures were made cannot always be discovered. The way in which a picture ended up in one particular newspaper, newsreel, archive or book illustration, often seems to have been due to chance or accident as much as to deliberate policy.[14] The fundamental questions (some of which may have to remain frustratingly unanswered) are about why pictures of *femmes tondues* were taken at all, who they were intended for, and the function they have played in the memory and the historiography of the Liberation.

Allan Sekula (1982: 87) has said that 'a photographic discourse is a system within which the culture harnesses photographs to various representational tasks'. The photographs participate in the story (fantasy?) France wished to tell about itself, to itself and to others. At a first level, these photographs help the historian to understand how the feminine was used politically and how particular visions of the feminine are written into the mythology of the Liberation.

Gendered imagery occupies a significant place in the memory of the Liberation and in its mythology. The female form provides some of the strongest, most evocative images of the time. In collections of images in history textbooks and monographs of the period, key aspects of the Liberation are encapsulated by images of women. The female form is identified with the euphoria of freedom: in paintings, drawings, posters, photographs and newsreels, we see girls and young women; they are waving, kissing soldiers on tanks, dancing, able to enjoy some frivolity legitimately at last.[15] The female body was used allegorically to triumphantly represent Liberty, or the Republic itself. At the Liberation, the preferred role of the female in political posters was maternal – represented usually in a mix of stylized semi-allegory and semi-realism – protecting the child in the family grouping which was to represent the harmonious and stable future of France. There were photographs of women Resisters, most obviously in Communist Party publications and at the meetings of the Communist-dominated women's organization, the Union des Femmes Françaises, where huge portraits of women Resistance heroines hung behind the platform.

But photographs of *femmes tondues* were (and are) far better known. They are the necessary opposite of the pictures of maternal and political virtue. They instantly signify the purges and collaboration, in a way that pictures of women Resisters do not instantly signify the Resistance, whose dominant image (visual and narrative) is masculine (Reynolds, 1990; Laborie, cited in Rouquet and Voldman, 1995). They draw on archetypes of female imagery from myth, history and fiction: Eve, woman-as-sex, woman-as-weak, both tempted and temptress; the witch as archetypal outsider; prostitutes and adultresses with hair shorn as punishment; aristocrats waiting before the guillotine. The sexually and politically deviant woman has always been singled out, looked at, desired, punished. If the female body is ever-present in Liberation imagery, it is in this culpable, sexually-marked way, linking the political with the erotic, that it has its greatest impact.[16] It represents that against which the new French Republic will be defined.

Photographs of *femmes tondues* confirm the equation of Resistance as male, collaboration as female;[17] male as heroic, female as guilty; male as combative, female as passive.[18] The attribution of collaborationist guilt to all women is achieved by the contemporary use made of the pictures in the press and in newsreels, by the anonymity of the women captured on film, by the lack of precise information accompanying the images. Some of the captions are bland or terse ('Photograph of a *femme tondue*'); some confirm guilt ('Photograph of collaborators having their heads shaved'); some are explanatory ('The man on the left explains to the public what it means to have your head shaved'); some are intended to be jocular ('Doesn't she look awful without her hair'); others are triumphant ('This is what the French think of their collaborators').[19] The caption may give the name of the victim or the village or town where the shaving took place, but many of the pictures give no indication at all of specific individuals or locations.

The caption or lack of caption universalizes the scene and thereby universalizes the feminine associations with collaboration. It reinforces collective rather than individual responsibility; specific individuals were targeted for headshaving but the women in the pictures could have been any women, anywhere in France. The way the photograph makes specific women anonymous and representative of all women confirms the mythic status of the image. Its symbolic significance far outweighs the actual incidence of headshaving. To misquote Roland Barthes (1957: 229), the photograph without context transforms history into myth; myth then turns history into nature. These women become all women, their particular history becomes myth. Women traditionally have been represented as body, sentiment, moral and physical weakness; men as mind, intellect, strength. *La femme tondue* as 'woman' draws on these stereotypes, confirming the associations. The repeated circulation of the photographs served to implant the image in the public consciousness and, over time, in the collective memory of the French.

Just looking

Fifty years later, the pictures tell a different story or rather tell the same story differently. Gone is a comforting story of France as told in 1944 or 1945 (the righteous men punishing the wicked women; the cleansing of France; the return of the morally and politically virtuous to authority) which might have emphasized the women's misdeeds and satisfied the viewer's sense of justice. Fifty years later, just looking at the pictures undermines this reading. Analyses of the headshaving can suggest that it was an integral part of the return to a Republican patriarchal order; it can be described as part of a 'distasteful carnival' (Brossat, 1992) or as a catharsis necessary for the reconstruction of the country. Maybe it was all these things. But the scene also shows a form of bullying, a public humiliation seemingly enjoyed by everyone but the victims themselves. The pictures show ordinary women, young girls in dowdy coats, skimpy frocks, short socks and clumpy shoes, with faces as expressionless as possible (Plate 3). The crowd provides a compelling sight of collective sadism, taking vicious and petty pleasure in the proceedings (Plate 4). The photographs carry the resonances of photographs used for surveillance purposes, or for anthropometric studies. They parody the accepted genres of photography (the portrait for the family album, the holiday snap, the pin-up girl). The woman is sometimes practically turned into an animal trophy – the fish, the deer's head – won by the crowd surrounding her (Plate 5). In some cases, the photographer seems to be complicit with the crowd and the act of photographing itself becomes the centre of attention (Plate 6). The contemporary viewer is made profoundly uncomfortable by witnessing the scene through photography. Spectators are turned into voyeurs, looking at an image of a public yet intimate act.

The anonymity that had tainted all French women with the guilt of collaboration paradoxically encourages a re-reading of the scene fifty years later, calls up the sympathy of those who were not there, turns the tables on thepunishers. From the standpoint of fifty or so years later, the waters of vice and virtue are muddied. The surrounding figures become as significant as the women

Plate 3 Axis collaborationists denounced in Cherbourg. A French Resistance member displays the shorn hair of young women of Cherbourg accused of violating rules set down by the Resistance for conduct with the Germans. The women were rounded up on Bastille Day morning, 14 July 1944, shorn and paraded through the streets. Photograph courtesy of the Imperial War Museum, London.

themselves. The photographs, over time, pass guilt from victim to victimizer; no one occupies the moral high ground. The spectator's ambivalence punctures the vision of the morally unassailable new France.

The silences and *lacunae*, which make the photograph such an unhelpful witness in certain respects, now become useful and prompt the historian's questions which pour forth once the lid of this Pandora's box is opened:

- What was the relationship between the various actors in the headshaving – *tondeurs*, *tondues*, accusers, onlookers? Were they neighbours, friends, colleagues? What does this tell us about sociability and community? What happened afterwards? Did they all live together again? The women involved have tended to deny any wrongdoing, but nonetheless continued to live with the shame of the accusation. Some women were driven to suicide; others were forced to leave town, as in the film *Hiroshima, mon amour*; yet others faced their victimizers daily and simply carried on.
- Why did sexual relationships constitute collaboration? How has collaboration been defined? Men bore the weight of political, economic and ideologicalcollaborationist activities because of the dominant role they played in public life; women seemed to carry the guilt of collaboration at the level of daily life and personal relationships. No distinction seems to have been made between

Plate 4 'Normandy haircut' for anti-French women. Members of the French Resistance mete out punishment to all known 'Axis collaborationists'. Housemaids, servants, etc. of the Germans were gathered together, shorn of all their hair, and paraded through the streets of Cherbourg, their hairless heads the symbol of their violation of the rules of the organization. Photograph courtesy of the Imperial War Museum, London.

different types of relationships between French women and German men. For instance, if a woman was a prostitute, plying her trade with the available clients in the interests of making a living, she was usually (but not always) considered guilty. A young woman who had 'really fallen in love' with a German was equally guilty, if not more so. Why was her behaviour a crime and not a tragic love story? Women were punished for failing to recognize that during war,

Plate 5 Collaborationist in Paris. French civilians wave the victory sign after shaving the head of a French woman accused of collaborating with the Nazis in Paris. A swastika is painted on her forehead. Photograph courtesy of the Imperial War Museum, London.

private life is far from private and that the very personal becomes very political. And whereas women who joined the Resistance were commonly said to have done this for personal rather than political reasons – following a boyfriend or husband – women who probably had little interest in politics had deeply political implications attached to their personal actions.

- What was the intended message of the photograph? Who was the intended audience? Were the pictures of *femmes tondues* intended for French women, to tell them unequivocally how to behave in the future? Were they for foreigners, to demonstrate that the French had recognized their guilt and were punishing the guilty? Or were the French simply indulging in some self-flagellation by displaying their own sinners to the world? What is striking here

Plate 6 Montereau (no date). Photograph courtesy of the Imperial War Museum, London.

is the emphasis on the visual. In most cases the purges have been examined via court records, written accounts, memoirs. Where ordinary people are concerned (as opposed to the trials of politicians and intellectual celebrities or public figures - civil servants, lawyers, journalists), there has been little interest and particularly little visual interest. In the case of *femmes tondues*, however, attention is paid less to the identity of the victims and the nature of their crimes than to the sight of the punishment itself. The photograph is an integral part of the punishment. The traditional role played by female imagery as incarnating virtues and vices, together with prurient interest in the sexual transgressions and in the downfall or misfortune of others, have ensured this prominence.

These photographs now invite the historian to rewrite the story, recast the *dramatis personae*, reassess the villains and heroes, shift the relationships visible in the pictures. Fifty years later, images of *femmes tondues* contribute to the destruction of the myth they originally helped to create. In one sense, the historian's duty is to reverse the semiotic alchemy and turn myth back into history, all women into some women. For this to be possible, the anonymity of the individuals and the locations has to end. Only by learning more about who did what to whom and why, individualizing and attributing some actions (sexual or not) to some women, can the association of women and collaboration be undone. This laborious process, undertaken via local and national police archives, Prefectoral reports and court reports, is now underway as material becomes available to researchers (Virgili, 1995: 112 n. 4).

The photographs also contribute to rewriting history in a broader sense. Confronting the unease provoked by the photographs means recognizing the gendered dimension of the purges and examining the unacknowledged relation between sexuality, violence and politics that is present in the images. More than that, it means working towards new readings of the sexual politics of war and peace, and reconsiderations of the relationship between the image, society and the writing of history.

Notes

1. An estimated eight to nine thousand people were executed without trial.
2. Information is simply not available or research has not yet been carried out in the remaining Departments; no known reported incidence of headshaving does not mean that none occurred.
3. Here are two short examples:

> A cortège of four shaven women ... is moving towards the rue du Bac, more and more people are joining the crowd. One of the women tries to escape. She is caught, people hit her, hurl insults at her, the crowd is inhuman. The poor woman is stripped ..., on her knees, in front of 102 rue du Bac. A member of the Resistance points his machine gun at her, to kill her. People force her to say she is sorry, she is kneeling there, half-naked, on her knees. It is said that she killed three Frenchmen, that she shot them from her window. What can be done in front of a half-mad crowd? are they going to kill her? No – a French officer arrives and says that she must be taken to prison and tried.

Emmanuel d'Astier de la Vigerie reporting on what one woman – a bourgeoise living in rue de Varenne – reported to him, *De la chute à la Libération de Paris* (Paris: Gallimard, 1965).

> Eugène de Brocard: Rue de Rennes, a car passes quickly. In the car, next to the driver, a French officer. Behind them, a German general in full military dress. He is dignified, quite haughty in fact, with an air of disdain for the passersby who are booing him. Further along, piercing cries. Down on the ground, a woman is defending herself from a wild crowd. 'Friend of the Germans' someone says. A local hairdresser shears her head. He leaves her a long lock by which she is dragged along by some shrieking women. They tear her clothes off. Completely naked, she runs away. A charitable soul opens a door for her. That same night, I saw ten women like that, surrounded by guards, paraded through the streets, carrying a Nazi flag. Luckily, the next day, spectacles like this were categorically stopped (Brossat, 1992: 157).

4. Apart from Robert Aron, whose many volumes on the history of the purges (Paris: Fayard, 1967–1975) fed the 'bloodbath' version of events.
5. In the twentieth century the French have not had the monopoly on headshaving: Republican women soldiers had their heads shaved by Nationalists during the Spanish Civil war; Irish girls risked tarring and feathering if they went out with British soldiers in Northern Ireland in the 1970s.

6. As well as those historians mentioned above, see Henri Amouroux *La grande histoire des Français après la Libération*. vol. 9 'Le règlement des comptes' (Paris: Laffont, 1991); and the work of journalists and commentators such as Catherine Gavin, Janet Flanner and Alexander Werth.

7. Other avenues still to pursue which stress the metaphoric over the literal include the psychoanalytical approach to the question of hair and its sexual symbolism, from headshaving as castration to hair as fetish; the Biblical and historical echoes, linking headshaving with sexuality and transgression across cultures and through time; and the arguments, developed by many scholars, over the masculinity of the Republican ideal.

8. Leclerc and Weindling in fact suggest that the alleged sexual nature of the *femmes tondues*' offence, and indeed the attention paid to the *tondues*, has completely obscured other forms of female collaboration and other ways in which women were punished. Françoise Leclerc and Michèle Weindling 'La répression des femmes coupables de collaboration pendant l'Occupation' in *Clio: Histoire, Femmes et Société* No. 1 'Résistances et Libérations, France 1940-1945'. Toulouse: Presses Universitaires du Mirail, 1995, 129–50.

9. See also Lynn Hunt's arguments in *The Family Romance of the French Revolution* (University of California Press, 1993).

10. When deportees returned from concentration camps the women survivors, mostly with no hair, wore turbans and scarves, as did women who had had their heads shaved. To avoid confusion between the women, some local Resistance authorities called for a law forbidding *femmes tondues* to wear turbans (Virgili, 1992: 30).

11. For his thesis *La tonte et les tondues à travers la presse de la Libération*, Fabrice Virgili consulted photographs at the Bibliothèque Nationale in Paris. He notes that of the 5000 or so photographs of the period, only six represented *femmes tondues*. For this chapter, the photographic collections at the Imperial War Museum (London), at the Musée d'Histoire Contemporaine (Paris), the Agence Roger Viollet and the Agence de la Documentation Française were consulted. The Imperial War Museum photographic archive contains a large number of photographs of *femmes tondues*, while the collections in Paris have a much smaller number. Many of the photographs are duplicated in each collection.

12. Caption writers were probably quite unconnected to the scene, sitting in some newspaper office far away. After receiving a copy of the picture from the Allied War Pool they could easily attach a more-or-less appropriate but invented caption.

13. Before 1948 press photographers were usually not given a credit for their pictures.

14. I tried to pin down a few answers to some of these questions. Each service in the military had photographers attached to it; there were also press photographers like Robert Capa working at that time for *Life* magazine and freelancers like Henri Cartier-Bresson, Margaret Bourke-White and Lee Miller. The nature of the individual pictures partly depended on the objective of the photographer. Press photographers, and freelancers hoping to sell pictures independently, tended to focus on 'human interest' stories; military photographers focused on images to be used for official recording purposes or for propaganda (Hilary Robert, Deputy Curator of Photographs, Imperial War Museum, London, in conversation 12 July 1994). All photographs were sent to Allied headquarters for approval or refusal by the censors. It appears that the

photographs were all placed in the Allied War Pool. Some of the pictures I saw at the Imperial War Museum had 'Not for publication in the Western hemisphere' stamped on the back; others gave no indication of eventual publication, while yet others were clearly marked by the name and date of publication.

15. Of particular interest are the images chosen for the catalogue of an exhibition held in Paris in 1984: *La France et les français de la Libération*, Musée des Deux Guerres Mondiales, Paris: BDIC 1984.

16. See Marcia Pointon, *Naked Authority: The Body in Western Painting 1830–1908* (Cambridge: Cambridge University Press, 1990) for a discussion of 'reading the body'.

17. The association of women with collaboration has been noted by Sîan Reynolds in 'The Sorrow and the Pity revisited, or, Be careful, one train can hide another' (*French Cultural Studies*, vol. 1, Part 2, No. 2, 1990, 149–59), in which she analyses this famous film in terms of its gender bias and shows how Marcel Ophuls makes an unspoken but obvious association between women and collaboration. See also Pierre Laborie, quoted by François Rouquet and Danièle Voldman: 'France, saved from Pétainism and collaboration by the spirit of struggle and "insoumission" of the Resisters, is assimilated to a symbolic form of political passivity, encapsulated by "horizontal" collaboration … The violence against women exalts the verticality of resistance opposing the horizontality of passive collaboration' (Rouquet and Voldman, 1995: 9).

18. Pictures of male collaborators that have had as much exposure as those of women have been pictures of named individuals, famous men whose activities were known; the women photographed are generally un-named, their punishment unofficial, their crimes alleged.

19. This is a selection of captions from the collection at the Imperial War Museum.

References

Amouroux, Henri (1991) *La Grande Histoire des Français après la Libération.* vol. 9, *Le Règlement des comptes.* Paris: Laffont.

Bakhtin, Mikhail (1968) *Rabelais and His World.* Cambridge, MA: MIT Press.

Barthes, Roland (1957) *Mythologies.* Paris: Le Seuil.

Barthes, Roland (1980) *La Chambre claire: note sur la photographie.* Paris: Le Seuil.

Bourdrel, Philippe (1988) *L'Epuration sauvage: 1944–1945, vol. 1.* Paris: Librairie Académique Perrin.

Brive, Marie-France (1986) 'L'image des femmes à la Libération'. In Rolande Trempé (ed.), *La Libération du Midi de la France.* Toulouse: Eché Editeur.

Brossat, Alain (1992) *Les Tondues: un carnaval moche.* Paris: Editions Manya.

Brossat, Alain (1994) *Libération, fête folle.* Paris: Editions Autrement.

Brothers, Caroline (1996) *War and Photography: A Cultural History.* London: Routledge.

Burgin, Victor (1983) 'Seeing sense'. In Howard Davis and Paul Walton (eds), *Language, Image, Media.* Oxford: Blackwell, pp. 226–44.

Burgin, Victor (1982) *Thinking Photography.* Basingstoke: Macmillan.

Capdevila, Luc (1995) 'La collaboration "sentimentale": antipatriotisme ou sexualité hors-normes?' In François Rouquet and Danièle Voldman, *Identités féminines et violences politiques (1936-1946)*. Les cahiers de l'IHTP. No. 31, Octobre, pp. 67-82.

Conan, Eric and Rousso, Henry (1994) *Vichy, un passé qui ne passe pas*. Paris: Fayard.

Douglas, Tom (1995) *Scapegoats: Transferring Blame*. London: Routledge.

Duchen, Claire (1993) '1944-1946: women's liberation?.' In Dave Berry and Alec Hargreaves (eds), *Women in 20th Century French History and Culture*. Loughborough: Loughborough University, European Research Centre, pp. 49-64.

Duchen, Claire (1994) *Women's Rights and Women's Lives in France, 1944-1968*. London: Routledge.

Einhorn, Barbara (ed.) (1996) 'Links across differences: gender, ethnicity and nationalism'. *Women's Studies International Forum*, 19 (1/2).

Foucault, Michel (1977) *Surveiller et punir: naissance de la prison*. Paris: Gallimard.

Girard, René (1982) *Le Bouc-Emissaire*. Paris: Grasset.

Higonnet, Margaret and Higonnet, Patrice (1987) 'The double helix'. In Margaret Higonnet *et al.* (eds), *Behind the Lines: Gender and the Two World Wars*. New Haven: Yale University Press, pp. 31-47.

Hunt, Lynn (ed.) (1991) *Eroticism and the Body Politic*. Baltimore: Johns Hopkins University Press.

Kaspi, André (1995) *La Libération de la France*. Paris: Librairie Académique Perrin.

Kedward, H. R. and Wood, Nancy (eds) (1995), *The Liberation of France: Image and Event*. Oxford: Berg.

Kelly, Michael (1995) 'The reconstruction of masculinity at the Liberation.' In H. R. Kedward and N. Wood (eds), *The Liberation of France: Image and Event*. Oxford: Berg, pp. 117-28.

Kupfermann, Fred (1985) *Les Premiers Beaux Jours*. Paris: Calmann-Lévy.

Laurens, Corran (1995) 'La femme au turban: les femmes tondues'. In H. R. Kedward and N. Wood (eds), *The Liberation of France: Image and Event*. Oxford: Berg, pp. 155-79.

Leclerc, Françoise and Weindling, Michèle (1995) 'La répression des femmes coupables de collaboration. *Clio* no. 1, 'Résistance et Libérations: France 1940-1945', ed. Françoise Thébaud, pp. 129-50.

Lottman, Herbert (1986) *The People's Anger: Justice and Revenge in Post-Liberation France*. London: Hutchinson.

Novick, Peter (1968) *The Resistance versus Vichy France*. New York: Columbia University Press.

Outram, Dorinda (1989) *The Body and the French Revolution: Sex, Class and Political Culture*. New Haven: Yale University Press.

Pointon, Marcia (1990) *Naked Authority: The Body in Western Painting 1830-1908*. Cambridge: Cambridge University Press.

Reynolds, Siân (1990) '*The Sorrow and the Pity* revisited, or, Be careful, one train can hide another'. *French Cultural Studies* 1 (pt. 2)(2), 149-59.

Rouquet, François and Voldman, Danièle (eds) (1995) *Identités féminines et violences politiques, 1936-1946*. Paris: Insitut d'histoire du temps présent, 1995.

Rousso, Henry (1992) 'L'Epuration en France: une histoire inachevée'. *Vingtième Siècle*, Jan–Mars, 8–105.

Scott, Joan (1987) 'Rewriting history' in Margaret Higonnet *et al.* (eds), *Behind the Lines: Gender and the Two World Wars.* New Haven: Yale University Press, pp. 21–30.

Seifert, Ruth (1996) 'The second front: the logic of sexual violence in wars'. *Women's Studies International Forum*, 19(1/2), 5–44.

Sekula, Allan (1982) 'On the invention of photographic meaning'. In Victor Burgin (ed.), *Thinking Photography.* Basingstoke: Macmillan, pp. 84–109.

Sontag, Susan (1973) *On Photography.* New York: Delta.

Stiglmayer, Alexandra (1994) *Mass Rape: The War against Women in Bosnia-Herzegovina.* Lincoln: University of Nebraska Press.

Virgili, Fabrice (1992) *La Tonte et les tondues à travers la presse de la Libération.* Unpublished thesis, Paris.

Virgili, Fabrice (1995) 'Les "tondues" à la Libération: le corps des femmes, enjeu d'une réappropriation'. *Clio*, no. 1 'Résistances et Libérations. France 1940–1945, ed. Françoise Thébaud, 111–27.

Warner, Marina (1985) *Monuments and Maidens: The Allegory of the Female Form.* London: Weidenfeld and Nicolson.

Yuval-Davis, Nira (1997) *Gender and Nation.* London: Sage.

Bibliography

Women, war and history: general and theoretical

Allen, M. (1983) 'The domestic ideal and the mobilization of womanpower in World War II.' *Women's Studies International Forum*, 6(4), 401–12.

Baumel, J. T. (1998) *Double Jeopardy: Gender and the Holocaust*. London: Valentine Mitchell.

Bridenthal, R. *et al.* (eds) (1998) *Becoming Visible: Women in European History* (3rd edn) Boston: Houghton Mifflin.

Brothers, C. (1996) *War and Photography: A Cultural History*. London: Routledge.

Cooke, M. and Woollacott, A. (eds) (1993) *Gendering War Talk*. Princeton: Princeton University Press.

Dex, S. (ed.) (1991) *Life and Work History Analyses: Qualitative and Quantitative Developments*. London: Routledge.

Ellis, C. and Flaherty, M. G. (eds) (1992) *Investigating Subjectivity: Research on Lived Experience* London: Sage.

Elshtain, J. B. (1987) *Women and War*. New York: Basic Books.

Elshtain, J. B. and Tobias, S. (eds) (1990) *Women, Militarism and War: Essays in History, Politics and Social Theory*. Lanham: Rowman and Littlefield.

Felman, S. and Laub, D. (1992) *Testimony: Crises in Witnessing in Literature, Psychoanalysis and Representation*. New York: Routledge.

Fuchs, E. (ed.) (1999) *Women and the Holocaust: Narrative and Representation*. Lanham: University of America Press (vol. 22, *Studies in the Shoah*).

Gluck, S. B. and Patai, D. (eds) (1991) *Women's Words: The Feminist Practice of Oral History*. London: Routledge.

Higonnet, M. R., Jenson, J., Michel, S. and Weitz, M. C. (eds) (1987) *Behind the Lines: Gender and the Two World Wars*. New Haven: Yale University Press.

Huston, N. (1985) 'The matrix of war: mothers and heroes'. In S. R. Suleiman (ed.), *The Female Body in Western Culture*. Cambridge, MA: Harvard University Press, pp. 119–36.

Isaksson, E. (ed.) (1988) *Women and the Military System*. New York: St Martin's Press.

Klein, Y. M. (ed.) (1997) *Beyond the Home Front: Women's Autobiographical Writing of the Two World Wars*. New York: New York University Press.

Laurentzen, L. A. and Turpin, J. (eds) (1998) *The Women and War Reader*. New York: New York University Press.

Linden, R. R. (1993) *Making Stories, Making Selves: Feminist Reflections on the Holocaust*. Columbus: Ohio University Press.

MacDonald, S., Holden, P. and Ardener, S. (eds) (1987) *Images of Women in Peace and War: Cross-Cultural and Historical Perspectives.* Basingstoke: Macmillan.

Ofer, D. and Weitzman, L. J. (eds) (1998) *Women in the Holocaust.* New Haven: Yale University Press.

Passerini, L. (ed.) (1992) *Memory and Totalitarianism.* Oxford: Oxford University Press.

Rittner, C. and Roth, J. K. (eds) (1993) *Different Voices: Women and the Holocaust.* New York: Paragon House.

Samuel, R. and Thompson P. (eds) (1990) *The Myths We Live By.* London: Routledge.

Seifert, R. (1996) 'The second front: the logic of sexual violence in wars'. *Women's Studies International Forum*, 19(1/2), 5–43.

Townsend, C. and Townsend, E. (eds) (1989) *War Wives: A Second World War Anthology.* London: Grafton Books.

Warner, M. (1985) *Monuments and Maidens: The Allegory of the Female Form.* London: Weidenfeld and Nicolson.

Wiener Philosphinnen Club (ed.) (1997) *Krieg/War: Eine philosophische Ausein-andersetzung aus feministischer Sicht.* München: Wilhelm Fink Verlag.

Women in Europe 1940-1956 (country-specific)

Bandhauer-Schöffmann, I. and Hornung, E. (1992) *Wiederaufbau Weiblich: Dokumentation der Tagung 'Frauen in der österreichischen und deutschen Nachkriegszeit.'* Wien: Geyer-Edition.

Bandhauer-Schöffmann, I. and Hornung, E. (1996) 'War and gender identity: the experience of Austrian women, 1945–1950'. In D. F. Good, M. Grandner and M. J. Maynes (eds), *Austrian Women in the Nineteenth and Twentieth Centuries.* Oxford: Berghahn Books, pp. 213–33.

Bridenthal, R., Grossman, A. and Kaplan, M. (eds) (1984) *When Biology Becomes Destiny: Women in Weimar and Nazi Germany.* New York: Monthly Review Press.

Chaperon, S. (2000) *Les Années Beauvoir.* Paris: Fayard.

De Grazia, V. (1992) *How Fascism Ruled Women, Italy 1922–1945.* Berkeley: University of California Press.

Diamond, H. (1999) *Women and the Second World War in France 1939–1948: Choices and Constraints.* Harlow: Pearson Education.

Duchen, C. (1994) *Women's Rights and Women's Lives in France 1944–1968.* London: Routledge.

Fishman, S. (1991) *We Will Wait: Wives of French Prisoners of War, 1940–1945.* New Haven: Yale University Press.

Freier, A.-E. and Kuhn, A. (eds) (1984) *'Das Schicksal Deutschlands liegt in der Hand seiner Frauen': Frauen in der deutschen Nachkriegsgeschichte: Frauen in der Geschichte V.* Düsseldorf: Schwann.

Frevert, U. (1988) *Women in German History: From Bourgeois Emancipation to Sexual Liberation.* New York: Berg.

Hancock, E. (1994) 'Employment in wartime: the experience of German women during the Second World War'. *War and Society* [Australia], 12(2), 43–68.

Hart, J. (1996) *New Voices to the Nation: Women and the Greek Resistance, 1941–1964.* Ithaca: Cornell University Press.

Heineman, E. (1999) *What Difference Does a Husband Make? Women and Marital Status in Nazi and Post-war Germany.* Berkeley: University of California Press.

Jancar-Webster, B. (1990) *Women and Revolution in Yugoslavia 1941–1945.* Denver: Arden Press.

Koonz, C. (1987) *Mothers in the Fatherland: Women, the Family and Nazi Politics.* New York: St Martin's Press.

Kuhn, A. (ed.) (1984/86) *Frauen in der deutschen Nachkriegszeit. vol 1: Frauenarbeit 1945–1949, vol. 2: Frauenpolitik 1945–1949.* Düsseldorf: Schwann-Bagel.

Kuhn, A. (1977) *Les Femmes dans la Résistance.* Actes du colloque UFF. Paris: Editions du Rocher.

Moeller, R. G. (1993) *Protecting Motherhood: Women and the Family in the Politics of Post-war West Germany.* Berkeley: University of California Press.

Owings, A. (1993) *Frauen: Women Recall the Third Reich.* New Brunswick, NJ: Rutgers University Press.

Pollard, M. (1998) *Reign of Virtue: Mobilizing Gender in Vichy France.* Chicago: University of Chicago Press.

Riley, D. (1983) *War in the Nursery: Theories of the Child and Mother.* London: Virago.

Rossi-Doria, A. (1996) *Diventare cittadine: Il voto alle donne in Italia.* Firenze: Giunti.

Rupp, L. J. and Taylor, V. (1990) *Survival in the Doldrums: The American Women's Rights Movement, 1945 to the 1960s.* New York: Ohio State University Press.

Slaughter, J. (1997) *Women and the Italian Resistance* Denver: Arden Press.

Summerfield, P. (1989) *Women Workers in the Second World War: Production and Patriarchy in Conflict.* London: Routledge (first published 1984).

Summerfield, P. (1993) 'Approaches to women and social change in the Second World War'. In B. Brivati and H. Jones (eds), *What Difference Did the War Make?* Leicester: Leicester University Press, pp. 63–79.

Summerfield, P. (1998) *Reconstructing Women's Wartime Lives: Discourse and Subjectivity in Oral Histories of the 1940s.* Manchester: Manchester University Press.

Swindells, J. (1995) 'Coming home to heaven: manpower and myth in 1944 Britain'. *Women's History Review,* 4(2), 223–34.

Thébaud, F. (ed.) (1992) 'Le XXe siècle'. Vol. 5 of G. Duby and M. Perrot (eds), *Histoire des femmes dans l'Occident.* Paris: Plon.

Withuis, J. (1994) 'Patchwork politics in the Netherlands, 1946–50: women, gender and the World War II trauma'. *Women's History Review,* 3(3), 293–313.

General works on post-war Europe

Alapuro, R. (1988) *State and Revolution in Finland.* Berkeley: University of California Press.

Bennett, G. (ed.) (1996) *The End of the War in Europe 1945.* London: HMSO.

Borneman, J. and Peck, J. M. (1995) *Sojourners: The Return of German Jews and the Question of Identity.* Lincoln: University of Nebraska Press.

Crampton, R. J. (1994) *Eastern Europe in the Twentieth Century – And After.* London: Routledge.

Ellwood, D. (1992) *Rebuilding Europe: Western Europe, America and Post-war Reconstruction.* London: Longman.

Ellwood, D. (1985) *Italy 1943–45.* Leicester: Leicester University Press.

Emsley, C., Marwick, A., Purdue, B. and Aldgate, T. (eds) (1990) *War, Peace and Social Change in Twentieth Century Europe. Book 4: World War Two and Its Consequences.* Oxford: Oxford University Press.

Gati, C. (1986) *Hungary and the Communist Bloc.* Durham: Duke University Press.

Gilbert. M. (1995) *The Day the War Ended.* London: HarperCollins.

Herf, J. (1997) *Divided Memory: The Nazi Past in the Two Germanys.* Cambridge, MA: Harvard University Press.

Judt, T. (ed.) (1989) *Resistance and Revolution in Mediterranean Europe, 1939–1948.* London: Routledge.

Kedward, H. R. and Wood, N. (eds) (1995) *The Liberation of France: Image and Event.* Oxford: Berg.

Marrus, M. (1985) *The Unwanted: European Refugees in the Twentieth Century.* New York: Oxford University Press.

Mayne, R. (1983) *Post-war: The Dawn of Today's Europe.* London: Thames and Hudson.

Mazower, M. (1993) *Inside Hitler's Greece: The Experience of Occupation, 1941–1944.* New Haven: Yale University Press.

Mazower, M. (1998) *Dark Continent: Europe's Twentieth Century.* London: Penguin.

Milward, A. (1984) *The Reconstruction of Western Europe 1945–51.* London: Methuen.

Noakes, J. (ed.) (1992) *The Civilian in War: The Home Front in Europe, Japan and the USA in World War Two.* Exeter: Exeter University Press.

Urwin, D. (1997) *A Political History of Western Europe since 1945* (5th edn). London: Longman.

Index